A COMM____

on   Saint Ignatius'

RULES FOR THE DISCERNMENT OF SPIRITS

—

JULES J. TONER, S. J.

A COMMENTARY

on

SAINT IGNATIUS' RULES

for the

DISCERNMENT OF SPIRITS

A Guide to the Principles and Practice

THE INSTITUTE OF JESUIT SOURCES

This is the
First Edition, for the Americas, Western Europe,
Australia, and New Zealand
First Printing, 1982
Second Printing, 1991

Note: There is a *Second Edition*, authorized for
sale ONLY IN ASIA AND AFRICA which
can be ordered from Gujarat Sahitya Prakash,
Anand 388 001, India

CONTENTS

PART I. A GUIDE IN TIME OF CONSOLATION AND OF DESOLATION

Contents

Contents

viii

EDITOR'S FOREWORD

Father Jules J. Toner, S.J., the author of the present book, has had the teaching of philosophy as his basic occupation since he received his doctorate in that branch from the University of Toronto in 1952. He has published articles in *Thought*, the *Journal of Religion*, the *Review for Religious*, and two issues on discernment in *Studies in the Spirituality of Jesuits*. He has also published two books, a historical study entitled *Modern Ethical Theories* (coauthored with James V. McGlynn, S.J.) and a phenomenological study, *The Experience of Love*. For some twenty-five years, too, he has been very much involved in spiritual counseling of lay persons, seminarians, priests, and men and women religious. From 1969 to 1971 he was Director of Novices for the Detroit and Chicago Provinces of the Society of Jesus. Since 1970 he has devoted much time to lecturing and directing workshops on Ignatian spiritual discernment.

Simultaneously with these activities he has pursued a special interest in St. Ignatius' principles for discernment of spirits and discernment of the will of God. He has studied Ignatius' "rules" or directives constantly and analytically, read about them extensively, and used them practically in spiritual counseling and lecturing. Manifestly, therefore, he is in the present book offering to others a study in depth which is the mature fruit of this long investigation and experience.

He presents his treatise in the form of a commentary which interprets and explains St. Ignatius' rules one by one, as well as their interrelations with one another, their context in the *Spiritual Exercises*, and the principles of spirituality underlying them. He does all this, however, with a very practical purpose: to produce a treatise helpful for use today by the many persons who have a special interest in this topic, such as directors of retreats, retreatants, spiritual counselors, students of spiritual theology, and others interested in pursuing the spiritual life. He aims to aid these readers to understand St. Ignatius' principles correctly and apply them skillfully in practice, whether in time of retreat or in daily living.

Especially among religious since Vatican Council II, there has been a growing interest in the topic of discernment, and specifically in the guidelines to it which are found in St. Ignatius' *Spiritual Exercises*. But there has also been more than a little difference of concepts about what discernment is, divergent phrasing, and terminology which is sometimes loose or imprecise. Father Toner's *Commentary* will aid considerably toward bringing clarification into this often puzzling situation. Noteworthy here is his clear distinction, too often little stressed or even overlooked, between Ignatius' directives for discerning spirits and those for discerning the will of God. The two topics naturally overlap and reciprocally illumine each other. But in the present book the author wisely focuses chiefly on discernment of spirits, and he plans to compose another book giving similar treatment to discernment of the will of God. It is when each type of discernment is itself accurately understood that it throws more light on the other.

St. Ignatius' two sets of Rules for the Discernment of Spirits, a little treatise only some twenty-two paragraphs long, may in a rapid reading seem misleadingly simple. One can quickly pick up a few principles which he or she can with some confidence apply in practice. But there are also many statements which have depths far beyond what first meets the eye. They lead one into that area where theological knowledge, while still uncertain, is eminently worthy of exploration. Confronted by that uncertainty, many commentators on the *Exercises* have tried to clarify Ignatius' Rules merely by selecting the chief ones and paraphrasing them. Others have laudably and courageously attempted extensive careful investigation.

All the commentators have approached Ignatius' Rules with their Catholic faith as the presupposition of their interpretations. Beyond that, they have used different methods which sprang largely from their varying purposes or methodologies. Some have sought, with great benefit to their readers, to gain further light by studying the Rules in the light of philosophical systems such as Hegelianism or Existentialism. Thus they have shown that Ignatius' thought is harmonious with the good in these systems, and that it can to no small extent be expressed within their framework and in their terminology; or they have found Ignatius' text a source leading to discovery of new theological knowledge, whether as yet solidly established or still tentative and suggestive, which is beyond what Ignatius himself possessed or explicitly expressed. All this is good.

In such search for truth the more light we can gain from any source the better off we are.

The chief sources and methods which Father Toner has used in the present *Commentary*, however, are those of exegetical study of Ignatius' text. He has carefully analyzed the thought of each rule, the structure of the collection of rules as a whole, and their meaning within the context of the *Spiritual Exercises*. When relevant and possible, too, he has sought further clarifications from other passages of Ignatius' writings which deal with the problem or idea in question. His guiding aim in commenting on each rule has manifestly been to ask: What did Ignatius intend to communicate here to a sixteenth century director, exercitant, or advisee? and how can that be accurately understood by us today and properly applied in practice?

It is only natural that after four centuries divergent and controversial views have arisen among commentators on Ignatius' terse texts. Not surprisingly, therefore, Father Toner too has arrived at interpretations different from those of other competent scholars. But he manifestly aims to express their views with accuracy and his own criticism with fairness and respect. Such discussion of differences is the ordinary means of progress in the search for truth. The Institute of Jesuit Sources is happy that its publications can serve as a forum for exploration of this kind.

There are, too, some problems which by their very nature can be handled in depth only through subtle and even technical discussion. For some readers they are very important, but for others a relatively brief exposition made in the body of the book is sufficient—even better lest the moving thought be too much encumbered and complicated. Those interested in them, however, will find a lengthier treatment in the Appendices, where the author tackles them with clarity and a firm grip. Prominent among them, and perhaps most important for the majority of the readers, is that about the existence of created personal spirits good or bad, angels or devils. In recent decades many doubts about their existence have been spread—more by insinuations than by a clear and comprehensive presentation of the pros and cons. This has left many retreat directors or retreatants in uncertainty and sometimes embarrassment. If perhaps devils and angels do not really exist, what good can come from an attempt to discern them? And what is a retreat director to say about them, woven as they are into Ignatius' text? What happens to his teaching as a whole? Other special topics especially interesting to some readers are the comparison of spiritual desolation as conceived by Ignatius with the dark night of the soul in the writings of St. John of the Cross; disputed questions on the nature of spiritual consolation or desolation as described by Ignatius; and similar problems about the nature and frequency of what Ignatius calls "consolation without preceding cause."

Theological discussion about the disputed questions mentioned above will go on for decades before a common agreement is reached —if it ever will be. Father Toner makes no claim to saying the last word. But by his careful analysis of Ignatius' text, by his expounding the controverted questions so clearly in the present book, and by taking a position about them, he does advance our knowledge. The Institute of Jesuit Sources is happy to present his *Commentary on Saint Ignatius' Rules for the Discernment of Spirits* as a book in its Series III, Original Studies about the Jesuits, Composed in English.

George E. Ganss, S.J.
Director and General Editor
The Institute of Jesuit Sources
Pentecost, 1979

AUTHOR'S PREFACE

Many persons striving to grow in the Spirit and many who are experienced as teachers of the spiritual life or as spiritual counselors have expressed a need for the kind of book this is meant to be, whatever may be the success of my effort. What seems to be one important need at present is neither a historical account of the none too rich literature on the subject, nor a highly speculative theology of discernment of spirits, nor another undeveloped restatement of some traditional fundamental principles.[1] To say this is not to minimize the value of historical accounts or of theological speculation on this subject. Both are greatly needed. What I find at present more urgently needed and desired is something which meets a more immediately practical need.

---

[1] Only after my own manuscript had been several times revised and was in the hands of the publisher did the recent book of Father Thomas Dubay, S.M., come to my attention: *Authenticity: A Biblical Theology of Discernment* (Denville, N. J., 1977). Otherwise it would have merited much more attention than mention here in this footnote and in the select bibliography, page 216 below.

Father Dubay's book and mine necessarily overlap; but nevertheless the two differ widely in scope, purpose, and method. Father Dubay has written a theology of discernment—all modes of spiritual discernment, including the manifold forms of discernment of spirits, as also discernment of God's will, and the spiritual dispositions requisite for discernment. His wide-ranging treatise even leads him, naturally enough, into many pages of theological controversy regarding the relationship of theology in general, and moral theology in particular, to the Church's teaching authority. I, for my part, have limited myself to an exegetical study of St. Ignatius of Loyola's teaching in his rules for discernment of spirits for the most part leaving aside for a further study his teaching on how to discern God's will and the necessary dispositions for such discernment. As will be made clear in chapter 1, the Ignatian rules are concerned with a very narrow sector of discernment of spirits. These rules with their narrow focus limit my study accordingly; and they call for an effort at deeper understanding of that narrow sector than would be possible for Fr. Dubay to undertake and still include all the other important matters he deals with—and which need to be dealt with. On the other hand, one of Ignatius' principal aims in his rules for discernment of spirits, one treated at length in this book, is to teach maturing Christians how to deal with spiritual experience once they recognize it. This aim seems to lie outside the scope of Fr. Dubay's book. Given such differences, the two studies may hopefully

Neither do I want to belittle the value of the many restatements of traditional practical principles (usually paraphrases of Ignatius' rules) which have been given us in recent years. There is, however, among those already familiar with these principles, a need for fuller understanding of their meaning, for more precise understanding of how to apply them in the concrete, for deeper practical understanding of how discernment of spirits fits into Christian life, and of how to respond to a situation once discernment of spirits has been made. This book has been written with a hope of contributing in some measure toward growth in such understanding.

Even though too brief and dense to be always clear and sometimes misleadingly imprecise in their wording, the rules of St. Ignatius of Loyola have for centuries now proved to be the most complete and practically helpful set of directives for discernment of spirits that has as yet been formulated. His set of rules is the most widely known and used. This book is an effort to throw light on these rules by careful analysis of them in their context within Ignatius' *Spiritual Exercises*, which contains them, and by study of Ignatius' other writings. My aim is to present a coherent body of Ignatian teaching and to exhibit the authenticity of what I present. The reason for adopting St. Ignatius as the preeminent teacher of discernment of spirits and for adhering closely to what he says will be expanded in the first chapter.

An aim such as that just stated cannot be achieved without some detailed scholarship and sometimes difficult textual analysis, or without critical discussion of conflicting interpretations. All this makes it difficult to achieve another aim, secondary but very important, that of writing a book which can be widely readable. I am unwilling to sacrifice the first aim for this second, but have done what I could to achieve it along with the primary aim. One help toward doing so has been to put into footnotes and appendices,

complement each other (even though we might have divergent views on some questions which Fr. Dubay takes up but which are not touched upon in my book).

Even more recently, on the very eve of sending this manuscript to the typesetters, still another long treatise has appeared which would merit more attention than this brief notice, if that were possible: Father Brian O'Leary's "The Discernment of Spirits in the Memoriale of Blessed Peter Favre" (*The Way, Supplement* no. 35 [Spring, 1979]). Beyond doubt the present book would be much enriched by this study of discernment in this early companion and disciple of Ignatius, but it would also be unduly delayed. For every author a moment arrives when he must say of his work: This must be it, at least for the present.

whenever possible, whatever would not be of more general interest. As a consequence, for some readers, it is the footnotes and appendices that will be of special interest.

Since references to the *Spiritual Exercises* of St. Ignatius are plentiful and many readers will like to have them easily available, I have kept them, along with references to Sacred Scripture, in the body of the text, abbreviating *Spiritual Exercises* to *SpEx* and giving in brackets the paragraph numbers, now standard, which were wisely added to St. Ignatius' text in 1928.

If the reader finds some repetition of what I see as basic and critically important ideas, I do not apologize for it; but I think I should give a prenotice and a word of justification. My intention, whatever the results may be, is to write a book which has a coherent line of development but is also one which can be consulted on this or that point when needed. Without some repetition of key ideas, a book to be used in this way could be misleading unless the reader has mastered and remembered the contents so well that every main step is seen in relationship with any other main step that may be necessary to qualify or balance it. A spiritual counselor may find it convenient to recommend a chapter or a few pages to someone who does not have time to read and assimilate a whole book right now but would profit from having something in writing on a particular point to go over and ponder at leisure. Unless key ideas are repeated, it would be difficult to use the book in this way.

Acknowledgments

To all those who have helped me by their encouragement and practical assistance while writing this book I desire to express my gratitude. To a few I owe special thanks: to Lois Gilbert, Sister Peggy Burns, and, most of all, John McAuliffe, S.J., for their generosity in typing several versions of the manuscript; to Robert Voglewede, S.J., for not allowing me to give up when I was ready to do so; to George E. Ganss, S.J., the Director of the Institute of Jesuit Sources. To the latter thanks is due for many improvements of the manuscript as a result of his advice. To his work he brought not only his expertise as an editor but also long and deep reflection on the writings of St. Ignatius along with a broad and critical knowledge of secondary sources. From his rich background he has been able not only to draw many fruitful suggestions for my exposition of Ignatius' teaching, but also to add significant scholarly information. Some of the footnotes owe so much to his scholarship that I feel obliged to mention them here: footnote 15 of chapter 1, on the meaning of the term "discernment"; footnote 4 of chapter 2, on the meaning of *sentir* in Ignatius' writings; and footnote 4 of chapter 7, on the formulation of Ignatius' principle of trust-and-act. Further, in the section of chapter 7 where I deal with that principle of trust-and-act, Father Ganss' suggestions led to extensive revision in order to show more clearly the documention of it in Ignatius' writings.

Jules J. Toner, S.J.
University of Detroit
July 31, 1979

A COMMENTARY

on Saint Ignatius'

RULES FOR THE DISCERNMENT OF SPIRITS

PART I

A GUIDE IN TIME OF CONSOLATION

and of

DESOLATION

ABBREVIATIONS

used in the footnotes

Ascent	*Ascent of Mt. Carmel*, by St. John of the Cross
Autobiog	*The Autobiography* of St. Ignatius
Cons	*The Constitutions of the Society of Jesus*
*Cons*MHSJ	*Constitutiones Societatis Iesu*, four volumes in the series Monumenta historica Societatis Iesu
ConsSJComm	*The Constitutions of the Society of Jesus, Translated with an Introduction and a Commentary*, by George E. Ganss, S.J.
Dark Night	*The Dark Night of the Soul*, by St. John of the Cross
DeGuiJes	De Guibert, Joseph, *The Jesuits: Their Spiritual Doctrine and Practice*
*DirSpEx*MHSJ	*Directoria Exercitiorum Spiritualium*, in MHSJ
LettersIgn	*Letters of St. Ignatius*, translated by W. J. Young, S.J.
Living Flame	*The Living Flame of Love*, by St. John of the Cross
MHSJ	the series Monumenta historica Societatis Iesu
SpEx	The *Spiritual Exercises* of St. Ignatius of Loyola
*SpEx*MHSJ	*Exercitia Spiritualia S. Ignatii...et eorum Directoria* (1919), in the series MHSJ
*SpEx*MHSJ*Te*	Sti. Ignatii...*Exercitia Spiritualia. Textuum antiquissimorum nova editio* (Rome, 1969), in MHSJ

Chapter 1

THE NEED FOR A GUIDE

The working of the Holy Spirit within the individual Christian consciousness is the focus of this book. Human life is Christian life in the measure that it is lived under the inspiration of the Holy Spirit of Christ. The Spirit is given to the Church and to each individual Christian within the Church. The Spirit teaches and moves each of us through the Church, through those who have authority from the Church, through those who have gifts for spiritual leadership in the Church, through historical events; but he also acts within the heart of each individual, his or her own thoughts and affections, leading and guiding each without the mediation of others—though not usually without the help of others in recognizing and responding to him.

Not all the good thoughts and affections in our hearts are the work of the Holy Spirit in his role as the indwelling Paraclete, the gift of Christ to believers. Every thought and affection, of course, in its created reality is his work as Creator and is what his providence positively intends or allows as it rules all the details of life in time for the glory of God in those who love him. The direct promptings of the Holy Spirit as Paraclete arise within our complex, flowing, conscious life that is hidden from all but God and self; and they have to be distinguished from our own spontaneous impulses (egoistic or generous), and from the promptings of our environment (good or bad) or of the evil spirit.

Listening to the Spirit Is Essential for Full Christian Life

"The depths of a man can only be known by his own spirit, not by any other man" (1 Cor. 2:11).[1] Can even his own spirit know?

---

1 All quotations from Scripture, unless otherwise indicated, are taken from the Revised

For "more tortuous than all else is the human heart, beyond remedy; who can understand it? I, the Lord, alone probe the mind and test the heart..." (Jer. 17:9-10). Yet we must, with the Lord's help, come to understand our own hearts. For it is from our hearts that we bring forth good or evil actions (Luke 6:43-45; Matt. 15:19). It is in our hearts that God writes his law (Heb. 8:10; Jer. 31:33), into our hearts that he gives his Spirit. (Gal. 4:6).

We cannot know our own or anyone else's heart only by overt actions. That is why only God, who reads the heart itself, can finally and justly judge us. Good or evil overt acts are often ambiguous. Good ones are sometimes done for a wrong reason, with a sinful motive, even as a way of deceiving ourselves as well as others. Sometimes evil overt acts are done through ignorance, with a good intention coming from a pure heart. What is more, even if such acts did reveal the heart adequately, in order to act rightly we would need to read our hearts *before* acting. To give God intelligent service, to escape the malice and deceptions of Satan and our own sinfulness, to open ourselves to the Holy Spirit, to recognize and yield to his gentle and subtle breath, we have to learn as best we can how to read our own hearts. We can do so but only in the power of the Spirit, who not only sees into the depths of every heart, but also inspires our thoughts, moves our affectivity, and illumines our minds to perceive and understand what he does in us. "The spirit reaches to the depths of everything, even the depths of God" (1 Cor. 2:10)—and certainly to the depths of the human person. "Now...we have received the Spirit that comes from God, to teach us to understand the gifts he has given us..." (1 Cor. 2:12).

To recognize, by the power of the Holy Spirit given to me, when he is inspiring my thoughts and feelings and urging me to action; and to interpret these rightly, so that I can freely open myself to receive them and respond truthfully to his inspirations, this is essential to living a full Christian life. Only in this way can I fully answer God's unique call to me to enter into a unique union with him and make my singular gift to the whole body of Christ. Recognition of God-given authority and the evident calls of charity in concrete situations are not enough if I am to live as fully as I can a life of Christ-like obedient love. Only the Holy Spirit who speaks to me in my own heart as well as through authority and the evident needs of my neighbor can lead and guide me to such a life.

This book is concerned with how to live such a life. Before taking up the main concern, it will be important to reflect on the Holy Spirit, who he is or at least wants to be to each one of us, to me personally, and what he is working in each individual life, in mine. Only against this background can we approach the question of how to recognize, understand, and respond to his inspirations.

Who Is the Spirit to Me?

The Spirit of God appears in Holy Scripture as power, creative power, the outgoing, life-giving breath of God. It is the Spirit that hovers over chaos and brings forth creation, that calls forth the stars and sets them in their course, that gives life to all the living, that constantly renews the face of the earth, that can dry up the sea and turn the desert into a garden. When the Spirit is given to the prophets, kings, and judges of God's people, power is given—power to lead, to rule, to conquer overwhelming foes, to prophesy, to raise the dead. The Spirit has power even to change the human heart, to cleanse it, recreate it. By this Spirit, God is always lovingly and powerfully present to his creation and to his people, destroying what stands in the way of his kind purpose and ruling all wisely and sweetly despite evil. In the fullness of time, the Holy Spirit comes upon Mary and in her brings forth the supreme wonder of God's love and wisdom and power, Jesus Christ, joining God and man so that God is a man and a man God—for all, for each, for me. The Spirit that hovered over the waters at creation, who hovered over Mary at the Incarnation, hovers over Jesus throughout his life. In the human consciousness of Jesus, it is the Holy Spirit who leads to a clearer and clearer reflective awareness of who he, Jesus, is. Through the Spirit, Jesus knows himself as the anointed servant of Yahweh, hears and understands what the Father says: "You are my Son, my Beloved" (Mark 1:11). He is consciously filled with the power of the Spirit to bring healing and freedom to men through his person, through his life, his words of teaching and promise, his miracles, his passion, death, resurrection, and glory. In it all, the Spirit leads, guides, sustains, empowers him—for all, for each, for me.

The glorified Jesus having now the fullness of the Spirit baptizes us with the Spirit, gives us his Spirit to drink, so that we may be immersed in his Spirit, filled with his Spirit, and by that Spirit made one life with him, destined to consciously live his life as ours even as he now lives our life as his. In him we are begotten of the Father, through the Spirit, sons and daughters of God, heirs of God's joy—all of us, each of us, I.

The power to believe and hope and love, to understand who I am, and to live in accord with the truth of who I am is from the Spirit. He teaches me to know Jesus intimately. He opens to me the Scriptures, enabling me to encounter Jesus and to understand his words to me. He assures me of what I am, God's son or daughter, who can never be separated from his love revealed in Jesus Christ. He draws forth within the depth of my being the word that expresses Jesus' life and my deepest reality in him: "Abba," that is, "dear Father." He defends the Christ-life within me, bearing witness to Christ before my consciousness, showing me that the unbelieving world sins by unbelief, that Jesus is the righteous one and is in the Father's glory, that the enemy of Jesus is already judged and condemned, that if I persevere to the end, I shall drink from the river of life and be given the bright morning star in glory.

In light and darkness, in life and death, he is my counselor, comforter, friend. He shows the way in life, the direction for the whole of my life, and the way in every concrete situation. He brings courage to endure darkness and pain with fidelity and patience. He brings light when I need it, consolation, joy, singing in my spirit. He is the wind that makes springtime in me, the fountain of living water at which I drink life, the living flame that conquers the power of death and darkness that stands against me. He is, as St. Augustine states, the infinitely sweet "consubstantial communion of the Father and Son" (*communio quaedam consubstantialis Patris et Filii...*)[2] given as gift into my heart as pledge of eternal life in its fullness, the beginning of full sharing in God's life of communion in perfect love, freedom, peace, and joy.

It is the Holy Spirit who draws me into union with all others in the body of Christ so as to share life with them. He gives to me a gift for the sake of all; and he wants to lead me to know what my gift is and when and where and how to use it.

To do all he has been given to do in me, for me, for all through

2 *De Trinitate*, XV, 27, [50], in Patrologia Latina, 42, col. 1097.

me, he not only governs the daily events of my life and world in order to make all work to his loving purposes; he also, day after day, touches directly on my mind and affectivity, speaks to me through my own thoughts and affections as well as through the providential situations and events of my life in the world. Directly and through others he teaches me how to recognize his voice and understand his words.

All that has been said about who the Holy Spirit is to me is found in Holy Scripture and is confirmed by the experience of those who over the centuries have most fully lived the Christian life.

The Need for a Guide

If I am going to hear his voice, perceive his touch as distinct from all others, open myself to him to do what he wishes, listen and understand so as to respond to whatever he speaks in me, I must cooperate in many ways. I must attend and perceive, listen to and interpret, what he is communicating through my thoughts, impulses, and feelings and through the events to which I am responding.

To do this is not easy. There are obstacles within me even to hearing him at all, to sensing his touch in my heart. He usually speaks quietly. My heart is full of other clamorous voices. He touches very gently. I am pushed and pulled from all sides. What comes from the Holy Spirit easily remains at the periphery of attention and sinks into a confused flow of multitudinous elements in consciousness—one indistinguishable from the other and none very significant to me, like the sound of far off music or the murmur of traffic outside my room when I am conversing or reading. Even when I do take particular notice of some inner movement, I may still be like one who cannot tell who is speaking; the voice is only another voice in a crowd. How do I tell when it is the Holy Spirit speaking and not merely myself or the world or the evil spirit? If I am able to recognize the Holy Spirit in my inner experience, I may still be confused or mistaken about his meaning, like one listening to words in a foreign language. Even if I correctly interpret the thoughts and affections which are prompted by the Holy Spirit, I may easily fail to remember the implicit and most important message in every illumination, impulse, or feeling from the Holy Spirit, namely, that he loves me.

What is very difficult for human nature can be made easy by a special "gift of recognizing spirits" (1 Cor. 12:10). By this the gifted person intuitively knows whether the good or the evil spirit is moving someone, self or another, without a need for noting the evidence one way and another, evaluating it by norms and weighing the results so as to reach a reasoned judgment—as others have to do. Among these others, some seem to arrive at great sensitivity and skill, through reflection on their own experience or the experience of those who confide in them, without being taught by any human master. The Holy Spirit himself seems to guide their thoughts. However, such persons are rare. Most of us have no charism to make intuitive judgments, and most of us are incapable of ever learning how to discern spirits, even with the principles we might glean from Holy Scripture, unless we have the teaching of a human master.

It might be thought that any intelligent Christian could by study of Sacred Scripture learn how to discern spirits, or at least that he or she could do so with the help of good Scripture scholars who gather and organize the scattered materials on discernment of spirits in the Old and New Testaments. For some forms of discernment of spirits, this seems to be true. But for the sort of discernment of spirits which we are talking about, the spiritual experience and teaching of those who have lived by the Scriptures under the influence of the Holy Spirit and developed a doctrine seem almost necessary. Study of Scripture alone would be an altogether ineffectual way for most of us to learn.

We must look, therefore, for a teacher among those who have had long, intense, and profound experience of the Holy Spirit acting in them; who also as spiritual counselors have had the opportunity of knowing the inner experience of many others; who have had power of reflecting on that experience in themselves and others in such a way as to grasp the dynamics peculiar to it; who have been able to express all this in accurate descriptions and sound directives; and preferably, who have left a teaching which has proved fruitful for many in generation after generation of those dedicated to living Christian life in the Spirit. Such great masters of spiritual life are rare indeed in the history of the Church, and even rarer in any particular age. Some of these great spiritual teachers of the past have left us writings which are precious; but in most of them, it must be said, there is little on discernment of spirits and discernment of God's will that is easily intelligible or at all adequate for most contemporary readers who are in need of practical help. On the other hand, the need is widespread and rapidly increasing in our time.

Some others, not gifted by God with the experiences and charisms of mind and heart given to the great masters of the spiritual life for the sake of the whole body of Christ, may mediate the teaching of those masters. But to be truly capable for this, they must themselves have had enough spiritual experience, have adequate theological background fresh in mind, and have had opportunity for prolonged study of the masters. For anyone without the rare and precious charism of intuitive discernment of spirits, it would be rash and irresponsible to assume the enormous responsibility of helping others discern what spirit moves them before he or she submits himself or herself to long and demanding preparation and experiences a call from God to do such a service. One of the main elements in preparation for such work is learning the teaching of some of the great masters of the spiritual life. Without that, one may have a sound academic grasp of theology, or skill in psychological counseling, or both, and still be quite incompetent as a spiritual counselor.

St. Ignatius and His Rules for Discernment of Spirits

Where, then, do we find a person who by the gifts of the Spirit is a teacher in his own right of the way to recognize the diverse spirits that move us, and also of the way to hold ourselves always open to the Holy Spirit? We think of Cassian, Gregory, Bernard, Thomas a Kempis, Teresa, John of the Cross, Francis de Sales, and the like.[3] We think, too, of St. Ignatius of Loyola. Other masters may surpass his teaching in value and influence regarding other matters of Christian spiritual life. But when there is a question of discernment of spirits and discernment of God's will, Ignatius' name comes to mind as at least one among the preeminent teachers— and perhaps as one of unparalleled influence.

Among those who know him only by popular legends, which are frequently caricatures of the real Ignatius, he is thought of as a stern and effective organizer and executive. If those who know him in this way should read the account of his early years in his *Autobiography*, they would find a personality and a life strikingly similar to St. Francis of Assisi: a romantic, a mystic, a beggar for Christ by choice, a pilgrim, teaching in all simplicity the gospel to everyone

---

3 For a historical survey of teaching on discernment of spirits, see "Discernment des Esprits," *Dictionnaire de Spiritualité: Ascétique et Mystique* (Paris: Beauchesne et Ses Fils, 1957), III, cols. 1222-1291 (hereafter abbreviated *DSp*). There is an English translation by Sister Innocentia Richards; *Discernment of Spirits* (Collegeville, 1970).

he met, rejoicing to endure the hardships and humiliations and dangers of being actually poor with Christ; a person threatened with blindness by the tears of love, joy, and tenderness beyond his control when he contemplated the beauty and love of God; an utterly selfless man, capable of sternness when true kindness demanded it but otherwise gentle and cheerful. They would find a man taught immediately by the Holy Spirit just as a schoolteacher teaches a little boy. As he told us about himself:

> At this time God treated him just as a schoolmaster treats a little boy when he teaches him. This perhaps was because of his rough and uncultivated understanding, or because he had no one to teach him, or because of the firm will God himself had given him in His service. But he clearly saw, and always had seen that God dealt with him like this. Rather, he thought that any doubt about it would be an offense against His Divine Majesty.[4]

They would find a man anointed with a most unusual charism to discern spirits and give spiritual counsel. It was his charism of spiritual leadership that most impressed those who knew him personally.

The work of writing constitutions for the Society of Jesus and governing it during its early years of growth was thrust upon him late in life, very much against his inclinations, and accepted only because his confessor convinced him that it was God's will for him to do it. To sit behind a desk reading and answering letters, making policy decisions, and writing constitutions was not at all a life to the taste of this romantic dreamer, wanderer, and mystic—one to whom God had given the gift of finding him in all things, of discerning the movements of the Spirit and discerning God's will, and of inspiring in others something of his own flaming love for God revealed in Jesus. If he turned out to be a great legislator, organizer, and executive, nevertheless his greatest endowments for serving his fellow men and his most characteristic gifts were not these. Rather, his most important endowments and gifts were those of communion with God and of spiritual counseling which he

---

4 *Autobiography*, no. 27 (hereafter abbreviated *Autobiog*). The translation here is that of W. J. Young, S.J., in *St. Ignatius' Own Story as Told to Luis Gonzalez de Cámara* (Chicago, 1956, now obtainable from Loyola University Press), p. 22. This is Ignatius' autobiography from the time of his conversion (1521) to the time just before he and his companions determined to form the Society of Jesus in 1539. The story was wrung from him by Luis Gonçalves da Câmara and dictated in brief scattered sessions. He speaks of himself always in the third person, frequently as "the pilgrim."

embodied in the *Spiritual Exercises*, along with his spiritual leadership. These made his legislative work and his governing spiritually fruitful.

Within the *Spiritual Exercises*⁵ there are two sets of instructions in which his wisdom about how to distinguish inner movements of the Holy Spirit⁶ from those that come from any other source, and about ways of maintaining openness to the Holy Spirit at all times, is codified for the use of others. Ignatius intended these guidelines first of all for use by the directors of the Spiritual Exercises, and then by others whom they teach, in the measure that each of them is capable. These instructions have proved to be more readily intelligible and widely used than any document on the subject before or since Ignatius wrote them. They are useful both during crucial spiritual experiences and during ordinary daily Christian life.

They are commonly entitled "Rules for the Discernment of Spirits." It is probably impossible to change that misleading usage. I shall not try to do so. But while employing that title myself, I shall do two things to counteract the possible bad effects: first, point out the discrepancies between the title and the contents and, second, use various other ways of referring to these instructions which are more in accord with the contents.

The word "rules," although it is a literal translation of what Ignatius wrote, has a connotation in ordinary usage of rigid directives imposed by authority. Such connotation, however, completely belies the content. That content is, often enough, simply a description or explanation of spiritual experience, or a statement of norms for judging such experience. When directives are given, they are, like all else in the *Spiritual Exercises*, flexible and adaptable to each individual person and situation.

5 Throughout this book, *Spiritual Exercises* (in italics) refers chiefly to Ignatius' book and Spiritual Exercises (in roman type) to the activities within a retreat. Reference, to Ignatius' book, such as *Spiritual Exercises*, [21], are abbreviated to *SpEx*, [21]. For other usages pertaining to the term "Spiritual Exercises," see the Editorial Note on page 319 below.
6 It is surprising to us today how little Ignatius refers explicitly to the Holy Spirit in his *Spiritual Exercises*. There is an explanation of this puzzling fact in Harvey D. Egan, S.J., *The Spiritual Exercises and the Ignatian Mystical Horizon* (St. Louis, 1976), pp. 120-122 (hereafter abbreviated as *Mystical Horizon*). Nowadays we often speak of the Holy Spirit in many contexts where Ignatius speaks of God or a good angel; but it seems clear that in these instances we are still following his mind.

Further, the phrase "discernment of spirits" is both too broad and too narrow to cover the contents of Ignatius' instructions. Consider the diverse kinds of discernment of spirits. In the Gospels, Jesus teaches his listeners how to discern between true and false prophets[7]: they can be told "by their fruits" (Matt. 7:15-20). He says that good and evil hearts can be discerned through the words that flow from them (Matt. 12:33-35; Luke 6:43-45). His true disciple can be discerned: it is the one who "listens to these words of mine and acts on them," the one "who does the will of my Father in heaven" (Matt. 7:21-27). That will is that we should love one another as he has loved us (John 13:15; 14:21-24). And that love is discerned by what we do for others (Matt. 25:31-46). Jesus also calls his listeners to discern the signs of the times, the spiritual meaning of what they see happening in the world. To the Pharisees and Sadducees who asked for a sign he said: "When it is evening, you say, 'It will be fair weather; for the sky is red,' and in the morning, 'It will be stormy today, for the sky is red and threatening.' You know how to interpret the appearance of the sky but you cannot interpret the signs of the times" (Matt. 16:2-4). To those who came to him from John the Baptist asking whether he was the one who is to come, he answered by pointing out to them the signs of the times: "Go and tell John what you hear and see: the blind receive their sight, and the lame walk, lepers are cleansed and the deaf hear, and the dead are raised up, and the poor have the Good News preached to them. And blessed is he who takes no offense at me" (Matt. 11:4-5). He condemned the Pharisees for not discerning between the commands of God and mere human traditions (Matt. 15:1-9). In the Church after Jesus' ascension there was the problem of discerning authentic from inauthentic beliefs and doctrines. In 1 John 4:1-3,6, we read:

> Beloved, do not believe every spirit, but test the spirits to see whether they are of God; for many false prophets have gone out into the world. By this you know the spirit of God: every spirit which confesses that Jesus Christ has come in the flesh is of God, and every spirit which does not confess Jesus Christ is not of God. This is the spirit of anti-Christ, of which you heard that it was coming, and now it is in the world already.... Whoever knows God listens to us, and he who is not of God does not listen to us. By this we know the spirit of truth and the spirit of error.

In one way or another all of us have to exercise these forms of dis-

---

7 For a discussion of such discernment, see the treatment by Jacques Guillet, S.J., in *Discernment of Spirits* (trans. I. Richards, 1970), pp. 21-24.

cernment of spirits. Some have to use others, for example, to discern whether or not some person is diabolically oppressed or possessed, and to discern what is to be prayed for at any step in the "deliverance" of such a person.[8]

None of the kinds of discernment mentioned just above are what Ignatius is concerned with in his rules. There will be, of course, overlapping in some respects between his instructions and those which pertain to other forms of spiritual discernment; but no one of these forms and his set of directions can serve for each other. For Ignatius is not concerned with judging anyone's claim as a prophet, or the authenticity of any prophet's particular prophecy.[9] Neither is he giving any way of discerning whether a person's heart is good or evil, or whether a person is a true disciple of Christ. Such discernment is presupposed by what he says, and Ignatius is telling us how to interpret the *experiences* of those whose hearts are set on God and those who are going from bad to worse (Rules I:1 and 2). Discerning the signs of the times has no place in the Ignatian rules, and the rules are not suitable for such discernment. For that sort of discernment one has to observe the external events and interpret them in the light of prophecy already given or use them to foresee the future.

Ignatius' rules are concerned with inner, private events, the movements in the individual discerner's own mind and heart prior to even his own overt acts which flow from these inner movements, whether spontaneously or subject to the agent's free choice. They tell us how to discover whether the movements are prompted by the good or evil spirit. There is in them no direct interest in discerning extraordinary experiences such as mystical prayer or diabolical possession, or in telling us how to deal with them.[10]

8 Francis MacNutt, O.P., *Healing* (Notre Dame, 1974), pp. 218, 223, and ch. 17.
9 For Ignatius' way of discerning true and false prophets and prophecies, see his letter of July, 1549 to Francis Borgia, in *Letters of St. Ignatius of Loyola*, trans. William J. Young, S.J. (Chicago, 1959), (hereafter abbreviated *LettersIgn*), pp. 196-211.
10 There are solid reasons for the opinion of some commentators that what Ignatius in Rules II:2 and 8 calls "consolation without preceding cause" is a high and unusual mystical experience (see pp. 299-300 below). But if this is true, it is also true that Ignatius is at no pains to emphasize its mystical character. All he wants to do is to warn us against a way in which such consolation can be the occasion for a deception about divine counsels. This entire matter is discussed at length in chapter 11 below.

In regard to these inner movements, Ignatius is not content to let them go and see what their fruits may be in our lives. His aim is that we learn to judge them, as far as this is possible to us, prior to choice and action—and even to judge them in their very beginnings, before they can gain momentum. In some instances, he is aware that all we can do is to be watchful as a course of thoughts and affections unfolds, and to look for any sign to show up which retrospectively reveals something about the beginning, about the spirit from which the whole process had its origin (II: 4-5; *SpEx*, [333]). But when this happens, he urges that the person having this experience immediately reflect on it, to see how it happened and so to learn for the future how to pass judgment at an earlier point of the inner process—as nearly as possible to the very start (II: 6; *SpEx*, [334]). He is also aware that sometimes we have to make the best discernment we can and put our ideas and desires into execution with readiness to change when any sign appears to call for it. But always his rules aim at discerning as much as may be whether the first movements of mind and affectivity are from the Holy Spirit or not.

Discernment of Spirits as Distinct from Discernment of God's Will

One final clarification is important regarding the limited scope of Ignatian discernment of spirits: His discernment of spirits must also be distinguished clearly from discernment of God's will.

Directions for discerning spirits aim at helping us (1) to discriminate, among the mass of inner movements, those which are merely from ourselves and those which are prompted in us by some spirit and (2), among these spirits possibly involved, to discriminate those which are prompted by the Holy Spirit from those prompted by an evil spirit. Such discernment is not by itself a discernment of what is God's will in a concrete situation for choice that is facing us. Ignatius' directives for discerning God's will are found in other places—clearly, for example, in the conclusion of the First Principle and Foundation (what is "more conducive" to our end), and in his directives for making an Election (*SpEx*, [23; 169-189]). These directives of Ignatius for discerning God's will include his directions for discernment of spirits but also go beyond them. They show us how to use not only the movements of the spirits, but also such factors as the signs of the times, the lessons of our own and others' past experience, and reasonable projections of future consequences

from alternative good courses of action, in order to judge which of
these courses of action or options is likely to be "more conducive"
to the glory of God.[11]

Although distinct, discernment of spirits and discernment of
God's will are nevertheless so closely related and even overlapping
that to treat the first in isolation from the second is sometimes difficult and unsatisfactory. On the other hand, however, it is not only
difficult but even impossible to present Ignatius' teaching on discernment of God's will without presupposing a sound knowledge of his
teaching on discernment of spirits. But it would take a volume twice
as large as the present one to give a satisfactory treatment of both
these topics. Hence it seems best to write this study on discernment
of spirits first and then to follow it with a companion study on
Ignatian discernment of God's will. If on occasion, therefore, the
progress of thought in this book stops short when it might be
expected to flow into discussion of discerning God's will, the reader
will understand that this results from problems both of pedagogy
and of publishing.

We see, then, that in many ways the purpose of the Ignatian
rules for listening and responding to the Holy Spirit is notably
narrower than what is indicated by calling them merely "rules
for discernment" or even "rules for discernment of spirits." On the
other hand, it is equally true that in a different way their purpose is
wider in scope than what is indicated by those commonly used titles.
For they do include practical counsels which follow from but lie
outside of the proper scope of discernment of any sort. The rules
which contain these counsels to which I am referring do help us to
discern the hidden action of the Holy Spirit during times of darkness or of desolation and temptation, when the influence of the evil
spirit and our own sinfulness are easily discerned. But they also
explicitly counsel us about what to do at such times in order actively
to receive the power of the Holy Spirit, and in that power to resist

11 Neither in his counsels on discernment of spirits nor in his counsels on discerning
God's will is Ignatius concerned to instruct us on how to discriminate between
intentions and actions which are in accord or in discord with material moral precepts, and much less on how to go about establishing such precepts. He assumes
that his reader has an ordinary sound knowledge of moral precepts; he calls on it as
a help in discernment of spirits and as a way of eliminating alternatives unfit to
deliberate about in discernment of God's will of the sort which he is teaching. His
way of discerning God's will is for finding the better among alternatives not forbidden
by any material moral precept.

and conquer the power of darkness. Eight of the fourteen rules in Ignatius' first set[12] of rules are of this sort. Two others touch on how, in times of spiritual peace and joy, to prepare for meeting spiritual darkness and temptation or in some measure to prevent it. Only four rules in the whole fourteen are exclusively rules for discernment of spirits. The second set of eight rules is entirely concerned with such discernment of spirits.

These Ignatian rules, therefore, in some respects need a more specific title than rules for discernment or even rules for discernment of spirits; and in other respects they need a more inclusive title. Therefore it would be better to call them "rules or instructions for discerning and opening oneself to the Holy Spirit in light and darkness" or "for listening and responding to the Holy Spirit." Or, since responding presupposes listening, they could be termed simply "instructions for responding to the Holy Spirit"; or, since they are all calculated to dispose us for receiving or retaining the peace of Christ, "counsels or guidelines for living in spiritual peace."

These counsels appear in Ignatius' *Spiritual Exercises*. Nevertheless, whether there is question of discerning spirits or of taking action with the Holy Spirit against the influence of evil in our affections and thoughts, the experiences in which these rules are intended to help us are not only those which occur during the Spiritual Exercises or some other special time but also those which occur in everyday life—where principally we succeed or fail as Christians. To see them as useful only while we are making the Spiritual Exercises, or in making some crucial decision about our lives, or in trying to understand some extraordinary spiritual experience, would be a serious misunderstanding. They also have a broad value in their application to everyday experience while we are living out the aims embraced at some privileged moment of inspiration or decision.

12 It is by design that we speak, throughout this book, respectively of Ignatius' "first set" or "second set" of Rules for Discernment of Spirits. Ignatius' own titles in *SpEx*, [313 and 328], on pp. 18 and 22 below, are admittedly wordy, but they are also precise. Many commentators, speakers, and even translators have shortened them to "Rules for the First Week" or "Rules for the Second Week," but this loses important nuances and easily leads to misunderstandings.

Ignatius did not intend his first set of rules (I:1-14) merely for the First Week nor his second set (II:1-8) merely for the Second Week. They are more likely to be useful, and the need to explain them is more likely to arise, respectively, in those weeks, but not exclusively. What is more, the second set is unusable without dependence on the first. Consequently, to call them "rules for the First Week" or "for the Second Week" can easily result in misleading ideas about their application. See also below, pp. 17, 214-216, and fn. 3 in chapter 10.

This is not to deny that they do have a peculiar value at times which are turning points in spiritual life or times of extraordinary opportunity for growth or for major decisions in regard to God's service. For at such times the opposing forces of good and evil, which are continually at work, will be more intensively active in order to support or block some especially significant event of conversion or growth or some important decision about apostolic work. This is far from saying, however, that they are exclusively or even principally given for those times. We need to discern daily and respond in such ways as are indicated in these rules if our lives are not to drift or to lose their firm direction; if we are not to miss God's grace, or to be weakened, misled, and plagued with vexing uncertainties or confusions; or, finally, to be brought to discouragement and disinterest in any intense Christian life.

Christian, Ignatian, and Jesuit Spirituality

The basic content of the Ignatian instructions on how to discern spirits and how to respond to them when they are discerned is not peculiarly Ignatian. It belongs to the whole Christian tradition. It is true that the biographical evidence seems to indicate that what Ignatius has given us was drawn mainly from personal spiritual experience, understood and tested in the light of Sacred Scripture and the teaching of the Church, rather than put together from things he read in books or heard others say. Nevertheless, what he learned through reflection and the light of the Holy Spirit agrees with what is found scattered throughout the Christian tradition.[13] The ordering of the elements for practical purposes, the emphasis on active energy in discerning and responding, and the imagery— all these are characteristically Ignatian; but only the ordering, the codification if you will, is his peculiar contribution. Strangely enough, no one before him succeeded in giving us such an organized set of practical counsels, and no one since his time has provided anything which could replace it. The content, as has been said, accords with Christian tradition and with all spiritualities in the Church. To think these rules are not suitable for those led by God in a different spiritual tradition than the Ignatian would be a mistake. Other great religious personalities may have a different empha-

---

13 Interesting in this connection is Hugo Rahner's "Be Prudent Money Changers: Toward the History of Ignatius' Teaching on the Discernment of Spirits," in *Ignatius of Loyola: His Personality and Spiritual Heritage*, 1556-1956, ed. F. Wulf, S.J., (St Louis, 1978), pp. 272-279; also H. Bacht's study, ibid., pp. 200-230, "Early Monastic Elements in Ignatian Spirituality."

sis and style, but the substance of what they say in a less organized and usable way is the same as what Ignatius teaches.

Least of all should anyone see these rules, or the *Spiritual Exercises*, or even Ignatian spirituality as specifically Jesuit in character, calculated to form a specifically Jesuit spirit and direct one in that particular way of life among all the other ways of life in which one can serve God. It is the Jesuit *Constitutions* which do that. The *Spiritual Exercises*, with the rules for discerning spirits and responding to the Holy Spirit, are no more peculiarly for Jesuits than the *Summa Theologiae* of St. Thomas Aquinas is peculiarly for Dominicans or St. Augustine's *Confessions* and others works are peculiarly for Augustinians. Each of these is a part of the heritage of all Christians, which Dominicans, Augustinians, and Jesuits respectively have a special responsibility to preserve and adapt and make effective in contemporary Christian life. It is true that the Jesuit spirit and way of life does have its source in the *Spiritual Exercises*; but it is also true that these *Exercises*, even though not yet printed or in their final form, were substantially completed and in use years before Ignatius and his companions decided to form a religious order. Before the Jesuit order began to exist as an order and since, the Spiritual Exercises have been used and found fruitful by popes, bishops, diocesan priests, laymen and laywomen, married or single, and men and women of many diverse religious orders and congregations whether chiefly contemplative or apostolically active. All of these have found the *Exercises* a means of meeting Jesus and of absorbing the gospel message in a manner that enabled them to find and to live out better their diverse vocations from God. Some of these, too, have understood the *Exercises* far better than most Jesuits.

The Intent of This Book

For several related reasons, it is not possible simply to refer the reader to these rules and expect him or her to be able to understand and use them. First, while they look deceptively simple at first reading, in reality, as anyone quickly finds out who tries to use them, they are frequently very difficult to understand or apply in practice; they need much explanation, qualification, and knowledge of the presuppositions underlying the rules. Growth in understanding them and skill in applying them are possible only through lengthy interacting activities: repeated reflection on experience in the light of them, reiterated recurrence to the text in the light of that experience, study of other writings of Ignatius, and discussion with others who have experience and have studied the rules. Secondly, the terse style of Ignatius' writing adds to the difficulty. His style does have the advantage of calling the reader's attention to the main point without having to sift it out of a mass of less important material; but it also often leaves his meaning uncertain and open to misinterpretation. Thirdly, what he has said that helps us to understand the rules (exposition, illustration, reasons, different ways of restating what is in them) is scattered here and there in his other writings but never brought together in a coherent development of thought, for example, in his *Autobiography*, letters, *Spiritual Diary*, the *Spiritual Exercises*, and the *Constitutions of the Society of Jesus*. Only those who read widely in Ignatius, raise questions and search for answers, ponder what is found and strive to synthesize the scattered elements can read the rules with confidence of understanding Ignatius' meaning correctly or, at least, with any fullness— unless they have someone else to do this work for them. Most of those who need and want to understand and to use the rules do not have the background or time to do the required research, and then to do the thinking necessary to interpret what they find and synthesize it with the rules. It was with the hope of meeting the needs of such persons that this book was undertaken.

For reasons obvious in the light of what was said earlier, I have not dared to write on discernment of spirits except as a disciple clarifying the teaching of Ignatius. His "rules" have been kept throughout as the focal point. My understanding of their developmental structure, of their coherent unfolding from beginning to end, will appear as the exposition progresses. A careful reading of the table of contents will suggest what that structure is. However, since each rule has to be read within the context of that structure, a brief statement of the overall structure may be of value even before one begins to analyze any rule.

The Structure of Ignatius' Two Sets of Rules

Ignatius' rules are commonly spoken of by abbreviated titles, such as "Rules for the Discernment of Spirits," . . ."for the First Week," or "for the Second Week." Such simplifications, like many other abbreviations, unfortunately lose many of his nuances and are all too open to misunderstanding or oversimplified conclusions. For precise thinking or analysis a literal translation of his own text is necessary, made usually from the Spanish "autograph" text.[14] Such a translation of his titles is desirable to show the structure of his rules, and it can be given as follows.

RULES TO HELP PERSONS GET IN TOUCH WITH AND UNDERSTAND IN SOME MANNER THE DIVERSE MOTIONS WHICH ARE PROMPTED IN THEM, SO THAT THEY MAY RECEIVE THE GOOD ONES AND EXPEL THE EVIL ONES. THESE RULES ARE MORE APPROPRIATE TO THE FIRST WEEK (*SpEx*, [313]).

RULES FOR THE SAME PURPOSE, WITH MORE ACCURATE WAYS OF DISCERNING[15] SPIRITS. THESE RULES ARE MORE SUITED FOR USE IN THE SECOND WEEK (*SpEx*, [328]).

In Rules I: 1-4, Ignatius treats of the opposing spirits of light and darkness, how they affect maturing Christians, what the signs are of their influence on those who are striving to be free from sin and to grow more like Christ in their lives, as opposed to these spirits' influence on those who are gradually moving further away from the ideal of Christ. In Rules I:5-14, Ignatius is aiming to help

---

14 All the rules are given below on pages 22-30 in my translation from the Autograph text.

15 *Discreción*, the substantive form of *discernir*, is Ignatius' Spanish term here. From it has arisen the abbreviated title which is common in many translations of the *Exercises*, such as "Rules for the Discernment of Spirits"—"for the First Week" or "for the Second Week." Such abbreviation, while convenient, all too easily loses important nuances of Ignatius' meaning. In any scholarly study of Ignatius' writings, it is important to grasp with precision what his term "discern" meant to him and his contemporaries, and to avoid anachronistically reading modern meanings back into his text.

In much conversation or writing of the past decade or two, especially among religious, there has been a growing practice of applying the term "discern" to almost any deliberations about religious options, or discussions, or weighing of pros and cons, or explorations of opinions. These are, however, modern usages, often rather loose and not yet recognized in dictionaries. But there is by now danger for many that they will read these new meanings back into Ignatius' words and through this anachronism miss the precise meanings which the term had for him and his contemporaries. One who desires to grasp his genuine meanings will be much helped by a brief historical survey of the meanings, as listed in well-known dictionaries, which Ignatius' term *discernir* (with its related forms *discernimiento*, *discreción*, *discreto*) had gradually acquired up to his day, and even beyond into modern times before these present and often imprecise usages began.

  1. Ancient Latin (Lewis and Short). *Cerno. . . .cretum:* I, to separate. II, A. To

us be aware of and respond to the Holy Spirit even in the darkness of spiritual desolation and temptation. Part of doing this is to show in more detail than noted in the earlier rules how the spirit of darkness attacks us, his strategy, so that we may know better how to repel him with the power of the Spirit of Light who is always lovingly present with us.

In Rules II: 1-8, on the other hand, Ignatius shows us how to discern the spirit of darkness working even in or through the light of spiritual peace and joy and holy thoughts, all rooted in faith. He distinguishes two special ways in which the evil spirit tries to use these experiences in order to deceive us and shows us how to uncover his activity in each of them.

separate, perceive by the senses, see (syn. *video*). B. Transferred to intellectual objects: to perceive, understand.

Hence, manifestly, arose the compound: *discerno*,...*discretum*: I. to separate, divide. II. to distinguish between, discern.

2. Medieval Latin (Blaise). *Discerno:* 1, separate, divide....4, discern, distinguish. 5, judge, decide (Ps. 67:15).

3. Spanish (Covarrubias' renowned *Tesoro*, published in 1611 and therefore often our best guide to Ignatius' sixteenth century meanings). *Discernir*, to distinguish one thing from another and to form a judgment about them; hence arises the term "discreet" (*discreto*): the prudent man with good understanding, who knows how to weigh things and to attribute its proper place to each. In religious institutes, the members call "discreet" those whom they choose and separate from the community in order to send them to the chapters. In apostolic briefs the term "discreet man" is used of one to whom some charge is entrusted. *Discreción*, something said or done with good understanding.

4. Modern Spanish (Real Academia Española, *Diccionario* [1875]). *Discernir:* to distinguish one thing from another on account of the difference between them. *Discernimiento:* right judgment by means of which things different among themselves are distinguished. *Discreción:* rectitude of judgment by means of which things are qualified and distinguished. It aids toward governing one's activities.

5. English (*Shorter Oxford English Dictionary*). Discern, 1. To separate as distinct (1645). 2. To recognize as distinct; to separate mentally (1483). 4. To distinguish by the intellect, to perceive distinctly (1622).

Against that background we observe that two basic ideas constantly recur in connection with Ignatius' terms pertaining to discernment of spirits in the *Exercises* (*discernir, discreción*): (1) perceiving the respective spirits as good or bad, with a view to (2) separating or distinguishing them. These two ideas sprang naturally from the developing history of these words up to his death in 1556. In his *Spiritual Exercises*, first published in 1548, the word occurs only three times: *discernir* in [336], and *discreción* in [176 and 328]. In the *Constitutions* the word occurs far more frequently. These considerations will also have an application to Ignatian discernment of God's will. In that connection, discernment pertains especially to clear perceptions of the options before one, with a view to distinguishing them and choosing the one likely to result in greater praise or glory to God.

Each of the rules must be interpreted not only within the context of this structure but also within the structure of the *Spiritual Exercises* as a whole and must be illuminated by what Ignatius says in his other writings, especially his letters. While trying to stay as close as possible to Ignatius' own writing, interpreting Ignatius by Ignatius, I have still found it necessary to add descriptive analyses of certain experiences which are not drawn from Ignatius. Whenever I have done so, I have made clear what I am doing and have made sure that my analyses in no way conflict with anything Ignatius has said.

The main point of this chapter can be put summarily: This book aims at providing a practical Christian theology of openness to the Holy Spirit based on the writings of St. Ignatius of Loyola; and it uses as a focal point the rules for this purpose which he included in his manual for making the Spiritual Exercises. It is a *Christian* theology inasmuch as it is governed by the teaching of Christian Scripture and tradition and rooted in Christian experience of living out that teaching under the lead and guidance of Christ's Spirit. It is a *practical* theology. It is not concerned with purely speculative theological matters, not even with those which are presupposed by a practical theology, except insofar as these are necessary for understanding what Ignatius counsels us to do in order to live an examined Christian life—a life reflectively and actively involved in the struggle between Christ and Satan, recognizing the forces at work in oneself, actively cooperating or counterattacking with the understanding and freedom befitting the sons and daughters of God.

Chapter 2

THE TEXT OF ST. IGNATIUS' RULES FOR THE DISCERNMENT OF SPIRITS

After the preliminary considerations presented above in chapter 1, we are in position to read Ignatius' Rules for the Discernment of Spirits accurately and with clearly defined expectations as to what we can—and cannot—expect to find in them. For this, however, and for drawing out and analyzing their threefold aim, we must use an accurate English translation which, as far as possible, faithfully preserves even the nuances of Ignatius' own words. For this purpose we print just below one made by the present writer which aims at this fidelity rather than at a grace of style which is not in the original Spanish.

Ignatius, whose mother tongue was Basque, composed the *Exercises* in Spanish in his own rough and difficult style, in which he often uses words with meanings peculiarly his own. His original Spanish text, called the "Autograph," was preserved for us in a manuscript written by a copyist, probably in 1544. But it was used and corrected by Ignatius himself and gives us his original and authentic thought.

There are also two ancient translations into Latin. The first, the *Versio prima* of 1541 (called P1) and of 1547 (called P2), is rough and unpolished and may be from Ignatius' own hand, at least in part. The second, called the Vulgate (*Versio vulgata*), was produced in 1546 and 1547 by the humanist André des Freux and, after approval by Pope Paul III, was published in 1548. Des Freux, however, was more concerned to use the flowing style of Renaissance Latin than to express Ignatius' nuances.[1]

---

1 For authoritative discussions on the texts of the *Spiritual Exercises*, see *Obras completas de san Ignacio de Loyola* (Madrid: Biblioteca de Autores Cristianos, 1977), pp. 191-196; *SpEx*MHSJ (Madrid, 1919), pp. 83-139; *SpEx*MHSJ*Te* (Rome, 1969), pp 83-139.

Saint Ignatius' Rules for the Discernment of Spirits

The Autograph and the Vulgate are the two principal ancient texts which call for the attention of serious students of the *Exercises*. The Autograph is quite generally considered the most reliable expression of Ignatius' thought, and the basic one to be used.[2] The translation given below is made from it. Time and again, however, in commenting on it, the Vulgate will be used to throw light on what Ignatius means. For, although the Vulgate does not have the same authority as the Autograph, we should not forget that it was examined and approved by Ignatius, that it was the text presented for papal approval, that it was the first published text, and that after publication it was used by Ignatius and all the early Jesuits in directing the Spiritual Exercises.

The Text of Ignatius' Rules, Literally Translated

[*S E T I*]

[313]. RULES TO HELP PERSONS[3] GET IN TOUCH WITH[4] AND UNDERSTAND IN SOME MANNER THE DIVERSE MOTIONS WHICH ARE PROMPTED IN THEM,

---

2 For a minority opinion that has considerable force, see Lewis Delmage, S.J., *Spiritual Exercises of St. Ignatius Loyola* (New York, 1968), pp. iii-iv. For reasons supporting the autograph and answering the reasons accepted by Delmage, see *SpEx*MHSJ pp. 135-139.

3 Here Ignatius' Spanish word is *ánima*. On translating it by "person" or "persons," see footnote 6 just below.

4 *...para en alguna manera sentir y cognoscer:* a very literal translation of Ignatius' text is "for helping in some manner to perceive and understand..."; his thought here moves from an initial perception (*sentir* in its primary or root meaning) of the interior motions to a better understanding (*cognoscer*) of them. Hence I translate by "get in touch with and understand." The Spanish word *sentir*, like the Latin *sentire* from which it came, has the primitive meaning of perceiving by the senses (e.g. by feeling) and then by the mind (e.g. by observing or judging); and thereafter the acquired meanings in new contexts become too numerous to list here. Ignatius used *sentir* frequently and with many meanings, some of which are peculiarly his own, especially in passages which record his mystical experiences. His shadings are treated in depth and with copious references by Iparraguirre in his *Vocabulario de Ejercicios Espirituales: Ensayo de hermeneutica Ignaciana* (Rome: Centrum Ignatianum Spiritualitatis, 1972), pp. 192-197. In the *Exercises* Ignatius uses *sentir* in its verbal form 32 times, with the meanings and nuances varying according to the context (*SpEx*MHSJ*Te*, p. 781).

Usually present in the meaning is a cognition which is basically intellectual; and often emotional or even mystical overtones are added. In various Ignatian writings *sentir* indicates cognition savored so repeatedly that it becomes a framework of reference instinctively or affectively used to guide one's thinking, deciding, and acting— for example, in *SpEx*, [352] on the directives *para el sentido verdadero que en la Iglesia debemos tener*, "toward acquiring the genuine attitude which we ought to maintain in

SO THAT THEY MAY RECEIVE THE GOOD ONES AND EXPEL THE EVIL ONES. THESE RULES ARE MORE APPROPRIATE TO THE FIRST WEEK.⁵

[314]. Rule 1. In the case of those persons who go from mortal sin to mortal sin, the customary tactic of the enemy is to put before them illusory gratifications, prompting them to imagine sensual delights and pleasures, the better to hold them and make them grow in their vices and sins. With such persons, the good spirit employs a contrary tactic, through their rational power of moral ¹udgment causing pain and remorse in their consciences.

[315]. Rule 2. As for those persons who are intensely concerned with purging away their sins and ascending from good to better in the service of God our Lord, the mode of acting on them is contrary to that [described] in the first rule. For then it is connatural to the evil spirit to gnaw at them, to sadden them, to thrust obstacles in

the Church militant...." (see Leturia, *Estudios Ignacianos*, II, 153; Ganss, *Studies in the Spirituality of Jesuits*, VII, no. 1 [Jan., 1975], 12). Ignatius' *Spiritual Diary*, [63] for February 21, 1544, in the words "During the Mass I was knowing, deeply feeling, or seeing, the Lord knows..." (*conoçía, sentía, o veía, Dominus scit...*), presents an instance where the basically intellectual cognition is savored amid circumstances of infused contemplation, and where all this together is used as a frame of reference in Ignatius' effort to discern God's will.

The affective and sometimes mystical overtones of *sentir* in Ignatius' works are well discussed by John Futrell in his *Making an Apostolic Community of Love* (St. Louis, 1970) pp. 111-116, and more succinctly in his brochure "Ignatian Discernment" (*Studies in the Spirituality of Jesuits*, II, no. 2 [April, 1970], 56-57). "In the process of discernment," he states on p. 57, "*sentir* comes to mean above all a kind of 'felt-knowledge,' an affective, intuitive knowledge possessed through the reaction of human feelings to exterior and interior experience."

This is undoubtedly true of many passages of Ignatius; but our present instance of Ignatius' title for his rules (*SpEx*, [313]) is not one of them. For to translate *sentir* here by "to feel" or "to have a felt-knowledge" would not make good sense. These rules for discerning spirits are certainly not calculated to help one feel anything. They presuppose feeling and other "interior motions," and are calculated to help us become aware of these and understand them, not to feel them. In the context of *SpEx*, [313], "for perceiving" or "for getting in touch with" seems to be accurate.

Futrell's two works mentioned above are highly important for the study of Ignatian discernment. However, they refer almost entirely to Ignatius' discernment of the will of God, whereas our present book is concerned with discernment of spirits. This difference of focus explains why Futrell's books do not appear more prominently in this present work.

5 The *Spiritual Exercises* are divided into four periods called "weeks," but these are not understood as periods of seven days. The distinction between the First and the Second Week is not to the point here; it will be taken up in discussing the difference of the second set of rules from the first. See below, page 319.

their way, disquieting them with false reasons for the sake of impeding progress. It is connatural to the good spirit to give courage and
active energy, consolations, tears, inspirations and a quiet mind,
giving ease of action and taking away obstacles for the sake of
progress in doing good.

[316]. Rule 3. Concerning spiritual consolation. I name it
[spiritual] consolation when some inner motion is prompted in the
person,[6] of such a kind that he begins to be aflame with love of his
Creator and Lord, and, consequently, when he cannot love any
created thing on the face of the earth in itself but only in the
Creator of them all. Likewise [I call it consolation] when a person
pours out tears moving to love of his Lord, whether it be for sorrow
over his sins, or over the passion of Christ our Lord, or over other
things directly ordered to his service and praise. Finally, I call
[spiritual] consolation every increase of hope, faith, and charity,

6 The Spanish is *en el ánima*. Here, as in *SpEx*, [313], and also in other occurrences in
these rules where the context warrants, I translate Ignatius' *ánima* by "person" rather
than "soul." Ignatius did not have a Platonic or Cartesian notion of man; he uses
ánima merely in the figurative sense of taking the part for the whole (synechdoche).
Important for understanding rightly Ignatius' use of *ánima* is the following commentary of George E. Ganss, S.J., in his translation of St. Ignatius' *Constitutions of the
Society of Jesus* (St. Louis, 1970), (hereafter abbreviated as (*ConsSJComm*), p. 77:
"...*ánimas* in Ignatius' Spanish, here means the persons, the men considered as their
entire selves. This was a frequent meaning of the word for 'soul' in all the languages
of Christendom, as it was of the Latin *anima* in classical times (e.g., *Aeneid*, xi, 24;
Horace, *Satires*, i, 5, 41) and in Christian writers too. Ignatius also uses *ánima*, soul,
in contrast to *cuerpo*, the body, e.g., in *Cons*, [812-814].
   "The use of the Latin *anima* and Spanish *ánima* to mean the living man, the self,
the person, is scriptural and occurs very frequently in the Latin Vulgate, especially
in texts frequently quoted such as Matt. 16:26; Mark 3:48, 8:36 (Cf., e.g., Gen
2:7, 12:5, 49:6; Exod. 1:5; Acts 2:41; 1 Cor. 15:45). Hence this usage was common
in all the languages of Christian Europe throughout the Middle Ages (see, e.g., Blaise,
Dictionnaire...des auteurs chrétiens, s.v. 'anima', 4; also, Peter Lombard's *Sentences*
II, 1, no. 8). Awareness of this usage is a key necessary for accurate interpretation of
virtually all Christian writers on spirituality. Because of their heritage of Greek philosophy, medieval theologians and later spiritual writers regarded this, more frequently
than modern scriptural scholars, as the figure of synecdoche by which the part
(*anima*) was taken for the whole, the living man (*homo*). Even this synecdoche, however, has a scriptural basis (Wisd. 3:1, 8:19-20). In the Spanish of the 1500's (as we
gather s.v. from the *Tesoro* [A.D. 1611] of Covarrubias, who refers to Gen. 12:5 and
14:21), *ánima* and its synonym *alma* have among their meanings 'that by which we
live' and are 'often used for the persons.' Ignatius' use of *ánima* rather than *hombre*
or *homo* has occasionally been taken as evidence of exaggerated dualism or even of
Neoplatonism in his thought. In the light of the pervading influence of the Latin
Vulgate and its use of *anima* throughout the Middle Ages, this interpretation appears
to be farfetched and groundless."

and every inward gladness which calls and attracts to heavenly things and to one's personal salvation, bringing repose and peace in his Creator and Lord.

[317]. Rule 4. Concerning spiritual desolation. I call [spiritual] desolation everything the contrary of [what is described in] the third rule, for example, gloominess of soul, confusion, a movement to contemptible and earthly things, disquiet from various commotions and temptations, [all this] tending toward distrust, without hope, without love; finding oneself thoroughly indolent, tepid, sad, and as if separated from one's Creator and Lord. For just as [spiritual] consolation is contrary to [spiritual] desolation, in the same way the thoughts which spring from [spiritual] consolation are contrary to the thoughts which spring from [spiritual] desolation.

[318]. Rule 5. The time of [spiritual] desolation is no time at all to change purposes and decisions with which one was content the day before such desolation, or the decision with which one was content during the previous consolation. It is, rather, a time to remain firm and constant in these. For just as in [spiritual] consolation the good spirit generally leads and counsels us, so in [spiritual] desolation does the evil spirit. By the latter's counsels we cannot find the way to a right decision.

[319]. Rule 6. Granted that in [spiritual] desolation we ought not to change our previous purposes, it helps greatly to change ourselves intensely in ways contrary to the aforesaid desolation, for instance, by insisting more on prayer, on meditation, on much examination, and on extending ourselves to do penance in some fitting manner.

[320]. Rule 7. Let one who is in [spiritual] desolation consider how the Lord has left him to his natural powers, so that he may prove himself while resisting the disturbances and temptations of the enemy. He is, indeed, able to do so with the divine aid, which always remains with him even though he does not clearly perceive it. For, although the Lord has withdrawn from him his bubbling ardor, surging love, and intense grace, nevertheless, he leaves enough grace to go on toward eternal salvation.

[321]. Rule 8. Let him who is in [spiritual] desolation work at holding on in patience, which goes contrary to the harassments that come on him; and, while taking unremitting action against

such desolation, as said in the sixth rule, let him keep in mind that he will soon be consoled.

[322]. Rule 9. There are three principal causes which explain why we find ourselves [spiritually] desolate. The first is that we are tepid, indolent, or negligent in our spiritual exercises; and, as a result of our own failings, [spiritual] consolation departs from us. The second is that it serves to put our worth to the test, showing how much we will extend ourselves in serving and praising God without so much pay in consolations and increased graces. The third is this: spiritual desolation serves to give us a true recognition and understanding, grounding an inward experiential perception of the fact that we cannot ourselves attain to or maintain surging devotion, intense love, tears, or any other spiritual consolation, but rather that all is gift and grace from God our Lord. So, we do not build a nest on another's property, elevating our mind in a certain pride or vainglory, giving ourselves credit for devotion or other constituents of spiritual consolation.

[323]. Rule 10. Let him who is in consolation think how he will bear himself in the desolation which will follow, gathering energy anew for that time.

[324]. Rule 11. Let him who is [spiritually] consoled set about humbling and lowering himself as much as he can, reflecting on how pusillanimous he is in the time of [spiritual] desolation without God's grace or consolation. On the other hand, let him who is in [spiritual] desolation keep in mind that, drawing strength from his Creator and Lord, he has with divine grace sufficiently great power to resist all his enemies.

[325]. Rule 12. The enemy acts like a shrewish woman, being weak and willful;[7] for it is connatural to such a woman in a quarrel with some man to back off when he boldly confronts her; and on the contrary when, losing courage, he begins to retreat, the anger vengeance, and ferocity of the woman swell beyond measure. In like manner, it is connatural to the enemy to fall back and lose courage, with his temptations fading out, when the person performing spiritual exercises presents a bold front against the temptations

---

7 My version perhaps takes a slight liberty with the text, translating Ignatius' *muger* by "shrewish woman" (which in this context is clearly his meaning) rather than merely by "woman." The text, I think, as well as Ignatius' respect for and friendship with women, calls for such a qualification.

of the enemy, by doing what is diametrically the opposite. If, on the contrary, the person engaged in spiritual exercises begins to be fearful and to lose courage while suffering temptations, there is no beast on the face of the earth so fierce as is the enemy of human kind in prosecuting his wicked intention with such swelling malice.

[326]. Rule 13. Likewise he behaves as a seducer in seeking to carry on a clandestine affair and not be exposed. When such a frivolous fellow makes dishonourable advances to the daughter of a good father or the wife of a good husband, he wants his words and seductions to be secret. On the contrary, he is greatly displeased when the daughter discovers to her father or the wife to her husband his fraudulent talk and lewd design; for he readily gathers that he will not be able to carry out the undertaking he has initiated. In like manner, when the enemy of human kind insinuates into the faithful person his wiles and seductions, he intensely desires that they be received in secret and kept secret. It dispirits him greatly when one discloses them to a good confessor or to another spiritual person who is acquainted with his trickery and malice; for when his evident trickery is brought to light, he gets the idea that he will not be able to realize the evil plan he has set in motion.

[327]. Rule 14. So also, in order to conquer and plunder what he desires, the enemy of human kind acts like a caudillo. For, just as a military commander-in-chief pitching camp and exploring what the forces of a stronghold are and how they are disposed, attacks the weaker side, in like manner, the enemy of human kind roves around and makes a tour of inspection of all our virtues, theological and cardinal and moral. Where he finds us weaker and more in need of reinforcement for the sake of our eternal salvation, there he attacks us and strives to take us by storm.

[*SET II*]

[328]. RULES FOR THE SAME PURPOSE [AS THE FIRST SET], WITH MORE ACCURATE WAYS OF DISCERNING SPIRITS. THESE RULES ARE MORE SUITED FOR USE IN THE SECOND WEEK.[8]

[329]. Rule 1. It is connatural for God and his angels, when they prompt interior motions, to give genuine gladness and spiritual

8 See note 5 above.

joy, eliminating all sadness and confusion which the enemy brings on. It is connatural for the latter to fight against such gladness and spiritual consolation by proposing specious arguments, subtle and persistently fallacious.

[330]. Rule 2. To give a person consolation without preceding cause is for God our Lord alone to do; for it is distinctive of the Creator in relation to the created person to come in and to leave, to move the person interiorly, drawing him or her totally into love of his Divine Majesty. I say without [preceding][9] cause, that is, without any previous perception or understanding of any object such that through it consolation of this sort would come by the mediation of the person's own acts of understanding and will.

[331]. Rule 3. With a [preceding] cause, an angel, good or evil, can console a person. In doing so, the good and evil angels have contrary purposes. The purpose of the good angel is the person's progress, that he may ascend from good to better. The purpose of the evil angel is the contrary—and thereafter, to draw the person on to his damned intent and cunning trap.

[332]. Rule 4. It is characteristic of the evil spirit to take on the appearance of an angel of light, so that he can begin by going the way of a devout person and end with that person going his own way. By that I mean that he first prompts thoughts which are good and holy, harmonious with such a faithful person, and then manages, little by little, to step out of his act and lead the person to his hidden falsehoods and perverse designs.

[333]. Rule 5. We ought to pay close attention to the progression of thoughts. If the beginning, middle, and end of it are altogether good and tend entirely to what is right, that is a sign of the good angel's influence. It is, however, a clear sign that the line of thought originates from the influence of the evil spirit, the enemy of our spiritual progress and eternal salvation, if the thoughts which he prompts end up in something evil or distracting or less

---

9 Careful reading of the text shows that "without cause" is simply a contraction of "without preceding cause." First, the Vulgate version and both the *Prima Versio* texts always speak of a cause that precedes. Secondly, in the autograph version of Rule II:2, where Ignatius first makes the shift, he writes, "*I say*, without cause," (emphasis mine) obviously referring back to the phrase "without preceding cause." He then adds a phrase to explain "without cause": "without any *previous* perception or understanding of any object such..." (italics mine).

good than what the person had previously proposed to do, or if they weaken, disquiet, or confuse him, doing away with the peace, tranquility, and quiet experienced beforehand.

[334]. Rule 6. When the enemy of human nature has been perceived and recognized by his telltale train of thoughts terminating in the evil to which he leads, it is useful for the person who was tempted by him to look immediately at the course of good thoughts which were prompted in him, noting how they began and how, little by little, the evil spirit contrived to make him fall away from the earlier sweetness and spiritual joy until he led him to what his [the spirit's] own corrupt mind intended. The purpose is that observing such an experience and taking mental note of it will be a safeguard for the future against these customary hoaxes of the evil spirit.

[335]. Rule 7. Persons who are going from good to better the good angel touches sweetly, lightly, gently, as when a drop of water soaks into a sponge, while the evil spirit touches them sharply, with noise and disturbance, as when the drop of water falls on a rock. Those who are going from bad to worse the aforesaid spirits touch in a way contrary to the way they touch those going from good to better. The cause of this contrariety is that the disposition of the one touched is either contrary to or concordant with each of the said angels. For when it is contrary, the angels enter perceptibly, with clamor and observable signs; when it is concordant, they come in quietly. as one comes into his own house through an open door.

[336]. Rule 8. Granted that when consolation is without [preceding] cause, it has no deception in it, since, as has been said, such consolation is from God our Lord alone; nevertheless, a spiritual person to whom God gives such consolation should, with great alertness and attention, examine his experience to discern the precise time of the actual consolation [without preceding cause] as distinct from the following time, in which the person is still glowing and still graced by the residue of [actual] consolation that is now over with. The reason for making this distinction is that frequently in this second period, either through one's own reasoning about the relations of concepts and judgments and the conclusions to be drawn from them, or through the influence of a good spirit or of an evil spirit, various purposes and opinions take shape which are not given immediately by God our Lord. Inasmuch as that is

29

the case, these purposes and opinions are in need of prolonged and careful examination before full assent is given to them or they are put into execution.

Theological Perspectives

In the introductory heading or title for his first set of rules, Ignatius says that they are for helping us to get in touch with and to understand in some manner the diverse motions which are prompted in persons, that they may receive the good ones and expel the evil ones. Since this heading contains several fundamental concepts and states the scope and purpose of the rules, it deserves more than passing attention. However, in order to interpret this statement of scope and purpose for all the rules that follow, it is necessary beforehand to sketch in large outline the theological perspective within which Ignatius is speaking, and to clarify what he means by "diverse motions."

Any vision of human life which does not see it as a life of conflict between good and evil, light and darkness, spirit and flesh, Christ and Satan, has lost the Scriptural vision within which Ignatius is speaking. It is above all in the conflict of Christ and Satan, not as personifications of forces, but as persons[10] struggling over the everlasting destiny of persons—it is in this conflict that Ignatius sees Holy Scripture reaching its profoundest revelation of what is going on underneath all the turmoil and peace, the misery and exultation, of human history in peoples and in every individual life.

Among the Scriptural metaphors of Christian life in time, we find, for example, seeds planted and growing to the harvest, a journey, military warfare. All of them present life as a matter of struggling and dying in order to attain and to give life. The warfare metaphor is most obviously of this sort. But the others are used in Sacred Scripture to bring out the same idea. The seed has to die if it is to bring forth more life; the early growth has to contend against weeds and thorns; the enemy plants cockle, while the good farmer or vinedresser protects, waters, and prunes. The journey is an exodus from slavery beset with suffering, danger, and enemies who have to be fought with in the strength given by the Lord who is always near.

---

10 See below, pp. 34-38, and Appendix I below, pp. 260-270; also, Raymond E. Brown, S.S., in *Jerome Biblical Commentary*, 78:127 on p. 787.

Among all these Scriptural metaphors, Ignatius finds that of warfare the most apt. By it he can make the conflict of opposing powers more obvious, dramatic, and above all personal. This metaphor highlights the role of personal reason, free decision and responsibility, in being with Christ against the power of darkness. It highlights the need for loyalty, courage, energy, promptness and generosity in making any sacrifice for responding to his call, the need for fidelity through times of darkness and apparent defeat, with complete trust in God to be with us always. Ignatius finds this metaphor more suitable to stress his ideal of utterly selfless service so as not only to reach his personal salvation but with Christ and in the power of Christ to conquer "the enemy of the human race" and bring all men to happiness in God.

The struggle is individual and cosmic. Each human person is divided within self (Romans 7; Galatians 5:16-17, 26) and the struggle within self is part of a larger struggle between the spiritual forces of Christ and Satan (Mark 1:12-14; 3:22-27; Matt. 12:24-28), each having some hold within the person and each able to bring influence to bear on him. This vision of human life is graphically expressed in Ignatius' meditation on the Two Standards (*SpEx*, [136-148]) and runs through the rules for discernment of spirits (*SpEx*, [313-336]). Ignatius sees that God has an immeasurable love for each of us, for me personally, creating the universe as a gift for me, dwelling in the creatures which he gives as gift, and serving me in them, wanting to give himself as much as I can receive him (*SpEx*, [232-237]), becoming man in Jesus for me, laboring, suffering, dying, rising, all for me personally (*SpEx*, [116]). Because of his infinite and infinitely delicate power, God can enter into and influence the human mind and heart as he wills (*SpEx*, [330]). Because of his love he enters into intimate and direct dealing with the created person to influence his life while respecting his freedom and appealing for a freely given response of generous love (*SpEx*, [5, 15]). Any diluting of the intimate dealing of God with each created person renders the *Spiritual Exercises* in general and these rules in particular unintelligible.

Ignatius does not wish us to become *illuminati* who think to get daily direct divine revelations in a supernatural mode. He does not, however, think that the way to avoid such illuminism is the denial of what he was sure Scripture, the experience of others, and his own experience taught him, namely, that God, over and above his action as creator and conserver of the whole universe, does enter into direct personal dealing with us (*SpEx*, [15]). He also believes that, in his dealing with us, God sometimes acts through his angels. This, however, is of no crucial importance. Whatever an angel from God does is what God does through the angel; so it makes no big difference for practical purposes, save for one case (which will be treated in chapter 11 below).

Ignatius shows no hesitancy in accepting in its fullness the central truth of Christian faith and all its consequences—unlike most of us who, if not in theory, at least in practice, are hesitant to accept the full astounding truth. If God so loves us as to send his Beloved, Jesus Christ, to be one with us in the flesh; to be a sacrifice for our sins; to give us all that the Father gave him, his life, his truth, his love, his joy, his glory; to give us his body to eat, his blood to drink; to give us the Holy Spirit who makes us children of God in Christ, who lives in us, enlightens us about Jesus and his teachings, pours out God's agape, defends and cherishes the Christ-life in us—if God so loves us as to do all this, then after that there is no problem in believing that God is constantly attending to each of his children, calling each of them by name, speaking to them, listening to them, sometimes in extraordinary ways but usually through the ordinary motions of their own minds and hearts, and giving them power to discover when it is he who is speaking and what he is saying. Given what a Christian is called to believe about his relationship with God, is it not surprising to our way of thinking that God does not speak and act in our lives even more obviously than Ignatius, with all genuine Christian tradition, has said he does?

Ignatius also sees a personal force of evil, trying in opposition to God to make those who have turned to God to lose heart and turn back again, or at least to give up on striving toward a life totally open to the Holy Spirit. In other words, he sees an anti-spiritual force extrinsic to the human persons but able somehow to instigate interior motions, thoughts and affections, calculated to hinder the work of the Holy Spirit. Ignatius never, at least in the *Spiritual Exercises* (except for one or two quotations from the New Testament), refers to this anti-spiritual force as Satan or the devil or the demon. In one exercise he speaks of "Lucifer, the deadly enemy of our human nature" (*SpEx*, [136-138]). Several times he uses "evil spirit" or "evil angel" when contrasting these created spirits with the "good spirits" or "good angels"(*SpEx*, [315-318]).[11] The usual name occurring over and over in his writings is simply

11 Brian O'Leary, S.J., has given us a valuable study of discernment of spirits as carried

"the enemy" (*SpEx*, [8, 12, 217, 274, 314, 320, and others]);
sometimes, but infrequently, varied as "the enemy of human
nature" (*SpEx*, [7, 10, 135, 325, and others]), "the leader of all the
enemies" (*SpEx*, [140]), that is, of the "innumerable demons"
(*SpEx*, [141]). "The enemy" seems to be a very good translation of
"Satan" as used in the New Testament.

The effect of this enemy on our minds and hearts with which
the Ignatian rules are concerned is emphatically not diabolical
possession or obsession or any other sensational experience whatever.
It is, rather, the experiences we all have day after day, sometimes
intensely, usually in a more quiet way, but always dangerous for
life in the spirit if we do not recognize what is happening, understand it, and know how to counteract it so as to maintain our
hearts open to the Holy Spirit during dark days as well as bright
ones. Ignatius on occasion uses dramatic images when speaking
of this hidden, inner struggle against the forces of evil—and with
reason, for it is dramatic in its significance for life. But it is not
usually experienced in a dramatic way. The descriptions of these
experiences and the directives given in the *Spiritual Exercises* and in
Ignatius' letters are thoughtful, balanced, peaceful, words of a man
who, through experience of struggle and pain, has himself won his
way to a quiet and assured mind filled with the peace and joy and
light of the Holy Spirit.

That we should become superstitious, tense, or obsessed with
fear of the demonic is the very contrary of all to which Ignatius
wants to lead us. Nevertheless, he does not think the way to avoid

on by a man who was a contemporary of Ignatius, his disciple and friend, in "The
Discernment of Spirits in the Memoriale of Blessed Peter Favre, "*The Way, Supplement 35* (Spring, 1979). Among other interesting contributions, O'Leary gives a
compendious sketch of Favre's belief's concerning good and evil created spirits
against a background of sixteenth century European modes of thought on this
subject (chs. 7-8). He indicates, and offers bibliographical aids for the study of,
the tradition leading up to the time of Favre and Ignatius, a tradition which was
basically orthodox but did at times fall into exaggerations and even absurdities
(p. 74). The then current modes of thought arising from this tradition influenced
Favre and cause us considerable discomfort when reading him (p. 79). No doubt
it is important for anyone reading Ignatius' texts on discernment of spirits to keep
the sixteenth-century background in mind. It is equally important, however, to
observe how carefully he avoids the exaggerations and absurdities which O'Leary
notes in the tradition, as also the conceptual complexities which bother us in Favre's
thought about spirits and, above all, the worrisome attitude toward evil spirits that
shows up even in so wise a man as Favre.

such aberrations is to deny or ignore the reality of evil spirits, any more than he would think that the way to avoid becoming health cranks is to deny the reality of dangerous germs or viruses. Anyone who follows Ignatian teaching will learn as he did to confront the evil spirit with vigilance and energy, but also with courage, calm, and a sense of humor, touched even with contempt for him. For in ultimate analysis, despite his cleverness and power, he is a futility, pitting his wickedness against an infinitely greater beneficent power and wisdom that uses even wickedness, demonic or human, for the good of those who love and trust God and do the best they reasonably can to let God rule over their hearts (Romans 8:28).

Satan and Discernment: Two Problems

No one who has a sober belief in a personal malevolent spiritual power and an emotionally healthy attitude toward him will have problems with Ignatius' teaching about Satan. Account must be taken, however, of the current uncertainty expressed by some Scriptural exegetes and theologians regarding angels, good or bad, who influence human lives. Whether these exegetes and theologians are many or few but very vocal is hard to know. One thing, however, is certain. It is hard to find much serious theological writing on the question of whether these spirits exist and are an object of Christian faith.[12] In any case, account must be taken also of the effect this uncertainty has had on many without theological or Scriptural training or without time for research and reflection on the question. Those who are interested in the current state of theological opinion on angels, good and evil, will find a brief discussion of it below in Appendix I.

What more directly concerns us are the *practical* problems or questions which arise in this situation. There are two which touch on what we are doing. The first is: Should good or evil created spirits be taken into consideration or left aside when discerning spirits? The second question is this: How should a commentator on Ignatius' rules deal with what he says about these spirits?

Regarding the first question, we should keep in mind that leaving good and evil spirits out of account in discernment of spirits does not necessarily imply a denial of their existence or of their influence on human lives. One may decide to omit them from consideration because of uncertainty. Or one may believe with certainty in their

12 See Appendix I below, pp. 260-270.

existence and influence and in the value of recognizing their influence if we could, but remain so dubious of being able to discover when and in what way they are involved that it seems useless to try. Or again one may think that in any case this problem concerning the existence and influence of the good and evil spirits is not worth bothering about; for, one may think, whatever the solution reached, it will be of little or no significance for the ultimate practical purpose of discerning spirits. The ultimate purpose is to open ourselves to be led and guided by the Holy Spirit and to reject any influence contrary to his, whatever the source of that influence may be. To do this, it seems enough to recognize: (1) the signs of the Holy Spirit prompting us, whether with or without the mediation of a good angel; (2) the signs of whatever force is opposed to him, without need to discern whether this force includes the promptings of a personal evil spirit or not; and (3) the naturally good promptings of our own hearts which, like all else in the universe, are under God's providence but are not what is meant by movements of the Spirit. For some persons, believing that a temptation or spiritual desolation is prompted by an evil spirit serves to call forth greater resistance (without unhealthy fear), more enthusiasm to conquer the movement. But that is not to say that such belief is necessary in order to respond well and to use the Ignatian rules as guides in doing so. For others, it may be that facing the sinfulness within themselves is helped by leaving aside the possible influence of an evil spirit. Or for still others, because of certain emotional conditions, their focusing attention on the influence of the evil spirits would have unhealthy consequences. And so on.

The answer to the first question, therefore, is that the better decision will vary with different persons; and each one, with whatever counsel seems needed and is available, has to make his or her own decision. Those who wish to leave Satan and demons out of the picture when discerning spirits can read Ignatius' references to these as personifications of the power of evil in self and the world. Only let it be clear that this is a practical decision which in no way decides the theological question about the reality of what is left out of consideration.

There is, however, one way of attempting to answer the first question which must be disallowed if Ignatius' own thought in its original form is to be presented, without any alteration to fit one's own or others' theological opinions. The way to which I am referring is that of identifying what Ignatius writes of as good and evil spirits with what he writes of as good and evil interior motions. Some recent writers have made this identification in their presentations of Ignatus' thought on discernment of spirits. They do this, so it seems, either because they themselves are uncomfortable with belief in angels and demons as real personal beings or because they hope in this way to keep the Ignatian rules for discernment of spirits acceptable to others who are sceptical of such beings. Unfortunately they have neglected to inform their readers of what they are doing and why they are doing it. Consequently, they leave the impression that they are presenting Ignatius' own thought and not an adaptation of it. Such an impression is, without question, a false one, even though unintended. Always, in Ignatius' own thought, the good or evil spirits are personal spiritual beings who prompt good or evil interior motions in us; and these motions in us are the signs by which Ignatius thinks we can discover whether a good or an evil spirit is moving us.

The second practical question noted above is this: Given the present state of thought on good and evil spirits and the diverse answers to the first question, what is the best way of proceeding in a commentary on Ignatius' teaching about discernment of spirits? He, along with most Christians then and now, obviously believed in these spirits as personal beings and in their action upon us. Would it be better in a practical presentation such as this one of Ignatius' teaching for contemporary readers, if the writer were to take a neutral stance on the question of the existence of good and evil personal spirits and of their influence upon us? and if he were also to neutralize the text of Ignatius by sifting out from it his belief in this regard? His belief is so fully woven into the fabric of his writing on discernment that to pull out the threads of it at every step of the exposition would become intolerably wearisome for the reader, certainly for the writer. If I were not trying to adhere as closely as possible to Ignatius' own thought as found in his own writings, but were, without constant reference to the text of Ignatius, merely presenting some Ignatian principles, it could be done without grave problems. The result, however, would be a different book, not the one I think is needed now. Much better, then, that I should hold to Ignatius' own point of view, and to his concepts and expressions, so as to present a more faithful interpretation of his text. The reader who finds Ignatius' treatment of Satan and demons uncongenial can, without painful complexity, readily understand them as personifications of the force of evil in self and in the world; and with this interpretation too Ignatius' Rules will remain wise,

valid, and useful. Li.tle will be said in any case about good angels;
and what is said will, I think, cause no problem for the reader, no
matter what his or her decision on the first question or even on the
theological question.

The *"Diverse Motions"*

Within the foregoing perspective of struggle between the forces
of Light and Darkness, we can now understand what Ignatius means
by good or evil motions which are caused in us and what the scope
and purpose of these rules are. Since all the rules are about these
motions, any obscurity or inaccuracy about the motions will
obscure or falsify our understanding of the scope and purpose of
the rules.

What Ignatius refers to by motions in the soul is the flux of
thoughts (such as judgments about God, self, the world, plans,
lines of reasoning, lines of association, or imaginings), and of
affective acts (such as love, hate, desire, or fear), and of affective
feelings (such as peace, warmth, coldness, sweetness, bitterness,
buoyancy, or depression). Among all these motions Ignatius sees
some to be of special interest for anyone who is trying to open himself to the Holy Spirit and to resist the influence of the evil spirit.
These are motions which *of themselves,* and therefore in every instance,
tend to build up or to tear down the Christ-life in us. Their unvary-
ing thrust is toward having a beneficial or harmful influence on
faith, hope, charity, prayer, personal relationships, apostolic work,
decisions that give direction to our life as Christians, and the like.

It must not be thought that we have no natural or acquired dispositions for impulses to good acts, and that thus without the direct
prompting of the Holy Spirit we would have no inclination to do
what is humanly good. Neither should it be thought that without the
prompting of the evil spirit we do not have enough sinful tendencies
which are quite capable of leading us toward sin, independently
of the influence of the evil spirit. We do have such tendencies,
arising spontaneously from our fallen nature and our acquired
habits, or from the weakness of our intelligence: our ignorance,
inability to perceive reality, to understand, to think logically.
Further, whenever we are moved by a good or evil spirit, it is we
ourselves who act under this influence. Therefore the motions of
which Ignatius speaks should be understood neither as produced
in a person who is totally passive, nor as always arising altogether

spontaneously and without any spiritual agents ever taking advantage of human dispositions and tendencies in accord with their own good or evil intentions. There is no possibility and no need to know in every instance how much of whatever experiences we have is due to our own spontaneous good or evil or neutral inclinations, and how much is due to the influence of God or a good angel or an evil spirit or the world. But there are some experiences which, Ignatius thinks, can be known as prompted by God, and others as prompted by the evil spirit, or as arising spontaneously from our own sinfulness.

In regard to these which can be thus recognized, it is necessary to stress something that was said above, namely, that these motions *tend*, of themselves, to have good or evil effects on our faith life. That means: They are such that, if they are accepted and allowed to work or are cooperated with, they will inevitably have such effects; but they do not necessarily, of themselves, have an actual constructive or destructive effect. Those which of themselves tend to a destructive effect can be resisted and become the occasion of actual spiritual growth. Those which of themselves tend to have a constructive effect can be ignored, resisted, or even misused, and so be the occasion for sin and regression in Christian life. What effect they actually have depends on what we do with them. No person who experiences them is worthy of praise or condemnation only for having had one or other of them. "I am not going to be saved," Ignatius writes elsewhere in reference to these motions, "because of the good works of the good angels"—that is, because of the good motions they prompt in me— "and I am not going to be condemned because of the evil thoughts and the weaknesses the bad angels, the flesh, and the world bring before my mind."[13]

The Context of These Rules in the Spiritual Exercises

Understanding what Ignatius means by "motions," and seeing these within the perspective of conflict between the powers of light and darkness, we can take up the purpose of these Rules for the Discernment of Spirits as he himself states it. If we are to understand that purpose as clearly as we can, we must take account of the fact that the rules are not a separate work of Ignatius which stands by itself. They appear within the *Spiritual Exercises*. Their purpose and meaning can be fully gathered only when kept within the context of that document. To say this does not mean that they have

13 Letter of Sept. 11, 1536 to Sister Teresa Rejadell, in *LettersIgn*, p. 25.

The Text of Ignatius' Rules and a Perspective

no value outside the time of making the Spiritual Exercises. Rather their main value, like all else which occurs when one' makes the Spiritual Exercises, is for living a Christian life after the Exercises are completed. Neither does their place in the *Spiritual Exercises* mean that anyone who wants to understand and use them has to have made the Exercises and then studied the book. (Studying the book without making the Exercises is of questionable value; no one can truly understand the book without the experiences to which the book supplies directives.) Nevertheless, since the rules were written as an integral part of that book, light for interpreting them will be found in it.

Before we even look at the stated purpose of the rules, then, it will be of great help to place them within the aims or goals of the whole *Spiritual Exercises*—both the book and the exercises it proposes. The overall goal is the removal of obstacles in us to the one certain expression of love for God, our seeking sincerely to find and do his will (*SpEx*, [1]), and so enabling us to grow toward the ideal of hearts so pure as to experience God's revelation of himself in all things, and to live lives in Christ totally dedicated to thanksgiving, praise, and service, or, in other words, to doing always what is for the greater glory of God (*SpEx*, [230]). The way to such purity of heart is mainly contemplation of God's love revealed in Jesus as he is seen in the Gospels—contemplating in such a way as to experience his personal love "for me" and so to enter into intimate personal relationship with him, taking on his mind and heart.

Growth into such purity of heart is God's work in us, impossible to achieve merely by our own efforts, but not to be effected by God without our free response and effort. So it is of essential importance to be able to recognize when God is acting on our consciousness and to know when it is not God, but our own selves, or the prodding of the world, or of Satan. Only so, can we by our free choice open ourselves to God's influence and close out anything opposed to it.

The Threefold Purpose of the Rules: to Notice, to Understand, to Accept or Reject

Accordingly, when he comes to write his Rules for the Discernment of Spirits, Ignatius states that they are "to help persons get in touch with and understand in some manner the diverse motions which are prompted in them, in order to receive the good ones and expel the evil ones." If we analyze this statement, we can see that

39

it proposes three aims in an ordered series: (1) to help us get in touch with—that is, to become reflectively and discriminatingly aware of—the spiritually significant motions among all those in the whole mass of motions swarming in our consciousness; (2) to help us to a practical "understanding" of these perceived motions; and (3) to enable us intelligently to receive or expel these spiritually significant motions. The first purpose is for the sake of the second and makes it possible; the second in turn is for the sake of the third and makes it possible. The first two are so closely bound together that they can be discussed as one combined purpose. Since the first takes its meaning by relationship to the second and the second by reference to the third, the latter purpose had better be taken first in the order of explanation. Then later we shall work back from the third purpose to the explanation of the first and second.

Ignatius assumes that those who study these rules will truly desire their third and ultimate purpose; they will want to open themselves wide to the movements from God and allow them to influence their lives in whatever way God intends by giving them; they will respond with decision and action when this is called for. On the other hand, he assumes that such persons will be ready to resist the movements from Satan and thrust them out.

In order to reject or receive these motions intelligently, we must first understand them—the second purpose of the rules. There are, of course, different understandings possible and desirable, but all are not relevant to the purpose of these rules or, at least, not adequate for it. Thus, a psychological or sociological or philosophical understanding is not what Ignatius is talking about, though these understandings may, of course, also be of great value. Neither is he concerned about a speculative theological understanding.[14] For his practical purposes, understanding a motion comprises

---

14 Although Ignatius' own aim is purely and directly practical and his own knowledge largely experiential, there does seem to be implied a schema of inner motions and their relationships. Michael J. Buckley, S.J., has made a penetrating essay at theoretical analysis of this schema in *"The Way, Supplement* no. 20 (Autumn, 1973), pp. 19-37. This essay may be of practical as well as speculative value to those who master it. I might add that I find myself in disagreement with his understanding of what Ignatius meant by spiritual consolation and desolation (as is clear from my chapters 4, 5, and Appendix III below). Even if my criticism of Buckley's interpretation should be valid, his schematization of inner motions, the main point of his study, need not, it seems to me, lose its value. His essay is one of the most learned and most interesting to be found in the literature on Ignatian discernment of spirits.

at least three things. First, we recognize the characteristic features by which it is distinguished from other motions. Second, we see the direction in which it of itself points or leads us, its likely or actually effected consequences. Third, we know its origin. In a spiritual understanding, we recognize those features which distinguish spiritually significant motions from others; and among the former, we distinguish one sort from another. We see the good or evil consequences for a Christian life to which the motion of itself tends; and from these two elements of spiritual understanding, we infer the good or evil origin.

An obvious condition for the possibility of understanding the spiritually significant motions within our minds and affectivities is our becoming aware of them. This is, therefore, the first purpose of the rules, to help us become perceptively aware of what is going on within us. This purpose involves more than mere consciousness of the motions; it involves reflective and discriminating attention. All the motions of which Ignatius speaks are conscious acts or feelings, but generally most of them are not attended to reflectively. In fact, when we make the effort to attend to them we find it very difficult to do so.

There are a number of reasons why it is so difficult for the ordinary person to become perceptively aware of his or her own inner experiences and then to understand them. In regard to spiritual motions, not the least of these reasons, according to those most experienced in reflecting on their spiritual experiences, are the blinding and distorting effects of our own sinfulness and the deceptions of the evil spirit. Ignatius has much to say about these. However, underlying all other reasons are two natural and universally operative ones: first, the natural bent of our attention and, second, the complexity and mobility of our psychic experience.

The bent of our attention is, perhaps, the most basic reason. Our power of attention is not easily disciplined. It tends to wander aimlessly, responding to any present stimulus, especially any sensible one; and among all objects of attention, the motions of our own mind and affectivity are in general the hardest to bring into focus. So, we get into the focus of reflective and discriminating attention very little of what goes on in our conscious life. As a consequence, we ordinarily have little understanding of what goes on in us, only a superficial awareness that some state of consciousness is pleasant or unpleasant, tranquil or disturbed. Sometimes we have only a vague awareness that it is good or bad. Why it is this way or that, how the inner motions arise, what they reveal about ourselves, where they may be leading us, what their value or disvalue is for the main purpose of our lives—all this we rarely wonder about; or, if we do, we feel rather helpless to answer the questions which occur to us.

It would be a serious mistake to think that because our interests are mostly self-centered our attention is reflectively and evaluatively centered on our own thoughts and affections. We are, it is true, very much concerned with what is to our advantage, concerned to satisfy our self-centered desires; but we rarely reflect on and understand these desires, their origin, their moral character, their significance within a Christian life. For instance, when we deliberately set about trying to surface our motivations for some way of acting, we frequently find it very difficult. The self-knowledge so prized by moral philosophers, by psychologists, and by the saints, is hard to come by.

Even when we do get attention focused on our inner motions of mind and heart, these motions themselves are so manifold and mobile, so complexly interrelated in a swift flux, that a distinct perception of any particular motion within the flow is difficult to achieve except in the case of unusually intense or prolonged motions.

For these two reasons, the complex and mobile character of our psychic experience and the centrifugal and wandering character of our attention unless we learn to discipline it, many inner motions which are more powerful for spiritual good in our lives, more significant for showing us what God is doing in us, fade into the unreflected and eventually forgotten flux of consciousness. They are never brought to the scrutiny of faith-enlightened intelligence and integrated into our Christian life of free choice and love. On the other hand, we let ourselves be moved about and badly harmed or impeded by evil or destructive forces without understanding what is happening, much less doing anything about it.

The foregoing stress on the difficulty of noting and understanding the workings of our minds and hearts is not intended to discourage anyone from undertaking it by suggesting that it is next to impossible to do. Quite the contrary. My intention is, first of all, to save from discouragement those who begin trying to discern what goes on within themselves and find they do not easily succeed. Awareness of how difficult this project is for anyone at all will free them from false expectations, from thinking they should find it all as easy as looking at and describing an external scene or event. If one finds it difficult to be attentive to inner experience and describe it to a spiritual counselor or a director of the Spiritual Exercises, that is a common experience. Repeated efforts over a long period may be required to grow in the capacity to carry it out, but it can be done. Secondly, my intention is to warn those who think that they do readily discern what is going on in themselves, that they are an open book to themselves. They are probably reading their hearts very superficially, finding what they want to find or what they have been led to expect to find. Their easy confidence may be a barrier to real self-knowledge, which is not easily achieved. Thirdly, my intention is to point out the need for prayer, for openness to and trusting in the Holy Spirit, if we are ever to discern and, much more, if we are ever to understand how he and the evil spirit and our own selves are acting and interacting within our consciousness. It is the Holy Spirit who can and will sensitize and enlighten those who sincerely seek such knowledge through prayer, reflection, and the acceptance of human help when it is available. It is he who will give them understanding and protect them directly or through a counselor from deceptions. Only he can enable us to understand his actions. Finally, and most immediately important in the present context, we need some help such as we can get from the rules which Ignatius gives us. The Holy Spirit expects us to use the human aids he has provided for us.

In his terse style Ignatius warns us, in a single phrase, against any exaggerated notion of what is contained in these rules. These are, he states, rules for getting in touch with and understanding "in some manner" the diverse motions prompted in us. The corresponding heading in the Vulgate version (and the other Latin versions) is, "A few rules for Discerning the Motions...." (*Regulae aliquot ad motus...discernendos,...*). He is not merely saying that the first set of rules is inadequate without the second, or that all these rules taken together without learning and experience and the help of the Holy Spirit are inadequate for the stated purpose. What he is saying is that both series of rules together are still far from an adequate set of rules, *even as rules go,* for discerning what spirit is moving the one discerning and how to act in response. This is a core set of rules which is sufficient for his purposes in the *Spiritual Exercises,* but needs to be expanded for other experiences than those taken account of in these rules themselves. Moreover, the rules serve, even in regard to what they do treat, only "in some manner"; they need discreet adaptation to meet the infinite variations of concrete individual experience. No rules can substitute for discretion. No one was ever more keenly aware of that than Ignatius. On the other hand, discretion may be impossible for most of us without the help of some basic set of principles, descriptions, explanations, and counsels such as Ignatius offers us.

PART II

THE GOOD SPIRIT AND THE EVIL SPIRIT.
THEIR CONTRARY EFFECTS AND SIGNS.

Rules I:1-4

Chapter 3

THE FUNDAMENTAL PRINCIPLES FOR DISCERNING SPIRITS
Rules I:1 and 2

In form, the first two rules of Ignatius' first set are merely statements of fact. They are not telling us what to do or how to do anything. When they are read in context, however, the reader easily understands that these are rules for discerning what spirit is moving the person who experiences certain interior motions. They give us in a first rough form the fundamental things to be noted and understood by one who wants to discern whether any spirit is moving him and, if so, whether it is a good or an evil spirit. These rough statements will have to be made more precise, qualified, explained, and nuanced; but all else in the rules builds on them.

The Kinds of Persons Envisaged in Rules I:1 and 2

The two things pointed out as fundamentals to be noted and understood are, first, the sort of persons experiencing the motions in question and, second, the ways in which good or evil spirits affect such a person. For his purpose in this context, Ignatius classifies persons into two kinds, devoting one of these rules to each of them. He illustrates what inner motions may be prompted in each and lays down the general principle for judging what is the source of such motions.

[314]. Rule 1. In the case of those persons who go from mortal sin to mortal sin, the customary tactic of the enemy is to put before them illusory gratifications, prompting them to imagine sensual delights and pleasures, the better to hold them and make them grow in their vices and sins. With such persons, the good spirit employs a contrary tactic, through their rational power of moral judgment causing pain and remorse in their consciences.

Saint Ignatius' Rules for the Discernment of Spirits

[315]. Rule 2. As for those persons who are intensely concerned with purging away their sins and ascending from good to better in the service of God our Lord, the mode of acting on them is contrary to that [described] in the first rule. For then it is connatural to the evil spirit to gnaw at them, to sadden them, to thrust obstacles in their way, disquieting them with false reasons for the sake of impeding progress. It is connatural to the good spirit to give courage and active energy, consolations, tears, inspirations and a quiet mind, giving ease of action and taking away obstacles for the sake of progress in doing good.

Contrariety in Ignatian Thought

In these first two rules, one is immediately struck with the multiple relationships of contrariety involved. The fundamental attitudes of the two types of persons are not merely unlike but contrary. Their lives move not merely in different but in contrary directions. The effects in them when they are under the influence of the Holy Spirit are not merely different but contrary; so also when they are under the influence of the evil spirit.

This notion of contrariety is used all through the rules. It functions not only in Rules I:1-2, but also in the more detailed descriptions of spiritual consolation and desolation (I:3-4), not only in all rules for discerning what spirit is counseling a person (I:5; II:5-8) but also in the rules on how to act once one has discerned the sort of motion he is experiencing and its source (I:6-13). It is worth our while to get the notion of contrariety and its implications clearly.

The term "contrary" is used by Ignatius in its most exact meaning, a meaning which goes beyond "different" or "diverse" or "contradictory." Contraries are not merely different in any sort of way, nor merely the negation of each other; they are diametrically opposed, opposite extremes. They always imply a mean which is the contradictory, the simple negation, of both contraries. There is no mean between contradictories; and most differences are not in the same line so as to make possible any opposition at all. Thus, love and hate, desire and aversion are contraries; indifference is the mean, which is a negation, the contradictory, of both extremes. There is no mean between indifference and love or indifference and hate. Elevated and depressed moods are contraries; untroubled calm is the mean, the negation or contradictory of both these extremes. There is no mean between calm and exultation, between calm and depression.

Now, when I know something about one reality, I do not ordinarily by that very fact have any implicit positive knowledge of something which is different, precisely in its difference. When the difference is one of contrariety, I do have implicit positive knowledge of the very differences in the contrary. If I learn something about love, I am not by that very fact any better off in my effort to understand mathematical reasoning; for love and mathematics are simply diverse. But by the very fact that I know something about love I am able to understand hate more deeply, and vice versa. All I have to do is to extrapolate in the diametrically opposite direction.[1] To illustrate, if love is an affirmation of another, issuing in care and desire for what will truly and ultimately bring the beloved fullness of being, then hatred is a negative response, issuing in desire for what will harm the one hated. It is commonly said that love makes one present to another. If that were true without qualification, then we would have to say that hate makes one absent. This is simply untrue to experience. One who hates is very much present to the one he hates. Indifference is affective absence. Knowing this throws light back on love and makes us aware of a *kind* of presence which is the contrary of presence constituted by hatred.[2]

Keeping in mind the strict meaning of contraries and how their relationship can function to throw light on each other, let us look at the contrary types of persons referred to in the first two rules and then at the contrary effects in them when they are acted upon by the contrary spirits.

The Two Contrary Types of Persons: Maturing and Regressing Christians

All else in discernment of spirits depends on first knowing what sort of person is experiencing the diverse motions. That is to say, what sort spiritually, whether one basically in accord with the Holy Spirit or basically in discord. Until that is known, no rule for discerning the source of inner motions or for responding can be intelligently applied. The very first step, therefore, toward understanding the rules is to grasp as accurately and clearly as possible what sort of person Ignatius is talking about in each of the first

---

1 One must be careful about doing this with metaphorical descriptions. For example, if love is said to be warm, that does not mean that hate must be spoken of as cold, that we cannot speak of a burning hatred.
2 See Jules Toner, *The Experience of Love* (Washington, 1968), pp. 121-123.

two rules. To do so, we will have to study them in conjunction; for any understanding or misunderstanding of one clarifies or obscures, rectifies or distorts, our understanding of the other. The reason for this is that Ignatius is dealing with contraries; and contraries, as we saw, are understood by relation to each other, each by implication illuminating the other.

Ignatius speaks in Rule 1 of persons who "go from one mortal sin to another." These words may at first blush lead a contemporary reader to think that the persons are sensationally bad. There are reasons to think, however, that they are not necessarily that evil. For there are grounds for interpreting Ignatius' term "mortal sin" here as meaning one of those which we are accustomed to call the seven "capital sins" or "deadly sins," with "sin" used in an analogous sense. These are primarily sources or tendencies giving rise to sinful acts,[3] to sins in the proper and ordinary meaning of the word. These acts may be either grave or light sins. Among the passages in the *Spiritual Exercises* where "mortal sin" is used, there are a number in which this is clearly the case,[4] and this could be another such text. If so, the picture we get of these persons is toned down very much. For, if we read "capital" in place of "mortal," we get a description which certainly includes those who are piling one grave and fully deliberate sin on top of another but also other persons. The description could include sinners who, little by little, through a life of petty egoism, trivial and selfish ambition, pleasure-seeking, or the like, drift away from God and grow uninterested in him. Their faith gradually choked out by cares and riches, they move toward a practical atheism in which God ceases to count, with self taking his place in a practical idolatry. All this happens so

3 On the "capital" or "deadly sins," see the *Catholic Encyclopedia*, XIV, 5; or St. Thomas, *Summa theologiae*, I-II, Q . 84, a. 3-4; II-II, Q . 153, a. 4; or H. Jone, trans. U. Adelman, *Moral Theology* (Westminster, Md., 1958), p. 55, who after stating that these "sins" are inclinations, thus sums up the traditional doctrine: "These sins are called "capital," not because of their gravity, but because of the greatness and extent of their influence. Whenever these inclinations produce their corresponding acts they become sins in the proper sense of the term."

4 *SpEx*, [18, 238, 244, 245]. See William A. N. Peters, S.J., *The Spiritual Exercises of St. Ignatius: Exposition and Interpretation* (Jersey City, 1967), p. 62, with note 8 of ch. 6 p. 190. He is ready to read "capital" for "mortal" in a number of other texts where I find it hard to fit such a translation with the context, even though I should like to because such a reading would be more congenial to any contemporary reader. The Vulgate version of the rule speaks of those who "easily sin mortally and add sin to sin." The sin they add to sin could be lesser sins by which they grow weaker and weaker so that, when on rare occasions they are tempted to grave sin, they easily fall.

subtly perhaps as to escape their attention, but so effectively as to render them incapable of being deeply disturbed when they discover their real condition—if and when they do. Such a condition can be far more harmful and dangerous in the long run than dramatic sins which are clearly known to be sinful and from which a person may readily repent when grace touches him or her.

What may turn out to be of more significance than the adjective "mortal" is something suggested by the phrases "from sin to sin" and "grow in their vices and sins." The full significance of these phrases comes out only by parallel with the contrary description of persons in Rule I:2 and by what is said in Rule II:7. So, we will go to these and then return to I:1.

The persons described in Rule I: 2, are neither saints nor even necessarily well on the road to sanctity—unless we go by the adage that well begun is half done. For these persons are well begun: They have turned to God, and the thrust of their lives is toward greater purity from sin and greater service of God. Certainly, this rule applies not only to beginners in a spiritual life. But it does apply to them also, and not only to those who have already grown very much in union with God and are already serving him with Christ-like wisdom, love, and courage. To stress this is important for understanding Rule 1 as well as this rule; for if we read into the description of Rule 2 any more demands than are actually there we will surely misunderstand by contrast what is said in Rule 1 (as also in Rules II:1-7) and let the range of application for all the rules become exaggeratedly narrow.

Perhaps as good an illustration of the lower limit of this type of person as we can find is Ignatius himself at the beginning of his conversion to God. In his mind, too, the sinner spoken of in Rule 1 could be exemplified by himself before his conversion. At that time he was experiencing and beginning to recognize the diverse motions in himself from good and evil spirits, in accord with rule 2.[5] He had just repented from a life of loose morals and selfish, worldly ambition, and set his heart on following in the footsteps of the saints, especially Francis and Dominic. However, even his good desires were as yet shot through with egoism, with a spirit of vainglorious competition.[6] At that time, he says, "He never took a spiri-

5 *Autobiog*, nos. 6-8, in *St. Ignatius' Own Story*, pp. 9-10.
6 Ibid., nos. 7, 14, on pp. 9-10, 13-14.

51

tual view of anything, nor even knew the meaning of humility or charity or patience or discretion as a rule and measure of these virtues. His whole purpose was to perform these great external works...," such as fasting and going on pilgrimages. The one thing that could be said in his favor was that he would not fall back from his purpose of serving God, but he kept striving to be free of sin, and, "although still blind, had a great desire to serve him [God] to the best of his knowledge."[7]

The above understanding of the persons described in Rule 2 implies something of critical importance for expanding the application of Rule 1. Just as the essential characteristic of persons in Rule 2 is not high holiness of life already achieved but a genuine desire for it issuing in some actual growth toward it, in parallel manner the essential characteristic of those described in Rule 1 is not having a heart already steeped in vice but having a growing disposition toward self-indulgence, a weakened resolution, a lack of any earnest *effective* desire to grow in charity and generous service of God, with a consequent declension toward a more and more sinful life. This may be accompanied even by a velleity for spiritual growth. In fact, there seems no reason to think that the first rule would not apply to one who had been leading a life of holiness, and has now settled into a slow but definite decline into mediocrity, the direction of development pointing beyond mediocrity toward final spiritual collapse, even though that collapse as yet seems far off. We are not talking here about a brief lapse, a passing incident in a life of genuine Christian growth, but of a relatively enduring, even if very gradual, regression that has momentum. The life of a person who is moving in this way may be in some obvious ways more Christian than one who has recently repented and is moving with a generous desire and effort in an upward direction.

The essential question is not at what point a person would be on a scale from serious vice to high virtue if the progress or regress should be stopped. It is rather this: What is the presently stable direction or thrust of his or her life? The way each spirit's action affects a person depends not so much on how good or bad the person is at the time as on the fundamental disposition and direction of development. It is the clashing or meshing of opposing or harmonious tendencies that explains the experiences Ignatius speaks of in these rules.

7 Ibid., no. 14, on pp. 13-14.

If by a good Christian we mean one who already has a notable measure of firm growth in faith, hope, charity, and humility, then Rule 2 does not apply only to "good Christians" but also to "bad Christians" who are now seriously desiring and striving to grow in a life of repentance. By the same token, if a "bad Christian" is one who is prone to grave sins and easily falls into them, whose faith, hope, charity, humility are notably fragile and indiscreet and shot through with egoism, more even than the ordinary good Christian's, then Rule 1 does not apply only to bad Christians but also to others who, though still relatively good, now have a downward impetus toward becoming bad Christians.

That the understanding of Rule 2 given above is correct, and that it should influence our reading of Rule 1 is confirmed by Rule II:7. This rule is placed where it is in the second series of rules for a very good reason, as we shall see. But it would *also* fit very well right after Rules I:1-2. For in II:7 Ignatius explains why the spirits affect the two types of persons in opposite ways; and this explanation explicitly stresses, as the key to understanding their respective dispositions, the set or drift of their hearts which underlies their progression or regression in Christian life.

> [335]. Rule 7. Persons who are going from good to better the good angel touches sweetly, lightly, gently, as when a drop of water soaks into a sponge, while the evil spirit touches them sharply, with noise and disturbance, as when the drop of water falls on a rock. Those who are going from bad to worse, the aforesaid spirits touch in a way contrary to the way they touch those going from good to better. The cause of this contrariety is that the disposition of the one touched is contrary to or concordant with each of the said angels. For, when it is contrary, they come in perceptibly, with clamor and observable signs; when it is concordant, they enter quietly, as one comes into his own house through an open door.

Whatever way one may interpret Rules I:1 and 2, this much is sure, that the distinction of the persons in these first two rules is the basis for the two wholly different, even contrary, fundamental principles of two contrary lines of discerning what spirit is prompting any motions which are respectively from a good or an evil spirit. Yet, this difference easily slips out of mind in theorizing, and especially in the practice of discerning spirits. Ignatius devotes his attention in the rest of the rules almost exclusively to the kind of persons described in Rule I:2, the maturing Christians. Our forgetting the distinction of the persons with which he begins can easily lead us to try to understand by these rules the experience of one whose motions must be judged in a contrary way.

There is then a critically important practical conclusion which issues from the foregoing discussion. The first step in discernment of spirits has to be taken warily and without easy assumptions, by seeking first to find out whether the inner motion under examination occurs in one who is, in the overall picture and without regard for the incidental variations, generally and steadily going forward or backward within the Christian perspective of what is forward or backward. If spiritual directors should think that, since Ignatius after Rule 2 centers his attention on those described in that rule, they can safely forget about Rule 1 in practice, they are in grave danger of misunderstanding those whom they want to help; and they may even give them irrelevant or harmful advice. Before attempting to interpret the inner motions, they must always try first of all to know not only where the other *is* spiritually, but much more importantly whether the other *is progressing or regressing* spiritually, maturing or decaying.

It will help very much both to keep the contrary kinds of persons in mind and to refer to them readily in discussion if we have a set of terms that serves both to emphasize what constitutes their essential point of contrast and to keep them unconfused. For our purposes, "maturing and regressing Christians" or "spiritually maturing and regressing persons" will serve best. The terms "maturing" and "regressing" convey exactly the understanding of the persons dealt with in Rules 1 and 2. Our speaking of *spiritually* maturing and regressing persons prevents a merely psychological understanding, because it points to a life lived in relation to the Holy Spirit of God. Our speaking of maturing or regressing *Christians* is apt, since Ignatius is certainly speaking to and about Christians. We shall, then, from here on use these terms in referring to the contrary types of persons Ignatius is concerned with in these rules.

The Effects of the Two Spirits on a Regressing Christian. Rule I:1

The second point Ignatius makes in each of the first two rules, after distinguishing persons with contrary directions in their lives, is that these persons experience contrary inner motions from good and evil spirits. In the first rule, he looks at the regressing Christian.

The evil spirit finds no serious opposition from the fundamental disposition of spiritually regressing persons. He needs only to go along with that disposition and propose what accords with it. He commonly proposes, Ignatius says, "sensual delights." What he commonly does, he does not do exclusively; and the term "sensual" is sometimes used by Ignatius in a much more inclusive meaning than we give it. What the evil spirit has to guard against is over-reaching himself, tempting the person to what is beyond the evil or the lesser good to which he is ready to move at the next step, and thus coming into open conflict with the person's good even if not dominant dispositions. Always alert for a fatal frontal attack when that is possible, the evil spirit is still content patiently to destroy little by little, even by hardly perceptible degrees. To keep the regression going, whether by inches or by leaps and bounds, that is the essential thing for him, "to hold them and make them grow in their vices and sins." Take them where they are and keep the momentum going—this is his aim.

The good spirit affects the regressing Christians "in a contrary way," that is, the good spirit comes into collision with the regressive direction of their fundamental tendency, and enters "perceptibly, with clamor and observable signs" (*SpEx*, [335]). Even though he cannot use the fundamental disposition and overall tendency in such persons for his purposes, he can and does still appeal to their reason, and through it cause a truthful and healthy even if painful sense of guilt.[8] He afflicts them through their moral judgment on the irrationality of their way of life, with the intention that their pain will lead to a change in direction.

If reason were all the Holy Spirit could appeal to in regressing Christians, there might be no effectiveness in such an appeal. The fact that right reason can cause moral anguish in them shows that there is in them an affective ground for experiencing the call of conscience to the goals of the Holy Spirit. They are regressing, that is true; the anti-spiritual disposition of egoism is growing in their lives; but there is still a spiritual dimension to their affectivity, subdued and declining but real, a subdued but actual desire for truth, for goodness, for God. When all else is gone, there is always the ineffaceable natural longing of the human heart for God, which can be covered over and muted but never erased.

---

8 Ignatius has great respect for human reason. He knows well that it can be misled by one's own emotions and the deceits of Satan. Nevertheless, he tends to see it as basic-ally on the side of God. See e.g., *SpEx*, [2, 87, 96, 180-182].

The Effects of the Two Spirits on a Maturing Christian. Rule I:2

All that has been said so far on Rules I:1 and 2 is preparatory for that to which we can now turn our attention, the way good and evil spirits affect the maturing Christian, the one for whom Ignatius principally drew up these rules.

In Rule I:2, when treating of how the diverse spirits affect spiritually maturing persons, Ignatius says that it is connatural to (*proprio es*)[9] each of the spirits to prompt in such persons the kind of motions attributed to him in this rule. To say this means more than to say that each spirit customarily or usually acts in this way. It means that the tendency to act in this way necessarily flows from his benevolent or malevolent set of will, which is so deep and firm as to be in some sense natural to him, as if joined to his very nature. As a consequence, he cannot in ultimate analysis act otherwise. Not that an evil spirit is created by God with an evil nature or that a good created spirit could not have become evil. By nature as they came from God, Ignatius believed, these spirits were only good and beautiful; but they were endowed with freedom by which they could express and complete what God made them to be, or they could sin and make themselves forever wicked. By reason of what an evil spirit's sin has made of him, he could not now intend to effect any motions in human persons except those which will immediately or at least ultimately tend to destroy human goodness and happiness, especially the Christ-life of faith, hope, and charity. He is a "murderer and liar" (1 John 8:44) through and through and irrevocably. The good angel, on the other hand, is totally yielded to the Holy Spirit; and the Holy Spirit, with or without the mediation of a created spirit, could never cause any motions in us save those which of themselves tend to our growth in Christlife, because he is immutably a life-giving spirit, who is truth and unselfish love.

If God is life-giving truth and agape, then the motions he prompts in one disposed toward these, insofar as he is so disposed by living faith, are light, clarity, right reason, truthfulness in affections and

---

9 *Proprio es* can bear other translations: "it is the way of" (Rickaby) or "it is characteristic of" (Puhl) or "it is typical of." None of these bring out as clearly and emphatically as "it is connatural to" what Ignatius means here and in Rule II:7, namely, that these effects flow from the good or evil spirit by reason of what they are—understanding, of course, that created spirits have become what they are by their free choice. English dictionaries define connatural by words such as connected by nature, innate, inborn, congenital.

actions, increase of faith and charity, and also of the consequences of charity (which include hope and courage and active power). There will sometimes be concomitant feelings of spiritual joy and peace, warmth, sweetness, contentment, repose of mind. If Satan on the contrary, is a murderer and a liar, anti-God, anti-Christ, anti-mankind ("the enemy of mankind," in Ignatius' phrase), then his influence will be just the contrary. He will cause darkness, fear and confusion, unbalanced affections, unreasonable judgments and actions, feelings of coldness toward God, of apathy about serving God, all tending toward discouragement, toward decline in faith, hope, and charity.

1. Effects of the Evil Spirit

All the above mentioned motions in the mind and heart of a maturing Christian are mentioned one place or another in Ignatius' writings.[10] Here in Rule I:2 he refers only to a few of them. Consider first the motions from the evil spirit. The evil spirit, he says, gnaws at maturing Christians, saddens them, tries to wear them down by putting obstacles in the way, urging disturbing falsehoods as truth. He does whatever he can, not only to make maturing Christians turn back but, if he cannot do that, to impede their progress—and, if he cannot do even that, merely to make them miserable. Satan is malicious, full of hate, the enemy. As Ignatius states in a letter of June 18, 1536, to Teresa Rejadell:

> If he [Satan] finds one whose conscience is easygoing and who falls into sins without a thought of their gravity, he does all he can to make venial sins appear no sins at all, and mortal venial, and a very serious mortal sin a mere trifle. In this way he takes advantage of the failing he perceives in us, I mean this excessively lax conscience. If on the other hand he comes upon one whose conscience is delicate (a delicate conscience being in itself nothing faulty, however) and sees that such a person avoids not only all mortal and all venial sins (as much as the latter is possible, for we cannot avoid them all) but even tries to keep from himself the very appearance of slight sin, imperfection, and defect, he tries to darken and confuse that good conscience by suggesting sin where there is none, changing perfection into defect, his only purpose to harass and make one uneasy and miserable. When, as frequently happens, he cannot induce one to sin, or even hope to do so, he tries at least to vex him.[11]

10 For a parallel of what Ignatius says about these signs of the spirits with what is given in the Fathers of the Church, see Hugo Rahner, trans. Michael Barry, *Ignatius the Theologian* (New York, 1968), pp. 164-180; or the abridgement in Wulf, ed., *Ignatius: Personality and Heritage*, pp. 272-279.

11 *LettersIgn*, p. 21.

In this passage from Ignatius' correspondence, as also in Rules I:1-2, and wherever he speaks of Satan's works, untruth and deception are stressed. Sometimes it is said that Ignatius treats Satan's deceptions only in the second set of rules, and that in the first he deals only with Satan's frontal attacks—those which are without subtlety, without deception, head-on efforts to break down his victim by main force of darkness, pain, weariness, frustration. This is not an accurate statement of what is in the rules. What is peculiar to the second set of rules is a special kind of deception, an especially subtle one in which Satan disguises himself as an angel of light and begins his deception with holy thoughts and consolation or by engendering confusion about the time when an experience of consolation from God has ended. Even in the first set of rules there is great stress on Satan as a deceiver in other ways. Wearing us down by prolonged frontal attacks, he gets us into a condition where we are more vulnerable to the false reasonings he prompts. Merely an incidental fall, even a serious one, under his attack would ultimately achieve little for his purpose. It might even in the event defeat that purpose, unless he could deceive us into misunderstanding our relationship with God, or misinterpreting our experience in such a way that we become discouraged, ripe for the lie that it is impossible to follow what we thought was God's call, and thus become ready to turn back or to give up trying to ascend from good to better for the greater glory of God.

The way in which Satan goes about wearing us down and leading us to false and discouraging thoughts about our lives will be discussed at length in commenting on Rule I:4. Two observations, however, seem to fit better here, observations on obstacles put mainly, but not exclusively, in the way of beginners. The first obstacle comes through those with whom life has until the present been most closely shared. Persons now trying to center life intensely on God are subjected to unreasonable demands for attention and time, for involvement in vacuous or sinful entertainments, ambitions, or projects. They are subjected to scorn or to heartfelt advice "for their own good." They are told that they are unreal, unbalanced, religious fanatics (and there are, it is true, enough of such people round about us to give anyone pause about oneself). No one who begins to love and to serve God with his or her whole interest and energy should be surprised at such an experience. It happens over and over in the lives of those who make a serious conversion or begin to follow a religious vocation. It happens also later on when God calls to and gives grace for a more total conversion and a fuller union with him.

What are even more common and dangerous than obstacles raised by other persons are the illusory obstacles (deceptions!) which the evil spirit prompts us to conjure up in our own imagination. These blot out joyful past experiences and all reasonable expectations for the future, make everything look dark, devoid of any contentment or delight, or too hard and too dangerous to be endured with hope of success. As Ignatius states in the same letter:

> In the first place, then, the enemy as a rule follows this course. He places obstacles and impediments in the way of those who love and begin to serve God our Lord, and this is the first weapon he uses in his efforts to wound them. He asks, for instance: "How can you continue a life of such great penance deprived of all satisfaction from friends, relatives, possessions? How can you lead so lonely a life, with no rest, when you can save your soul in other ways and without such dangers?" He tries to bring us to understand that we must lead a life that is longer than it will actually be, by reason of the trials he places before us and which no man ever underwent. He fails to remind us of the great comfort and consolation which our Lord is wont to give to such souls, who, as new recruits in our Lord's service, surmount all these obstacles and choose to suffer with their Creator and Lord.[12]

Ignatius had just such an experience when he first began to turn seriously to God.[13] All who set their hearts on serving God must expect such thoughts, so obviously false to an experienced observer, so specious to the subject under stress.

To counteract Satan's discouraging deceptions, one truthful conviction about the nature of the motions he incites must be held fast. It is this. All the motions from the evil spirit are for the sake of leading the person into sin, into regression in God's service, or at least for the sake of preventing progress. Of themselves these motions tend to these goals; of themselves they always make faithfulness and progress hard. What must be emphatically noted, however, is that they are not themselves sins or regression in God's service, nor even necessarily a sign of any regression already taken place. Neither do they of themselves alone actually impede progress. All depends on how the person responds to the situation. If he responds badly, without resisting these motions, some evil effects will follow. If he responds courageously and vigilantly,

12 *LettersIgn*, p. 19.
13 *Autobiog*, no. 20, in *St. Ignatius' Own Story*, pp. 17-18.

using heart and head to combat Satan, love will grow faithful and pure in ways that are possible only through temptation and desolation. Then God will give him the grace and glory that is given only to those who have endured faithfully with brave and watchful love. It is primarily to help us do this that Ignatius wrote this first set of rules.[14]

2. Effects of the Good Spirit

Paralleling his list of evil effects from Satan in the affectivity and intelligence of the maturing Christian, Ignatius lists some examples of the good effects or fruits from the Holy Spirit. All of them are just the contrary of what Satan effects: courage, strength, consolation in the affectivity, finding expression in tears of tenderness or joy; inspirations and quiet in the mind; obstacles removed or made to seem easily overcome—all for the sake of making it easy to progress in God's service.

In Ignatius' illustrative list of effects produced by the Holy Spirit in the maturing Christian, two related features are noteworthy. First, he omits the absolutely fundamental and essential effects of the Holy Spirit, faith, hope, and charity,[15] as also such *necessary* manifestations of faith, hope, and charity as humility, gentleness, patience, forgiveness, and the like. All except the first one of the effects he does mention, namely, "courage and energy," are *contingent* to maturing Christian life in this world—effects which may or may not at any particular time be experienced by one whose fundamental and essential acts of faith, hope, and charity, with their necessary consequences, are intense and firm and pure. By such fundamental and essential acts I mean those which necessarily arise in the intellect and will of anyone insofar as he or she is living a Christian life at all, and which find expression in desires, choices, and actions. These acts are without dependence on any special kind of feelings, and they need not find expression through such feelings.

14 This will become clear in Rules I:5-14. See the discussion of this point below, at the beginning of ch. 7.

15 A reader who is familiar with these rules will immediately think of Rule I:3, where, under the rubric of "spiritual consolation," Ignatius speaks of inflamed love, which is clearly charity, and of "every increase of hope, faith, and charity." Let me only assert here what I hope to show later (see ch. 5, esp. pp. 103-107; also pp. 60-63 here), that while spiritual consolation always includes faith, hope, and charity as its subjective ground, faith, hope, and charity do not necessarily constitute or bring on spiritual consolation *in the way that Ignatius uses the word.*

The second feature worthy of note in Ignatius' list of effects produced by the prompting of the Holy Spirit in the maturing Christian is a correlative of the first. Ignatius in no way indicates that of themselves these effects of the good spirit which he does mention constitute any increase, even transient, of the Christ-life which is actuated in acts of faith, hope, and charity, and in the necessary consequences of these in a person's life. These two features are noteworthy because the common tendency among all save the most experienced in leading a reflective spiritual life (and even among them at times) is to think that spiritual life is flourishing when they experience these contingent effects of the Holy Spirit which Ignatius mentions; and also to think that it is regressing when these contingent effects are absent; or especially, when they are replaced with their contraries, the effects of the evil spirit.

Omission of the essential effects of the Holy Spirit in Rule I:2 appears as altogether inexcusable unless we understand that Ignatius is assuming these essential effects in the person about whom he is writing. The rule is dealing with a maturing Christian, one who is going from good to better. No one goes from good to better as a Christian except by performing better acts of faith, hope, and charity, and other acts which presuppose greater faith, hope, and charity. Assuming that we are considering such a person, Ignatius wants to point out further effects of the Holy Spirit which can be a positive help to his or her growth in faith, hope, charity, and the necessary consequences of these (humility, patience gentleness and the like). Some of these helps, those summed up in the term "consolation," can also be an occasion for harm if the person responds with vainglory or becomes attached to them. They can also be of service for seeking and finding God's will if they are rightly perceived and interpreted; but they can be misinterpreted and serve as an occasion for self-deception.

Such effects of the Holy Spirit are not the only ways this Spirit has of helping us grow in faith, hope, and love; he can also help us by allowing desolation and giving power to endure it with unselfish, courageous, and energetic love through darkness and sadness. So, the effects of the Holy Spirit mentioned by Ignatius in Rule I:2 can be absent without in any way necessarily indicating a decline in Christian life and the fundamental acts in which it finds expression. It is true that St. Paul tells us that Christian life is "a matter...of righteousness, peace and joy given by the Holy Spirit "(Romans 14:17). Nevertheless, it would be simplistic

61

and possibly tragic in its results to think that righteousness always actually issues in peace and joy—unless a peace and joy so deeply inward as to be unnoticed by the subject or drowned out in awareness by confusion, anguish, and dread and, consequently, compatible with even the most excruciating concurrent desolation.[16]

a. Spiritual Consolation (Peace and Joy)

Ignatius does stress the great value of spiritual peace and joy from God as an aid to growth in holiness of life,[17] but not a constitutive factor of such growth. Nevertheless, it results in a harmful distortion of his teaching if such stress on the value of consolation is not understood in the light of his more fundamental teaching. This stresses what he says is "more to the purpose," and strongly asserts the encouraging truth that growth in the essentials of Christian life does not depend on consolation, and can go on "with or without many consolations." What is more to the point is what he calls "solid virtues" such as "patience, humility, obedience, charity, and other virtues." One who takes care of these more important matters need not be disturbed about how much consolation he has but can be content to "accept from the hand of God whatever he disposes in this regard."[18] Spiritual consolation is of importance in the life of a Christian just insofar as it helps to growth of living faith and of agape. Ignatius explicitly tells those making the Spiritual Exercises to reject spiritual consolations of a sort that do not fit in with and help toward achieving the desired goal of any phase of those Exercises (*SpEx*, [78, 206]). He also sees some consolations, even spiritual consolations, which are prompted by the evil spirit (*SpEx.* [331-332]).[19] Great as its value can be, spiritual consolation should not be overestimated, or made an end in itself, or made *the* sign of a good Christian life. It is one means among others by which the Holy Spirit helps us to grow and which Satan and our own selfishness can use to harm us. We have to be "indifferent," in the Ignatian meaning of that word, to spiritual consolation or spiritual desolation in the same

---

16 See also pp. 227-235 in ch. 10 below, where this is further developed. There is always what we have called "essential consolation" of Christian life, a structural element of Christian consciousness, a state that necessarily flows from Christian faith (see below, at the end of ch. 4). There is also a correlative desolation which is a structural element of Christian consciousness in time. Neither of these is what Ignatius is writing about.

17 *LettersIgn*, p. 181.

18 Ibid., p. 342.

19 See also pp. 227-235 in ch. 10 below, where this is further explained.

way that we have to be indifferent to long life or short life, health or sickness, and so on (*SpEx*, [23]).

On the one hand, we should, Ignatius thinks, try to be always disposed to receive consolation, and we should even intensely desire it insofar as having it would be for God's greater glory — but only insofar as it would be so. On the other hand, we should be ready to bear and struggle against desolation if that should be what God wills to allow for our spiritual growth. As we shall see in chapter 7, what Ignatius will not approve is our merely enduring spiritual desolation without striving to conquer it, without reaching out for God's peace and joy.

A number of the effects which Ignatius in Rule I:2 attributes to the good spirit acting on a maturing Christian will be considered when we comment on the following rules, especially Rule I:3, on spiritual consolation. But two of these effects call for consideration before we take up spiritual consolation and desolation, because they are more fundamental than consolation and desolation; they are effects of the Holy Spirit which Ignatius holds can be present at all times in a Christian's life, and should be present insofar as it depends on him to be open and to cooperate with the Holy Spirit. These basic effects are "courage and energy," along with clarity and truth of spiritual reason (that is, reason led by faith and charity). The first of these is stated explicitly in Rule I:2; the second is, in context, clearly implied, as I shall show when we come to it. Discussion of the latter will necessarily include discussion of another effect of the good spirit, "taking away obstacles."

The basic importance of these two works of the Holy Spirit can be seen if we recall the basic contrary aims of Satan. In the maturing Christian, faith, hope, and charity are alive and growing no matter whether the person is in consolation or desolation or calm. Satan's goal is to destroy that life or, failing that, to stunt it. His immediate aims, his most powerful and basic ways of achieving his goal are two: discouragement and deception. Directly contrary to these are the Holy Spirit's most powerful and basic ways of helping the Christian grow to the fullness of faith life: energy with courage and truth with clarity. Let us look at each of these.

b. Courage and Energy

Animo y fuerzas, "courage and energy," is a phrase which occurs more than once in the *Spiritual Exercises;* but it is the word *fuerzas* that comes up over and over and expresses something basic to Ignatian spirituality. In Ignatius' thinking it seems to have special significance in regard to our response to temptations and desolations, or to any sort of obstacle to growth in and expression of faith and love. When the director of the Spiritual Exercises finds the exercitant desolate or tempted, he should, Ignatius says, be gentle and kind, giving *animo y fuerzas* for the future (*SpEx*, [7]). If, when making a decision, a person is strongly inclined to one alternative rather than to another for any reason other than God's greater praise and service, then he should stir himself up and put forth all his energies (*todas sus fuerzas*) in order to arrive at a contrary inclination (*SpEx*, [16]).[20] In time of spiritual consolation, Ignatius wants us to consider how we will bear ourselves in the coming desolation, drawing in renewed energy (*tomando nuevas fuerzas*) for that time (*SpEx*, [323]). In the actual time of desolation, we should consider that we can do much with God's grace, which always remains with us, to resist all spiritual enemies, drawing energy (*tomando fuerzas*) from our Creator and Lord (*SpEx*, [324]).

Gathering together these varied contexts in which Ignatius speaks of *fuerzas* enables us to see two things: the crucial importance in Christian life which Ignatius attributes to it and the precise meaning of the word. First, its importance. Growth or regression depends on whether the Christian puts out this energy. Without it he or she will collapse at the moment of truth, making decisions on the basis of selfish inclinations and fears rather than unselfish love for God and desire for his glory. Without it he or she will be swept along by desolation into discouragement and, in discouragement, turned back from striving to become a true disciple of Christ.

Secondly, these uses of *fuerzas* in varied contexts enable us both to draw out the richness of the word and to make very exact its meaning in the Ignatian vocabulary. *Fuerzas* can carry a number of closely related, even overlapping meanings: force, strength, power, vigor, energy. All relate to acting.[21] Now, one may be powerful or strong or forceful without being vigorous or energetic (as, in the physical order, an elephant gives the appearance of

20 See also *SpEx*, [157] and below, pp. 160-162.
21 The Vulgate text uses *vis* and *vires*. It is significant also that in Rule I:14 Ignatius uses the same word in referring to military forces. Satan acts, Ignatius says, like a military commander who explores what the forces (*fuerzas*) of the enemy are and how they are disposed.

being) or may be the reverse (as a chipmunk is). Ignatius seems to have both strength and energy in mind, force and vigor in using it. It would not be taking a liberty to translate *fuerzas* as strength (power, force) *and* energy (vigor). What is more, in context, it seems to carry also the note of courage—which may be lacking in one who is forceful and energetic in action. *Fuerzas* could be taken as a contracted form of *animo y fuerzas* in the Ignatian idiom. This full meaning should be kept in mind when we use only one word such as "energy" or "strength" or "power." Ignatian *fuerzas* is courageous, energetic, active power.

The contexts also make it possible, and necessary for an exact understanding, to add a number of defining phrases, qualifications, which limit the extension of the term. In these texts, Ignatius is always referring to energy or active power *under control of the agent*, to be used as he chooses. This energy is *volitional* rather than corporal.[22] It is *directed to activating desirable affections and thoughts* (*SpEx*, [116, 195]), and *to deactivating or at least restraining the influence of undesirable thoughts and spontaneous affections already in act* (*SpEx*, [16, 155]), or both (*SpEx*, [7, 323, 324, 327]). Putting all these qualifications together, we see that *fuerzas* refers to courageous volitional energy (force or active power) which is subject to the agent's decision. It is up to him to exert it in order to initiate and confirm, or to resist and change, his own inner motions—such as thoughts, desires, aversions, joy, sadness—insofar as this can be done; and insofar as it cannot be done, to conquer any unreasonable inclinations to choice and action which flow from these.

We would miss the meaning of *fuerzas* as it is used by Ignatius in the *Spiritual Exercises* if we did not add two other features: (1) it is *spiritual* energy, and (2) it has no necessary bond with spiritual consolation.

Fuerzas designates spiritual strength or energy inasmuch as it is a gift of the Holy Spirit. It is connatural for the good spirit to give it (*Proprio* [*es*] *del bueno espiritu dar animo y fuerzas*). Perhaps it is not unintentional that Ignatius puts courage and energy first in the list of the effects connaturally worked by the good spirit to help the life of faith grow (*SpEx*, [315]). Further, this energy is spiritual inasmuch as it functions only in the recipient's faith life. It is courageous strength and energy to perform the acts of that

---

22 For an illustration of using *fuerzas* for bodily energy, see *SpEx*, [213].

life by which it expresses itself and grows. It is active power to resist and attack all that threatens faith life. The thoughts and affections it activates or deactivates or resists are spiritual or anti-spiritual thoughts and affections.

Fuerzas has no necessary bond with spiritual consolation. This second feature points to the fundamental, even essential, place of this gift of spiritual energy in Christian life. It is necessary and possible in all spiritual affective conditions: in consolation, or desolation, or calm. In fact, just because he is in the first set of rules principally concerned with the spiritually maturing person in desolation and under attack by the evil spirit, Ignatius speaks more about this spiritual energy in time of desolation than in consolation. As will be evident especially in Rules I:6-9, 11-12, the most immediate need of the Christian in desolation is courage and energy to take hold of himself and set in motion an intelligent and vigorous counterattack. All the texts we gathered above confirm this and show that courage and energy from the Holy Spirit are not spoken of as including or springing from, or by their very nature issuing into, what Ignatius means by spiritual consolation.[23] This gift of courage and energy does not constitute consolation, and it does not of itself and directly erase or lessen desolation. It does give the person power to resist and ultimately conquer spiritual desolation. This is not to suggest that courage and energy are not given also in consolation; it is rather to sever any necessary bond with consolation — as though to give courage and energy were to give consolation, as though the Holy Spirit were not lovingly present and generously giving during time of desolation as well as the time of consolation.

In no way does desolation exclude a courageous and energetic life of faith, hope, and charity under the loving and powerful action of the Holy Spirit. Sometimes even more intense and pure acts of faith, hope, and charity flourish during affective darkness and dryness. At the core of the personality, where one exercises intelligence, loves in the most proper sense (distinct from feelings), and has power of free choice, at this core where one's life is given

---

23 John of the Cross notes how in the aridity experienced in the dark night of the senses, "the spirit feels the strength and energy to work" *fortaleza y brio para obrar* (*The Dark Night of the Soul* I, 9, 6 [hereafter abbreviated as *Dark Night*]). All translations of John of the Cross will be taken from the translation by Kieran Kavanaugh, O.C.D. and Otilio Rodriguez, O.C.D., *The Collected Works of John of the Cross* (Washington, 1973), (hereafter referred to as *Works*).

its dominant thrust, there the Spirit gives courage and energy. These gifts from him work in desolation as well as in consolation. They keep alive and growing the life of faith, hope, and charity, which of itself, when our weakness is supplied for by the Spirit and the barriers within us are removed or temporarily overcome by him, floods into the sensibility as consolation.[24] Spiritual courage and spiritual energy are necessary fruits of faith, hope, and charity; their measure is the measure of the essential acts of faith, hope, and charity from which they spring. To intensify the latter is to intensify the former. To experience an intensification of spiritual courage and energy in finding, doing, or enduring God's will is a sign of the intensification of living faith by the Holy Spirit, a more certain sign than anything else in spiritual consolation and a sign which can be experienced without consolation.

Severing any necessary bond of spiritual courage and energy with spiritual consolation has great significance for discernment of spirits. If the gifts of faith, hope, and charity are themselves left aside, there is a tendency to take joy or consolation as *the* sign, or at least as the most important sign, of the Holy Spirit working in our lives. One reads instances of this in books and hears them in preaching. It serves to exacerbate the false negative self-image which those in desolation already tend to have, because it implies that if one does not experience joy in God, it is the person's own fault, that he or she must have hindered the work of the Holy Spirit. This is the only possible conclusion to be drawn from saying that whenever we are under the influence of the Holy Spirit, we experience spiritual consolation. The conclusion and the premise are utterly false and either spring from or go along with diabolical deception leading to despair of spiritual growth. Some speak scornfully of loving and serving God and neighbor "with gritted teeth" — as if there were any alternative at times for those who want to be faithful. Those who speak this way seem uninformed about Christian experience or else blinded by a thesis of joy as the sign of the Holy Spirit. They also seem blinded to the splendor of courage and fidelity through times of dryness, desolation, and temptation. We should, of course, always be striving to grow toward the ideal of being totally integrated persons, whose affective feelings as well as affective acts are easily and joyfully integral with faith, hope, and charity. Nevertheless, to identify that ideal image with the image

---

24 A fuller treatment of this relation between faith and spiritual consolation will be found in ch. 4 below.

of a person being led by the Spirit is altogether in discord with Christian experience, opposed to the whole Christian tradition, and, in particular, to Ignatian teaching.[25]

When Ignatius' statements are read without great care to interpret his meaning and make them more exact in the light of what he states elsewhere, his own ways of writing can give rise to this wrong and harmful way of thinking. Before one studies out the meaning of "courage and energy," the overall impression of Rule I:2 misleads in this way. Or consider what he says in Rule I:5: "For just as the good spirit shows us the way and counsels us in consolation, so in desolation does the evil spirit." Again, in Rule I:7: "Let one who is in desolation consider how the Lord has left him to his natural powers." In the light of the rest of this Rule I:7, and of other rules, the passages just now quoted take on an altogether different meaning than they have when read in isolation. After stating in Rule I:7 that the one in desolation is left to his natural powers, Ignatius adds in the very same rule that he is able to resist all the disturbances and temptations of the enemy "with the divine aid which always remains with him even though he does not clearly perceive it." The assistance of the Holy Spirit is *always* with him. Spiritual desolation is a sign that one is in some way being influenced by the evil spirit, but not a sign that one is not being influenced by the Holy Spirit in other ways than consolation.

As will be shown, to be in desolation merely means that one's affective sensibility is to some extent under the influence of the evil spirit. Because of that, the person "does not clearly perceive" that God is with him, so dependent is perception on our feelings, at least generally for most of us.[26] That the Holy Spirit is truly active in the life of one in desolation is assumed in Rule I:6, when the person is urged to act against desolation in ways which require the power of the Holy Spirit to make them effective. The active power of the Holy Spirit is necessary to effect the purification and spiritual growth which Ignatius sees in Rule I:9 as a major reason for God's allowing desolation in the lives of those who are neither unfaithful to him nor indolent in his service.

25 Note what Ignatius says in Rule I:4 on the thoughts that flow from consolation and those that flow from desolation, and see the discussion of that part of the rule found in ch. 4 below.

26 Something parallel to this must be said about decision-making during the actual time of consolation, at least of high consolation. See *SpEx*, [14].

The Fundamental Principles. Rules I:1 and 2

As will be explained later on, what Ignatius states in Rule I:5 about the counsels or inspirations from the evil spirit in time of desolation takes on a much more limited meaning than an isolated reading would give it. Ignatius is writing here only about those counsels which are *rooted in desolation.* Thus, the person who is spiritually desolate may receive counsels which clearly spring from living faith and are directly opposed to the counsels rooted in spiritual desolation: counsels to trust God, to hope and be patient under the test (I:8), to be courageous and energetic (I:2) in living out decisions made under better circumstances (I:5), in combating desolation by prayer, meditation, reflection on what is going on, and suitable penance (I:6).

c. Clarity and Truth

As noted above on page 63, Ignatius sees two principal helps from the Holy Spirit for preventing or overcoming the two principal works of the evil spirit in those who are maturing spiritually. The first work of the Holy Spirit we have just considered, "courage and energy" as opposed to discouragement. Now we can consider the second, clarity and truth about our spiritual experiences; and this work of the Holy Spirit is opposed to the deceptions and confusions which the evil spirit tries to effect. It is true that, among the few illustrations which Ignatius gives, in Rule I:2, of how the Spirit influences maturing Christians, he does not mention this one in so many words. But recall what Ignatius states in Rule I:1 about how the good spirit influences those who are regressing, going from sin to sin: He appeals to their power of right reason, which in the light of truth judges their own lives and effects a truthful sense of healthy guilt. Is it likely that the good spirit will influence reason in those who are departing from God and not do so in Godward persons? The fact is that the work of the Holy Spirit in giving clarity and truth to our reason is very clearly implied in Rule I:2 by the statement that the good spirit removes all obstacles. For in the first part of this rule, where Ignatius describes the influence of the evil spirit, he says "it is connatural to the evil spirit to...thrust obstacles in the way, disquieting with false reasons, for the sake of impeding progress." To remove obstacles involves conquering false reasons with true ones, confused reasons with clear ones.

Further, throughout the whole first set of rules, Ignatius time and time again explicitly refers to the false counsels of Satan

Saint Ignatius' Rules for the Discernment of Spirits

(I:2, 4, 5, 13). He calls for careful examination and reasonable consideration to find out what is going on within one, why, and what to do about it (I:6-9). He calls for accurate and expansive thinking in order to combat the narrowed and erroneous perspective of desolation — the perspective which leaves out the encouraging and energizing truths learned from Christian doctrine and Christian experience, such as God's power, wisdom, love, presence, and providence over our lives (I:7-11). He provides our reason with descriptions that can serve as models for identifying kinds of experiences, and also criteria for judging their source.

The power to think truthfully, clearly, and comprehensively about spiritual experience is, like spiritual courage and energy, a gift of the Holy Spirit — not only during consolation but also during desolation and time of calm. The negative feelings of desolation can make such thinking more difficult; and therefore during desolation it is best to avoid changing any significant decisions about our spiritual lives which seemed sound in previous time of calm or consolation (*SpEx*, [318]). But the understanding of what is going on in us, the unmasking of deceptions and fallacies, the application of guiding principles on discernment of spirits and on the way of responding in desolation or in consolation — all such acts of reason are of essential importance during desolation as well as during consolation. In fact, they may be even more important during desolation than during consolation. Accuracy and clarity about these fundamentals are powerful helps toward resisting and conquering desolation, arriving at calm, and disposing oneself to receive the gift of spiritual consolation.

Concrete Complexities in Contrast to Pure Cases

The foregoing discussion has touched on all the principal elements in Rules I:1 and 2 which need clarification: the two contrary types of persons in whom the spiritual and anti-spiritual motions are experienced, and the contrary motions prompted respectively in each by the good and evil spirits. However, before we take up the following rules, something needs to be added, a qualification of what Ignatius has said. It is not in conflict with his rules, but it goes beyond what he states while it remains fully consonant with the movement of his thought. In fact, unless this qualification is kept in mind, what Ignatius has written could easily be applied to concrete experience in a way that would defeat the basic intent of his rules.

70

In Rules I:1-2, Ignatius, as a good pedagogue, has stated pure cases in order to communicate an initial understanding which is unconfused by complexities. Such complexities have to be faced, but they can be unraveled only by the use of concepts and principles clearly understood in his pure cases. If, on the other hand, discernment of spirits were all as easy as a first reading of these fundamental rules for the pure cases would lead some to think before they consider the cases found in concrete experience, there would be no reason for one of Ignatius' important concerns. He thought that the trained and experienced director of the Spiritual Exercises, not the inexperienced exercitant, should do the discernment of spirits. He should do it, of course, on the basis of data supplied by the exercitant.[27] If Ignatius' concern were unfounded, anyone could read Rules I:1-2 and then discern spirits pretty well without help. Neither would there be any reason to think of the director's work during the "Election," the process of decision-making, as calling for greater skill and discretion than anything else in the *Spiritual Exercises.*[28] Failure to take careful account of the complexities involved in actual cases of discernment of spirits can lead to naive confidence, to erroneous and harmful interpretation of inner motions, and thus to erroneous and harmful discernment of spirits.

Ignatius will himself bring up one source of complexity: spiritual consolation which at first bears the marks of the Holy Spirit, and then only as its consequences unfold in the person involved reveals itself as the work of the evil spirit disguised as an angel of light. In cases such as these, Rules I:1-2 simply do not hold up without qualification. But they are, when qualified, seen to be perfectly sound. The required development of these fundamental rules to unravel this particular complexity is taken care of in the second series of rules.[29]

There are other sources of complexity for discernment of spirits in the concrete which Ignatius does not take up at all in either set of rules. This should not be surprising if we recall what the heading says: "rules for perceiving and understanding *in some manner* the

---

27 See Ignatius' Autograph Directory, [19], on p. 76 of *Directoria exercitiorum spiritualium* (1540-1599), Vol. 76 in MHSJ, (Rome, 1955), (hereafter referred to as *DirSpEx-* MHSJ).

28 See the Directory of 1599, XXII, 1 [162], in *DirSpEx*MHSJ, p. 683. There is an authorized English translation, *Directory to the Spiritual Exercises* (London: Manresa Press, 1925). See also Hugo Rahner, *Ignatius the Theologian*, p. 140.

29 See in particular Rules II:4-7.

diverse motions...." (*SpEx*, [313]) or, as it is put in the Vulgate version, "some (*aliquot*) rules...." Ignatius has no intention of writing anything more than some fundamental directives put together in a coherent and useful order. What we find is that the additions which need to be made can be made in the light of his fundamental principles — and that without calling the validity of the latter in any way into question.

Among the other sources of complexity in concrete discernment of spirits, there are two which are even more fundamental than those which Ignatius takes up in the second set of rules; for these two sources of complexity should come into consideration in *every* discernment of spirits. The one source is found in the motions experienced by the person himself or herself, and the other is found in his or her spiritual condition. In the motions experienced by the person, the similarity and interweaving of spiritual and non-spiritual motions makes it easy to confuse the two. When this confusion does take over, the whole discernment is falsified from the very start. Within a commentary on the Ignatian rules this problem can best be dealt with when we take up Rules I:3-4; there Ignatius describes spiritual consolation and spiritual desolation as distinct from any other consolation or desolation. From the side of the person experiencing these movements, the fundamental source of complexity in concrete discernment of spirits is the spiritually unintegrated condition of the maturing Christian as well as the regressing one.

A classical description of this condition can be found in St. Paul's account of the tension within the human person between the "law of God" or "law of my mind" and the "law of sin." He is describing the person without Christ and the Spirit of Christ. Even in this person's inmost self, Paul sees a harmony with God's law. There, this person approves what God commands; in his deep heart, he delights in it; but he is overcome by the law of sin which the "flesh" serves.

> I do not understand my own actions. For I do not do what I want, but I do the very thing I hate. Now if I do what I do not want, I agree that the law is good. So then it is no longer I that do it, but sin which dwells within me. For I know that nothing good dwells within me, that is, in my flesh. I can will what is right, but I cannot do it. For I do not do the good I want, but the evil I do not want is what I do. Now if I do what I do not want, it is no longer I that do it, but sin which dwells within me. So I find it to be

a law that when I want to do right, evil lies close at hand. For I delight in the law of God, in my inmost self, but I see in my members another law at war with the law of my mind and making me captive to the law of sin which dwells in my members. Wretched man that I am! Who will deliver me from this body of death? Thanks be to God through Jesus Christ our Lord! So then, I of myself serve the law of God with my mind, but with my flesh I serve the law of sin (Rom. 7:15-25).

When by faith we are joined to Christ and receive his Spirit, then we have power to conquer the law of sin, which the carnal self serves, and to obey the law of God, which the spiritual self is delighted to serve. However, the struggle between the two laws and the two dimensions of self is not ended. The redeemed person is still both "spiritual" and "carnal"; and the possibility of the "flesh" overcoming the "spirit" is still real.

Neither "spirit" and "flesh" nor "spiritual" and "carnal" in this text are to be taken as referring to constitutive principles of human nature, each ontologically distinct from the other, as we speak of soul and body. "Spirit" and "spiritual" refer to the whole person inasmuch as he is in Christ by living faith and led by the Holy Spirit of Christ. "Flesh" and "carnal" refer to the whole person inasmuch as he is ruled by egoism and is not in Christ. In order to avoid the misleading connotations of the word "carnal," some translations use the word "unspiritual." The term which catches Paul's meaning more exactly seems to be "anti-spiritual." For, as both Romans (7:14-25; 8:2-13) and Galatians (5:16-26), as also our own experience, make clear, these two aspects or dimensions of the concrete human person in history are in mortal conflict. Each tends toward the destruction of the other: "For the desires of the flesh are against the spirit and the desires of the spirit are against the flesh" (Gal. 5:17).

From the description of the two types of persons in Rules I:1 and 2, from the stated preliminary goal of the *Spiritual Exercises,* the removal of disorderly affections (*SpEx,* [1]), from Ignatius' constant awareness of how difficult it is to arrive at that goal in any measure adequate for finding God's will (*SpEx,* [1, 23, 150-157, 166-167, 169, 179-180, 184]), from the descriptions of spiritual consolation and desolation in Rules I:3 and 4 — from all these indications it is evident how keenly aware Ignatius was of our spiritually unintegrated condition. Nevertheless, for the peda-gogical reason given above, when he speaks of how the good or evil spirit affects the spiritually regressing or maturing person, he takes no account of how this condition complicates discernment. The good spirit acting on the person going from good to better is said to be experienced only as harmonious and agreeable, while the evil spirit is said to be experienced only as clashing and disagreeable. The effect of these spirits on the person going from bad to worse is just the opposite.

If intended as a full and final statement about the persons involved in discernment of spirits, Rules I:1-2 would be dangerously simplistic guides, or even certainly harmful. Something needs to be added to take account of the fact that in the one who goes from sin to sin, the spiritual dimension with its spiritual thrust is weakening but still there; and this person can find the action of the good spirit harmonious and pleasing in some measure, in some dimension of his being, even though the painful clash with his dominant carnal thrust of life usually tends to drown out the harmony and delight. Contrariwise, the action of the evil spirit, harmonious with this person's dominant carnal dimension, can be experienced as in discord with what remains of the spiritual dimension. In the same way, and more importantly for the purpose of these rules, in the person who is going from good to better, the carnal dimension with its anti-spiritual tendencies is weakening but still functioning, sometimes powerfully, usually very subtly. As a consequence, this spiritually maturing person can, in that carnal dimension of his personality, experience carnal motions as harmonious (otherwise temptation would be impossible), and spiritual motions from the action of the good spirit as violently disturbing, or as a subtle malaise.

Recall Christ's encounter with the rich young man in the Gospel:

> And as he was setting out on his journey, a man ran up and knelt before him, and asked him, "Good Teacher, what must I do to inherit eternal life?" And Jesus said to him, "Why do you call me good? No one is good but God alone. You know the commandments: 'Do not kill, Do not commit adultery, Do not steal, Do not bear false witness, Do not defraud, Honor your father and mother.'" And he said to him, "Teacher, all these I have observed from my youth." And Jesus looking upon him loved him, and said to him, "You lack one thing; go, sell what you have, and give to the poor, and you will have treasure in heaven; and come, follow me." At that saying his countenance fell, and he went away sorrowful; for he had great possessions (Mark 10:17-22).

Surely the young man fits the description given in Rule 2 of what we have named the spiritually maturing person. He has kept the commandments, he desires eternal life, he comes to Jesus to be taught. His goodness and sincerity is attested to by Jesus looking upon him and loving him. Surely he has experienced contact with Jesus and his teaching as a source of courage and energy, of joy and peace, of inspirations, making attainment of eternal life seem possible, even not too difficult with Jesus' help. All this accords with Ignatius' description of how such a man is affected by the good spirit.

Suddenly, however, the picture changes. What should not happen, if we read Rule 2 without qualification, to such a person when acted on by God does happen. When Jesus calls the man to renounce his wealth and follow him, we may assume that the Holy Spirit touched him inwardly in accord with Christ's invitation. The effect, however, is not courage and energy, joy and peace, making all seem easy, as it did to Andrew and Peter, John and James. On the contrary, the result is disturbance, depression, discouragement. Jesus has touched on the carnal, the anti-spiritual dimension in this man, his attachment to wealth; and the affective response is that which comes from Satan according to Rule 2. Truly, Satan could have been, likely was, active. But even without his prompting, the thrust of Jesus' call clashes with one thrust of the young man's life which is still anti-spiritual, and the results are the contrary of what should happen in a spiritually maturing man according to Rule 2. They are what should characterize the experience of the spiritually regressing person of Rule 1 when he is affected by the good spirit. The young man became sad, his face fell. Because he was a spiritually maturing man, he felt the anguish of failing to do what in his inmost self he knew God wanted him to do, and what he wanted to do but did not want it enough to conquer his carnal self. If he were not a spiritually maturing person, he would not have experienced sadness in turning down Jesus' invitation.

The rich young man's response is in striking contrast with the apostles who readily, with courage and energy, joy, heedless of difficulties, left all to follow Jesus — that is, all worldly possessions. These men are surely among those "ascending from good to better." However, they had their own strains of the anti-spiritual still alive, not love of wealth, but egoism, vanity, ambition. Only let Christ's words or actions come into conflict with that in them which was still carnal and the results are again, in these men going from good to better, what Ignatius says happens in the man going from sin to sin when the good spirit acts on him. It does not seem reasonable to think that they experienced no disturbance, pain of remorse, or embarrassment when Jesus rebuked them for their ambition or their blindness to his way of thinking and loving; or when, during the passion of Christ, the Holy Spirit and their own love for Jesus accused them of cowardice. No doubt Satan could take advantage of these situations and affect them as he is said to affect the spiritually maturing person in order to harm him; but independently of that, they were affected by Jesus and his good spirit in the way these are said, in Rule 1, to affect the spiritually regressing person for his good.

The foregoing illustrations are of those whose dominant disposition and tendency is Godward. St. Augustine in his early life is an example of a regressing Christian, to whom Rule 1 clearly applies but not to the exclusion of Rule 2. He tells how, when he began his steady decline away from God, sinful desires "clouded over and darkened my soul, so that I could not distinguish the calm light of chaste love from the fog of lust. Both kinds of affection burned confusedly within me..."[30] A few years later, sunk more deeply in lust, full of vainglory over his success as the leading student in the school of rhetoric, and filled with worldly ambitions, he could still, on the occasion of his reading Cicero's *Hortensius*, be suddenly touched into flame, forgetting all worldly desires and wanting only to love and to pursue wisdom itself. Even that was astonishing, but the one reason for his hesitation about this experience says even more to our purpose.

> In so great a blaze only this checked me, that Christ's name was not in it. For this name, O Lord, according to your mercy, this name of my saviour, your son, my tender heart had holily drunken in with my mother's milk and kept deep down within itself. Whatever lacked this name, no matter how learned and polished and veracious it was, could not wholly capture me.[31]

There was always in Augustine, through all the years of wandering away from Christ which followed this experience, a deep dimension of his personality which harmonized with the good spirit, and was in conflict with the evil spirit and with the dominant disposition

---

30 *Confessions*, II, 2, as translated by John K. Ryan, (Garden City, Image Books, 1960), on p. 65. See also III, 1, on p. 77.

31 Ibid., p. 82.

and tendency of his life. In that limited area of his personality, Rule 2 could apply to him. Books 3-8 of his *Confessions* are the story of the struggle between these two dimensions acted on by God and the evil spirit. To interpret his inner experiences during that struggle only in the light of Rule 1 would make a muddle of them.

The apostles, then, the rich young man, and Augustine are in varying measures and in different ways all such that both the Rules, 1 and 2, apply to them. So are all of us, unless someone is totally purified of carnal inclination or totally voided of Godward tendencies (if that is even possible). Consequently, when we are trying to understand the significance of certain motions and to discern what spirit is moving anyone, we must be very careful to find out not only what sort of person (spiritually maturing or regressing) is having the experience, but also whether the experience is being described from the side of the spiritual dimension or the anti-spiritual; and whether the feelings that arise from harmony or discord of the motion with the person are from harmony or discord with his spiritual or his anti-spiritual dimension. To be disquieted, to have peace destroyed, or the like is a clear sign of the evil spirit only if the disquiet arises because of an opposition between the spirit and the Godward inclination or tendency of the person. The disturbance, even in a very good and maturing Christian, could be from the good spirit in conflict with the person's remaining egoistic tendency. All we know before determining which tendency is being affected is that one of two things is happening: either an evil tendency of the person is in conflict with the good spirit or a good tendency is in conflict with an evil spirit.

Besides the two sources of complexity we have noted in every concrete discernment of spirits, there is another one which occurs in relatively unusual cases, but is of special importance. It is a surprising one in the light of Rules I:1-2. That source is the fear and disturbance, or even prolonged desolation, in good Christians progressing intensively from good to better when they encounter the divine in unusual ways. Two instances come to mind. One is the initial and quickly passing dread and disturbance at unexpected and intense religious experience. Another is the prolonged and painful darkness, aridity, anxiety, or seeming loss of God which is experienced in the passive nights of the senses and of the spirit as described by John of the Cross and found verified in the accounts we have from many whom God has drawn into these nights. To apply the Ignatian rules without understanding the difference between desolation caused by the evil spirit and that caused by divine light in the passive nights of the soul would surely cause added pain and possibly grave harm. This matter is discussed below in Appendix II. If the reader is interested in it, it will be better to delay reading it until after he has studied what Ignatius means by spiritual consolation and spiritual desolation in chapters 4-6. (on pages 79-144 below).

Chapter 4

SPIRITUAL CONSOLATION AND DESOLATION
PRELIMINARY ANALYSES
Rules I:3 and 4

In Rules I:3 and 4, Ignatius takes up two contrary experiences in spiritual life which are for him, in the rest of his rules for responding to the Holy Spirit, the focus of his attention. His focus on spiritual consolation and desolation[1] should not lead us to conclude that for him spiritual movements other than faith, hope, and charity are exclusively, or even principally, constituted by these two. For example, among the motions from the good or evil spirits, there are inclinations and counsels, but these are not counted as constitutive elements in consolation or desolation properly speaking. This is clear from the fact that the same inclination or counsel can arise either in consolation or in desolation, and these consolations or desolations are signs of what spirit prompts the inclination or counsel (*SpEx*, [318]); in some cases, it is the other way around (*SpEx*, [332-333]). Then, too, as we have seen, there are motions from the Holy Spirit more fundamental than consolation, such as "courage and active energy"; and there are certain forms of light and clarity. The spiritual life goes on and can go on vigorously in the affective sensibility during a time of spiritual calm, a time when one is "not moved by diverse spirits" (*SpEx*, [177]) to spiritual consolation or desolation. The fundamental and essential acts of

---

[1] To a contemporary reader not familiar with the traditional vocabulary of Christian spiritual theology, these terms "spiritual consolation" and "spiritual desolation" may sound archaic and somewhat affected. When we try to find a more widely acceptable pair of contemporary terms, however, we run into problems. Neither joy and sadness, nor peace and trouble, nor comfort and distress, for example, can carry all that is involved in the notion of consolation and desolation. Moreover, "spiritual consolation" and "desolation" have gathered such a wealth of connotation and are so deeply ingrained in the speech of all those formed in Ignatian spirituality, that it would be an unreasonable risk to exchange them for any other set of terms.

Christian spiritual life, along with other non-consoling or non-desolating motions, can most certainly go on in a time of calm. Some persons read *SpEx*, [6] and then draw from it the conclusion that, in Ignatius' opinion, spiritual life has died down when consolation and desolation have died down, or when one finds oneself in the state of calm described in *SpEx*, [177]. But this, although rather common, is a totally unjustifiable reading of Ignatius' text in *SpEx*, [6]. One only needs to read *SpEx*, [177-188] to see what great faith and charity Ignatius assumes as possible during spiritual calm. During such an affective state, a person may be more faithfully and generously obedient to God's will than someone having intense spiritual consolations and desolations.

Neither may we think that these two experiences are more fundamental and more certain criteria for discernment of spirits than all others. Certain external criteria, (the teaching of Sacred Scripture and the Church, the directives of just authority acting justly, the clear call of charity, and the like) are, when available and applicable, far more reliable; and they override any judgment based on experiences of spiritual consolation or desolation. They can be used to judge the source of spiritual consolation and desolation, rather than be judged by the consolation and desolation (*SpEx*, [170]).

On the other hand, to understand these two affective poles of spiritual experience is of cardinal importance for the particular kind of discernment of spirits with which Ignatius is concerned, and also for leading a life open to the Holy Spirit. There are several reasons why this is so. Most, even if not all, of the motions which are relevant for Ignatian discernment of spirits can be in one way or another integrated into the total complex experience of spiritual consolation and spiritual desolation. The truth of this reason will become apparent as we describe these experiences themselves. A further reason why it is of cardinal importance to understand spiritual desolation in particular can be found in something we have already seen: Discouragement is Satan's principal aim in his attack on a spiritually maturing person, and everything in spiritual desolation leads up to discouragement. Hence arises the crucial importance both of recognizing spiritual desolation as distinct from any other and of knowing how to deal with it once it is recognized. As we have also seen, consolation in particular has a cardinal value as a way in which the Holy Spirit encourages us and prepares us to receive and recognize his inspirations. On the other hand, spiritual consolation not fully understood can be used by Satan to deceive and mislead us. Further, we ourselves, unless we understand how to respond, can misuse it to the frustration of God's purpose and to our harm. Finally, our understanding of spiritual consolation is of cardinal importance for discerning when God is leading and counseling us to make some decision. Any failure to discern genuine spiritual consolation and desolation from non-spiritual could open wide the door to decisions which are not in accord with the counsel of the Holy Spirit.

Ignatius' Intention in Rule I:3

The heading of every rule except the third and fourth in the first set is merely "the first," "the second," and so on. The headings of the third and fourth rules read: "The third rule, concerning spiritual consolation" and "The fourth rule, concerning· spiritual desolation." While we should avoid blowing up little things into undue importance, these headings do help us to understand what Ignatius intends to do in these rules and so to determine how we should read each statement in them. It will make discussion simpler if at present we attend only to Rule 3. The parallel in Rule 4 will be obvious and noted when we take up that rule.

Clarity about what Ignatius is intending to do in Rule 3 and what he is not trying to do will clear away confusions that otherwise could plague the rest of our study. It will also giᴠe us our bearings as we set about descriptive analysis of spiritual consolation rooted in Ignatius' description.

He is not intending to analyze or explain what is meant by "consolation" in its general meaning. He assumes the reader knows that; it is, after all, a very ordinary word. His whole effort bears on identifying a specific kind of consolation, namely, *spiritual* consolation. The heading of the rule is "concerning spiritual consolation," and every part of it is calculated to show what specifies consolation of the sort which he calls "spiritual." What might confuse the reader is that frequently in the rules, and more often than not elsewhere, Ignatius uses merely the word "consolation" instead of "spiritual consolation." However, there is no doubt that every phrase in the rule refers to a very special sort of consolation which is called spiritual. Also, Ignatius does on occasion employ the term "spiritual" again to modify "consolation" or some element in spiritual consolation (*SpEx*, [322, 329]).[2] It is significant that in

2 See also *DirSpEx*MHSJ, [11] on p. 72 and [18] on p. 76.

Saint Ignatius' Rules for the Discernment of Spirits

Rule I:9 (*SpEx*, [322]), where Ignatius is stressing that the consolation about which he is speaking is beyond man's power to initiate
or sustain, that "all is gift and grace of our Lord," there he uses
"spiritual consolation" three times instead of merely "consolation."

That Ignatius is assuming the ordinary meaning of consolation,
that is, an agreeable, delightful, affective experience, and that he
is intent only on specifying what sort of consolation is spiritual,
this is clearly indicated in the Vulgate text, and it is also confirmed
by two passages in his Autograph Directory of the *Spiritual Exercises*.
Rule 3 in the Vulgate reads: "[The third rule is] that consolation
is recognized to be spiritual properly speaking, when through a
certain interior motion...."[3] In his Autograph Directory all possible
hesitancy is removed. There he tells the director to explain to the
exercitant at the appropriate time what sort of thing consolation is
and suggests briefly what to say. In one passage the suggestion
reads: "...such as *spiritual* gladness, *love, hope* of *heavenly* things,
tears and interior movement which leaves the person consoled
in our Lord."[4] In the other passage, Ignatius' suggestion reads:
"interior peace, *spiritual joy, hope, faith, love,* tears and elevation of
mind, which are *all gifts of the Holy Spirit*."[5] Faith, hope, and love,
spiritual joy or delight (that is, from the Holy Spirit), all of these
"in the Lord," all "gifts of the Holy Spirit" — these surely are
indications of a very special sort of consolation

Descriptive Analysis of Consolation

So far we have seen that Ignatius takes for granted the ordinary
meaning of "consolation" and, in this rule, is concerned with
showing us how to identify a spiritual consolation. To do so, he
obviously had no idea of presenting any careful analysis of the
experience or any clearly stated set of criteria. He indicates in
short strokes a series of typical experiences or elements in experiences of spiritual consolation so that by these the reader may be
helped toward distinguishing a spiritual consolation from a non-
spiritual one.

Obviously, the items which he mentions, such as love, faith, a
feeling of peace, a desire for heavenly things, tears, are not all

---

3 *Quod spiritualis proprie consolatio tunc esse noscitur, quando per internam quandam motionem*
....(*SpEx*MHSJ, p. 376).
4 *DirSpEx*MHSJ, [18] on p. 76, emphasis mine.
5 Ibid., (11] on p. 72, emphasis mine.

spiritual consolations in the same sense. Neither do they play the same role in constituting a spiritual consolation. Nevertheless, Ignatius makes no formal effort to say in what sense the experiences or parts of experiences can be called consolations, or be related to each other in constituting a consolation. Consequently, before we try to understand with any depth and precision the significance of the several descriptions of consolations given in Rule 3, it seems necessary to make a descriptive analysis of consolation in general (whether spiritual or not). We must attempt to uncover the essential structure of such an experience, to see what the elements are, and how they are related. By so doing we shall see the different referents of the word "consolation" and have a structure in which to relate the various bits of experience which Ignatius sets down, somewhat incoherently. We do, of course, have to be very cautious lest we impose a meaning on Ignatius. We must make very sure that what we arrive at in this way tallies in all details with what he says. There is a risk in this, but there is a risk in any interpretation; and this way at least grounds the interpretation in an analysis of experience which can be checked in each one's own experience.

In order to achieve any clarity and precision in a descriptive analysis of consolation and desolation or of affective experience in general, it is necessary to distinguish affective acts and affective feelings. This distinction is commonly overlooked, not only in common sense thinking and speaking but even in the writing of philosophers and psychologists, with very confusing results. The distinction is especially needed when some affective act and affective feeling go by the same name. Then we have, for example, one saying that love is a warm feeling or a feeling of openness or of being in union, while another says that love is the affective act of willing good to or affirming someone or the act of desiring union with the loved one. The acts are clearly possible without the feeling. The same sort of confusion then arises in regard to dispositions for acts or feelings. For example, courage is thought of as a readiness to *feel* unafraid in the face of danger or pain, something very different from readiness to *actively accept and choose to endure* pain and danger despite feelings of fear. Any adequate treatment of the distinction between affective acts and feelings would take many pages. For our purposes, it will be enough merely to note that in any affective act, the person is in some true sense an agent, *does something* (immanently but virtually effectively). Thus, I affirm you, I fear embarrassment, I desire food. In an affective feeling, the person or subject is not what we would ordinarily speak of as an agent; rather, the subject's affectivity is actuated in a purely passive way. The feeling is, of course, grounded in the person's own cognitive and affective acts. A feeling is a purely passive actuation of affective sensibility, an affective *state* of conscious being, growing from conscious activity, accompanying it, influencing it, but not itself an activity. Thus, I have such feelings as those of warmth or coldness, of tranquility or excitement, depression or elation, heaviness or buoyancy, sweetness or bitterness.

Understanding the foregoing distinction between affective acts and affective feelings, we can say that "consolation," in ordinary usage, refers primarily to a conscious affective state, a feeling or a cluster of feelings of peace, gladness, sweetness, well-being, and the like, replacing or easing a feeling of disturbance, depression, bitterness, distress, and so on.[6] The word is then extended to an activity of the person which is the subjective ground for the affective feeling of consolation. Thus, if we find consolation in religious contemplation, in philosophical study, in making love, in playing music, in drinking and chatting with boon companions, we call these activities consolations. We then easily apply the word to the objects of these activities and say that God or a certain kind of music or poetry or the beloved or drink or companions is our consolation in life. Further, the word may also refer to the activity by which someone else consoles us, prompts in us an affective feeling of consolation, for example, by kind and wise words, by giving signs of love. From there it is an easy step to the one who performs such acts: "You are a consolation to me," we say to someone. Attentive observation of these usages will note that in all but the first "consolation" is used in one or another causative sense: What is consoling, what brings about consolation in the first meaning, is itself given the name consolation.

The conscious affective feeling (feelings) has primacy therefore over all the other referents so far mentioned; the others are called consolation in relation to it. After that primary meaning, the most important one is the cognitive and affective acts which are necessary (such acts as perceptions, judgments, imaginings, desires, hopes, loves). The other referents of consolation are such only inasmuch as they are objects of those acts from which the affective feeling of consolation arises. So, our concern is principally with that affective feeling and the acts which are subjective grounds for

6 See, e.g., 2 Cor. 1:3-7; 1 Thess. 1:6.

that feeling. This implies, of course, that whatever is an object of those acts is an objective ground of consolation in the primary meaning of the word.

It is not easy to describe affective states or feelings in themselves. The several concepts we use to describe this state of consolation overlap and often have only a shade of difference — a difference of emphasis or connotation, for example, peace, contentment, a sense of security or well-being, gladness, delight. Further, each of these has varied qualities which we describe as best we can by metaphors drawn from sensuous experience. Thus, we speak of them as warm, sweet, lucid, bright, quiet, deep, exalted, surging, swelling, and so on. Even then we find the description vague, unsatisfactory, revealing little of the peculiar quality of a feeling in the concrete; we have to describe as best we can the matrix of concrete experience within which it arises and from which it takes its special quality. For instance, consolation may be: contentment in some interesting work after the drudgery by which one earns a living, or after fulfilling dull social obligations; a delicious sense of relief from anxiety over a loved one now known to be saved from a painful and dangerous situation; the sweet, exultant joy in the assurance of being loved by a beloved one after having doubted; a sense of gladness because of renewed hope to achieve some desired goal; exaltation at hearing great music or reading about a heroic human life. All these are different consolations by reason of different sources.

Description by reference to the source is not merely an extrinsic way of distinguishing one experience of consolation from another, as if every peace or gladness or exaltation or the like were intrinsically univocal, and only extrinsically differentiated by relationship to a different source. The affective feelings of consolation are intrinsically differentiated by the different sources; they are rendered qualitatively different. Not only is the consolation arising from hearing great music qualitatively different from the consolation of being loved by a beloved one, but the consolation from hearing one musical composition can be intrinsically different from that which arises when hearing another composition, and the consolation at being loved by one person can differ intrinsically from the consolation which arises at being loved by another.

Not only do the affective feelings of consolation have sources in the conscious life of the person; they also have characteristic consequences. They dispose the person for, and so lead to, certain ways of perceiving, thinking, imagining, affectively responding, choosing. That the influence of acts and feelings is reciprocal, that all our conscious acts are influenced by our feelings, just as much as our feelings are influenced by our conscious acts, this is obvious in our experience. This or that feeling of consolation or desolation disposes us to remember some truths or experiences and to forget others, to note some elements in the concrete situation and to overlook others, to emphasize some aspects of what we note and to deemphasize others, to understand and reason well or to be blind and confused. In all these ways, such feelings shape our present vision of past and future and our present perception of the concrete situation in which we are. They also dispose us for more intense and more enduring affective acts of love, hate, desire, fear, trust, distrust, and so on, or make us indifferent. They dispose us to be reasonably decisive, precipitous, or indecisive; to be resolute or irresolute in initiating action on decision and carrying it through. They dispose us to find burdens light or crushing, or to find the endurance of suffering for a purpose easy and joyful or hard and dreadful.

We saw that the feeling of consolation is intrinsically differentiated by and consequently described by relationship to its source. So also the consequences of consolation are themselves influenced by the consolation. Nevertheless, they also serve as a way for us to describe the consolation from which they originate; for they manifest in some measure, even if at times vaguely or uncertainly, the nature of the affective feeling by which they are influenced, as also of the causes of that feeling.

To sum up what we have seen, consolation in its inclusive meaning has three related parts: first, consolation in the proper or exclusive meaning (affective feelings such as peace or gladness); second, the causes or sources, subjective and objective, of consolation properly speaking (cognitive and affective acts with their objects — or the objects as known and responded to); and third, consequences of consolation properly speaking (such as our ways of perceiving, of remembering, of responding affectively, for which the feeling of consolation disposes the person).

The description of the total complex experience referred to as consolation in the broad sense has practical implications in regard to our understanding of our experience of consolation and to our way of speaking about it. Failure to attend carefully to any element could leave the experience vague and its significance in the flow of life unknown or misunderstood. The significance of all this in relation to discernment of spirits in general hardly needs emphasizing. Of immediate and particular significance in relationship to interpreting Rule I:3 is the following point. We saw that the only or ordinary way in which we can most adequately describe our consolations properly speaking as they are in the concrete is by clarifying their subjective grounds and their subjective consequences. Therefore we tend to refer to any element in the total concrete experience as consolation, not discriminating what is consolation strictly speaking from its sources (consolation in the causal sense) or its consequences. Sometimes we simply refer to the subjective grounds (for example, contemplation of God's beauty, trust in his love and power) or to the subjective consequences (for example, ease in being kind or in enduring work and pain, or tears of tenderness and joy) as consolation, leaving the consolation properly speaking only implied. Or we say that the sort of consolation we are talking about is a feeling (for example, of peace, gladness, sweetness) which arises when one has certain experiences (causes) or from which certain dispositions follow (consequences).

The diverse ways of referring to the complex reality, all tumbled together, are certainly what we find in all the cases in which Ignatius says what spiritual consolation is by giving illustrations; and this is his ordinary, even his only, way of saying what he means by spiritual consolation. Keeping this in mind will enable us to read Ignatius with greater accuracy and less chance of drawing erroneous and dangerous conclusions in so delicate and critically important a matter.

The Meaning of Peace

Before we turn to Ignatius' description of spiritual consolation, one further clarification is needed. A whole cluster of feelings constitutes consolation properly so called, especially spiritual consolation. Among them one is always included; it seems to be the core of every such consolation. That feeling is what we call peace. However, the word "peace" and the concept of peace are ambiguous; and this ambiguity readily leads to considerable confusion in thinking and talking about the peace of spiritual consolation. Consequently, before we take up the Ignatian description of consolation, we shall act wisely if we distinguish and clarify several meanings of peace in general, and of spiritual peace in particular.

There is a purely negative way of speaking about peace as absence of turmoil, freedom from disturbance, without any necessary positive implications of rich and well-ordered activity. Thus, we call a gathering of people peaceful when there is no positive form of orderly interaction or personal communion but merely an absence of clashing and dissonance. Nations are said to have peace when not destroying each other by war. This mode of speaking reaches its limit in speaking of inactivity and motionlessness as peace. Thus, we refer to sleep or death as states of peace, even when these are thought of as the total cessation of a person's conscious life. This notion of peace is of interest only as one to keep unconfused with a positive notion.

There is peace in a positive sense when in conscious human life, individual or communal, each element of its complexity is acting tranquilly and gracefully (even though intensely and powerfully), and all the elements are well ordered (subordinated and coordinated, meshing with and balancing each other, without conflict or disturbance, with just the right degree of tension to avoid painful strain or dull slackness). This is peace as a condition or state or quality *of* conscious life, not a condition *for* it. It may be a condition for successful performance of some particular activity; but it is first of all a condition or state or quality of conscious life as an integrated whole, individual or communal.

In the context of our study, it is peace in the individual's conscious life that is our concern. On the one hand, there is freedom from disturbing thoughts and affections (such as anger or worry), or from the painful confusion and tension of conflicting thoughts and affections. On the other hand, there is the graceful integration of conscious acts (such as thoughts, loves, hates, or desires), actualized with some measure of intensity, depth, and power. Peace in this sense is some measure of true human well-being. Perfect peace of this sort would be the fullness of human life, all human activities at their peak and all fully integrated.

From the experience of peace as a condition of conscious life arises peace as a *feeling*. This is not an ordered state of all feelings, peace as a condition of affective life, the sort of peace we have just been talking about. It is one particular feeling. It is not merely the absence of disturbing feeling or the subjective causes of these. It is a positive actuation of affective sensibility. It overlaps with and is in concrete experience joined with one or another of the feelings referred to as gladness, sweetness, delight, contentment. It is commonly referred to in many contexts simply as "peace"; but for clarity's sake, let us call it the feeling of peace or peace as a feeling and reserve the word "peace" for the actualized and integrated condition of conscious activity described above.

Among all the concepts of peace these two are of special importance to us: (1) peace as an integrated condition of healthy conscious activities and (2) the feeling of peace. The former is the ground of the latter; the latter is the expression in affective sensibility of the former. These two concepts are of critical importance in any descriptive analysis of spiritual consolation. They are easily and commonly confused. Inasmuch as it also causes confusion, one other concept is also important for us, that of peace or tranquility in the negative sense, mere calm in the affective sensibility, absence of consoling or desolate feelings.[7]

Spiritual Peace

The foregoing clarifications of peace enable us to show the nature of *spiritual* peace as distinct from any other. By spiritual peace I mean peace inspired by the Holy Spirit. While well aware that the Holy Spirit can work in one who is not a Christian, in this discussion I mean by spiritual peace Christian peace, that is, peace which is rooted in Christian faith, hope, and charity, the primary works of the Holy Spirit in Christian life. This peace

---

7 The confusion of peace in this negative meaning with peace as a feeling conduces to a distortion of the Ignatian teaching on discernment of God's will. An illustration can be found in Karl Rahner's "The Logic of Concrete Individual Knowledge in Ignatius Loyola," pp. 84-170 in his *The Dynamic Element in the Church* (New York, 1964), (hereafter abbreviated as *Dynamic Element*). He first reads "time of tranquility" in *SpEx*, [177] according to the obvious meaning it has there, a time without movements of the spirits, good or bad, a time therefore in which the affective sensibility is becalmed, without consolation or desolation (pp. 95-96). Later on in this essay (pp. 168-169), when making a different point, he seemingly forgets what he has said earlier and now suggests that this tranquility spoken of in *SpEx*, [177] may somehow be thought of as corresponding with the "tranquility and quiet" of spiritual consolation, and therefore as a sign of the good spirit. This confusion is not without distorting effects on his interpretation of Ignatian discernment of God's will in the "third time" (*SpEx*, [177]). The question of what Ignatius meant by the "third time" for finding God's will and of its dependence on or independence of the "second time" will be more appropriately taken up in a separate study on Ignatian discernment of God's will.

is first of all a condition of conscious life insofar as it is Christianly actualized, and secondly a state of affective sensibility, a feeling of peace.

Christian peace as a condition of conscious life is freedom from anxiety and fear, because and insofar as one has faith in God's power, wisdom, and love for us revealed in Jesus Christ. It is also freedom from turmoil or disturbance insofar as our conscious acts, both those that are spontaneous and those that are freely chosen, are in accord with, integrated with, faith, hope, and charity, and consequently in accord with each other. Such Christian peace is, in some measure, a participation in divine life, a communion with God in Christ, in the members of Christ, and in the whole universe as joined to Christ — for all is from Christ as God — for all things are from him and through him and to him (Rom. 11:36). It is greater or lesser depending on the degree of faith, hope, and charity and on the extent to which these dominate and integrate all other elements of conscious life.

Christian peace as a feeling, or the feeling of Christian peace, is a state of sensibility which Christian peace as a condition of conscious life tends of itself to induce. Such peace can be, as we shall see, impeded or reduced by contrary forces in any dimension of consciousness which is not integrated with and dominated by Christian faith, hope, and charity. It is not merely an untroubled state of affective sensibility, a state of calm in the sensibility unactuated by feelings of anxiety, discouragement, uneasiness. It is a certain euphoric actuation of sensibility, basically a feeling of well-being (warm, sweet, lucid, secure, glad) which can be specified as different from any other feeling of peace by reference to its ground, the peace constituted by a life in which Christian faith, hope, and charity are actual and govern thoughts, affective acts, and decisions.

Essential and Contingent Spiritual Peace

The kingdom of God, which we enter or which enters us through Christian faith, hope, and charity, is, as St. Paul says, a matter of "righteousness and peace and joy in the Holy Spirit" (Rom., 14:17). Christian life in time alternates between consolation and desolation. The consolation is more or less fully and intensely suffused with a feeling of peace, and the desolation is suffused with feelings of anxiety, anguish, gloom. Hence the question arises: Do faith, hope, and charity (which make up righteousness) always issue in the peace and joy of the Holy Spirit? If so, how do we explain desolation in good Christians? If not, why not? For the kingdom of God is a kingdom of peace and joy; and it is hard to see how one could really believe and hope and love as a Christian does and still be in desolation. The foregoing description of the experience of peace and the analysis of the ways in which we use the word peace will now enable us to answer these questions. The answers will help us to understand our own experience as Christians and enable us to give an intelligent interpretation of the Ignatian rules for living with spiritual peace.

First, unless there is a split in the personality between understanding and affective appetite on one side and affective sensibility on the other, we have to grant that really believing what a Christian believes will necessarily issue in some sort of spiritual consolation, a feeling of spiritual peace and joy rooted in living faith. On the other hand, we have to grant the fact of spiritual desolation in Christians who believe and hope intensely and love generously. This is an inescapable fact which poses an apparent dilemma. The escape from this dilemma is provided by noting other facts about our affective responses in the spiritual life, both affective acts and affective feelings. Acts of faith, hope, and charity vary not only in their intensity but also in their extension, that is to say, in the breadth of conscious life which they dominate and integrate in relation to God. Recall that spiritual peace as a condition of spiritual life is constituted by such integration and, therefore, can also be of greater or less extent. Spiritual peace as a feeling, a basic element in every spiritual consolation, depends on having some measure of spiritual peace as a condition of spiritual life. However, and this fact is of fundamental importance for our purpose, the intensity and pervasiveness of spiritual peace as a feeling is not necessarily in direct ratio with the intensity and pervasiveness of spiritual peace as an integrated condition of spiritual life. These facts enable us to see how some otherwise puzzling spiritual experiences are possible.

For they show how it is possible to experience feelings of desolation concurrently with feelings of consolation, and how one of these feelings, when intense enough and extensive enough, can, in ordinary awareness, swallow up the other so that it is not noticed at all. Careful and methodical examination of consciousness can bring that other to attention, but to ordinary attention it is nonexistent. Thus, spiritual consolation (in the proper sense of feelings which flow from living faith) is sometimes dominant. It may be so dominant that we hardly notice the spiritual desolation in another area of conscious life; and then the whole experience is thought of as consolation. Sometimes we are quite conscious of both consolation and desolation. We take our stand in the consolation and combat the desolation from the area of peace and partial spiritual integration, and we even find joy in meeting the challenge with the energy and courage of faith and charity from the Holy Spirit. By the power of the Holy Spirit experienced at the limited center of tranquility and fullness of spiritual life, we are able to integrate even the experience of desolation into that life as an occasion for spiritual growth in humility, faith, hope, charity, courage, and self knowledge. (We shall see in detail how this is true when we study Ignatius' directions on how to resist and conquer spiritual desolation.) At another time spiritual desolation is so dominant and absorbs our attention so fully that the consolation which is really actuated in sensibility is hard to note; often it is not noted at all. Hence, this time is thought of simply as a time of desolation. Nevertheless, consolation, peace as a feeling (consolation properly speaking), is not totally absent so long as faith, hope, and charity are alive. The total state of consciousness is throughout different because of faith, hope, and charity; and there is in it — necessarily, I think we have to say — some measure of spiritual consolation, of peace as a feeling, even if in our limited power of reflective attention it gets drowned out or engulfed from view by the desolation.

This understanding of our spiritual experience leads us to see that in any maturing Christian there is an enduring feeling of peace, a spiritual consolation, which is an essential property of Christian life. It is an element in the essential structure of Christianly actuated consciousness. Let us call it essential spiritual consolation; and let us distinguish it from contingent spiritual consolation, which is in some measure an intensification, clarification, and sometimes expansion of essential consolation. It comes and goes. At times it has to go for the sake of Christian maturation. In the form in which it is given to us in this life, it is a means, not an end; and it is important only insofar as it helps the Christ-life which comes through faith to grow and to bring life to the world.

The peace with which Ignatius is principally concerned in his rules is contingent rathei than essential spiritual peace or consolation. What he calls "spiritual consolation" in his ordinary usage goes beyond the essential Christian peace which endures through all the vicissitudes of life in this world. It arises out of the essential peace as its spring or fountainhead, and it fades back into it. It is the rising and falling of the quiet song that always sings at the deep center of Christian life. It is an intensification of the taste of God's sweetness, a pledge of bliss to come, a viaticum. But it has its dangers for the sinful human person as well as its advantages. It is only one means among others which the Holy Spirit uses to help us along the way to eternal life. Spiritual calm and spiritual desolation are also means, and sometimes much more needful than contingent consolation. These can be experienced with essential Christian peace or consolation.

Chapter 5

THE DESCRIPTION OF SPIRITUAL CONSOLATION
Rule I:3

By now we have reached some clarity about the ordinary meaning of consolation in general; some clarity about the multiple states to which the words "consolation" and "peace" are referred; some clarity about Ignatius' intention, which assumes the ordinary general meaning of consolation and is directed to helping us recognize when it is spiritual; and, finally, some understanding of his indiscriminate way of illustrating spiritual consolation. Hence we are now in position to read his brief series of descriptive statements on spiritual consolation.

At first glance these statements, as also those on desolation, seem simple enough and not particularly enlightening. Those who have, through experience and study, become aware of the complex realities involved find these statements both full of difficulties and full of light.

To see the problems and to gather the light, every step in the study of Rules 3 and 4 must be taken carefully, with close attention to the text. We must stubbornly resist every urge to read our own assumptions, theories, or personal insights into Ignatius' words and to grasp at proof texts to justify what we have done. Further, as we read these descriptive statements, it is essential to keep in mind that Ignatius is describing how those experiences which he calls spiritual consolation or desolation[1] appear to the one experiencing them. I do not mean that he is describing what the experiencing person might name spiritual consolation or desolation (but which Ignatius would name non-spiritual). I mean that he is des-

---

1 See above, pp. 83-84, on the distinction between an affective act, e.g., an act of loving, and an affective feeling, e.g., warmth, sweetness.

cribing only such an experience as he, Ignatius, calls spiritual consolation or desolation; but he is describing that experience as it appears to the person experiencing it, no matter how the latter might name it. Particularly in desolation, much of what appears to the person in his reflection is not in accord with the reality of the experience reflected on. Sometimes grasp of our own experience is distorted, and we misinterpret our own acts and feelings. Ignatius will have to remind us of that.

The First Descriptive Statement

The first description speaks of a person's being moved to intense love for God, and of the repercussion of this on his or her love for creatures.

[316]. Rule 3. I name it [spiritual] consolation when some inner motion is prompted in the person of such a kind that the person begins to be aflame with love of our Creator and Lord and consequently, when he cannot love in itself any created thing on the face of the earth but only in the Creator of them all.

Ignatius immediately calls attention to the greatest work of the Holy Spirit in man's spirit, that to which all other works of the Holy Spirit lead or from which they follow, charity. The love to which Ignatius refers is not any ordinary love for God and for creatures in God. It is an unusual experience in which the nature of Christian love appears most obviously to the person who experiences it: the experience the person has when he begins to be "aflame with love of his Creator and Lord," when the act of love is enriched with intense feelings (*spiritual* and sensible) of warmth; when the affective sensibility is, so to speak, set afire. In such an experience, love shows its power more clearly to us — to us who are so dependent on feeling if we are to believe that our own love is genuine love for God and to find joy in the loving.

Such an experience is a more complete response of the whole personality to God, but the act of love in its essential reality is not necessarily purer or stronger or more enduring than it is in some other experiences which lack the flaming feelings. Love for God without any warmth of feeling may also render one courageous in enduring suffering for him, or daring and energetic in doing deeds expressive of love. Such love may remain faithful through times when the lover feels no sweetness, warmth, tenderness, or joy in loving, when, perhaps on that account, he is even tempted to

95

doubt his own love. One who loves with such love does not seem to himself to be aflame with love. Nevertheless it is genuine love; it can even be heroic love; but it is not *experienced* as aflame until the person feels it burning in his or her sensibility. When that happens, it is a consoling love. The lover is assured of truly loving, is filled with joy in God — and joy in loving God not only because of a faith-conviction that God is infinitely loving and lovable, but because of a faith experience of God's love and lovableness, by which he or she tastes and sees how sweet God is. As a consequence it is easier to love God intensely and purely.

Let us try to understand better the consequence to which the inflamed feelings of love are conducive. The subjective consequence of this love (while it lasts) is, Ignatius says, that the lover can love no creature in itself but only in God. The act of intense love for God to which the Holy Spirit moves the one consoled absorbs, as it were, all love for creatures so that they can be loved only in God and God in them. The flaming feeling in the sensibility more fully disposes for such love. Without loving creatures less but rather loving them even more, all the love is love for God, one love for one beloved. Any object of love which cannot form one object of love with God is not lovable as long as this movement of the Spirit endures.

Since self is a creature, the love could not be as Ignatius describes it unless for the moment self is lovable to self only because self can be loved in God and God in self. Love is for the moment utterly unselfish. For the moment, I say, because such love does not last in this life, not even in the lives of the great saints. Any reading of their own testimony about their lives makes this clear. A rare one may at the peak period of life have more or less frequent and enduring experiences of this sort; but that even the greatest Christians live constantly at such intensity and purity of love is hardly believable. Saint Bernard, whose opinion should carry some weight in such matters, was strongly of a mind that only the great saints, and they only for passing moments, ever came to a love in which self is loved *only* in God.[2] Many could reach a love in which God is

---

2 St. Bernard of Clairvaux, *De Deo Diligendo*, X, in Patrologia Latina, vol. 182, cols. 990-992; see esp. X, 26 in col. 990. English translation by Terrence Connolly, S.J. *St. Bernard on the Love of God* (New York, 1937) pp. 43-46, esp. 43-44. See also John of the Cross, *Dark Night*, II, 11, 2-4. It is clear that for John such a love as Ignatius describes is infused and unusual, given only to those who have gone through not only purifications of the active night of the senses and spirit, but also the passive night of

constantly loved more than self; but that is not at all the same as
to exclude even a lesser love of self independent of love for God,
so to transcend all trace of egoism as to have no love at all for self
or any creature except in God.

The sure sign and the test for Ignatius that the person is so disposed toward creatures by an all-consuming love for God is the
consequent disposition for desire and choice. In the *Spiritual Exercises*,
Ignatius sees this consequence of such unselfish love to be of pivotal
importance. If love is pure love for God and powerful enough to
unify all a person's love, at least while the consolation lasts, then
also, during that time, the lover will have one all-consuming desire
which unifies all desires, the desire for whatever is God's will.
As long as one loves in the way Ignatius describes in this first formula
of spiritual consolation, no object of desire can be attractive except
insofar as it appears to be God's will. Therefore, the lover will also
have one basic choice which in principle settles all choices, the
choice of whatever alternative in any concrete situation for choice
is God's will — or what comes to the same thing for Ignatius,
whatever is more for the glory of God, more for the praise and
service of God (*SpEx*, [1, 23, 166, 169, 177, 179-180, 184]).

Is it necessary that one's love for God and desire for his glory be
affectively inflamed in order to be so unified, and to render oneself
"indifferent" to all but God's will in matters for choice? Here one
must be careful not to begin by thinking of love merely as a warm
feeling. Then he will see that an *act* of love can be pure, intense,
and firm without inflamed feelings — as careful attention to experience shows, as all the saints and great spiritual directors have taught,
as Christ teaches in the Gospels. For he tells us that the sure sign
of loving him and the Father is not feelings, but doing the Father's
will; and for this the affective act of love, with or without warm
and sweet feelings, is necessary and is sufficient to move us to find
and do all else that is God's will. The flaming feeling may render
the person more joyful and sure of his love, capable of *more easily*
loving creatures only in God, and thus more ready to do his will
with ease and joy rather than with inner struggle. Nevertheless,
it is possible in the darkness and dryness of desolation to be so moved
by the Holy Spirit to love for God that no creature is lovable except
in God. During life in time, the heights and depths of Christian

the senses and are deeply in the passive night of the spirit. For a brief explanation of
what this involves, see Appendix II below on pages 271-282.

love, agape, do not essentially depend on consolation. To lose consolation is not by that very fact to lose anything of the act of love for God, but only the intense feelings of warmth and sweetness which make loving delightful — and which usually make it easier for the person to have a unified love and to be indifferent to all but God's will, that is, to all but his greater glory. The indifference to all options before God's will is known is something which can come more readily and be sustained more easily during spiritual consolation than it frequently can in time of calm or desolation. Without consolation a person may sometimes, not always, have a harder struggle in overcoming selfish desires and fears; but Ignatius clearly thinks that without consolation the goal of indifference to all but God's will can be reached and maintained.[3]

Ignatius speaks of God taking away consolation (Rule I:7 in *SpEx*, [320]), even without fault on the part of the person [322]. It would be strange indeed if God in so doing took away the power of charity, which he gave, when the receiver of the gift had not put up any new obstacles. That he would take away the feelings of warmth, sweetness, delight, and assurance of loving, that is altogether another matter and easily understood.

If all of this is true, then not every love for God, not even every intense and pure love for God, is what Ignatius means by spiritual consolation in this first description of it. To qualify as such consolation, the love has to be experienced by the person as "aflame." Love has to be love for God if the lover's experience is to count as *spiritual*, but love for God has to be love with delightfully inflamed sensibility if the lover's experience is to count as *consolation*. The passages where Igntius speaks of consolation are shot through with such feeling words as: satisfaction, contentment, sense of security, peace, tranquility, repose, delight, rejoicing, sweetness, warmth, tears (of love and joy).[4] Desolation is always spoken of in contrary terms,[5] never merely as a movement away from or in conflict with God.

---

3 The Ignatian directives for achieving this control presuppose the possibility of doing it (*SpEx*, [147, 150-157, 159]). In fact, the "Preamble" for directives on how to make any election (*SpEx*, [169]) demands indifference to all but God's will as a prerequisite for decision, both in time of calm and in time of consolation; and all the instructions on making a decision in time of calm (*SpEx*, [177, 179-181, 184]) or on reformation of life ([189]) assume that indifference to all but God's will is possible without consolation.

4 *SpEx*, [315, 329, 335]; *DirSpEx*MHSJ, [11] on p. 72; [18] on p. 76; and especially Ignatius' *Spiritual Diary*, passim.

5 *SpEx*, [317, 329, 335]; *DirSpEx*MHSJ, [12] on p. 72, [18] on p. 76.

In other words, when consolation springs from such love for God as Ignatius here describes, it is spiritual consolation. The source, the essential act of love, can be called consolation in a causative sense; and the affective feelings of warmth, sweetness, peace, joy from pure love of God constitute spiritual consolation in the proper sense. Ignatius makes clear in his Autograph Directory of the *Spiritual Exercises* that he employs this manner of speaking. For there he says that "consolation is...every inner motion which leaves the person consoled in our Lord."[6] This is not a mere tautology. As we saw in our analysis of consolation, the motion from which arises the conscious affective state of consolation (the state of being "consoled") is itself called consolation in a causative sense (the consoling). So here, when the person has a clear awareness of loving God purely and intensely with his affective sensibility aflame, the love is said to be aflame, and he is consoled.

One last remark before leaving the first statement in Rule I:3. Once we become alert to the extraordinary nature of the love in this experience of consolation, its surprising purity, we are not too surprised to note another feature in this first description. The transition to such love as just described is said to be prompted (*se causa*) in a person, presumably by some influence beyond his or her affectivity and awareness of its object. The motion is not purely and solely a spontaneous affective response.[7]

This first description of spiritual consolation, consolation grounded in the kind of love Ignatius here describes, seems to be the paradigm of all spiritual consolation: for Ignatius, any other consolation is spiritual precisely insofar as it is like this one, or integrated with it or with what is like it. The truth of this assertion will become clearer as we analyze the following descriptions and reflect on them.

The Second Descriptive Statement

The second descriptive statement speaks of spiritual consolation in terms of what moves one to love for God and leads to His praise and service: "Likewise [I call it consolation] when one pours out tears moving to love of our Lord, whether it be for sorrow over sins or over the passion of Christ our Lord or over other things

---

6 *DirSpExMHSJ*, [18] on p. 76.
7 All the Latin texts of the *Spiritual Exercises* suggest this aspect of the experience. The Vulgate uses *exardescit*: the person not only begins to be aflame but "is enkindled," "is set afire." The *Versio Prima* uses *accenditur* (*SpExMHSJ*, pp. 376-377).

directly ordered to his service and praise." There are several elements in the experience spoken of: tears, repentant sorrow, compassion for Christ, love, the service and praise of God. What kind of tears, sorrow, and so on these have to be in order to be elements in a consolation, what kind they have to be in order to be elements in a spiritual consolation, what place each has in the spiritual consolation, and how they are related to one another — all these are questions requiring our investigation.

Before we look into these questions, however, let us note a significant peculiarity in Ignatius' manner of speaking both here and in the first description. He says that he calls it consolation when one is set aflame with love and when one pours out tears and so on. Notice that just as in the first statement he did not equate love simply with consolation, so here he is not equating tears or sorrow (not even every sorrow for sin) with consolation. Tears of sorrow can be an element in the total complex of spiritual consolation if they are tears of a particular kind of sorrow from a particular source and with particular consequences. He is saying that when one has tears of sorrow with the appropriate source and consequence, then he is having a spiritual consolation.

What Ignatius is doing is similar to what a teacher of poetry might do in trying to tell beginners what a genuine aesthetic pleasure (consolation) is, as distinct, for example, from the sense pleasure of eating and drinking or the intellectual pleasure that comes from working through a challenging scientific problem, or even from analyzing the intellectual content of a poem. Instead of giving a careful analysis of aesthetic emotions as distinct from others, the delight that comes from beauty as distinct from the delight in achievement, or in certainty after doubt, the teacher might say something like this: "When your eyes get watery, when a shiver goes down your spine, when you want to hear the lines over and over, or when you become still and deeply silent after hearing them, then you have had an aesthetic experience of poetry." Now, aesthetic delight is certainly not constituted by water in the eyes or shivers in the spine or an urge to read the lines again or by deep silence. But when these things happen as a result of reading poetry or hearing music, you may be sure the pleasure or delight you have experienced is an aesthetic pleasure. You will see, once you notice it and reflect on it, how it differs in quality, in source, in consequence, from other pleasures. So with spiritual consolation. When you have tears of peace and joy for some reason related to God and when you are moved to love for God, or to praise and serve him, then the consolation is a spiritual one. Once you attend to it, you will see how different it is from other consolations.

Aware of how Ignatius is going about his description, let us look at the elements and try to see the nature of each and their relationship to one another. The key element is living faith, belief in God's love that flowers in hope and above all in charity toward one's neighbor. As we noted, charity is the Spirit's principal work. Any sorrow and tears or any other element in the experience that does not lead to or flow from charity cannot be spiritual.

What kind of sorrow springs from and leads to living faith? It is a sorrow about something that is directly related to the praise and service of God, for example, sorrow over my sins or sorrow over the sufferings of Jesus. In other words, it is a sorrow that is rooted in faith and love for God in Christ. Only faith and charity can explain such sorrow as Ignatius speaks of. Only one who already believes in and loves God can be concerned about the praise and service of God and can sorrow over what is opposed to God's praise and service. The phrases "moving to love of our Lord" and "directly related to his service and praise" eliminate a multitude of tender and tearful consoling experiences. Attention to those phrases will keep us from confusing genuine spiritual consolation colored by sorrow with any sweet melancholies and sorrows of a romantic or sentimental or aesthetic nature, and with the pleasure of self-pitying sorrow.

On the other hand, we must not let these two phrases lead us to think that every sorrowful affection which terminates in God is by that fact a spiritual consolation. Such affection may be spiritual but not consolation; or it may be consolation and not spiritual. We have just noted some non-spiritual experiences that are sad, sorrowful, and yet suffused with comfort, sweetness, even exquisite delight. Some spiritual experiences of sadness or sorrow are of this kind and are spiritual consolations. On the other hand, we are all familiar with non-spiritual experiences of sorrow that are bitter, painful, desolating. So also with spiritual experiences. Sorrow for sin in one who believes up to a point, enough to be sorry for sin but without a deep experience of God's forgiving and all-powerful love, will be bitter and depressing, not a consolation. Only when the sorrow becomes fused with realization of God's merciful, tender love conquering sin and turning it to his glory in us is it possible for one to find, as Augustine found, "more delight in weeping over my sins than I did in committing them."

What is more, there is a sorrow of compassion which springs from intense love for God and neighbor that is experienced as desolation, even in a person of great faith and charity. All that faith and charity can do in these cases is to strengthen one to endure with fidelity and courage. Think of Mary's sharing in Christ's desolation on Calvary. Surely, there was no consolation in it. Desolation with Christ in desolation is very different from the sweet sadness of consolation experienced over the sufferings of Christ as a revelation of God's love. The latter was possible to Mary after Calvary, when Jesus had transcended suffering and she was shedding tears in remembering the heroic and conquering love of her risen and glorious son. To speak of her anguish on Calvary, or worse yet of Christ's sorrow in Gethsemane or on the cross, as spiritual consolation because it was springing from faith and love of God is confusing even as technical jargon. What is more to the point here, it is in discord with Ignatius' thought.

All this leads to one last comment on the second description of spiritual consolation. It suggests two characteristics of every Christian consolation. The first characteristic is that Christian consolation springs from and moves to the love of a forgiven sinner for his saving God. Whether in temporal spiritual consolation or in final triumph, we are sinners, whose very sins are transformed into glory and grounds for our joy by God's infinitely creative and loving power. They become a source of glory for Christ and of joy for us over Christ's glory as redeemer. Peter is forever the man who denied Jesus, and who forever glories in the faithful, forgiving, transfiguring love that makes him the glory of his beloved Jesus. So, in the foretaste of bliss that the Holy Spirit gives in spiritual consolation during this life, a sense of our sinfulness and of God's redeeming love in Christ is always present. It is not always explicit, not always easy to detect, but, insofar as the consolation is truly Christian, always at least implicit and giving a special tone of humility and gratitude to the experience.

A second characteristic of Christian consolation during life in time is this: It is usually tempered by sorrow over the suffering of Christ in our sisters and brothers, and over our absence from and unfaithfulness to God. On occasion God may so overwhelm our consciousness with his joyful presence as to wipe out all sorrow for the moment. At other times, faith may be raised to a pitch where one sees suffering and sin taken up fully into the glory of God, and sees too that "all will be well, all manner of things will be well." But ordinarily Christian consolation will be tempered by the awareness of a world of pain and sin, one's own and all others' whom he loves in Christ.

The Third and Fourth Descriptions of Spiritual Consolation

In the third and final statement on spiritual consolation, Ignatius expands the range of experiences which he calls consolation: "Finally, I call consolation every increase of hope, faith, and charity and every inward gladness which calls and draws to heavenly things and to the salvation of one's own soul, bringing repose and peace in one's Creator and Lord." In this one sentence, we find a number of elements in the experience of consolation: increase of hope, faith, and charity; inward gladness; a drawing to heavenly things, repose, and peace. Two questions must be answered: what is meant by each of these phrases?_Are the descriptive phrases meant to be parts of one description, or are they meant to constitute more than one description of spiritual consolation? Since the second question can only be answered in light of the answer to the first, let us examine each of the phrases.

The first phrase, "every increase of hope, faith, and charity," brings together explicitly for the first time in Ignatius' description the fundamental acts of the spiritual life. In fact, this is the first explicit mention of hope and faith. These are clearly implied in the prior descriptions, but only implied. Further, love (*amor*) now becomes charity (*caridad*), a more proper word for the love found in spiritual consolation, a love of God in and for himself and of creatures in and for him and with him. Also, the "increase" of faith, hope, and charity, which is clearly implied in the first two statements, is now made explicit; and every such increase is said to be spiritual consolation.

This statement raises grave problems. It seems to conflict with what was said in chapter 3 and what Ignatius states in other rules and in other writings. If every increase of hope, faith, and charity is spiritual consolation, then it seems that these cannot increase during spiritual desolation; for at least in some measure they would not only dispel the desolation and give calm but would also, in fact, immediately bring consolation.

This is simply not our experience; and the contrary seems to be assumed by Ignatius when he tells us to strive patiently against desolation with trust in God. All his advice in Rules I:6-9 clearly calls us to stir up faith, hope, and charity in prayer, meditation, and examination, in order to resist the effects of desolation as long as it lasts and to ultimately conquer it. In Rule 7 he assures us that God's help is always with us during desolation. What is that help if not grace to intensify faith, hope, and love in spite of desolation? And can one be patiently faithful in resisting temptation (I:8) without growing in faith, hope, and love by doing so? Do not the second and third reasons attributed to God for allowing desolation (I:9) mean that he intends us to grow in unselfish love and in humility during desolation? And what can we make of what Ignatius says elsewhere about growing in charity and other solid virtues without dependence on spiritual consolation?[8]

We could perhaps escape the apparent conflict in Ignatius' thought if we understood consolation in the way rejected above, that is, as any motion which is toward God, and desolation as the contrary, without regard for delightful or contrary qualities. As we have seen, however, that would only lead to other and greater contradictions in Ignatius' teaching. The solution of our problem, as I shall now try to show, lies in understanding the manifold ways in which faith, hope, and charity can increase and then, in the light of the essential structure of consolation already worked out, in seeing what Ignatius means by his phrase, "increase of hope, faith, and charity."

The word "increase" in this context has manifold possible meanings, some overlapping with others, some referring to the conditions or grounds for others. Increase could refer to greater *depth* of faith, hope, and charity: that is, the acts become more interiorized, reach more profoundly into one's personality, and involve a fuller commitment of self to Christ, based on a fuller understanding of him and of his life and teaching. Increase could mean that the acts of faith, hope, and charity are *firmer*, more unshakable under trial. The increase could also be in greater *purity* of faith, hope, and charity, less admixture of one's faith life with merely natural understanding and good humanistic motivation, a nearer approach to the ideal of living purely by faith. Increase could also refer to *greater intensity* in the acts of faith, hope, and charity, or to greater intensity of affective feelings (spiritual and sensible) which are grounded in these acts, and so dispose the person as to make further acts easier. Another meaning, then, could be increased *ease* of the acts themselves of believing, of hoping, loving while, for the moment, all intellectual difficulties and all conflicting affections are put to rest. Another meaning of increase could be *greater diffusion* through the person's personality, coloring all his or her ways of perceiving reality, of reasoning, of judging, of imagining, all affective acts and feelings. Still further, the increase could be in *greater effectiveness*, increased influence on modes of choice and action, so that one's choices and actions better express the faith, hope, and charity which are in one's spirit. The agent more easily and readily is kind, patient, generous, peaceable in dealing with others, more courageous in bearing pain or undertaking risks for God's glory, more indifferent to everything except what is God's will. It is clear that increase of faith, hope, and charity in all these meanings moves toward an *increased integration* of the whole conscious life with living faith as the center and source. Such increased integration is what we have spoken of above as increased spiritual peace and is the source, as we saw, of the increased feeling of spiritual peace.

All these meanings of increase in hope, faith, and charity can be included in spiritual consolation taken in its broad meaning. The meaning of increase that seems most stressed by Ignatius is increased intensity, especially in the affective sensibility. (Without motion in the sensibility, we have seen, there is no consolation.) Thus, in a letter to Francis Borgia about God's "gifts and graces," Ignatius mentions "intensiveness (*intensión*) of faith, hope, and charity" and "intense consolation (*consolación intensa*)."[9] In the other rules of the first series for discernment of spirits, when he gives instances of what is taken away when God leaves the spiritual person in desolation, it is intensity that is stressed. Thus in Rule I:7 (*SpEx*, [320]) he says that although divine aid is still with the person experiencing desolation, he or she does not clearly perceive it, "because the Lord has withdrawn from him his bubbling ardor (*mucho hervor*), his surging love (*crecido amor*), and intense grace." In Rule I:9 (*SpEx*, [322]), Ignatius says that in desolation God teaches us inwardly and experientially "that we cannot of ourselves attain or maintain surging devotion (*devoción crecida*), intense love (*amor intensa*), tears or any other spiritual consolation." He seems to

9 *LettersIgn*, p. 181.

find words like *intensa, mucho, crecido, hervor,* and *devoción* most apt for expressing his meaning. They convey the images of swelling, dilating, billowing, rising in a bursting *crescendo* of intensity, a boiling or bubbling of affections at great intensity. There is no word more frequently used by Ignatius to signify consolation than the word "tears,"[10] which are a sure sign of intensified feeling in affective sensibility. When giving reasons why during studies divine wisdom suspends sensible "visitations," Ignatius says that, although the mind delights in them, the body is often excessively weakened.[11] It is surely the intensified feelings that would weaken the body, not intensified spiritual acts of pure faith, hope, and charity, experienced without any surging, swelling ardor, and sweetness.

If what is forcefully suggested by converging evidence from all these passages is joined with our earlier analyses of consolation, of peace, and of the first two descriptions of spiritual consolation given in this Rule I:3, then we can with confidence interpret the phrase "every increase of faith, hope, and charity" which Ignatius sets down as a third description of spiritual consolation. "Increase" in this context has to be taken in a fuller meaning than merely any greater intensity of the essential acts of faith, hope, and charity, with greater purity or even greater effectiveness for making decisions. This kind of increase is readily possible in a state of spiritual calm and even in spiritual desolation. The increase of faith, hope, and charity which constitutes spiritual consolation has to include further modes of increase for which those already mentioned can be the ground, that is, consolation causally understood. There is an experience of what Ignatius means by such consolation when the Holy Spirit so influences the Christian that living faith dominates his consciousness and integrates intelligence, imagination, and affectivity in relation to itself as a center. Then this intensified living faith and spiritual peace (as a state of conscious life) issues in intensified feelings of spiritual peace, joy, warmth, sweetness, and the like (which sometimes find expression in tears). This is spiritual consolation properly speaking. Such consolation makes it easy to believe, hope, and love, giving for the moment freedom of spirit and ease in praising and serving our Lord. Only then is the complete Ignatian consolation present. It may be of greater or lesser intensity. It may affect the consciousness more or less widely or deeply.

---

10 See especially the *Spiritual Diary,* passim, and the excellent gathering of data in Piet Penning de Vries, *Discernment of Spirits* (New York, 1973), pp. 16-19,
11 *LettersIgn,* p. 342.

But it has to comprise something of the above modes of increase. The truth of this conclusion will become clearer when we analyze the experience of spiritual desolation. There we shall see the part that living faith plays in constituting that experience.

When we turn to the phrases following on "every increase of hope, faith, and charity," we find that they all run together. Thus they resist separate treatment and form together a fourth[12] and final description of spiritual consolation: "and every inward gladness which calls and draws to heavenly things and to the salvation of one's own soul, bringing repose and peace in his Creator and Lord." In these phrases Ignatius is clearly doing the same thing he has been doing in the earlier descriptions, that is, pointing to the kind of experience in which consolation can be recognized as spiritual. Here, however, the consolation is identified as spiritual by its *consequences* instead of its causes. "Inward gladness" is itself consolation in the proper sense of the word. It is *spiritual* consolation when it is such that it "draws to heavenly things[13] and to the salvation of one's own soul, bringing repose and peace in one's Creator and Lord."

Although the spiritual character of the consolation is explicitly identified by its consequences, its grounding in faith, hope, and charity is implied. For if the gladness is such as to call and draw the person to heavenly things and to salvation, it must be gladness over God and all the wonders of creation and salvation as seen by faith, gladness because of hope in God's promises, gladness because of some present participation in heavenly life, some experienced presence of God, a foretaste, a pledge which rouses a yearning for the full consolation. In other words, when such heavenly longings together with a sense of repose in God and peace in God follow on gladness, then it is spiritual consolation. If the gladness leads to no such consequences, there is no sign that it is spiritual consolation.

---

12 The word "finally" at the beginning of the last sentence in the rule suggests only, *one* last reason, a third one. I have shown in the text why I think there are two· Grammatical analysis would also justify a fourth reason. The Vulgate Version, too, confirms such a reading.

13 On the rich meaning of "heavenly things" or "the things that are above," as opposed to "earthly things," to which one is drawn in spiritual desolation (I:4), see Col. 3:1-17. Heavenly things are all that belong to the "new man," renewed in the image of the Creator: loving kindness, compassion, forgiveness, peace, and so on. It encompasses also what we ordinarily mean by heaven, the new man completed in a universe full of glory, immortal, free with the freedom of God's sons and daughters (Rom. 8), knowing God as he himself is known in Christ.

The Order of the Descriptions

Ignatius has given us in this Rule I:3 four typical illustrations of consolation which is spiritual. With an understanding of these four descriptions of spiritual consolation, the second main question about this rule can be attended to very briefly: How are these four descriptions related? The question comes to this: Is there any discernible order or progression among them? or are they simply thrown out at random to give some general notion of what is meant by spiritual consolation — as Ignatius does elsewhere?[14] If there is an order, what is it?

What has been found in this series of descriptions does reveal an ordered progression. It begins with a description of consolation narrowly defined and relatively rare in human experience. It moves to descriptions which apply to a wider range of experiences which are more and more common,[15] reaching finally what could include the ordinary everyday peace from faith, hope, and charity which is hardly noticeable to the person but does color his or her consciousness and is noticed only when it is lost.

As shown above, it is not many persons, and they not often, who experience the sort of consolation which Ignatius describes in his first statement — a consolation grounded in faith and charity so inflamed that the person actually finds it impossible for the moment to love any creature, even self therefore, except in God.

The second description points out a consolation which is rooted in faith and charity. It also has some added affections such as sorrow, intense enough to find expression in flooding tears (provided the person is temperamentally and culturally uninhibited), and it moves to greater charity. In the consolation so described, the charity from which the feelings arise, and to which they move, can be less total than that in the first description. It can be mingled in conscious life with love of self for one's own sake, not only in and for God. It does not exclude the possibility of also loving other creatures for their own sake, apart from God even though not in

---

14 *DirSpExMHSJ*, [11] on p. 72, [18] on p. 76.

15 For an interesting interpretation of Rule I:3 which sees the order of these descriptions of consolation in a very different, even contrary, way to that presented here, and which is an interpretation based on what the author sees as steps of development in Ignatius' own spiritual life, see Piet Penning de Vries, *Discernment of Spirits*, pp. 14-28.

opposition to God. Obviously this description can cover a much wider range of spiritual consolations than the first; and any of these could be more commonly experienced than those in the first description.

The third description leaves aside every other note and mentions only the most fundamental subjective sources for any Christian spiritual consolation: hope, faith, and charity. The only qualification is that there be some increase, some intensification, such as described above. The range and commonness of spiritually consoling experiences is expanded enormously.

Only in the fourth description, however, does expansion reach the ultimate limit. For here even the qualification of increase is dropped; and any truly Christian gladness, with inclination to heavenly rather than earthly things, with repose and peace in the Lord, is said to be a spiritual consolation.

The Essential Structure of Spiritual Consolation

The descriptive analysis we made of the experience of consolation and of peace without regard for what specifies these as spiritual, and the following analysis of Ignatius' descriptions of spiritual consolation enable us now to state and explain the essential structure of every spiritual consolation. This statement is not Ignatian in the sense that it is found explicitly anywhere in his writing. It is Ignatian in the sense that it is implicit in what he says. If the reader should think that it goes beyond what Ignatius implies, it still begins with what he says and coheres and harmonizes with his description in all details.

What permeates Ignatius' thought on spiritual consolation, without being explicitated, is the Scripturally founded understanding of faith as the radical work of the Holy Spirit and of charity as his principal and crowning work. The Holy Spirit is given us to complete Christ's work of bringing us the Father's life through faith. He incorporates us into Christ by living faith. He enables us to grow in living faith: to know Jesus ever more intimately, trustfully; to understand his teaching and promises more clearly, more fully, more deeply; to realize who we are in Christ, God's children. He pours the charity of God into our hearts. He is the pledge that strengthens our hope based on belief in Christ's promises of eternal life. Besides what he does to bring us living faith, all else that the

Spirit effects in us is an expression of the life which we have by faith acting through charity. All the other motions he works in a Christian are rooted in and have life from living faith; and they tend toward the growth and propagation of that living faith.

To be spiritual, therefore, that is, to be a work of the Holy Spirit, the joy and peace of consolation have to be integral parts of a faith experience, the flowering of living faith in human sensibility. As we have seen, not every actualization of faith, hope, and charity brings spiritual consolation; but without it no consolation can be spiritual. Any act other than the acts of faith, hope, and charity (such as, for example, contemplation) can cause spiritual consolation only insofar as it is charged with living faith.

Some indications of how this is true may be helpful. Thus, for example, the feelings of peace, security, and repose of mind and heart experienced in spiritual consolation proper are generated from the basic act of trust in God, as he is revealed in Jesus Christ. The light of God shining on the face of Christ Jesus is received by faith; and God in Jesus is experienced by faith as a loving God who loves me and calls me by name, as the one on whom I may stake the meaning of life, the one in whom I may trust through all vicissitudes to bring that meaning to full actuality as he has promised; for he is wise, powerful, loving, faithful. Not that all this needs to be conceptually explicitated; but it is all there in the radical act of receiving the light of Christ and in trusting myself and my life to that light. Such belief tends of itself to issue in feelings of peace, joy, contentment, and exultation; and it does so unless impeded.[16] Trusting in Christ, I am opened to the light of his teaching and promises. I grow in understanding of God and the meaning of life, in understanding of God's presence, of the gift of union; hence arise the spiritual peace and joy. Agape, love for God who loves me and for the creatures whom God loves, tends to joyfulness, to the utter sense of well-being from loving presence to the one who is always lovingly present to me. I am, as a person, made for such loving union; and unless its power is inhibited from flowing into

---

16 Ignatius indicates one possible impediment from the side of the person, his or her negligence in serving God (Rule I:9). He also speaks of God's withdrawing the gift of consolation for his loving purposes in our regard (*SpEx*, [320, 322, 324]). This seems to imply that the Holy Spirit himself may move the intellect and will to the essential acts of faith, hope, and charity, and then may or may not extend the motion to the affective sensibility or, once it has been given, may withdraw the motion from the sensibility without withdrawing it from the intellect and will.

the whole affectivity, it will issue in a spiritual joy. So close is the relationship of love and joy that some see joy as the necessary consequence of love, or even mistakenly identify love and joy.[17]

The God-centered character of spiritual consolation is shown not only in the living faith which causes it but also in its consequences. The consolation of itself gives and makes easy a tendency toward expression of living faith in thoughts, affections, choices, and actions.[18] As we shall see in Rule II:5, if the thoughts and feelings in what appears to be a spiritual consolation lead to thoughts, affections, or actions not in accord with faith, then the very beginning is suspect as coming from the influence of the evil spirit. Spiritual consolation cannot be understood apart from the flow of life in time. All genuine spiritual consolation issues in further thoughts, affections, choices, and actions; and these, in turn, express and can reinforce the spiritual consolation and the essential acts of faith, hope, and charity on which spiritual consolation radically depends.

Some thoughts that characteristically flow from truly spiritual consolation are the very thoughts which found spiritual consolation and come now more easily, more clearly, and deeply — thus setting up a beneficent circle. The thoughts might be: of God's beauty and joy; of his redeeming love and power, his wisdom, and providential care; of his intimate loving presence and our union with him in Christ; of his presence and revelation of himself in all things; of all things as being his gifts. Spiritual consolation helps toward having kind thoughts, Christ-like thoughts about our neighbors and how to serve them. Some fundamental and spontaneous consequences in affectivity are: eager inclination to prayer and whatever draws us to God, strong and ready aversion from whatever in any way draws us away from God, disinterest in what seems unrelated to God, ease in maintaining purity of motivation (seeking first the kingdom of God, desiring to do God's will out of unselfish concern for his glory in ourselves and our neighbors), ease in being patient and gentle toward our neighbor. Along with these thoughts and affections arising from the influence of spiritual consolation and in dependence on them, is an easy readiness for energetic decision and action: We are able to execute with ease what would otherwise be difficult acts of divine service, without the

17 See Jules Toner, *The Experience of Love*, pp. 28-42.
18 *LettersIgn*, pp. 21-22, 181.

hesitancy that springs from selfish worry over possible failure or threatening consequences. We become concerned only to do the deeds of love that God calls for in the situation and to leave all consequences to his loving providence.

To sum up, spiritual consolation means for Ignatius an experience in which living faith is not only increased but is recognized by the believer as such faith now increased in depth or firmness or purity or intensity or diffusiveness or effectiveness, so that it issues in feelings of peace, joy, contentment, confidence, exultation, and the like. There is no spiritual consolation when living faith does in fact flourish but the believer has no assurance that it is so flourishing, or feels that it is declining. For then there is no feeling of peace or joy or exultation in his believing, hoping, or loving. Neither is there any spiritual consolation when there is an access of delightful feelings or consolations which are concomitant with living faith but do not spring from that faith. In short, spiritual consolation has to include an assured experience of living faith and the affective feelings of which such experience can be the source. Living faith without delightful feelings or delightful feelings without living faith as their source — neither of these is spiritual consolation. The former is not consolation in any sense of the term; the latter is consolation but not spiritual.

The foregoing explanation of spiritual consolation could be taken as a commentary on St. Paul's prayer for the Romans: "May the God of hope fill you with joy and peace in believing so that by the power of the Holy Spirit you may abound in hope" (Rom. 15:13); or as a commentary on Paul's statement that "the kingdom of God does not mean food and drink but righteousness and peace and joy in the Holy Spirit" (Rom. 14:17). For righteousness is from faith (Rom. 5:1-2; 3:28). Faith-life grows into fulness of love and hope under the action of the Holy Spirit, who thus brings us a peace and joy that are possible only in those who believe.

Perhaps as rich a statement as could be found of joy in the midst of trials as the flower of Christian faith, hope, and love under the power of the Spirit is that found in 1 Peter 1:3-9:

> Blessed be the God and Father of our Lord Jesus Christ! By his great mercy we have been born anew to a living hope through the resurrection of Jesus Christ from the dead, and to an inheritance which is imperishable, undefiled, and unfading, kept in heaven for you, who by God's power are guarded through faith for a salvation

ready to be revealed in the last time. In this you rejoice, though now for a little while you may have to suffer various trials, so that the genuineness of your faith, more precious than gold which though perishable is tested by fire, may redound to praise and glory and honor at the revelation of Jesus Christ. Without having seen him you love him; though you do not now see him you believe in him and rejoice with unutterable and exalted joy. As the outcome of your faith you obtain the salvation of your souls.

The joy spoken of in this passage is consolation in the most proper sense, joy given to one who is enduring trials. It is spiritual in the fullest sense, the joy caused by believing, hoping, and loving which come from God's mercy and power.

Some Gospel Paradigms of Spiritual Consolation

All that we have been saying in this integrated statement on the Ignatian meaning of spiritual consolation may be brought into clear focus and concretized if we follow a lead given by Ignatius in his directives for contemplating Christ in his appearances to his friends after his resurrection. There Ignatius draws attention to two special aspects of these events: first, how Christ's divinity, which was so hidden during his passion and death, now manifests itself so marvellously (*SpEx*, [223]); and second, how Christ exercises the office of consoler, "in the way friends are wont to console one another" (*SpEx*, [224]). Among all the aspects of the Easter events, what most of all preoccupies Ignatius' attention in the *Spiritual Exercises* is the joy which the risen Jesus, with the Godhead shining through, finds in consoling those whom he loves. So, we may hope to find in these events, more than anywhere else, the clearest models of what Igntius means by spiritual consolation.

The first thing to notice in all these events is that Jesus comes to those who are weak and sinful but who do love him, men and women such as those described in Rule I:2, who are striving to be free of sin and to ascend from good to better in God's service (*SpEx*, [315]).

Secondly, notice that in all these events Jesus comes to bring comfort and joy to those in desolation. Consolation in its fullest and strictest sense presupposes some kind of pain, trial, desolation. All these persons were desolate over the death of Jesus, were in bitter, discouraging sadness. For some, for example, Mary Magdalen, the only cause of sadness is separation from Jesus. For others, such as the apostles, and especially Peter, there was the anguish of having failed Jesus in his hour of need, the bitter awareness of how weak and cowardly their faith and love really were all along. Added to this was the apparent collapse of all reason to hope for the kingdom now: "But we had hoped that he was the one to redeem Israel" (Luke 24:21). The central meaning of their lives, put there by Jesus, seemed gone beyond recovery. All were in darkness, confusion, discouragement — tending toward loss of faith and hope if not love also, and actually bringing about lessening of faith in some (see Matt. 28:17; Mark 16:14; John 20:24-29).

To these fundamentally good persons, weak and desolate but reaching for the truth, Jesus comes. Sometimes he comes to them suddenly and frighteningly, having to assure, to calm, to give proof it really is he in the flesh and so bringing them finally to joy (Luke 24:36-43; John 20:19-23). At other times he is at first not recognized, but gently leads them to spiritual consolation and only afterwards reveals who he is: for example, the disciples on the road to Emmaus, whose hearts burned within them as Jesus talked and opened the Scriptures to them, but who did not recognize him until later (Luke 24:13-32).

In every instance the consolation is effected by calling forth renewed or intensified living faith. The hearts of John and Mary Magdalen leaped readily to faith in the resurrection and to over-flowing consolation because of it at the first signs that were given, the empty tomb for John, the voice of Jesus for Mary. The disciples on the road to Emmaus had Scripture opened to them so that they believed the meaning of the prophecies and their fulfillment in the passion and death of Jesus. As faith came more alive, their hearts burned with joy. Then by faith they recognized Jesus in the breaking of bread and returned with joy to Jerusalem. The apostles, especially Thomas, had to have faith revived by seeing, touching, hearing. No consolation of the kind given by Jesus in his risen life is given or even can be given except through faith. It is the flowering of living faith in the believer's sensibility. The peace and joy given is peace and joy in the risen Christ — in his reality, his triumph, his power and loving presence, his promises.

The moments of realized presence, gazing, hearing, and touching are brief. Jesus comes from they know not where and quickly goes where they do not know. But he leaves their minds and hearts fragrant of his presence, "burning," "aflame" with intensity of feeling, full of the peace and joy of faith that disposes for spiritual understanding, for praise, for living as Christ's followers, for growing in union with him and each other, and for carrying the Good News to others.

The moments of consolation in faith-realization given by the risen Christ seem always to bring a mission. The women, and Mary Magdalen in particular, must go and tell the apostles the good news. The disciples at Emmaus must hurry back to Jerusalem with the good news. The apostles are to forgive sins and bring the good news to every creature.

In all the paschal consolations concretely described in the Gospels, we find a perfect parallel which point by point confirms what we arrived at as the essential structure of spiritual consolation according to Ignatius: the subjective grounding in intensified living faith; the feelings of joy, peace, exaltation, and the like which flow from that faith to ease or replace the desolate feelings; the consequent subjective dispositions for spiritual understanding and for praise and service of God. One element is added. Although not involved in the essential structure of spiritual consolation, it is commonly a part of the experience. That element is the experience of mission, of a counsel or command to do some particular service for God which is needed in the concrete situation. This element will be considered at length further on, in chapter 7, when we shall discuss Rule I:5.

Illustrations of the Discernment of Spiritual from Non-Spiritual Consolation

In our own lives, we sometimes experience consolations that are to us as obviously spiritual as the consolations experienced by those to whom Christ appeared after the Resurrection. But with many of our consolations it is not that clear. A number of factors conspire in leading us to uncertainty or error. On the side of the one discerning, there may be a lack of sufficient learning and experience, carelessness and precipitousness in reaching a judgment. On the side of the consolation itself, there may be the superficial similarities of spiritual with non-spiritual consolation, or the simultaneity and even commingling of spiritual and non-spiritual consolation in the experience, or the commingling of spiritual consolation with desolation, whether spiritual or non-spiritual. Illustrating these causes of confusion may help to keener awareness of the need for careful observation, and help also toward carrying such observation into practice.

When reading the illustrations of discernment between spiritual and non-spiritual consolation, some readers may wonder why all this apparently excessive refinement is necessary. What difference does it make so long as the non-spiritual consolation is not sinful? Those with long and intense reflective experience of the spiritual life know by that experience why refined analysis for the sake of precision is needed in discernment of spirits. The consequences of ignorance and error can be disastrous, unless God's providence prevents it; and while we may trust God to care for what is beyond our limited perception and understanding, we are not to presume on God to do for us without us what it is within our reach to do with him. After one has seen enough people make important and (seemingly, at least) wrong decisions because they thought that they were prompted by the Holy Spirit when they were only experiencing a natural exhilaration at doing their own thing,[19] one begins to prize care and accuracy and to shudder at cavalier discernment of spirits.

For a start, consider a case which will immediately have associations for those familiar with the life of Ignatius. Consider the experience of someone without any religious vision of reality contemplating the stars. Let it be someone who has fine aesthetic sensibility, or a lively sense of wonder, or an adventurous spirit that dreams of voyages in space, or has an impressionable imagination so that all the troubles in our little world are dwarfed by the bright and serene vastness of the heavens with its multitudinous possible worlds. Contrast the peace, the delight, and the comfort which such a person might find in stargazing with the experience of Ignatius of Loyola. The consolation of the former may have none of the signs of spiritual consolation; but notice what Ignatius' experience was. He says of himself:

> It was his [Ignatius'] greatest consolation to gaze upon the heavens and stars, which he often did, and for long stretches at a time, because when doing so he felt within himself a powerful urge to be serving our Lord.[20]

---

19 Such natural exhilaration is, it should be said, data for the *third* Ignatian mode (*SpEx*, [177]) of finding God's will, not the second (*SpEx*, [176]). It is not a spiritual consolation and so not a sign of being moved by the good spirit; but it is a revelation of the person's personality which may have an important bearing on deciding, e.g., in what way of life or in what apostolic service he or she may better serve and praise God.

20 *Autobiog*, no. 71; in *St. Ignatius' Own Story*, pp. 11-12.

Obviously, looking at the stars is in itself no consolation properly speaking for anyone. It can however be a cause of consolation properly speaking, spiritual consolation for some, for others non-spiritual. To a man of faith, under the influence of the Holy Spirit, as Ignatius surely was at the time of which he is writing, the heavens could be a manifestation of the glory of the Creator; and contemplating them within the vision of faith could ground a spiritual consolation. Confirmation of the consolation as spiritual is found in its consequences. For the man who does not find God in the stars, the consequences may be simply a motivation to study astronomy or to write poetry or to let go of small ambitions or to become an astronaut. For Ignatius the consequence was "a powerful urge to be serving our Lord."

What can stand out clearly in two different subjects of consolation may become confusing in the case of some one person who has both a religious vision of reality with frequently prayerful responses, and also has one or more of the qualities ascribed to the non-religious person in the foregoing illustration. Unless this person is cautious, he may in retrospect read a spiritual meaning into a non-spiritual consolation, or he may have both responses at once and have difficulty discriminating between them.

Stars do not necessarily have reference to God in the mind of the beholder. Other objects of contemplation or meditation do so; but even these can give rise to non-spiritual as well as spiritual consolation. Consolation is not spiritual merely because it springs from thoughts and affections with a religious theme. Obviously, for example, listening to Handel's Messiah or Bach's Passion According to St. Matthew can give a purely aesthetic consolation. One may find great satisfaction and contentment in reading the Scriptures as a purely scholarly occupation, totally devoid of spiritual experience. In the book of Ezekiel we have an illustration of consolation grounded in religious themes but not in genuine living faith. The people find listening to Ezekiel a pleasing emotional experience. They have faith inasmuch as they theoretically assert God's existence. Their faith however is not a living faith, not a faith issuing in loving service of God and genuine hope. They are practical unbelievers who are having an experience comparable to the experience of those who listen to a moving love song.

> As for you, son of man, your people who talk together about you by the walls and at the doors of the houses, say to one another, each

117

to his brother, "Come, and hear what the word is that comes forth from the Lord." And they come to you as people come, and they sit before you as my people, and they hear what you say but they will not do it; for with their lips they show much love but their heart is set on their gain. And, lo, you are to them like one who sings love songs with a beautiful voice and plays well on an instrument, for they hear what you say, but they will not do it (Ezek. 33:30-32).

Another illustration would be consolations in a religious setting which prepare for reception of spiritual consolation, but are not themselves spiritual and do not of themselves assure such consolation. Thus, the joy or peace or contentment that comes in liturgy from moving words and music, from personal encounter with other persons who are participating — these feelings can be to a large extent or even wholly non-spiritual, for example, when the subjective ground is not living faith but only sensitivity to poetry, great thoughts, music, the charm of human persons. All these consolations from these sources are good, very good, a support for human living; they are gifts and even a preparation to receive the greater gift and grace of spiritual consolation. But they are not motions prompted by the Holy Spirit. Every innocent peace and joy is a gift from God, but not every gift from God is a spiritual consolation. Neither is every help to grow as a Christian a spiritual consolation; non-spiritual consolation can be such a help; so too can spiritual or non-spiritual desolation.

A yet more difficult case for the discernment of spiritual from non-spiritual consolation is that in which the latter can serve as the very matter for a spiritual consolation but does not always actually do so. Suppose, for instance, I find joy in some created beauty, a person or music or a landscape, and then remember it is a gift of God and give him thanks for it. Do I then have a spiritual consolation? I may or I may not. My joy prior to remembering and thanking God is not. It could even be an integral part of a sinful experience. Let us assume the joy is innocent, not integral with any sinful act. It is still not God-centered and does not spring from living faith. There is still no reason to think of it as a prompting of the Holy Spirit.

What about after remembering God and seeing the created beauty as God's gift and giving thanks to him for it—is my experience of joy then a spiritual consolation? Not necessarily. Not unless there is a new kind of joy, one rooted in faith. We have to ask: do I still have joy only in the created reality and give thanks for that reality and for my joy in it, or do I also have a joy now in the created beauty *precisely as a manifestation of God's beauty or precisely as gift of God*, joy in God's love for me? The difference is very great. Only insofar as I have joy centered on God, grounded, for example, in faith in God as creator revealing self in creation or faith in God's love for me shown in his gift, do I have spiritual consolation. The joy of aesthetic contemplation or of meeting with a lovable person is not itself a spiritual consolation. Giving thanks to God for it, as well as for the created beauty which I rejoice in, is not itself spiritual consolation. It *can* be a ground for it; but I can also give thanks in *spiritual* calm or even in spiritual desolation.

Similar cases may easily be thought of, ones that may have more immediately practical import. Thus, the joy I may have in doing a work for God that I like doing, and would have the *same* satisfaction in doing even if not doing it for God, can be confused with having a spiritual consolation in doing the work because it is for God, because it is God's will for me. I might even, without reflective awareness of it, really be doing my own thing and finding joy in that, rather than finding joy in doing what God wills because he wills it. However, joy in work just because it is congenial can be a good thing, itself also a gift of God, a help to serving God. Seen in this way by faith, it can become a ground for another joy which is a spiritual joy, joy in the loving kindness of God who gives me work that I delight in doing.

What Ignatius means by spiritual consolation can, I think, be highlighted in the case where it is given in the midst of bitter anguish or non-spiritual desolation which calls forth great faith to face the situation with courage. For then spiritual consolation stands clear of any confusion with non-spiritual consolation. I am not implying that spiritual consolation cannot arise concurrently with non-spiritual consolation or even be integrated in one experience with it. I have already illustrated how it can. What I am saying is rather that, when spiritual consolation comes as a surprise during a non-spiritual desolation, we escape most of the difficulty of discerning the true nature and source of the experience. One striking illustration which I have come across is that recounted by Dorothy Day.

There was a terrible situation which arose in one of our houses farther west. A family had a brain-damaged child, and that child, at the age of sixteen, was raped by three boys in the weeds out in the back of the house where she was wandering. You can imagine the family's anguish. The police blamed them and said they ought to put her in a mental hospital and that it was their fault for not taking better care of her. It was just so unbelieveable to them. They came East to talk to me about it, and I took them to this nun who is in charge of the Astor Home up there in Rheinbeck. At Astor Home they accept all the horrors and tragedies, knowing God will straighten things out; they have that sense of joy. The good sister had that, and she reassured them: "Of course, keep the girl at home, maybe lock her in on occasion, but watch her more carefully." They went home very much reassured. But the father said to me, "Strangely enough, through all this horrible tragedy, I had suddenly a sense of a strange supernatural joy that God was very close to us." He said, "It reminded me of Bernanos' book, *Joy*—which was a tragedy."

Bernanos had that sense that where there's great suffering there's also that great sense of hope and joy and knowledge that God is there. "Peace" might be a better word.[21]

This example leaves no doubt that the consolation comes from faith actuated by the Holy Spirit. It is joy despite tragic pain because of the faith-experience of God's loving presence.

Less easy to discern but no less clear when analyzed correctly is the experience of spiritual consolation which is in some sense partially grounded in spiritual desolation. Here, presented with permission, is a description of such an experience in the journal of one making the Spiritual Exercises:

In this retreat so far (fourth day), no profound desolation, little consolation of the tender affective sort (feelings of sweetness, warmth, tendency to tears, delight, peace, etc.), but a rather lasting sense or feeling of contentment, springing not from imaginative and emotional realization but from firm faith convictions about the reality of what I have been contemplating and meditating on and about its meaning in my life. This is not mere notional knowledge and abstract conviction. It is real knowledge, conviction about the concrete, which can be as effective for living as the sort which brings a powerful emotional response—sometimes even more effective in the long run, I have found by experience. This is a form of consolation, quiet and lacking warmth or sweetness, but a positive experience, which makes it easy to continue in prayer despite dryness in all other ways and despite distractions and tiredness. It is, strangely, a consolation in dryness even in desolation. Imagination and emotions gone dead, i.e., in regard to spiritual objects, sometimes gone wild in other ways, intellect not getting any interesting insights. Sometimes angry or sexually lustful or worrisome or having ambitious thoughts and affections during the prayer. Yet during all this, deep underneath

21 "An Interview with Dorothy Day," *National Jesuit News* (May, 1972), p. 10.

all this, a *contentment* in having to be faithful and trusting. A readiness to go on this way as a way of love, perhaps of enduring someone else's dryness or desolation for him or her; almost a backing away from consolation as a way of less love, as self-satisfying and not calling for generosity and fidelity during hard going. But, at the same time, paradoxically, this is itself a consolation, not only a consolation which is simultaneous with desolation, but a satisfaction in bearing desolation willingly for love of God.

Here is a consolation of a kind that can only be in one who is also experiencing desolation. It illustrates perfectly what was said above about the various dimensions or levels of conscious experience and also the integration of these into one fuller experience.

Chapter 6

THE DESCRIPTION OF SPIRITUAL DESOLATION
Rule I:4

In the fourth rule, Ignatius turns to the contrary pole of spiritual experience, spiritual desolation.

[317]. Rule 4. Concerning spiritual desolation. I call desolation everything the contrary of [what is described in] the third rule. Thus, in desolation we experience gloominess of soul, confusion, a movement to contemptible and earthly things, disquiet from various commotions and temptations, [all this] tending toward distrust, without hope, without love; finding self thoroughly indolent, tepid, sad, and as if separated from our Creator and Lord. For just as consolation is contrary to desolation, in the same way the thoughts which issue from consolation are contrary to the thoughts which issue from desolation.

The Intent of the Rule

What is most important about the heading of the rule is the use of the word "spiritual." We saw how, in Rule I:3, Ignatius uses the heading "Spiritual Consolation" and then for the most part thereafter speaks only of "consolation," leaving "spiritual" to be understood. He uses the term "spiritual desolation" and "desolation" in the same way. Also, in parallel with Rule I:3, his intention in this rule is not to describe desolation. Rather, assuming we know what desolation is, Ignatius aims at enabling us to tell, among our many sorts of desolations, when we are experiencing a spiritual one.

The Descriptive Analysis of Desolation

When we were drawing out the significance of Ignatius' sparse words on spiritual consolation, we had need of a descriptive analysis which would expose the main lines of the essential structure of every consolation, without any qualification as spiritual or non-spiritual. So also now, when reading his description of spiritual desolation,

122

we need to have in mind the essential structure of desolation, without qualification as spiritual or non-spiritual. It is obvious by a parallel that in the total complex experience of any desolation whatsoever there are three components: desolation proper, constituted by affective feelings; the subjective sources of the desolation proper, that is, the acts of the person which give rise in one way or another to the feelings of desolation; and the consequences, the influence of these feelings and their sources on the person's further cognitive and affective acts and his or her decisions. It is also evident by parallel that, while these components of desolation are distinct, they are related in vital continuity, form one total complex experience, and are not fully intelligible without reference to each other. Finally, one other parallel with consolation follows. There are different kinds of desolation, and each kind allows for many individual differences, because of the differences of their subjective causes and the objects of those acts which constitute the subjective causes. Feelings of desolation (desolation proper) because of a broken friendship, death of a beloved one, frustrated ambition, loss of status, and other similar causes — these desolations are qualitatively different; and the differences in the desolate feelings can be satisfactorily described only by including a description of the grounds (desolation causatively).

Having in mind this structure of the total complex experience of any desolation whatsoever as we read Ignatius' compact description of spiritual desolation, we can draw out his meaning with greater precision, penetration, and coherence than would otherwise be possible. We will be able to place the elements he mentions in relation to one another, and by their relation to one another to understand each one more fully.

While the structure of any desolation parallels that which was found in any consolation, the acts and feelings in the two structures are obviously all contrasting. Let us briefly note what seem to be the specifying features of any desolation. The term "desolation" in its widest meaning refers to a state of being devastated, bare, dreary, lacking that which gives fullness or beauty or life. Thus we speak of a desolate scene and call a barren or wasted land a desolation. As a state of consciousness, desolation properly speaking can in a general and initial way be spoken of as a state of affective distress, a negative and disagreeable state of affective sensibility. Not every disagreeable or distressing state is a desolation, however. Painful tension in a demanding or dangerous situation that stimulates to action, a distressing sense of injustice that stirs up anger and eager determination to right a wrong, feelings of painful disappointment and humiliation over a failure accepted without discouragement or depression — none of these or experiences like these are desolations. In desolation, the person is in a depressed and a gloomy mood. He or she experiences a notable or total loss of hope flowing from loss of trust in self or others, with a likely consequent tendency to inaction. In a word, he experiences feelings of discouragement. Anyone who suffers emotional distress but still *feels* courageous because he has easy spontaneous affective responses of trust and hope, who, as a consequence, tends to address the situation readily with zest and vigor, such a one is not in desolation.

It will be of essential importance for understanding spiritual desolation, and after that for understanding how to deal with it (Rules I:6-8), to notice one feature of the foregoing description of any desolation. The description is concerned with the dynamics of affective life insofar as it is not subjected to the control which a person can have, directly or indirectly, through reflection and freedom. Through these he can direct attention; and he can suppress or set in motion lines of thought and volition which promote or counteract, or at least impede the effects of, what happens in his affectivity and thought prior to his reflection and exercise of free choice. In the sphere of intelligent reflection and freedom and of volition under control of these, it is possible, even during desolation, to actuate a resolute act of hope despite all feelings of hopelessness. Likewise, a courage deeper than feeling can be actuated, a volitional strength to endure and dare despite fear, and thus to summon up energy to act vigorously and perseveringly despite feelings of discouragement and indolence. We touched on this matter before and shall do so again. The reiteration is conscious and intended. To let it slip out of the picture at any point of our reflection on the spiritual life can tragically falsify our whole understanding of ourselves and our lives,[1] can render Ignatius' rules for dealing with desolation senseless, and render his first set of rules for discernment of spirits of little practical value. What is the use of discerning what spirit moves me if I can do nothing about it? It might yield an interesting bit of speculative knowledge; but that is all.

1 See above, pp. 63-68.

Contrariety and Its Implications in Rule I:4

Keeping in mind the main lines of the foregoing descriptive analysis of every experience of desolation, we are ready to examine the Ignatian description of spiritual desolation. The first sentence after the heading does not strike one as being of any singular importance. The fact is, however, that this sentence determines how we read the rest of this rule. It puts Rules I:3 and 4 into continuity with Rule I:2; and, along with the latter, sets the way along which Ignatius will advise us to think and act in time of desolation (as we shall see in Rules I:5-14). The sentence reads: "I call [spiritual] desolation everything the contrary of [what is described in] the third rule."

That Ignatius, in this context, is using "contrary" in its strict sense (explained above on pages 48-49) is clear even at first glance, before any careful examination of his description. Thus we find: gloominess and sadness as opposed to the gladness of spiritual consolation; confusion and disquiet as opposed to peace and repose; spiritual indolence and movement to earthly things as opposed to desire for heavenly things and for salvation; a tendency toward loss of faith, hope, and charity as opposed to increase of these; tepidity as opposed to warmth; a feeling as if separated from God as opposed to the sense of union; dryness or coldness toward God and spiritual things as opposed to inflamed love. This contrary character of spiritual desolation and consolation is also made explicit and emphatic in the Autograph Directory. There Ignatius says:

> Prompted by the evil spirit and his gift, desolation is the contrary [of consolation]: contrary to peace, [there is] conflict; contrary to joy, sadness; contrary to hope in higher things, hope in base things; contrary to heavenly love, earthly love; contrary to tears, dryness; contrary to elevation of mind, wandering of mind to contemptible things. [2]

In order to grasp fully what it means to say that spiritual desolation is "everything contrary to [what is described in] the third rule," we have to note two aspects of the contrariety. First, as *desolation*, it is the contrary of consolation. Second, as *spiritual*, it is the contrary of spiritual consolation precisely inasmuch as the latter is spiritual.

2 *DirSpEx*MHSJ, [12] on p. 72.

That desolation is the contrary of consolation is evident in the descriptive analyses already made of consolation and desolation. Desolation is not merely the negation of consolation, not merely a state of being without consolation, any more than consolation is merely a state of being without desolation. There is plainly a state of calm or tranquillity between consolation and desolation. This state of calm is simply a negation (the contradictory) of both consolation and desolation; whereas consolation and desolation are contrary to each other, diametrically opposed extremes.

To say that spiritual desolation not only as desolation but also as spiritual is the contrary of spiritual consolation has implications. First, spiritual desolation is, strange as it may sound, an anti-spiritual experience. Second, inasmuch as spiritual consolation and desolation are contraries, anything we can know about one reveals something about the other. A word about each of these implications is in order.

That Ignatius saw desolation as an anti-spiritual experience is beyond doubt. For him it is anti-spiritual in its source: its grounds are anti-spiritual (though not totally, as we shall see). They are prompted by the evil spirit, only permitted by God for his kind purposes, never prompted by him (*SpEx*, [315, 318, 320, 329, 333, 335]). Coming from such a source, all the elements in the description converge, as we shall see, to produce an untruthful feeling of separation from God; all tend toward loss of faith, hope, and charity. Now a problem arises: How can an anti-spiritual experience be called a spiritual desolation? At first blush, this is a contradiction in terms. The solution, made possible by our descriptive analyses of consolation and desolation, leads to a deep and fruitful insight into spiritual desolation. However, the solution must wait for our study of the elements involved in the latter experience as Ignatius describes it.

The second implication of seeing spiritual desolation as everything the contrary of spiritual consolation precisely as spiritual is that anything Ignatius says about either of them shows us something about the other by contrast. This implication needs only to be noted and then taken into account when we are reading the rules; it has already been explained above.[3]

---

3 See above, pp. 48-49.

The Description of Spiritual Desolation

We are now ready to study in some detail the description which Ignatius offers of spiritual desolation. We shall try to make the meaning of each element in the description as precise and full as we can and to integrate it into the whole description, always looking for light by contrast with the contrary experience of spiritual consolation. What is said about each of these contraries will not only help to interpret what Ignatius says about the other but will also perhaps imply some things which he does not make explicit.

Ignatius first draws up in broad strokes some of the most obvious elements in spiritual desolation: "gloominess of soul, confusion, a movement to contemptible and earthly things, disquiet from various commotions and temptations." Some of these can appear even before the deep anti-spiritual character of the whole experience is reflectively manifest to the person. Nevertheless, since Ignatius is describing a spiritual desolation it seems reasonable, even necessary, to understand all these elements as concerned with spiritual life right from the start.

Gloominess (*obscuridad*) is a state of conscious life metaphorically described by a visual term, referring primarily to the person's affective condition and then to his imaginative and intellectual awareness as influenced by his affective condition. A "lightsome" mood is one characterized by brightness and cheerfulness. To use another metaphor, it is a mood in which our feelings seem to rise as if freed from a burden. "Light" as use of affectivity is opposed to "heavy" as well as to "dark," both of which characterize a "gloomy" mood, even though the latter word denotes only the dark quality. Darkness is oppressive. In a gloomy mood a person's apprehension and interpretation of his life-world, the world of his experience, are influenced so that he sees all as dark and oppressive. In such a mood, to be is to bear a burden; the journey of life is a groping of one's way through the night. In this context, it is the spiritual life that the person finds oppressive and darksome.

Associated with gloominess, and even a correlative of it, is "confusion" (*turbación*). This is a state of mind in which one's own ideas, judgments, principles, values, and emotional responses are so jumbled that one cannot discern distinctly or clearly what is going on or why. Such a state readily follows on gloominess somewhat as visual confusion of objects does in physical gloom.

The more confused the person becomes about the things that matter most in his life as a maturing Christian, the more is he liable to gloominess, and the less capable he becomes of dealing with the grounds of gloom. A vicious circle is set in motion. In this state it is difficult to take hold of self, to deliberate and make balanced judgments in accord with one's accepted principles, to respond intelligently by free choice to the present situation. The inclination comes to question beliefs that ground hope and joy; they seem unreal. The psychic energy to live out decisions and resolutions already made wanes. Those decisions made in a better frame of mind now seem unreal, and a change of decision seems called for to ease the situation. So, there is a tendency to make rash, emotionally determined decisions; or else an ineffective state of wavering ensues. There is a tendency to abandon good undertakings already begun or to leave them hanging in abeyance. A tendency to inconstancy colors the whole spiritual life.

Within the gloom and confusion, whether as a source of it or as a consequence or both, comes a "movement to contemptible and earthly things." This must not be understood as a movement to what is necessarily sinful or even in itself contemptible, but to what is, when put in tension with heavenly things, contemptible, for example, wealth, fame, status, power, sensual pleasure, (The drawing to what is sinful is noted in the next step of the description.) Apart from graced moments of consolation, to reach for heavenly things is for most persons an effort, a going up an incline often against human desire, which more readily tends to what is sensible, to what flatters the self-centered ego, to what is more immediately satisfying and meets the most obvious and intense (even if often superficial or sick) needs, whether physical or emotional. No struggle or prolonged education is needed in order to desire these things. The urge toward them is ready to assert itself in one way or another. Consequently, when one is gloomy and feeling a need for some immediate and intense satisfaction to brighten life or to lighten its burden, then the heavenly things can seem far away, rather unreal, and even hardly desirable in comparison with the objects towards which one is presently impelled. When a person is already confused, it becomes a great struggle to hold things in perspective according to his deepest faith convictions. So, inevitably, what in a faith-induced perspective is seen as relatively contemptible now, in this time of gloom and confusion, is seen as very desirable.

Most of what has been said so far about gloominess, confusion, inclination to contemptible things could be said of a non-spiritual desolation. The spiritual character of what is going on will emerge more and more as we proceed and see these elements of the description integrated with the later ones. What we already know about spiritual consolation and desolation could assure us that the gloom, the confusion, and the contemptible tendencies referred to spring either from some failure of living faith or from some inhibition of its influence, and that they tend to be destructive of such faith.

Sunk in gloom, confused, uncertain about directions, feeling the attraction of lesser goods which the person had thought of discarding when setting out to ascend from good to better, he or she is now subject to commotions and temptations that lead to "disquiet." Disquiet describes a condition of mind and heart which is the contrary of the peaceful, sweet tranquillity that characterizes consolation. The source of it is said to be "various commotions and temptations."

The kind of commotions which can contribute to the disquiet called spiritual desolation consists of those which are directly opposed to, which tend to effect the very contrary of the peace which flows from faith, hope, and charity. There are other kinds of commotions which are not of themselves and directly opposed to spiritual peace and joy but can be in some measure a distraction from such peace and joy, or can exacerbate the disquiet of spiritual desolation. The inner commotion sometimes caused by external turmoil or by the demands of administrative responsibilities is an example of what we are talking about. These commotions, however, are not grounds for a feeling of disquiet which is a constitutive element of spiritual desolation properly speaking. In a person whose life is moving from good to better toward God, the above mentioned tendency to earthly and contemptible things (without reference to the attainment of the higher) is bound to conflict, of itself and directly, with the central spiritual thrust of his life. Even though the latter may be somewhat dimmed in the person's awareness at the moment, or hidden under the gloom and confusion, or inhibited from areas of conscious life where it appears in time of consolation or calm, it is not dead or powerless. Thus there is commotion which disturbs precisely that peace which is the fruit of living faith and grounds a disquiet which is contrary to spiritual peace as spiritual. One who is uninterested in heavenly values, whose life is a search for earthly goods and satisfaction, will not experience such commotion. He would, however, experience a similar commotion if his earthly values became endangered or in conflict with one another, or if the good spirit shook him into a moment of insight about higher values.

Inclination to earthly things does not stop merely at what is in itself legitimate and good, even though contemptibly less than that which one has set his heart upon in his happier moments of spiritual light and peace. Human desire, no matter whether well or badly directed, is boundless. As a consequence, the desire for earthly things easily becomes temptation to sin. It becomes lust for sinful pleasure or status or power or success; it brings on envy of those who have the things we want, anger or resentment toward whoever hinders our egoistic fulfillment or fails to respond as we desire and so on — all leading to greater commotion, confusion, and gloom in a vicious circle.

In the midst of the struggle to hold out against such disturbing feelings and temptations, the thought often comes to the person: How can you go on in this way all your life without the satisfactions which your human nature needs? Does it make any sense? Would a kind God really want you to live this way? Are you not over-reaching yourself? Who do you think you are that you can do what others cannot? In those more firmly established in the spiritual life, those in whom the thrust toward ever greater praise and service of God has become more intense and more settled and is clearly based on trust in God's power rather than their own — in them more subtle commotions, confusions, and temptations arise. There may come a temptation to self-satisfaction, or vainglory in their having been faithful through the foregoing troubles. Or, when it at least seems to such persons that they have not successfully resisted, then they may back off from intimacy with God in prayer because they feel unworthy. Or they may be impatient with themselves for not living up to their own ideal, or even subtly refuse to accept God's forgiving love until they prove themselves worthy — as if they could do this without the strength of God's forgiving love received in prayer.

So these persons swing back and forth, from one temptation to its opposite. The ensuing painful confusion and disquiet blocks out the clarity, the peace, and the joy that in the very nature of things would flow from their living faith if it were not impeded in these ways.

The temptations which not only prevent spiritual consolation but also bring on desolation are already a clear sign that this desolation should be recognized as a spiritual one. Immediately following the phrase "disquiet from various commotions and temptations," in Rule I:4, Ignatius calls attention to an even clearer sign — the clearest sign of all — that an anti-spiritual power is at work prompting a spiritual desolation. It is, in fact, *the essential* sign by which a spiritual desolation can be distinguished from a non-spiritual one: The desolate feelings tend directly and by their very nature to destroy faith, hope, and charity. Ignatius speaks of the one in desolation as "tending toward distrust, without hope, without love."

Desolation grounded in physical exhaustion or physical sickness (such as headaches, nausea, after-effects of heart attacks) or in emotional tension from too many responsibilities or crises, or past emotional traumas repressed and never worked through, and the like — these are not likely to be cases of spiritual desolation. In many or most cases, they hinder spiritual consolation. They can even, indeed, at least indirectly, have a detrimental effect on faith-life. But unless the desolate feelings directly tend to be destructive of living faith, the desolation is not a spiritual one.

Two things in the Ignatian rules will help to make this clearer. Recall that Ignatius states that spiritual desolation is everything which is *contrary* to spiritual consolation. We saw what this means: that these two kinds of spiritual experiences are contrary in the strict sense of the word, diametrically opposite extremes; that spiritual desolation is contrary to spiritual consolation not only as consolation but also precisely as spiritual. We saw that what radically constitutes consolation as spiritual is its grounding in living faith and its consequent disposing of the person for expressing that faith in his or her life and thus growing in it. Therefore, if spiritual desolation is the contrary of spiritual consolation as spiritual, it must be subjectively grounded in motions which of themselves tend to destroy living faith. Further, the feelings of desolation must dispose the person in such a way, as to hinder the expression of living faith, in such a way as to promote, instead, the expression of what clashes with faith and tends toward loss of it.

Another confirmation of what has just been said can be found in a reflective reading of Rule I:5. In this rule Ignatius says that in spiritual desolation we should not make new decisions but stay with those made during a previous time of consolation or calm.

The reason given is that during spiritual desolation we are under the influence of Satan. Now, one may in the light of Holy Scripture maintain that all physical and psychological illness, and therefore any desolation grounded in these, is in ultimate analysis and at least indirectly the consequence of sin and the work of Satan. What Ignatius is talking about, however, is an immediate influence of Satan here and now. Ignatius does not think it possible to judge any inner motion to be here and now from the evil spirit (or one's own sinfulness) unless it is itself clearly anti-spiritual, or clearly leads by a continuous process to some anti-spiritual motion (*SpEx*, [333]).

Even when we understand the consequences of saying that spiritual desolation is the contrary of spiritual consolation, and anti-spiritual in its grounds and consequences, we still face a subtle danger. Unless we read Ignatius' words very carefully, we can swing to another interpretation and in a different way miss the significance of his description. First, if we read him as saying spiritual desolation actually leads to loss of faith, hope, and love, we not only misread him but make him utter nonsense. For, while desolation might have this effect in some instances, in others it does not. Of itself, it only *tends* toward such a consequence, and that is all Ignatius says it does. Second, it is not even exact to read Ignatius as saying that spiritual desolation tends to loss of faith (*fe*), hope, and love. It does do this, but what Ignatius says is that it tends toward "distrust" (*infidencia*), "without hope, without love."[4]

By stating this, he brings out the central element in faith and in spiritual desolation. At the heart of Christian faith is trust in God as he reveals himself in Jesus Christ; trust in his saving love, wisdom, and power, and in his providence for each person, for me. It is not usually the intellectual assent by faith to the truths of the Incarnation or divine providence that is immediately and explicitly imperiled by spiritual desolation; and much less is it the intellectual

---

4 Ignatius' words are usually translated so as to come out more gracefully than they do in the original. Thus, Puhl: "which lead to want of faith, want of hope, want of love"; Mottola: "which lead to loss of faith, loss of hope, loss of love"; Corbishley: "tending to loss of faith, hope, and love." Corbishley's use of "tending" avoids one distortion of the meaning; but his translation and the others' also lose two important nuances kept in a more literal translation: (1) the emphasis on the personal *trust* element in faith, which grounds the consequent element of assent to truths; and (2) the suggestion that being without hope and without love follow on distrust, or even qualify the distrust.

assent to other truths of the faith. Rather, what is imperiled is the *trust* in God's intellectually admitted salvific love for me personally. Distrust in spite of intellectual assent to the truth of God's love, wisdom, and power is possible and not unusual. The Vulgate text of the *Spiritual Exercises* confirms this interpretation of Ignatius' words by translating the Spanish *infidencia* as *diffidentia de salute*, distrust concerning my salvation.[5]

The gravest danger from all the elements noted in spiritual desolation up to this point is that they tend toward loss of trust in God. If the temptation to distrust is yielded to, the whole edifice of Christian life collapses. In the measure that it weakens, the whole edifice of Christian life weakens, growth is stunted, charity and hope wither. That is the principal reason why spiritual desolation must, as Ignatius will tell us, not only be resisted but also counterattacked boldly, thoughtfully, and perseveringly. When desolation is met in this way, far from losing faith, hope, and charity, one grows in them.

What, by the very nature of the case, does actually happen in spiritual desolation, and is necessary for the experience of it, is an inhibition of the power of actualized faith, hope, and charity to affect certain dimensions, especially the affective dimension, of the person's conscious life. Some of the consequences which living faith tends to have on the affectivity, and through affectivity on the whole person, are diminished or totally obstructed. Such inhibition of the influence of faith, hope, and charity in affectivity would by itself result only in spiritual calm. But something beyond such inhibition is involved. In place of the influence of living faith, other motions are caused which of themselves and directly tend to weaken faith, hope, and charity. In other words, spiritual desolation properly speaking springs from anti-spiritual motions; and these sources, along with the desolation properly speaking, have as their consequences a "tending toward distrust, without hope, without charity." This can then cause worse feelings of desolation, and so on in a vicious circle. But Ignatius is still writing only about a temptation, not an actual failure.[6]

5 All the Latin versions, both the Vulgate and the *Versio Prima*, translate the Spanish *infidencia* as *diffidentia*, and the Vulgate version makes it more precise as *diffidentia de salute*.

6 That spiritual desolation of itself tends to weaken faith, hope, and charity, but does not of itself necessarily do so, is confirmed also by the reading of Rules I:6-9. All of these counsels presuppose faith, hope, and love in the one counseled. Notice also a

As a consequence of all that Ignatius has just been describing, the person feels "thoroughly indolent, tepid, sad." With anti-spiritual motions swarming in his consciousness, he feels and spontaneously thinks of himself as spiritually dead or dying. He is thrown back on the more fundamental work of the Holy Spirit in him, on his tenaciously held faith-convictions and resolute determination to believe despite all appearance and feeling to the contrary, to hope against hope, and to love in deed and truth without the feelings of warmth, sweetness, and gladness that make it easy to love and act in consolation. A careful consideration of the sadness, tepidity, and indolence referred to by Ignatius is called for so as to see clearly which of the affective feelings that go by these names are really constitutents of the spiritual desolation.

As should be clear from our earlier consideration of sadness in spiritual consolation, not every sadness, not even every religious sadness, is spiritual desolation. The various forms of sadness which are sometimes present in spiritual consolation have characteristics such as these: They are rooted in faith, hope, and charity; they involve a sense of God's peace-giving presence and a warm realization of his love; they tend to foster a more intense faith life. The sorrow or anguish of spiritual desolation is depressing, discouraging, has no sense of God's presence, even has the feeling of being unloved by God, and, unless resisted, tends toward decline of faith life. This anti-spiritual character is what distinguishes the sadness of spiritual desolation from any sadness, sweet or bitter, which is merely non-spiritual.

In like manner, not every experience of indolence and emotional tepidity is anti-spiritual; it may be merely non-spiritual. Given that the indolence and tepidity which are elements in spiritual desolation are anti-spiritual, we must be on guard against two false interpretations; for these misinterpretations are common and dangerous, and need to be noticed and corrected. The first is the opinion that one must have fallen into an indolent and tepid manner of serving God, or else one would not be in desolation. As was noted before, actual tepidity in God's service is one possible cause of desolation (Rule I:9) but by no means the only one, nor one to

little further on in Rule I:4 where Ignatius states that the one in desolation finds himself "*as if* separated from our Creator and Lord." Clearly, a Christian is actually separated from God only in the measure that he declines in living faith. If to be in desolation is to find self "as if" separated from God, then to be in desolation is merely to be feeling *as if* living faith had declined.

be assumed. The second misinterpretation is that by the very fact of being in desolation one is actually here and now giving God an indolent and tepid service. What is actual in spiritual desolation is a *feeling* of spiritual indolence, a *mood* of spiritual lethargy and a consequent uncritical emotional judgment that one is indolent and tepid in loving and serving God. This feeling or mood of itself tends to make one act indolently, but by no means necessitates it. Such a feeling is compatible in concrete experience with generous initiative and loving service. In fact, such is the way in which Ignatius calls upon the person who is in desolation to respond (see Rules I:6-8, 12). He does not expect that such a response will immediately dissipate the desolation; it may be a prolonged struggle. Therefore he must be assuming that a generous, active love can endure through spiritual desolation along with feelings of indolence and tepidity.

Among all the affections and thoughts in any spiritual desolation which tend toward distrust and a collapse of Christian life, there is one which Ignatius has not yet mentioned. Within the vicious circle of elements which function in spiritual desolation, it is the most revealing source and consequence of the most painful feeling in spiritual desolation properly speaking — the more painful the more one loves God. It is a source and consequence of every feeling of gloominess, confusion, and disquiet, a source and consequence of every feeling and thought that living faith is dying, the source and consequence of every feeling of spiritual indolence, tepidity, and sadness. It is in some measure present, at least implicitly and obscurely, right from the start and grows as spiritual desolation grows. That one all-pervading and most vicious element, which most reveals the anti-spiritual character of spiritual desolation, and which most reveals the father of lies at work, is "finding oneself. . . as if separated from one's Creator and Lord."

Like "finding oneself thoroughly indolent, tepid, and sad," this experience of finding oneself as if separated from God is constituted by feelings and a consequent unreflected, uncritical, thought that is grounded on the depressed feelings, not on a calm and a clear-headed assessment of the evidence. Even in time of gloom, confusion, temptation, and disquiet, when one feels as if faith were dead or dying, powerful movements from the Holy Spirit can be discerned, movements of faith and love for God, of desire for union with God, desire to do his will, to pray, to do good works for love of the neighbor. These spiritual movements, occurring without

affective warmth, without any sweet, peaceful, joyful realization
of God's presence and love, occurring even during spiritual desolation, are clear signs of the Holy Spirit's loving presence and power.

What usually happens, however, during desolation in those who
are spiritually inexperienced or, when desolation is severe enough
even in those greatly experienced, is that they feel *as if* they had
sinned, as if they had become displeasing to God, had actually
declined in trust, hope, and love and are now on the verge of losing
these virtues altogether. So easily influenced is thought by emotion
that only those escape yielding more or less to this often rash view
of themselves who have learned better through long experience,
or those who during the time of desolation have a spiritually wise
and trusted person to help them gain a true perspective.

What makes matters worse, many persons have a psychological
tendency to think the worst of themselves. Hurt pride and self-
resentment make others judge themselves harshly, without charity
or even justice toward themselves. A hypersensitive and untruthful conscience can do the same. The evil spirit, of course, takes
advantage of these weaknesses and counsels such harsh and untrue
self-depreciation. (This is one illustration of how a source of non-
spiritual desolation can be a contributing cause to spiritual desolation.) Because of one or several of these influences, most of us are
in some measure in danger of this trap — the more so, the less
our spiritual experience or the greater the intensity of the desolation.

A passage in the *Spiritual Diary of St. Ignatius* shows how completely this sense of separation from God can in spiritual desolation
flood the consciousness even of a person who is without doubt
deeply in union with God, even when he has had recent prolonged
and intense experience of divine consolations. In fact, this experience of desolation by Ignatius is embedded in a series of over-
whelmingly tender and joyful mystical experiences of God.

> Finishing Mass, and afterwards in my room, I found myself
> alone and without help of any kind, without power to relish any
> of my mediators, or any of the Divine Persons, but so remote and
> separated, as if I had never felt anything of Them, or would never
> feel anything again. Rather, thoughts came to me sometimes against
> Jesus, sometimes against another, being so confused with such
> different thoughts....[7]

7 *Spiritual Diary*, [144]; in W. J. Young's translation, no. 40 (March 12), p. 32.

This experience of Ignatius gives us a warning and a hint. We must move cautiously here. Recall what has been stressed before, that Ignatius throughout Rule I:4 is assuming as understood the meaning of desolation in general, and is noting what is peculiar to spiritual desolation. When we remember what any desolation is, then we can see that finding oneself as if separated from God is an element in spiritual desolation only when such separation is experienced as painful, disheartening, and tending toward despair of God's merciful love.[8] Not every sense of separation from God in any person whatsoever is of this kind, but only a sense of separation from God constituted by feeling unloved or despairing of ever having the union desired by a person who does love God.

Love itself constitutes presence and union.[9] Nevertheless, the lover experiences painful separation and consequent desolation if the beloved does not return the love (or, at least, is thought not to do so) and is not expected to return it. When there is mutual love, mutually revealed, the experience of union and joy in the union is great in proportion to the greatness of the love. When added ways of fuller presence and union are not actualized, love then issues in yearning for these. Thus, when lovers are geographically at a distance, they long for visible, tangible presence; when so present they desire to share memories, thoughts, emotions, and the like with each other. So long as the fullest union is missing, there is along with the experience of union by mutual love a sorrowful, painful sense of separation. This, however, is not yet necessarily desolation. If the power of hope for fuller union also reaches into the sensibility intensely enough, the whole experience may even be a sort of consolation, a sorrow shot through with sweetness, warmth, delight, and so deeply fulfilling in some mature experiences of love, so actualizing the person as to make being without the painful, sweet longing seem a loss of self.

In spiritual life, longing for the face-to-face experience of God may be such. The lover of God might gladly face physical torture and death to escape the felt separation from God and to fully consummate union. But, on the other hand, if that consummation cannot be had now, then the next best thing is the union constituted by loving longing with hope. Despite all the pain of such longing

---

8 Note the Vulgate translation, *de ipsius Dei Creatoris sui, clementia prope desperare* (*SpEx*-MHSJ, p. 376).
9 See Jules Toner, *The Experience of Love*, pp. 116-136.

love, being without it and the incomplete union which it constitutes seems to the hopeful lover a sort of death, abhorrent even to imagine. It is when the true grounds of hope for the longed-for union become blurred, when hope appears to be incompatible with the reality of sinful self, when all support from feeling is lost, that lovers of God can experience desolation, sorrow without sweetness, absence of peace, and bitterness which seems a foretaste of death begun. With these thoughts in mind, let us turn to Ignatius' description and try to understand this all-pervasive and climactic element in spiritual desolation, when one is "finding self...as if separated from God."

Spiritual Desolation as a Faith Experience of a Maturing Christian

Again we must return to the contrary relationship of spiritual consolation and desolation. Recall some features of spiritual consolation. It is a God-centered experience in a person with living faith. It is, further, a God-centered experience in which the person feels God's loving presence, feels himself lovingly present to the lovingly present God. It is, in short, a conscious, affective, experience of loving communion with God.[10] Spiritual desolation, as the contrary of this, is not merely a non-religious experience, an experience without God as center. (That would be contradictory, not contrary, to spiritual consolation.) Spiritual desolation is also a God-centered experience of a contrary sort. It is, in fact, just as much a God-centered experience as spiritual consolation; only it is *God-who-seems-absent* at the center of it, God apparently not loving me, God the beloved from whom I feel separated, God by whom I feel abandoned. Since God is the center of life for a spiritually maturing person precisely insofar as he is spiritually maturing, the apparent separation from God leaves a sense of painful emptiness, of bitter loneliness, in the spiritual dimension of his personality where the basic attitude and dominant thrust of his life is Godward. The sense of separation from God leaves him feeling utterly frustrated, discouraged, depressed, tending toward despair. Only insofar as a person's conscious life is God-centered or Godward will a sense of separation from God generate spiritual desolation; but the greater the extent to which his conscious life is such and the more intensely it is such, the more completely and the more acutely will the sense of separation from God flood his consciousness with desolation.

10 See ibid., pp. 185-198, for a descriptive analysis of loving communion.

Not only is spiritual desolation a God-centered experience; it is also a faith-experience, with the desolation properly speaking grounded in faith! This statement and its explanation overlap with what has just been said about a God-centered experience; but it goes further, seemingly in contradiction to much of what we have been saying, by asserting that the desolation properly speaking is grounded in faith. Resolving the problem which this raises will enable us to bring out something crucially important for the understanding of the whole experience. In fact, the point to be made is so crucial that if we miss it, we could end up attributing nonsense to Ignatius and holding doctrine which in practice could cause untold confusion, pain, and harm. On the other hand, understanding it can be the source of courage and energy to resist and conquer desolation. Some weariness of repetition will be a slight price to pay for making this point clearer.

Only a person who has living faith, faith that works through charity, can experience spiritual desolation. Further, such a one can experience it only in the measure of his living faith, which finds its necessary expression in a desire to go "from good to better" in the service of God. The more intensely painful the sense of separation from God, the more intense must be the actual faith and love underneath all the darkness, confusion, and disquiet. Although they are without warmth, sweetness, and the like during desolation, faith and love are, nevertheless, necessarily strong. For otherwise there would be no desolating sense of separation from God. One for whom God is not a living, loving, and lovable reality cannot feel spiritually desolate over separation from him.

Imagine a man who has some faith but not a living faith, for whom God means nothing of any special value or interest, whose heart is not at all set on going from good to better in the service of God. For such a one, awareness of separation from God causes no affective desolation in his conscious life. One who has had faith and lost it altogether and looks back on it as an illusion might even regret the loss, much as in wistful moments he regrets the passing of his childhood illusions which gave him a sense of security and joy. But he will not now experience a painful sense of separation from the loving God, any more than he now feels a painful separation from the good fairies or Santa Claus — as he once did when he was a naughty child.

To some other person, an observer whose faith-life is flourishing, any person without faith and charity may appear as desolate; but the latter person without charity does not *experience* it that way.

The observer could, of course, say that from a religious point of view, the faithless person is desolate in the same way that we say a barren landscape or a bombed-out city is desolate. But then we are no longer talking about the latter's experience. We have left off Ignatius' purpose of describing things as the person experiences them and have entered on an objective religious ontological description.

The point being made can be strengthened by turning attention to some other elements which Ignatius has noted as sources or consequences of spiritual desolation. Inclination to what he means by contemptible things, distracting vanities, is not experienced as a cause of sadness by one who has lost his faith in God, or even by a seriously regressing Christian. This is also true of what Ignatius calls temptation, inclination to sinful acts. Insofar as the anti-spiritual tendencies of one's life are prominent, such desires will even be delighted in as stimulating, giving zest to life. Such a person, insofar as he is such, will not find the danger of decline in faith, hope, and charity to be something to worry or sadden him. He does not pay much attention to the condition of his faith, hope, and charity; and he is not much distressed if he does notice their decline. None of these factors run against his basic attitude or the main thrust of his life. Why should they cause him to experience desolation?

When he loses interest in what he is doing or fails in his projects, he will experience other forms of desolation than spiritual: frustration, emptiness, meaninglessness. He may even experience the gnawing of conscience when the Holy Spirit calls him to repentance. If one wants to call that a spiritual desolation (it is not clear that Ignatius does), it is still true that such desolation is experienced precisely insofar as the man is moved by the Holy Spirit to a transient spiritual experience of faith; and it is still true that the more he sins, the less he is receptive to such motions from the Holy Spirit.

The Twofold Cause of Spiritual Desolation: Spiritual and Anti-Spiritual

Understanding that spiritual desolation is in some sense a faith experience, and using our analysis of the essential structure of any desolation, we can now readily resolve the question raised earlier but left unanswered until we should have studied Ignatius' description of desolation. The question was this: How can an experience which is the contrary of spiritual consolation, both as consolation and as spiritual, be called spiritual instead of anti-spiritual desolation? It is, after all, prompted by the evil spirit and the anti-spiritual tendencies within the human person; it is subjectively and immediately grounded in anti-spiritual motions which tend to destroy the faith, hope, and charity which are the work of the Holy Spirit.

This desolation could be called spiritual if by that term Ignatius meant: prompted by some spirit, good *or* evil. That way out of the difficulty seems to be an evasion, giving the term "spiritual" a meaning it has nowhere else in Ignatius' writing and leading to absurd consequences if used consistently. For, to be consistent, Ignatius would then have to speak of the person in Rule I:1, the one going from sin to sin under the influence of the evil spirit, as a spiritual person. He would have to call the "carnal delights and pleasures" incited in this person by the evil spirit spiritual delights and pleasures. And so on.

However, when we remember the distinction between desolation properly speaking and its immediate subjective sources or consequences, and when, along with this distinction, we remember how what Ignatius calls spiritual desolation is in some true sense a faith experience, then we can see that this desolation is under one aspect a true spiritual experience, even though under another aspect it is an anti-spiritual experience. It has a twofold subjective cause: (1) the anti-spiritual motions and (2) also the spiritual motions of living faith, by reason of which the subject has desolate feelings over the anti-spiritual motions.

Thoughts from Consolation and Desolation

After completing his description of the affective components in spiritual desolation, which come to a climax in "as if separated from our Creator and Lord," Ignatius adds: "For just as consolation is contrary to desolation, in the same way the thoughts which issue from consolation are contrary to the thoughts which issue from desolation." Why does he begin this sentence with the word "For"? What has Ignatius said in the preceding passage for which this statement gives a reason? Remember that one's finding oneself indolent, tepid, sad, and as if separated from one's Creator and Lord involved not only feelings, but also thoughts, about oneself in relation to God, thoughts generated by the feeling of separation and in accord with it. Remembering that, we can understand Ignatius' last statement as one which expands his immediately previous statement about some particular feelings and thoughts in desolation into a generalization about all thoughts which arise under the influence of spiritual consolation or desolation.

In spiritual consolation our affective feelings flow from and harmonize with the truths of faith: that God loves us, that we have sure grounds for hope, for peace, for joy, that God is very near and, no matter what evils there are, all is safely under God's wise, powerful, and loving care. The feelings, in turn, facilitate our being in accord with faith; the thoughts which flow from consolation as its consequence are thoughts which are fully in accord with the truths that ground spiritual consolation.

It is true that, given our egoism, spiritual consolation also has its peculiar danger of issuing in untrue thoughts — not because of itself it tends to do so, but because it can be an occasion for our egoism to assert itself. Nevertheless, even the untruth which can arise in our thoughts on occasion of spiritual consolation is the opposite of the untruth to which spiritual desolation tends, as well as of the truth which is borne in on us by desolation. In consolation we are all too likely to forget our helplessness and attribute to ourselves what is purely a gift from God. We are likely to see ourselves as better than we are, even to look down on others who do not experience consolation and who are obviously weak and tempted to discouragement. We can get the idea that never again will we be down, depressed, or discouraged; that we are unshakably loyal followers of Jesus — like Peter: "Everyone else may fall away, but I will not....Even if I must die with you, I will never disown you" (Mark 14:30-31). We shall find Ignatius warning us about these untruthful and dangerous thoughts in Rules I:9-11.

In spiritual desolation, on the contrary, the truthful thoughts about our weakness and utter dependence on God are inescapable (I:9). But so also are untruthful thoughts. They are not necessarily genuine judgments, and are rarely explicit judgments, but thoughts which are always more or less in danger of becoming judgments if we yield to the deceptive power of affective feelings of desolation and start down the road toward actual distrust and despair. Our feelings are such as would be justifiable if God really were absent, or were present but not with merciful love. The consequence in our thoughts is at least forgetfulness of what we have believed so easily and intensely during consolation; and beyond mere forgetfulness, there is an implicit negation of God's presence, or love, or truthfulness, or faithfulness, or power. These implicit thoughts are often cloaked under explicit, exaggerated, thoughts of our own unworthiness. We are, the thoughts run, beyond the reach of God's love (which is, by implication, given because of our worthiness) or beyond his forgiveness (which is, by implication, limited). Or, we perhaps think that God does not remember us — for who are we that God should think of us? (Thus, God, by implication, is limited in power of attention or is not faithful in love.) And so on.

If the grossly untruthful character of these implications is uncovered by the one in desolation, then other less obviously but equally untruthful thoughts arise. A life thoroughly dedicated to God's praise and service, a life that calls for a sacrifice of so much the human heart desires, seems beyond one's power. We think that we do not have the grace from God to live it. Most others think that this way of life is foolish. Who are we to think that we know better? And so our thoughts run. In such ways as these the thoughts which flow from desolation bear the marks of Satan: deception leading to discouragement, with a tendency to turn back from the way that goes from good to better, that ascends from glory to glory, as in the Spirit we are transfigured into the likeness of the Lord. (2 Cor. 3:18).

Summary: Factors in the Dynamic Structure of Spiritual Desolation

Putting together all that has been drawn out of Ignatius' description of spiritual desolation, we find that such desolation in the proper meaning of the word, feelings, is generated by four factors in dynamic relationships. Two of them are spiritual and are in conflict with the two which are anti-spiritual. (1) The Holy Spirit (2) actualizes living faith in a human person. In the power of such faith that person intends and strives to grow in freedom from sin, to go from good to better in God's service, to experience God's love in Jesus Christ, to know and love Jesus more and follow him more fully. The two anti-spiritual factors oppose these spiritual factors. (3) The evil spirit, or simply the power of sin within the human person, (4) instigates thoughts and affective acts and feelings which are contrary to those which living faith of itself tends to generate. These motions from the evil spirit or the person's own sinfulness are various in kind and degree, but all tend in some measure toward loss of confidence in God's love and care. Thus, by degrees of discouragement, they tend toward making one despair of ever achieving the goal that had sprung from living faith. When these anti-spiritual movements so dominate some area of conscious life that the feelings of peace and joy flowing from living faith are suppressed, or are drowned out by feelings of anxiety, sadness, and discouragement *regarding faith life,* then the person experiences spiritual desolation. Only desolation in a person with faith, hope, and charity, which arises from inner movements contrary to faith, hope, and charity, only such desolation is a *spiritual* desolation. We may and do use the latter term in a restricted meaning when we refer only to the desolate feelings as distinct from the spiritual and anti-spiritual, objective and subjective, sources of these feelings. Nevertheless, the sources are elements in the essential dynamic structure of the total experience, and the term "spiritual desolation" in a larger meaning can be used to mean this total experience.

PART III

THE GOOD SPIRIT
IN TIME OF DESOLATION
Rules I:5-14

Chapter 7

DISCERNING AND RESPONDING TO THE HOLY SPIRIT
DURING SPIRITUAL DESOLATION:
FUNDAMENTAL COUNSELS
Rules I:5 and 6

In Rules I:1-4 Ignatius has distinguished two types of persons in their relationship with God, respectively those who are spiritually maturing or regressing. He has stated the fundamental signs for discerning what spirit is moving each type; and he has described in some detail spiritual consolation and spiritual desolation as two contrary experiences which are of special importance in maturing Christians.

From here on, he focuses his attention on maturing Christians, those who are striving to be cleansed more and more from sin and to go on from good to better in the service of God. Or, to state the matter in the traditional terms of the spiritual theology current in his day, in Rules I:5-14 and II:1-8 he is concerned with persons who are "advancing" (*proficientes* in *Summa theologiae*, II-II, Q. 24, a. 9) in the "illuminative way" or stage of growth or "life" (*vida illuminativa* in *SpEx*, [10]) by the prayerful pursuit of the Christian virtues, especially as exemplified in Christ.[1] It is natural that to such a person a good spirit will bring truths and motions which will encourage him or her, and an evil spirit, as father of lies, thoughts and motions which will discourage or deceive. All of these remaining Rules for the Discernment of Spirits are aimed at helping such a maturing person to discern the good spirit from the

1 On the three ways or stages of spiritual growth, see St. Thomas, *Summa theologiae*, II-II, Q. 24, a. 9; F. Cayré, trans. H. Howitt, *Manual of Patrology* (Tournai: Desclée & Co., 1935), I, 21; II, 521; A. Tanquerey, S.S., trans. H. Branderis, *The Spiritual Life* (Tournai: Desclée & Co., 1930), pp. 171-172, 297-303, 454-460; J. de Guibert, S.J., trans. P. Barrett, *The Theology of the Spiritual Life* (New York: Sheed and Ward, 1953), pp. 265-291.

evil one, and then especially to guard himself or herself against the evil spirit's temptations and deceits.

For regressing Christians, and even too for those who are static or lukewarm, Ignatius' remaining rules (I:5-14 and II:1-8) will have little relevance until these persons turn to God and begin to mature spiritually. For until then their problems and the solutions will be very different from those of the maturing Christians.

For the maturing Christians, in Ignatius' view, the most common and fundamental challenge to be met is that of spiritual desolation, with its temptations and deceptions, which leads to discouragement and a turning back from the way toward a total love and service of God.

Practical Steps for One in Spiritual Desolation

Rules I:5-14 — that is, all the remaining rules in series I — are aimed at encouraging and guiding the maturing Christian during this experience of spiritual desolation. None of these rules are concerned with discerning spiritual consolation or desolation from non-spiritual. None of them add to what has already been said about discerning spirits through consolation or desolation. The only discernment of spirits touched on here is discernment that the Holy Spirit of Light is lovingly present to us and powerfully active in us even during the darkness of desolation. He may be largely hidden to our darkened vision, but in fact he is shining undimmed in the depth of our being, giving sure signs of his presence to those who know what to look for. And Ignatius is concerned with telling us how to remain open to the Spirit and to cooperate with him during desolation, that thus we may resist and conquer the power of darkness. Even what is said about spiritual consolation is for the sake of preparing for desolation or preventing it.

Stress on the experience of spiritual desolation does not imply an obsession with the dark side of life. This would be surprising in one of the most joyful men who ever lived. The fact is that Ignatius did not intend that these rules should be brought up at all until one has experiences that make them needed (*SpEx*, [9]). Further, these rules appear within the context of the *Spiritual Exercises,* of which the central aim is to lead toward an intimate experiential knowledge of God's personal love for each person, as that love is revealed in all things, but especially in Christ, a knowledge that can bring spiritual consolation. Ignatius is, however, keenly aware that "the enemy" and our sinful egoism obstruct our way to such knowledge of Jesus and to the joy of pure unselfish love for him.

The times of spiritual desolation are not the peak experiences of Christian life, but they are the critical ones. When we are in consolation we are carried along effortlessly. But in the midst of darkness and apparent absence of God, feelings of discouragement, turmoil, attraction to what grieves the Holy Spirit, spiritual listlessness — in the midst of all this, we have to struggle in order to believe in God's love, to remember and remain open to the Spirit. If we do not learn how to do it and actually do it we shall never mature as Christians. We need to understand how the Holy Spirit uses this time for our growth in Christ. We need to know what to expect from him, how to recognize his movements without spiritual consolation as a sign, and how to correspond so that he may lead us to peace.

The counsels which Ignatius gives to guide us along the way to peace can be divided into three sections. Rules I:5-9 and the second part of Rule 11 tell us what to do or not to do during the time of spiritual desolation. Rule I:10 and the first part of I:11 tell us what to do in time of consolation in order to prepare for desolation in the future and to profit from past desolation. Rules I:12-14 describe several characteristics of Satan's style of attack and draw practical directives from these on how to counteract his influence.

Rules I:5-9 on how to combat spiritual desolation may be summed up in two general directives: (1) during desolation, do not change decisions or plans made in the time of preceding consolation or calm, but (2) strive to change yourself. Or, put another way: (1) hold fast to decisions and resolutions which seemed just before the desolation to be from the Holy Spirit, and (2) take active measures to remain open to the Holy Spirit so that by his power you may prevent or nullify the evil effects of desolation and even destroy it.

However, besides these two steps in dealing with spiritual desolation which Ignatius explicitly treats, and presupposed for each of them, there is another step which he leaves implicit, perhaps because it seems so obvious. Nevertheless, experience seems to show the crucial importance of explicitly stressing it; for, despite its obviousness, it is in actual experience easily and frequently missed — with the consequence that the subject of desolation does not remember the necessity of the two steps we have already mentioned. The very first step in dealing with spiritual desolation is becoming *reflectively* aware of it and *explicitly* naming it for what it is.

There are, then, three main and even absolutely necessary steps in dealing wisely and effectively with spiritual desolation: (1) to become reflectively aware of it, by explicitly recognizing it as spiritual desolation; (2) to resist any impulse coming from desolation to change previous decisions about our way of loving and serving God; and (3) to change ourselves in ways contrary to desolation, by doing whatever will open us more to the power of the Holy Spirit. For he is always lovingly and powerfully present to us, in spiritual darkness as well as in light.

The First Step: Become Reflectively Aware of Spiritual Desolation

Let us see more clearly what reflective awareness of spiritual desolation means and what its importance is. We can do this by considering two reasons for this step. The first reason is that success in doing whatever Ignatius recommends in these rules for dealing with desolation will be possible in the measure that we accurately and clearly recognize that we are not in just any kind of negative mood, but in *spiritual* desolation, the kind of desolation described earlier in Rule 4, the kind that is anti-spiritual in source and impetus. Unless we reflectively recognize what is going on in us, we may be ground down into a state of utter discouragement and lethargy; we may even be impelled into stupid and perhaps irreversible decisions, before we remember the advice given in Rules 5 and 6. We may in a confused, dark way be conscious that something is terribly wrong, but not bring the experience clearly and explicitly enough into focus to enable us to do anything about it. We will be like persons who are physically sick but only vaguely aware of the symptoms and unable to do anything about it until they become clearly aware of the symptoms diagnosed as signs of such-and-such a disease which needs such-and-such a treatment.

The second reason why prompt recognition of spiritual desolation is of crucial importance lies in the fact that such recognition itself begins to deprive desolation of its power to dominate thought and action, and begins to mitigate its intensity. Before I reflect-

150

ively and explicitly recognize my state as spiritual desolation, the space of my conscious life can be or tend toward being totally preoccupied by it. I become or tend to become fully identified with myself-in-desolation. As a consequence, I am utterly incapable of taking a stand against it, not only because I do not know what to do (first reason, above), but because I have no basis in my consciousness on which I can take a firm opposing stand; but by reflecting on the desolation, I expand my consciousness beyond it and escape full submergence in it.

Let us see how this is so. By reflection on my state of desolation, I set myself-in-desolation apart from myself-reflecting-on-myself-in-desolation. In this way I make the total concrete experience of desolation (the causes, the feelings of desolation, and the consequences) an object distinct from myself as a person, and I now take possession of my life, through my power of reflection and my striving to master myself through my power of freedom. By doing this, I have made space in my consciousness for something besides desolation with its causes and consequences. In that space I can now reconnoiter, maneuver my attention and reason and will, and thus attack and weaken or even destroy the sources of the desolation.

In fact, my simply being reflectively aware of spiritual desolation is already a beginning of weakening or destroying it. In reflection, whatever in my direct awareness causes or reinforces the desolation now becomes to some extent a mere object of reflective analysis; and by this its power is blunted. Similarly, reflection on my own affective response to that cause tends to weaken the response to it. There is a parallel here with what can go on in spiritual consolation. Suppose I am contemplating the beauty of God revealed in Christ or in some beautiful person and I experience a response of burning, joyful love for God. Or suppose I am experiencing peace and joy in the understanding of some revealed truth, for example, the Mystical Body of Christ. Now suppose I I turn back on myself and think to myself: See what a great spiritual consolation I am having, how deep and intense my emotions are, see how this revelation of God is affecting me. Immediately the beauty or the truth that grounds the consolation loses something, if not all, of its power; immediately the love, the peace, the joy, begin to die down. That, I think is what is meant by saying that we pray best when we do not know we are praying. The parallel with desolation and temptation to sin is obvious. Just as it is bad to

151

be consciously and reflectively aware of a desirable response, such as spiritual consolation, while it is actually happening; so also it is good to be consciously and reflectively aware of an undesirable response while it is actually happening. The reason is the same in both cases: the reflective awareness tends to destroy the response.

Finally, in reflective awareness of the experience not only as desolation but as *spiritual* desolation, I become aware of its evil instigating source and its likely evil consequences. Insofar as I love God and seek his reign, such awareness calls forth the energy of purposeful hate, such hate as is the necessary consequence of, the obverse side of love for God and desire for his Kingdom, his glory, in human lives. In the measure of that love and desire, I hate the inner motions which are in conflict with love for God and neighbor. I hate the instigating source, precisely as the source of these motions, as the enemy of the human race. Such hatred gives energy and courage to resist and conquer the power of evil once it is recognized.

The Second Step: Resist Change of Decisions

Once spiritual desolation is recognized and named, the first advice Ignatius gives is this: Resist any suggestion or impulse arising from desolation to change prior purposes. This advice is found in Rule 5 along with the reason for it:

> The time of [spiritual] desolation is no time at all to change purposes and decisions with which one was content the day before such desolation or the decision with which one was content during the previous consolation. It is, rather, a time to remain firm and constant in these. For just as the good spirit leads and counsels us in [spiritual] consolation, so in [spiritual] desolation does the evil spirit. By the latter's counsels we cannot find the way to a right decision.

Two explanations and a warning will help us to read this rule accurately. The meaning of a counsel from a good or evil spirit needs explanation; so also do the decisions which the rule says should not be changed during desolation. The warning concerns several false conclusions which readers could readily draw from this rule if they are not familiar with the whole of Ignatius' teaching on discernment of spirits and of God's will. These conclusions need to be pointed out and corrected.

First, the meaning of a counsel from the good or evil spirit can be clarified if we relate this rule to the previous one, Rule I:4

152

(*SpEx*, [317]); see also [314, 315, 329, 333]). There we saw that from spiritual desolation flow thoughts which are the contrary of those which flow from spiritual consolation. Given that spiritual consolation and desolation are respectively the work of the Holy Spirit and the evil spirit in a maturing Christian, the thoughts which flow from consolation or desolation may be taken as prompted by these spirits. In Rule 5, it becomes clear that thoughts from spiritual consolation and desolation, and thus from good or evil spirits, can be thoughts about decisions already made and yet to be made, plans for actions to be dropped or carried out. Thus, if I experience a sense of God's absence, sorrow that leads to spiritual discouragement, in short, spiritual desolation, I may be inclined to give up on a work or a way of life I had previously decided to undertake for God. Since the thought of doing so sprang from spiritual desolation, it appears to be from the evil spirit rather than the Holy Spirit. It should not be accepted or even deliberated about until I am again in spiritual consolation or at least in a time of spiritual calm. Once the desolation has passed, the thought of changing my decision will very likely appear to be non-sensical.

The second explanation called for in Rule I:5 concerns the kinds of decisions to which the rule is referring. Certainly the rule does not mean that during spiritual desolation no decisions should be made about any matters whatsoever. That would paralyze us. Three kinds of decisions may be distinguished. A first kind consists of those which touch most closely on our personal or communal spiritual life or our apostolic work, and which would change directions already set by well-made decisions. The impulse to change these during desolation should be firmly and promptly resisted. A second class of decisions are those that have to be made during desolation. As we shall see, some decisions have to be made about how we are going to combat desolation, and some decisions regarding current business that crops up obviously cannot be delayed. But we should take care not to allow them to be shaped by the desolation. A third class of decisions consists of those which do not change previous decisions regarding our spiritual life or apostolic work and do not have to be made now. The general principle implied by the rule is that such decisions should be put off until desolation has passed. There is too much danger of falling into some trap during a time when the spirit of darkness is influential on our feelings, and through our feelings on our thoughts and inclinations.

Besides the foregoing explanations, a warning is called for regarding apparently logical conclusions from what is said in Rule I:5. The sentence which seems clearly to imply these conclusions is the one that reads: "for just as the good spirit leads and counsels us in [spiritual] consolation, so in [spiritual] desolation does the evil spirit." A reader without a broad and integrated understanding of Ignatian writings on discernment of spirits and discernment of God's will might readily infer the following conclusions: (1) The Holy Spirit does not counsel us outside the time of spiritual consolation, and the evil spirit does not counsel us outside the time of spiritual desolation; (2) any counsel which comes to mind during spiritual consolation is by that very fact from the Holy Spirit; (3) therefore, this counsel surely reveals what God's will is. None of these conclusions is in accord with the integral teaching of Ignatius. We shall consider each of them in turn.

(1) Regarding the first conclusion, to say that in spiritual consolation or in spiritual desolation our decision-making is influenced by the good or evil spirit respectively is not at all to say that each of these spirits so influences us only at these respective times. As we have already seen and will have occasion to see again, the good spirit counsels us not only during spiritual consolation but also during spiritual calm, and even during spiritual desolation; and the evil spirit counsels us not only during spiritual desolation but also during spiritual calm, and even during spiritual consolation (see above, pp. 61-69 and below, pp. 177-178). There are more fundamental and sure signs than feelings of consolation and desolation by which the source of these counsels can be judged, for example, evident harmony or discord of the counsels with the clear demands of faith, hope, charity, and humility.

(2) The second specious conclusion from Rule 5 overlooks a number of important factors in Ignatian understanding of how to discern spirits. It overlooks the point just made immediately above, that the evil spirit can and does counsel us during spiritual consolation. It further overlooks the Ignatian teaching in Rules II:3-5, that sometimes the evil spirit himself prompts spiritual consolation as an occasion to deceive us (*SpEx*, [331-333], and see below, pp. 222-243). Ignatius' basic principle for discerning spirits in maturing Christians is the principle stated in Rule I:5, that consolation and desolation are signs of the good and evil spirits respectively. However, this principle has to be understood as qualified by other factors, in particular those stated in Rules II:3-5. There-

fore, the fact that a counsel comes in spiritual consolation justifies only an initial and tentative opinion that it comes from the Holy Spirit. Further evidence may support the opinion that the consolation and the counsel are prompted by the evil spirit.

(3) The third conclusion mentioned above as apparently following from what Ignatius says in Rule I:5 is that a counsel which comes during a spiritual consolation surely expresses what God wills. This third conclusion is already disproved by what we have seen regarding the second. But something more must be said. For one might still think that if all the evidence supports the judgment that this consolation and counsel are prompted by the Holy Spirit, then the person who experiences them can be justly confident of having found what God wills. But Ignatius would rarely if ever allow any one such experience to justify a judgment regarding God's will. Such a judgment, he thinks, requires "abundant light and knowledge" received through many such experiences critically evaluated by discernment of spirits (*SpEx*, [176] and *Spiritual Diary* [1-40]).

One last comment on Rule I:5: the importance of this rule and the need for calling it to attention can hardly be overestimated. To forget it in lesser matters, or to fail to follow it when it is remembered, can lead to entanglements and vexations that impede personal growth in Christian life, and also to waste of time and energy on projects that are irrelevant to God's work in the world or even a hindrance to it. To forget the rule in greater matters can lead to grave harm. Yet in time of desolation we so easily forget the guiding principle put down in this rule. Even those who know it well do this. It would be conservative to say that nine out of ten times any suggested change of decision about our spiritual life or apostolate which we thought of during spiritual desolation seems undesirable or even foolish when the desolation has passed; and that ten out of ten times we will be glad that we waited and do not have to live with consequences of a decision made in circumstances which call that decision into question.

The Third Step: Change Yourself Intensely in Ways Contrary to Spiritual Desolation

When spiritual desolation has been explicitly recognized (in the first step), and when the person has been secured against a rash change of decision (in the second step), then Ignatius, in Rules

I:6-9, gives him or her some counsels on what further to do. Carrying out these counsels constitutes the third step in responding to spiritual desolation. They are summed up at the beginning of Rule I:6 in a general counsel to change ourselves intensely in ways contrary to the thoughts and affections which characterize spiritual desolation. The rule reads:

> Granted that in spiritual desolation we ought not to change our previous purposes, it helps greatly to change overselves intensely in ways contrary to the aforesaid desolation, for instance, by insisting more on prayer, on much meditation, and on extending ourselves to do penance in some fitting manner.

The ways of changing ourselves which are instanced in this rule are, as we shall see, added to in the three following rules, namely, Rules I:7-9.

Two Principles Underlying Step Three

First, however, we need to consider two principles which underlie Rule I:6, principles which are of major importance in Ignatian spirituality. Let us name them here the principles of (1) trust-and-act and (2) counterattack. For present purposes they can be phrased as follows. The first is: Trust in God and pray as if everything depended on him alone [with your actions counting for nothing]; and act as if everything depended only on your own efforts. The second is: When negative forces attack you in the spiritual life, counterattack. The third step in responding to desolation is only an application of this second principle to one particular kind of negative force, namely, spiritual desolation. Let us examine in more detail these two principles behind step three.

1. The Principle of Trust-and-Act

Ignatius always attributed a primacy[2] of importance to God's action and to whatever unites us to God and opens us to receive

---

2 The primacy of reliance on God and so of prayer appears throughout Ignatius' writings, in every context. For several general statements about this, see *The Constitutions of the Society of Jesus* (Trans. by George E. Ganss, S.J. St. Louis, 1970), pp. 119 on [134], 331-333 on [812-814] (abbreviated hereafter as *ConsSJComm*). See also Ignatius' letter to John Pelletier, *LettersIgn*, p. 245. The fullest, most precise and painstaking statement by Ignatius of the primacy of divine grace and so of reliance on God, no matter how great one's natural gifts may be, can be found in the first draft of the *Examen*, in text *a*, which remained unpublished until 1936. It can be found in *DeGuiJes*, pp. 147-148.

his actions so as to be more fully instruments of his loving and wise power. Nevertheless, Ignatius also highly valued natural gifts and human effort inasmuch as they are from God, and have from God's action in us both their purpose and their power to achieve that purpose. The two-sided principle of trust-and-act flows from this view of the human agent's relationship with God. This principle is not found anywhere in Ignatius' writings in the precise wording that we have used a little above. However, with slightly varied wordings, its thought is often attributed to him by his disciples. They are correct in doing this, for that thought does underlie many of his statements and deeds. For example, it is clearly apparent only a little below the surface in two beautiful paragraphs of his *Constitutions of the Society of Jesus:*

[813]. 2. For the preservation and development not only of the body or exterior of the Society but also of its spirit, and for the attainment of the objective it seeks, which is to aid souls to reach their ultimate and supernatural end, the means which unite the human instrument with God and so dispose it that it may be wielded dexterously by His divine hand are more effective than those which equip it in relation to men. Such means are, for example, goodness and virtue, and especially charity, and a pure intention of the divine service, and familiarity with God our Lord in spiritual exercises of devotion, and sincere zeal for souls for the sake of glory to Him who created and redeemed them and not for any other benefit. Thus it appears that care should be taken in general that all the members of the Society may devote themselves to the solid and perfect virtues and to spiritual pursuits, and attach greater importance to them than to learning and other natural and human gifts. For they are the interior gifts which make those exterior means effective toward the end which is sought.

[814]. 3. When based upon this foundation, the natural means which equip the human instrument of God our Lord to deal with his fellowmen will all be helps toward the preservation and development of this whole body, provided they are acquired and exercised for the divine service alone; employed, indeed, not that we may put our confidence in them, but that we may cooperate with the divine grace according to the arrangement of the sovereign providence of God our Lord. For He desires to be glorified both through the natural means, which He gives as Creator, and through the supernatural means, which He gives as the Author of grace. Therefore the human or acquired means ought to be sought with diligence, especially well-grounded and solid learning, and a method of proposing it to the people by means of sermons, lectures, and the art of dealing and conversing with men.[3]

3 Translation of G. E. Ganss, S.J., in *ConsSJComm*, pp. 332-333.

Saint Ignatius' Rules for the Discernment of Spirits

Still further, something very close to the formulation used above is attested as Ignatius' thought by his contemporary who knew him so well, Ribadeneyra:

> In matters which he took up pertaining to the service of our Lord, he made use of all the human means to succeed in them, with a care and efficiency as great as if the success depended on these means; and he confided in God and depended on his providence as greatly as if all the other human means which he was using were of no effect.[4]

In accord with the teaching of Holy Scripture (for example, John 6:44, 65; 15:5; 2 Cor. 3:5; Phil. 2:13), Ignatius is always keenly aware that God does act intimately in our lives, that only God's action can do anything to bring about his greater glory in ourselves or give our efforts any power to help bring about his Kingdom among men. For this purpose, no human effort has the least value except insofar as the person acts in union with God

---

4 Ribadaneyara's *De ratione quam in gubernando tenebat Ignatius*, in *FN*, III, 631, and cited in fn. 55 of *DeGuiJes*, p. 148.

A century and a half after Ignatius' death, Gabriel Hevenesi (1656-1715) in his *Scintillae Ignatianae* (Vienna, 1705), p. 2, attributed to Ignatius a thought somewhat similar to the principle of trust-act as we and Ribadeneyra have formulated it, but with an inverted and paradoxical wording difficult for many to understand: "So trust in God as if all the success of undertakings depended on you and nothing on him; but so apply all your work to them as if God alone were to do everything, and you nothing at all" (also cited in *DeGuiJes*, p. 148)—a wording which more recent writers have simplified to "Pray as if everything depended upon you, act as if everything depended on God."

Since 1929 much lengthy discussion and differences of opinion in learned works have occurred about the two formulations of the aphorism, by writers on Ignatius such as C. A. Kneller, G. Fessard, J. C. Dhotel, Hugo Rahner, E. Pousset, and others. Fessard, in *La dialectique des Exercices Spirituels de S. Ignace de Loyola* (Paris, 1956) favors Hevenesi's formulation and shows that it has provenance from some two centuries before Ignatius; and this opinion is mirrored in Pousset, *La vie dans la foi et la liberté* (Paris, 1971), p. 159, and in its translation by E. L. Donahue, *Life in Faith and Freedom: An Essay Presenting Gaston Fessard's Analysis of the Dialectic of the Spiritual Exercises of St. Ignatius* (St. Louis, 1980), p. 238. One difficult passage from the first draft of Ignatius' *Constitutions* (a draft which was never published until 1936 and is cited in *DeGuiJes*, pp. 147-148), and another passage from Gonçalves da Câmara's *Memoriale* (1574) cited in *FN*, I, 663-664, are sometimes adduced to show that the complicated formulation given by Hevenesi was what lay beneath Ignatius' thought. But H. M. de Achával, in *Gregorianum*, XXXVIII (1957), 324-327, seriously doubts that Ignatius truly knew or used this formulation. See also J. W. Padberg, in *Studies in the Spirituality of Jesuits*, X (1978), 320. This controversy is perhaps not yet conclusively settled.

But even if Ignatius had Hevenesi's formulation in mind, the one which we have used above in our text as his principle of trust-and-act still stands along with it. The two formulations do not exclude each other. Both could be used on different occasions, even on occasions almost simultaneous.

and as an instrument of God. This is one side of the Ignatian two-sided principle: All depends on God. The other side is that we must do all that lies in our power, make every human effort to cooperate with God. For ordinarily God acts through us to achieve his purposes for us. He acts effectively through human intelligence, imagination, affections, freedom, initiative, bodily activity. So, all our power of acting in all the ways we can with "courage and energy" is to be summoned up for the praise and service of God. Such adjectives as "generous," "intense," "all," "every," "totally" along with "discreet," characterize Ignatian writing on spiritual and apostolic life.

All depends on God — this side of Ignatius' twofold principle holds primacy and determines what in our own activity directed to the praise and service of God is to have priority. When faith, hope, and charity are assumed as the root of all else, any striving to grow, whether in one's own life in Christ or in any Christian ministry to others, must begin and be carried on with prayer for God's help. All the while, too, we must constantly seek to know God's will in the concrete situation. We must have utter reliance on his wisdom to know what are the better goals and better ways to these goals, on his power to accomplish them, on his loving concern which assures us that he will hear our petitions and lead us to find his will; that then he will work in us and through us to accomplish his will. To seek and to trust in this way is also a grace of God for which we must pray. Without him we can do nothing.

To let the Ignatian demand for courageous and energetic action (as if all depended on us) get separated in thought from the other and more profound demand for reliance on God alone (even as if our action counted for nothing) inevitably leads to a caricature of the Christian relationship with God. So also, to let the demand for prayer and trust relieve us of the need to expend all our energy in the effort to find and do God's will would be equally misleading. His mind formed by the teaching of Holy Scripture and his own spiritual experience, Ignatius lived and taught neither activism nor quietism but rather an attitude constituted by a tension between the positive truth in both these excesses. Each of these one-sided attitudes negates the truth of the other; and this is the error of each. Ignatius does not resolve the problem by negating the truth found in either attitude; neither does he even try to diminish what is being positively asserted so as to resolve the tension by watering them down in a compromise at some middle ground.

Rather, he negates their mutually exclusive character, grasps both extremes, and holds them together in the spiritually healthy and truthful tension of his two-sided principle, never willing to let go or weaken either side.[5] The unrelieved tension enables us to see more fully the meaning of each extreme by relation to the other. Our reliance on God becomes such as to energize us for action; for our reliance is on a God who acts through our freedom, love, intelligence, and energy. Action becomes such that it is an expression of reliance on God and deepens that reliance; for the very action itself is seen to be from God, and any desired achievement for his praise and service through the action is seen to be dependent on God's loving power.

2. The Principle of Counterattack

When we put the principle of trust-and-act together with Ignatius' stress on courage and energy in the service of God[6] and on the contrary character of motions from good and evil spirits,[7] we can readily see how in the face of temptation and spiritual desolation his counsel is to counterattack (*agere contra*). In accord with the trust-and-act principle, the primary response to temptation and desolation is prayer of petition and total trust in God. Reliance on God, however, must accord with "the gentle arrangement of Divine Providence," which "requires the cooperation of his creatures."[8] This cooperation for Ignatius means more than merely refusing to yield to temptation or desolation; it means counterattacking, trying to conquer and destroy these. It means more than that: It means trying to draw good from evil, to gain and grow through the very desolation and temptation, to cooperate with God who "in everything...works for good with those who love him" (Rom. 8:28) and who moves us in ways just the contrary of the ways Satan moves us. To join ourselves by our free choice to God's work in us as fully as we can, we have to go beyond standing our ground and waiting for the temptation or desolation to pass. We have to

---

5 He does not attempt a theoretical or theological explanation, an explanation that would involve problems such as the relation of man's created freedom with the Creator's omnipotence or omniscience, or of nature to grace, of time to eternity, of which any explanation winning general acceptance has evaded the admirable speculation of great theologians through the centuries. Ignatius' rules were intended for practical use here and now, and he had to keep them free, as far as possible, from theoretical controversies.

6 See above, pp. 63-69.

7 See above, Rules I:1-2; II-7; and ch. 3.

8 *ConsSJComm*, [134] on p. 119.

seize the initiative with God and with him turn the apparently bad situation into an occasion for the greater praise and service of God.

The principle of counterattack is often referred to by Ignatius' disciples as the principle of *agere contra*. Like the principle of trust-and-act, it is not found in Ignatius' writings with the precise phrasing that I have used. But it does underlie many passages, such as that in the contemplation on "The Kingdom of Christ," from which it gets its name (*SpEx*, [97]):

> Those who have greater desire to show affection and in all ways to give outstanding service to the eternal King and universal Lord will not only offer themselves for work, but also, acting against [*haziendo contra, certando contra*] their sensuality and against their egoistic and worldly love, will make offerings of greater worth and importance...

Another example is found in Ignatius' directive for the spiritual training of the novices (*Cons*, [265]):

> Temptations ought to be anticipated by their opposites, for example, if someone is observed to be inclined toward pride, by exercising him in lowly matters thought fit to aid toward humbling him; and similarly of other evil inclinations.

When speaking of one who is committed to a full hour of contemplation and is tempted to shorten it, Ignatius states (*SpEx*, [13]):

> Likewise, it is to be noted that just as in time of consolation it is easy and a light matter to remain in contemplation for the full hour, so in time of desolation it is very difficult to fill out the hour. Therefore, the exercitant, in order to act contrary to the desolation and conquer the temptation, should always remain in contemplation somewhat more than a full hour. The reason for doing so is to train himself not only to resist the adversary but even to overthrow him.

For one who is seeking to find to what way of life God calls him or her and who feels repugnance toward a freely chosen life of actual poverty in imitation of Christ in his public life, a repugnance which is rooted in selfish fears and desires and could obstruct finding and following God's call — for such a person Ignatius has this advice (*SpEx*, [157]):

> ...it is very helpful toward extinguishing such a disordered affection to ask in the colloquies (even though it be contrary to sensual inclinations) that the Lord choose us for a life of actual poverty. We

161

should will for it to be so, beg and plead for the call, with only one condition, namely, that it be for the service and praise of his divine goodness.

The principle of counterattack, when formulated abstractly and its illustrations taken out of full context, can appear to be a grim expression of an agonistic personality that cannot brook human weakness. Seen in the context of the Ignatian spirit as it shines in his life and in his *Spiritual Exercises*, it is the inevitable expression of a burning, tender, courageous love that is ready to die to everything in self which hinders living all of life with Christ and for the neighbor, that wants with Christ to be totally yielding to the movement of the Father's Spirit, active with all possible energy in responding, and so eagerly aggressive against every manifestation in oneself of selfishness or of the power of evil.

The Application of the Two Principles, in Rule I:6, to Spiritual Desolation

Having experienced the depths of spiritual desolation in his own life, Ignatius is well aware of the anguish which one in desolation can sometimes endure. In his instructions to the director of the Spiritual Exercises he insists on all gentleness and kindness toward one in desolation or temptation and forbids all harshness, but at the same time he urges that the director bring the exercitant "courage and energy" (*SpEx*, [7]). He will not allow the director's gentleness to decline into sentimental and harmful pity that excuses him or her from calling the exercitant to courage and effort and in so doing leaves the exercitant mired in the darkness of spiritual desolation, closed to the energizing light of the Holy Spirit.

We can now look at the directives which Ignatius gives to show what this principle of counterattack can call for when, applied to the experience of spiritual desolation, it urges us "to change ourselves intensely in ways contrary to the aforesaid desolation." He suggests some ways in which the change may be effected: "by insisting more on prayer, on meditation, on much examination, and by extending ourselves to do penance in some fitting way." We shall have to consider in some detail the what and why of each of these suggested ways. But first of all we must consider the underlying assumption that when we are in spiritual desolation, we can effectively do something to change ourselves and, in changing ourselves, hope by God's power acting in us and through us to ease or eliminate the desolation. Note that Ignatius says that we can "change ourselves," not that we can by changing ourselves certainly get out of desolation and into a state of spiritual calm or much less get into spiritual consolation. Changing ourselves in the ways suggested, he says, "helps greatly" for overcoming the spiritual desolation; it is not said to be a sure cure. The darkness of desolation will lift when God wills. This will come out clearly in Rules 7-9. As for the passage beyond spiritual calm to spiritual consolation, that is, as Ignatius says time and again, "a gift and grace" of God.

It is also by God's grace (still with us in desolation, as we shall see), grace other than consolation, that we can change ourselves to receive God's consoling grace and by so doing grow in faith, hope, charity. But, as we saw, God's grace usually works in and through our created power and effort. From our side, changing ourselves depends first of all on the effort of willing it. Not that we can directly will ourselves to be changed and by that very fact be changed in the way we desire to be. No act of will, however intense, can do that. But we can insistently will to do things which spiritual desolation strongly inclines us not to do, and by doing them, not only resist but strive to undermine the desolation. In desolation we do not at all feel like praying, meditating, examining ourselves, or doing penance. The evil spirit and our own feeling of spiritual indolence suggest easing off until we feel like doing so. "Would it not be insincere, not being your true self, to pray and meditate and do penance when you do not feel like it?" Nothing could be more stupid and more fatal. This is the way to let go all defenses and all offensive power against the force of evil. Ignatius' advice is: Do what is diametrically the opposite; insist more on those very things which the desolation inclines you to drop.

"Insist more" is ambiguous. It could mean insisting with ourselves more intensely than we ordinarily do on the prayer, meditation, and so on which are usual in our lives. It could also mean that we insist on doing these more than we usually do. The first meaning is minimal. Certainly, at the time of desolation, we do have to be more sternly insistent with ourselves if we are not to fall away from a life of prayer and reflection and so become defenseless against the force of evil. But insisting on more prayer or other spiritual activities seems also to be included in Ignatius' meaning. It accords with the advice we found him giving in Annotation 13 (*SpEx*, [13]) for one who during desolation is tempted to shorten the time he has allotted for contemplation. The Vulgate version of Rule 6 explicitly urges that "those things be cared for *and increased* which tend to counteract the impetus of desolation."[9] Most clearly of all, the counsel is stated and explained in a letter of September 20, 1548, from Ignatius to Francis Borgia. In the letter, he is advising Francis to cut in half the time of his spiritual exercises; and he explains why he had before now approved of prolonged contemplation, severe penances, and so on for Francis, and why he now changes his advice.

> First, I should think that the time devoted to these exercises, both interior and exterior, should be reduced by half. We ought to increase these exercises, both interior and exterior, when our thoughts arise from ourselves, or are suggested by our enemy, and lead us to fix our attention on objects that are distracting, frivolous, or forbidden, if we wish to prevent the will from taking any satisfaction in them or yielding any consent. I say that, as a rule, we ought to increase these exercises, both interior and exterior, the more the thoughts are multiplied, in order to conquer them, keeping in mind the character of the individual and the varying nature of the thoughts or temptations, and being careful to measure the exercises to the capacity of the individual; contrariwise, when these thoughts lose their strength and cease, their place will be taken by holy thoughts and inspirations, and to these we must give the utmost welcome by opening to them all the doors of the soul. As a result there will be no further need of so many weapons to overthrow the enemy. From what I can judge of your lordship [Francis was still a Spanish grandee, not a Jesuit] in our Lord it would be better if you were to devote to study about half the time you now give to these exercises. In the future, learning will always be very necessary or certainly useful; and not only that which is infused but that also which is acquired by study. And some of your time should be given to the administration of your estates and to spiritual conversation. Try to keep your soul always in peace and quiet, always ready for whatever our Lord may wish to work in you. It is certainly a more lofty virtue of the soul, and a greater grace, to be able to enjoy the Lord in different duties and places than in one only. We should, in the Divine Goodness, make a great effort to attain this.[10]

This passage is followed immediately by a similar one in the same letter regarding bodily penance, quoted below on page 170. I have quoted this passage at such length because in it there is, in a few words, a coherent summary of several basic teachings and attitudes of Ignatius, expressed in a concrete way for application to an individual who was certainly one of those going from good to better, but also as yet certainly lacking the discre-

9 *SpExMHSJ*, p. 378. Emphasis mine.
10 *LettersIgn*, pp. 179-180.

tion which in Ignatius' opinion should govern all generosity. This paragraph is worth much study to understand all its many implications. These pertain to many topics: changing applications of principles to an individual in different circumstances; adaptations of principles to the needs and capacities of different individuals; the role of contemplation in our lives; the relationship of contemplation to apostolic preparation or action; and the basic aims of a peaceful, quiet mind and of finding God in all things.

Whatever is said about "insisting more on prayer" or other such means of changing ourselves during desolation must be understood within the clear, balanced doctrine expressed in this letter of 1548. We should not forget, however, what is implied about the period preceding this letter, when Ignatius had advised all these spiritual exercises which he now tells Borgia to cut in half, and all the penances which he now tells him to drop. Discretion may sometimes perceive that the counterattack principle calls not for increase of meditation, examination, penance, or work, but for a deliberately chosen lessening of these. It may call for much rest and recreation, or for physical or psychological therapy if physical or psychological illness seems to be a large contributing factor to the desolation or to mark it as non-spiritual altogether. From here on, in explaining Rule I:6, it will be assumed that the reader keeps these counsels of discretion in mind; also, that there will be no need to bring them up again, unless they arise quite naturally from what Ignatius says.

Ways of Changing Oneself against Desolation

In the light of the principles of trust-and-act and counterattack, then, we see the general justification for urging our own efforts to change ourselves in ways contrary to spiritual desolation. In the light of what we have just seen about how Ignatius applies these principles in practice, we are ready to turn our attention to several fundamental ways he suggests by which we can effect such a change.

As the trust-action principle would lead us to expect, the first and most essential step in changing ourselves with the hope of conquering desolation is prayer — in this context, prayer of *petition*. God, for our own sakes, requires our cooperation in such ways as will be called to our attention after prayer; but without God acting in and through our efforts, these efforts to cooperate would be useless. Our following the counsels of sound psychology or of sound common sense can help us to overcome non-spiritual desolations. We can escape the strain of prolonged spiritual desolation by turning away from the spiritual life, ceasing to make God and the Kingdom of God the center of our attention and concern, much as we can be relieved of enduring temptation by yielding to it. But if we are to be faithful and conquer spiritual desolation rather than merely escape from it by running away from the struggle, and if we are to conquer it in a way that brings growth of faith, hope, and unselfish love for God, then we must have God's help and open ourselves to receive it by intense, insistent, perservering, trusting, pleading with him.

Such prayer may be with or without words. Essentially, this prayer is simply a desire springing from faith in God's power, love, and wisdom, a yearning before God for him to rescue us. God reads our hearts. Words formed in imagination or spoken are, however, oftentimes needed by us to keep our attention turned to God in prayer and our desire alive; or at times they serve to relieve a little the tension and anguish in our hearts. Some lines in the Psalms inspired by the Holy Spirit in persons who were experiencing spiritual desolation express this desire perfectly and have a power in them to sustain us, to keep our suffering in union with Christ and the body of Christ. Examples are found in Psalms 13, 22, and 25.

After prayer, Ignatius urges meditation and much examination. Many persons are surprised to find what great attention Ignatius gives to the feeling dimension of Christian life, what great importance he attributes to its power to invigorate or debilitate that life, and also to its value for discerning God's will. Several forms of prayer which he teaches are calculated to touch the affectivity principally through phantasms or the sense imagination. It is, however, equally true that he never weakens in his emphasis on the necessity for a reasoned understanding of Christian truths, for intellectual convictions, for knowing ourselves and the concrete situation in which we find ourselves. He never loses his concern for balanced judgment and straight practical reasoning. So, in the present context of dealing with spiritual desolation, immediately after looking to God for his aid in escaping it, Ignatius tells us to go contrary to the darkness, confusion, and deceit involved in the desolation by meditation and examination. Let us consider these to see more clearly what is meant and how they contribute to changing ourselves in ways contrary to desolation.

Meditation means recalling God's words to us in Scripture and experience, pondering on them and applying them to our present situation, responding with the will and affections (*SpEx*, [56]) in conversation with God as friend with friend, child with father, and so on (*SpEx*, [54]). Taking meditation in its broad sense,[11] Ignatius is telling us also to contemplate in our imagination the events in Christ's life as related in the Gospels (*SpEx*, [101-117]).[12] He even tells us to put ourselves imaginatively as actors within the events (*SpEx*, [114]), and to reflect on what is contemplated, thus drawing from it understanding and inspiration to love and follow Jesus, and entering into conversation with him.

Subjects of meditation should be chosen with a view to what will most meet our needs in this particular experience of desolation with its particular sources, feelings, and consequences. In one experience of desolation we may need meditation on God's presence in all creation, his power and love shown in creating, in the history of God's people before Christ. In another experience of desolation, we may need to meditate on Christ forgiving sin, in another on his resurrection and promise of our resurrection, in still another on his suffering, and so on. In every spiritual desolation, one way or another, we need to meditate on that revealed truth which is most fundamental to our peace, God's infinitely wise, powerful, tender, and faithful love for us in Christ Jesus, and his loving presence to us at all times and in everything.

By thus opening ourselves to God's word, we may hope to experience something of its life-giving light and warmth, to experience God present in it, and so to overcome the spiritual darkness and coldness and the feeling of separation from God which characterize spiritual desolation. The least we may expect is to draw from God's word "courage and energy" to be faithful and patient as long as the desolation lasts.

In order that meditation may be most fruitful for the purpose of counterattacking spiritual desolation, it is necessary that we should have a clear and accurate grasp of what is presently going

11 In this sense it includes what Ignatius calls "contemplation." He does ordinarily distinguish contemplation and meditation; but the distinction is elsewhere made equivalent to two types of meditation, meditation on visible things and meditation on invisible things. See *SpEx*, [47].

12 Two models of contemplations are given here, respectively in the contemplations on the Incarnation and the Nativity.

on in our own conscious life, what led up to it, where it is moving, what light is thrown on it by past experiences. Until we reflectively grasp our own lives, there is no way of knowing how to change them, no way of knowing what the truths of faith or the life of Jesus Christ have to say to us about them. That is why, along with meditation, Ignatius recommends "much examination." The examination he has in mind is not merely a matter of knowing sins and mistakes, though it does include that. It is, rather, a matter of noting thoughts and affections of all sorts which constitute or affect spiritual life, their origin and progression and direction for the future, the whole dynamism of spiritual life. We need to understand what are the sources of this desolation, why we feel sad, disturbed, and discouraged, how the evil spirit is deceiving us through false premises or bad reasoning or through feelings that generate untrue thoughts. Such self-knowledge enables us to bring our present selves to the word of God to be lovingly judged by it, enlightened and healed; to be strengthened and encouraged by it in just the way we need. It enables us to know how best to counterattack the desolation.

Commonly, especially with those inexperienced in seeking self-knowledge, such examination can be carried out successfully only with the help of an experienced spiritual counselor. He or she can, by listening well, help us to notice and say for ourselves what we might never clearly uncover for ourselves unless we were trying to tell some trusted and interested listener — a listener who has adequate learning and experience to be of help.[13] Such a counselor can by questioning help us to notice and bring out much significant data which we might otherwise overlook. He or she can help us relate and interpret what we find so as to reach not only an awareness of the facts but an understanding of them.[14]

What has just been said about reflection on oneself in the Ignatian manner should be enough to distinguish such a response to desolation as he urges, not only from any unreflective, blind thrashing about, but also from any unhealthy self-reflection. For this can be a cause or a consequence of desolation, whether spiritual or non-spiritual. There is a kind of reflection which is a turn-

---

13 See below, comments on Rule I:13, pp. 199-201.
14 For a classical illustration of how a spiritual counselor can relate and interpret data and, in doing so, teach another how to deal with spiritual experience, see Ignatius' letter to Teresa Rejadella, *LettersIgn*, pp. 18-24.

ing in on ourselves in order to feel sorry for ourselves, or to castigate ourselves for not fulfilling our own unreal ideals of ourselves. Unreasonable self-pity or self-blame, swallowing the lies about myself in my relationship with God that flow from spiritual desolation, these only exacerbate the desolation. Reflection in the manner recommended by Ignatius is not for the sake of self-pity or self-blame (unless truth demands it and it helps to attain true peace). It is for the sake of seeing oneself in the light of Christ in order to bring my real self to God in prayer, and in order to understand what further means I must take in order to intelligently apply remedies which may help to conquer the desolation or, in any case, to enable me to grow in faith, hope, and charity during it, and even through it by courageous endurance. Ignatian reflection on oneself during desolation has an active intent. It is part of the whole response that springs from courageous, energetic, discreet charity.

Besides insisting with ourselves on meditation and examination when we are in spiritual desolation, Ignatius also recommends that we insist "on extending ourselves to do penance in some fitting way." Let us ask how he conceives of penance, of its relationship to countering desolation, and what he means by doing penance in a fitting manner. The answers to these questions can be found principally in the *Spiritual Exercises*, [82-89].

Penance, he says, may be interior or exterior. Interior penance is grief over one's sins with a firm purpose of not sinning again. Exterior penance is the fruit of the former and is done in three principal ways, by fasting from food, by shortening sleep, by chastising the body. Regarding food, to retrench from a diet that is too much or too rich is temperance, not penance; penance requires retrenching from what is a temperate diet. Similarly with sleep. By chastising the body, he means wearing a hair shirt, scourging, or something similar. This last mode of penance should, he says, never be done publicly but only in private.

None of these forms of penance are to his mind reasonable if they go beyond causing discomfort and cause any infirmity, or if they conflict with more important activities such as contemplation, apostolic labor, or works of charity. In the letter to Francis Borgia to which we referred above, we see how Ignatius applies his principles. At the beginning of Borgia's conversion to an intense spiritual life, Ignatius had encouraged a program of exterior penance and with excellent results. When, however, these penances (which Borgia seemingly carried to excess) showed signs of being detrimental to his health, Ignatius took a firm stand against them.

> Second, as to fasts and abstinences, I would advise you to be careful and strengthen your stomach, for our Lord, and your other physical powers, rather than weaken them. My reason is that, in the first place, when a soul is so disposed to lose its own life rather than offend God's majesty by even the slightest deliberate sin, and is moreover comparatively free from the temptations of the world, the flesh, and the devil (a condition of soul which I am sure your lordship by God's grace enjoys), I should like very much to see your lordship imprint in your soul the truth that, as both body and soul are a gift from your Creator and Lord, you should give him a good account of both. To do this you must not allow your body to grow weak; for if you do, the interior man will no longer be able to function properly. Therefore although I once highly praised fasting and abstinence even from so many ordinary foods, and for a certain period was pleased with this program, I cannot praise it for the future, when I see that the stomach because of these fasts and abstinences cannot function naturally or digest any of the ordinary meats or other items of diet which contribute to the proper maintenance of the body. I should rather have you seek every means of strengthening the body. Eat, therefore, whatever food is allowed and as often as you find it convenient. But it should be done without offense to the neighbor. We should love the body insofar as it is obedient and helpful to the soul, since the soul with the body's help and service is better disposed for the service and praise of our Creator and Lord.[15]

Note how Ignatius sees a time for us to be hard on ourselves and a time to be gentle, all with a discretion that measures everything for the sake of attaining the goal of God's greater praise and service through our whole being — "a reasonable service."

It is interesting to note that Ignatius makes a special case of sleep. We should, he says, never go beyond temperance in denying ourselves sleep, that is, never do penance in this way, unless it is necessary to do so for a time in order to overcome (*agere contra*) "the vicious habit" of sleeping too much (*SpEx*, [84]). Sticking to the limits of temperance in denying ourselves sleep does not, of course, forbid one from imposing hardship on oneself, for example by rising at night or early in the morning to pray or by putting off sleep in order to meet the demands of charity. It only means that we get overall the sleep we need to carry on prayer and work.

---

15 *LettersIgn*, p. 180. For an excellent statement on the meaning and effects of fasting, see George T. Montague, S.M., *Riding the Wind* (Ann Arbor, *Word of Life*, 1974).

What has been said provides two basic conditions that have to be met if any penance is to be "fitting": it must not cause any infirmity and it must not impede any greater good. However, as Ignatius points out in *SpEx*, [89], we are so easily misled by our fear of discomfort or by rash enthusiasm that meeting these conditions is not easy. Further, what one may be able to bear without causing infirmity or impeding greater good may still for other reasons turn out to be unfitting for this individual at this time. Ignatius is aware of how complex human nature is and how complex are the workings of God's providence in human life. The only way he sees to make sure of what is fitting for the individual is to experiment and see what turns out to be more helpful. More penance may prove fruitful for one person's prayer and work for the neighbor at this time of his life; less may prove more fruitful for another. At another time, the results may be different. One kind of penance may suit one and not another; or the same person at different times may find different kinds of penances helpful. Only God knows with certitude what is best in regard to amount or kind. If we pray for light and do what we can to learn by experimenting, he will lead us to do what is fitting. The one sort of penance we may be sure is fitting is that which is demanded by discreet charity for our neighbors, the sacrifice of food, drink, rest, and comfort in order to supply their needs, physical, psychological, or spiritual.

Fitting penance, therefore, not only respects the reasonable demands of psychic and physical health needed for a life of prayer and charitable works, and the limits set by time and energy needed for these greater goods; but it is also adapted to certain purposes and is positively helpful for these. In *SpEx*, [87] Ignatius mentions three: (1) subjecting the sense appetites to reason, (2) making satisfaction for sin, and (3) our joining penance to prayer in order to open ourselves to receive some grace desired for the praise and service of God. None of these reasons have any necessary relationship with conquering a desolation here and now. They may move us to do penance when we are in spiritual calm or in spiritual consolation. All, however, can have some bearing on changing ourselves in ways contrary to spiritual desolation. Let us look at each one of them.

The first reason is an evident application of the principle of counterattack. If you are intemperate on the side of self-indulgence, then the principle demands: For a time, do not be satisfied with trying to resist the tendency to eat or drink too much, to sleep too much, or to live too comfortably and softly. Rather, go beyond temperance and do penance in order to conquer the evil tendency by doing what is diametrically the opposite. It must be understood, of course, that this is done as an expression of the faith and charity which motivates you to do it and so tends to strengthen the disposition for living in accord with faith and charity. This first reason for doing penance deals with counterattacking desolation when the yielding to self-indulgent tendencies shows up, in the examination, as a likely contributing cause for the loss of divine consolation and the fall into desolation.

The second reason, to make satisfaction for sin, most clearly emphasizes the relationship of exterior penance to interior, the turning to God and away from past sin, with resolution to stay so turned with God's helping grace. This reason for penance is evidently and perennially a part of prophetic teaching and the experience of God's people. It bears directly on countering spiritual desolation only insofar as actual sin has been seen to be a reason for such desolation; there are other reasons for desolation, as we shall see in Rule 9.

The third reason for doing penance is that of joining it to prayer for a desired grace from God, such as sorrow for sin, increase of faith, light to resolve a problem, or the like. This is a reason Ignatius surely has in mind when in Rule 6 he recommends penance as a way of changing ourselves; for, no matter what the cause of spiritual desolation may be, we must always turn to God with prayer for help to overcome it and grow spiritually through it; and we always do well to add some fitting penance to the prayer for God's grace.

Penance is the last suggestion made by Ignatius in this basic rule for dealing with spiritual desolation. It seems clear in the statement of the rule that all the suggestions listed in it are illustrative, not a complete list — even though presumably the principal means Ignatius thinks of for attacking desolation. One additional remark comes to mind, suggested by the final remarks concerning penance, namely, works of charity, especially for those who are suffering mentally and physically. This manner of going against desolation is so fully in accord with the Ignatian spirit and so effective for getting attention off one's own suffering that the question seems worth asking why Ignatius does not include it.

One reason might be that, since the rules are embedded in the *Spiritual Exercises*, Ignatius is thinking above all of those who are going through these exercises in solitude. Further, those who are not in the solitude recommended in *Sp Ex*, [20] for making the Spiritual Exercises will be doing such works of charity as are consonant with their vocations; if not, they are included among the persons to be mentioned in Rule 9 who are experiencing spiritual desolation as a result of negligence and tepidity in the service of God. If they are already doing the works of charity that until now have seemed to be God's will for them, desolation is not a time to change what they are doing by reason of a previous decision (I:5); to do so would open them to some deception, such as that of undertaking works which would weaken their health, withdraw them from what God calls them to do, or make them withdraw from the desolate prayer through which God is purifying and forming them for the sake of helping others.

Such considerations as these lead us to the conclusion that, unless it is clear we have been failing God in our neighbor through indolence in work, we should not by our own initiative undertake new works of any great extent during spiritual desolation—unless, of course, charity clearly demands it. What is important during desolation is to examine our own motivation in works already undertaken and our generosity in carrying them out. We need to purify our motivation from self-seeking, to direct our attention to the needs and sufferings of others, to stir up unselfish sympathy for their sorrows and joys, unselfish concern for their needs, and to carry on generously in serving them. Joined with the work, and even holding priority over it (in accordance with the principle of trust-action) should be constant unselfish prayer for other persons in the midst of serving them. There is so much in the lives of people we know to call forth unselfish compassion, and also unselfish satisfaction in the good that comes to them, and praise and thanks for it. Also, through the news media the tragedy and joy of the whole world are brought near to us, that they may be touched by our love, healed by the power of prayer, and made reasons for our thanks and praise. Christian meditation on the newspaper may make one's own desolation seem a slight matter, and also inspire self-forgetful prayer of praise, thanks, and petition (with or without appropriate feelings).

In these ways we break away from absorption in our own suffering, from the danger of self-pity. We also go contrary to the spirit

173

of indolence and prove in act the untruthfulness of the thoughts which come with desolation—thoughts that our faith, hope, and charity are being lost, that we are separated from God. Our lives of love expressed in unselfish prayer and service will be a testimony from the Holy Spirit and our own spirits that God is surely with us, acting in and through us. Even if such ways of acting do not disperse the cloud of desolation, they will help us endure it without harm, even with great profit for ourselves and others.

Chapter 8

DISCERNING AND RESPONDING TO THE HOLY SPIRIT
DURING SPIRITUAL DESOLATION:
DEVELOPMENT OF THE FUNDAMENTAL COUNSELS
Rules I:7-14

The phrase, "let him think (consider, ponder, meditate on)" or
the equivalent occurs time and again in the rules following Rule
I:6, always involving some form of what Ignatius refers to in this
rule as "meditation" and "examination." Emphasis in these rules
on meditation and examination does not mean that prayer for
God's help loses its primacy among the means for combating
spiritual desolation. Such prayer needs no separate explanation in
relation to the aspects or elements of spiritual desolation focused
on in these rules which follow Rule 6; it will take its coloring from
meditation and examination.

It is these which need elaboration. We must use our intelligence,
Ignatius keeps reminding us, to remember and understand what
we believe as Christians, to see the relationship of this to spiritual
desolation, to note concrete realities both interior and exterior, to
judge these in the light of faith, and to guide our responses accordingly insofar as these are under our direct or indirect control.
Since these rules following on Rule 6 are all elaborations of that
rule, they may to some extent overlap not only with Rule 6 but
also with one another. Nevertheless, each one brings out a special
facet or element in spiritual desolation and temptation; and each
stresses some intelligent way of dealing with it based on Christian
faith and Christian experience.

Spiritual Desolation as a Challenge. Rule I:7

The facet of spiritual desolation brought out in Rule 7 is its
meaning as a challenge, a chance to prove loyalty when the going

is rough and to grow in living faith despite the loss of all delightful feelings in doing so, despite all the painful harassments which the evil spirit musters to deter us from God's praise and service.

> Rule 7. Let one who is in [spiritual] desolation consider how the Lord has left him to his natural powers so that he may prove himself while resisting the disturbances and temptations of the enemy. He is, indeed, able to do so with the divine aid, which always remains with him even though he does not clearly perceive it. For, although the Lord has withdrawn from him his bubbling ardor, surging love, and intense grace, nevertheless he leaves enough grace to go toward eternal salvation.

As we shall see, this same challenging character of spiritual desolation comes up in Rule 9 as one of the main reasons why God allows it. In order to meet the challenge, Ignatius indicates in a general way some suitable content for the meditation and examination of the desolate person.

He calls the desolate person to consider the truth of Christian faith that God is faithful, that he never deserts us, no matter how it seems to us at the moment, that he is *always* lovingly and powerfully present, keeping us sheltered in the shadow of his wings, putting his power at our disposal in the measure and in the way it is needed in every situation to accomplish the glory he plans for us.

An unreflective reading of the first sentence in Rule I:7 could easily mislead us into thinking that Ignatius is saying that God withdraws His grace and leaves us on our own. He tells the one in desolation to "consider how the Lord has left him to his natural powers." This is an unfortunately inaccurate expression of his thought, which, taken literally and without interpretation by the context, would contradict all the rest of Rule 7 and the last part of Rule 11 (which is really a restatement of Rule 7). Only consider the immediately following assertions, that the desolate person is able to resist all disturbances and temptations "with the divine aid, which always remains with him even though he does not clearly perceive it," and that God "leaves enough grace to go on toward eternal salvation." Clearly, in the light of these assertions what Ignatius says in the earlier statement means one of two things, or both. He may mean that we *feel as if* left to our natural powers. Or else he may mean that we are left without the grace of *consoling feelings*—which is truly a grace, but by no means the only or even most important grace God gives to keep us faithful and growing from good to better. Recall, for example, what was said above[1] regarding "courage and energy" to live the life of faith. This point will become clear as we see now what sort of examination this rule calls for.

We saw, when commenting on Rule I:6, that examination is needed in order to let the truth of God's revelation, which we assimilate in meditation, have its full effect on our lives, judging, guiding, inspiring, and supporting us in living as Christians. For that purpose we need to note what is really going on. For instance, we need to see whether we are letting the truth of God's faithfulness shape our thoughts and affections or allowing the evil spirit through our desolation to shape them in a contrary way. We need to take note of the evidence other than spiritual consolation that the Holy Spirit is present and acting in us—evidence such as the faith we truly do have, the charity shown in deeds, and shown too in the very anguish of spiritual desolation. (For, as we saw, only one who believes and loves can experience *spiritual* desolation.) We need to see whether or not it is negligence and tepidity in our love for and service of God that is hindering reception of his spiritual consolation. We need to investigate how our feelings are distorting our thoughts, how objective reality as we can apprehend it through faith and prayerful reflection on inner experience is being blocked out by feelings which give rise to thoughts that are not in accord with reality.

It will help us toward apprehending the realities of our situation when we are in spiritual desolation, and thus also help toward meeting the challenge of such desolation, if we now recall something of practical consequence which emerged from our study of spiritual consolation and desolation when we were commenting on Rules I:2-4. We were led to the conclusion that consolation is not itself an increase in the essential acts of faith, hope, and charity, any more than desolation is necessarily a decrease. Rather, because of the intensified contrary feelings in each of these experiences, faith and hope and charity are *experienced as if* intensified or *as if* dying out. So, we must understand that what Ignatius refers to in Rule 7 as withdrawn by God in time of desolation is not the essential acts of love, but the warm surging *feelings* of love. To be without these is to be without an "intense grace," because they are from

1 See above, pp. 63-69.

the Holy Spirit through living faith and, of themselves, they tend toward and make easier more intense acts of faith and hope and charity, as also acts which express these—just as, by parallel, the coldness and deadness of spiritual feelings make difficult and, of themselves, tend toward a decrease in those acts. However, to have the gift and grace of the sweet, ardent, joyful, powerful feelings of consolation withdrawn is not the same as being left without any graces of the Holy Spirit that help us live an intense Christian life.

There are other graces, less obvious to us in desolation, which, if recognized, accepted, and cooperated with, can be at least as effective as consolation. Ignatius indicates this truth in Rule 7. It is even clearer in Rule 11: "On the other hand, let him who is in desolation keep in mind that, drawing energy from his Creator and Lord, he has great power, with the grace offered him, enough to resist all enemies." The Vulgate version is stronger yet. There the one in desolation is assured of being able, by God's power, "to conquer easily all his adversaries."[2] By grace other than consolation not only can those who are in desolation successfully resist the evil spirit and the desolation he causes; they can triumph over him and do so easily. In spiritual desolation, we can still do what Paul says no one can do except under the influence of the Holy Spirit, that is, say in all sincerity of living faith "Jesus is Lord" (1 Cor. 12:3). In spiritual desolation, "charity, . . . patience, kindness, goodness, trustfulness, gentleness, and self-control" (Gal. 5:22), the fruits of the Spirit, can be obviously in our lives and manifest to others the hidden "peace and joy" that are essential to actuated Christian consciousness, but are drowned out of the subject's self-awareness by the waves of desolation.

Patience and Expectation. Rule I:8

As long as the conviction of God's faithful love giving grace at all times, and also the clear-headed insight into the realities in our experience of desolation are sustained, we can meet the challenge of desolation with courage and energy rooted in faith. However, certain aspects of desolation make it difficult to sustain such conviction and insight. Without these aspects of desolation in mind, Rule 8 can sound like a useless repetition of Rules 6-7 with a routine exhortation to patience added on.

Rule 8.   Let him who is in [spiritual] desolation work at holding

2 *SpEx*MHSJ, p. 382.

on in patience, which goes contrary to the vexations that come at him; and, while taking unremitting action against such desolation, as said in the sixth rule, let him keep in mind that he will soon be consoled.

There is here no explicit mention of those aspects of desolation which make Rule 8 significant, and which enable the reader who understands them to see the significance of the rule. Let us, then, look for those aspects of desolation which are implied by the need for patience of a very special sort in anyone who is going to come through a serious spiritual desolation a better rather than a weakened Christian.

One presupposition of the need for patience in desolation is that the latter can be prolonged. Usually, however, it is not. Usually what Jesus said to the apostles can be said in an applied meaning about what goes on in the consolation and desolation of Christian life. "A little while and you will see me no more; again a little while, and you will see me" (John 16:6). Consolation and desolation come and go in a rhythm like the crests and troughs of waves and, like these, are of varying heights and depths. Unlike waves in physical nature, however, the rhythm of crest and trough in spiritual experience is an irregular one. Sometimes the periods of consolation and desolation that succeed each other are both prolonged. Sometimes they follow each other so rapidly as to bewilder the person.[3] Sometimes the desolation can be brief and the consolation long; sometimes the consolation brief, preceded and followed by long desolation. Obviously, in long desolation the patience of which Ignatius speaks in Rule 8 is called for if we are to sustain faith in God's faithful love and insight into the realities of our faith-life during that time.

Patience, however, is not only needful when desolation is prolonged by an objective temporal standard. Any intense desolation which is brief by such a standard is long by the standard of human time, the time of human experience. For one in pain, how long "a little while" may be! For one in love, when feeling separated from the beloved, especially when tempted to doubt about being loved or about his or her own love, and while waiting for assurance and for presence and union, how long "a little while" may be! (Recall again in this respect what we already saw about spiritual desolation, that it is possible only in proportion to one's love for

3 *Autobiography*, no. 21; in *St. Ignatius' Own Story*, p. 18.

God.) Patience of the sort which Ignatius has in mind, and which we shall consider in a moment, is necessary even for a brief spiritual desolation of unusual intensity.

Not only is a little while a long while when spiritual desolation is acute; there is a feeling in such desolation that consolation will never come again in this world, that life will go on to the end being desolate—even though the subject may have an intellectual judgment that such feelings and the thoughts which spontaneously arise from them are untrue. In fact, spiritual desolation tends to blot out not only the expectation of future consolation but even the memory of past experiences of consolation which might ground hope for the future. Those who keep a spiritual diary are sometimes amazed when, during desolation, they look back over the record of the preceding period of their life and find it studded with spiritual consolations. Spiritual desolation seems to cause amnesia regarding spiritual joy. Recall the experience Ignatius relates in his *Spiritual Diary* and to which we referred above on page 136 in our earlier description of desolation. In the midst of a long series of intense mystical consolations, he suddenly experienced a brief but overwhelming spiritual desolation and during it felt "remote and separated [from the presons of the Trinity] as if I had never felt anything of them or would never feel anything again."[4] In one case, past consolation comes back by the very impetus of desolation, namely when the memory of it adds to the present pain of desolation; for then the memory of lost consolation is a constituent of desolation.

Reflection, and examination of one's present experience of desolation in the light of all we have been noting above, will surely help to grasp the real situation to which desolation tends to blind us. It will help us to place it in the flow of temporal life where past and future consolation are real. Joined with meditation on God's faithful love and with all that Ignatius recommends in Rules I:6 and 7, such reflection will surely help us to be patient.

The patience we need, however, as Ignatius is careful to indicate, is not just any sort of patience. It is patience of a very special sort, specially apt for meeting desolation as a challenge. A patience that merely renders us willing to wait passively for release from desolation is good but by no means adequate. We need a patience in

4 *Spiritual Diary,* [144]; in W. J. Young's translation, no. 40 (March 12), p. 32.

accord with the principle of counterattack, a patience that enables us to persevere energetically in "unremitting action against such desolation," in order to blunt its impetus and cut off its source of power. We need a patience which is "contrary to the harassments" of desolation or, as the Vulgate version of Rule 8 puts it, which is "dead set precisely against the harassments of desolation and resists them from a diametrically opposite stance."[5]

Ignatius assumes that such patience will not be given without prayer, and that even in answer to prayer it will not come without our effort. The desolate person is not only to pray but, he says, to "work at holding on in patience." The *Versio Prima* reads: "let the desolate person work *with all his might* to possess himself in peace."[6] In the Vulgate version we are told: "The hope and thought of consolation to come in a little while must be *summoned up*" by our initiative and effort.[7] Patience, like God's other gifts, is ordinarily given through our own free, energetic exertion (which is also his gift). Our effort or work to achieve patience during and against desolation is, presumably, after prayer, constituted principally by the meditation, examination, and penance recommended in Rule 6. Insofar as such patience is attained, it enables the desolate person to live in darkness with trust in God's faithful love, to hope for the coming light, to act meanwhile with courage and energy against the inclinations and thoughts that derive from desolation.

The moving exhortation in 1 Peter, 5:6-11, if read with reference to the inward suffering of desolation, says with the power of God's word what Ignatius is telling us in Rules 7 and 8:

> Humble yourselves therefore under the mighty hand of God, that in due time He may exalt you. Cast all your anxieties on Him, for He cares about you. Be sober, be watchful. Your adversary the devil prowls around like a roaring lion, seeking someone to devour. Resist him, firm in your faith, knowing that the same experience of suffering is required of your brotherhood throughout the world. And after you have suffered a little while, the God of all grace, who has called you to his eternal glory in Christ, will himself restore, establish, and strengthen you. To him be the dominion forever and ever. Amen.

---

5 *SpEx*MHSJ, p. 380.
6 Ibid., p. 381 (emphasis mine).
7 Ibid., p. 380 (emphasis mine).

If we meet desolation in this spirit of patient faith and hope, we may or may not immediately lessen the desolation, but we will certainly shatter its power to harm us; and we will grow stronger and more pure of heart through the struggle, able to receive God's consolations, when he gives them, unselfishly and humbly. This result Ignatius brings out in the following rules.

God's Reasons for Allowing Desolation. Rule I:9

After looking at its challenging aspect and its seeming endlessness, Ignatius calls attention in Rule I:9 to a third facet of the experience of spiritual desolation; and he offers a way of meditating and examining in order to respond most appropriately. The facet of desolation under consideration is the questioning which spontaneously arises in us and tends toward doubt: Why does a God who loves me leave me in darkness and pain and danger of failing him when he could rescue me? The way Ignatius shows us of meeting this distressing and sometimes dangerous question is to consider several reasons why God's very love for us leads him to act in this way.

> Rule 9.   There are three principal causes which explain why we find ourselves [spiritually] desolate. The first is that we are tepid, indolent, or negligent in our spiritual exercises; and as a result of our failings, [spiritual] consolation departs from us. The second is that it serves to put our worth to the test, showing how much we will extend ourselves in serving and praising God without so much pay in consolations and increased graces. The third is this: spiritual desolation serves to give us a true recognition and understanding, grounding an inward experiential perception, of the fact that we cannot help ourselves attain or maintain surging devotion, intense love, tears, or any other spiritual consolation, but rather that all is gift and grace from God our Lord. So, we do not build a nest on another's property, elevating our mind in a certain pride or vainglory, giving ourselves credit for devotion or other constituents of spiritual consolation.

If we read this rule within the whole context of Ignatius' teaching on how to act during spiritual desolation, we shall see that it is not meant to accuse us or to justify God by telling us that we are getting what we deserve and therefore ought to keep quiet and take our punishment. Rather, like all the other rules, it is meant to take some of the sting out of spiritual desolation, to be a source of encouragement. A careful analysis will show this intention, and also show us how to draw out of the rule the comfort intended for us.

To do this, a number of likely misunderstandings must be eliminated. When Ignatius talks about "the causes which explain why we find ourselves desolate," he is not intending to take up again what he has done in Rules I:2 and 4, where he says that the instigating or prompting cause of spiritual desolation is the evil spirit. The purpose here is to point out some reasons why God who gives us spiritual consolation allows us to lose it; and even, beyond that, allows the evil spirit to instigate spiritual desolation. Since the reasons are God's reasons, they are reasons of infinite wisdom and infinite love for us. Consequently, what Ignatius is telling us in this rule is to meditate on desolation in the light of our faith in God's love and wisdom, in order to understand how it is not despite God's love, but *on account of it*, that we find ourselves in spiritual desolation. This is one form of the meditation he calls for in Rule I:6.

We are all somewhat like the apostles when Jesus told them he was going away and they would see him no more. They were sad. All they could think of was their loss of Jesus. Their emotions fixed their attention there on the source of their sorrow. Consequently, they could not respond in a way that would go along with the heart of Christ who was telling them what would give them his joy. They could not even think to ask why he was going. So, Jesus finally said: "I tell you the truth: it is to your advantage that I go away, for if I do not go away, the Counselor will not come to you; but if I go I will send him to you" (John 16:7). He is trying to get their minds off the sorrow of anticipated separation and on to the reasons for it, reasons springing from his love and the Father's love for them. If they could only grasp why Jesus is going away, then they could deal with their sorrow; and they could also respond to Jesus' departure in such a manner as to cooperate with what he was doing, and grow through it in the way his love intended. In like manner, Ignatius is telling us, when in desolation, to turn our attention to the reasons why God in his loving providence lets it be. We must try to see our experience of desolation from God's side, as he sees it with immeasurable love for us.

To do this we must first clear away any misunderstanding about God's causing desolation, and then get clearly and firmly fixed in our minds the basic principle controlling any conjectures about God's reasons for taking away his consolation and letting us endure spiritual desolation.

Although it is God who takes away consolation, it would be a grave error to think that God actively causes desolation just as he causes consolation. There can be no question of God's being the prompter or instigator of desolation. In Rules 1 and 2 Ignatius asserts quite simply that it is the evil spirit who prompts or instigates those feelings which constitute spiritual desolation in a maturing Christian, while the good spirit prompts all that is contrary to desolation. The good spirit, it is true, influences reason in the regressing Christian, and through reason he causes pangs of conscience; but that is not the same as spiritual desolation and, in any case, Rule 9 is not addressed to regressing Christians.

Is there any sense in which God does cause spiritual desolation? He does directly withdraw, or cut off, the gift of spiritual consolation and thus leaves us in a state of calm. This is a step in the direction of desolation. He also allows or permits spiritual desolation to be prompted by other agents; but that is not the same as his instigating it himself. One may be responsible for allowing something that he or she could prevent. To be responsible for allowing the active cause to act is not the same as actively causing. There seems to be only one way in which God can be said to contribute actively toward effecting spiritual desolation: He may, in his providence over human history, actively lead us into situations where we will be subjected to forces that prompt desolation in us. Perhaps there is a parallel here with the Spirit leading Jesus into the desert to be tempted by Satan or leading him into the final crisis of his life on earth in which, at Gethsemane and on Calvary, he experienced the depths of spiritual desolation.

Now, let us ask why God would withdraw spiritual consolation and allow spiritual desolation to be caused in us, why he would even lead us into a situation where this will take place. If spiritual consolation is a fruit of living faith, inspired by the Holy Spirit and of itself tends to support and bring about a life of fuller faith, hope, and charity, why would God want to take it away? Why would he not rather give it all the time? If, on the other hand, spiritual desolation is anti-spiritual in origin and tendency, why would God even want to allow desolation? In answer to these implied questions, Ignatius in Rule 9 gives three principal reasons that occur to him. Before looking at these reasons, we need to have firmly fixed in mind what our faith in God's love, wisdom, and power requires us to hold as the guiding principle to which every specific reason suggested to explain why God allows spiritual desolation has to conform. In one of his letters, Ignatius states it firmly, clearly, and without qualification: "For we must always suppose that whatever the Lord of the whole world does in the souls of men is either to give us greater glory or to lessen our evil if he does not find better dispositions in us."[8]

If God withdraws spiritual consolation which he could continue to give and allows spiritual desolation which he could prevent, it can only be because at certain times in our lives he sees desolation serving his loving aims for our good better than consolation would. Spiritual consolation as we experience it in this life is not an end, is not for its own sake; it is merely a means, a very precious one when suitable, but only one means among others employed by the Holy Spirit to help us grow into union with God and each other in Him, to bring about the greater glory of God in us, to help us come fully alive. Sometimes spiritual consolation is needed to help us grow. At other times, he sees that it is better to allow us to suffer spiritual desolation; and during it to continue to encourage, teach, and inspire us. In this way he gives increase of purity and depth to our faith, hope, and charity in a way that would be impossible during spiritual consolation. At still other times, the Spirit sees that it is better for us if he withdraws consolation and works in us while we are in a state of spiritual calm.

While Ignatius does seem to be more uneasy about prolonged calm than spiritual desolation during the Spiritual Exercises (*SpEx*, [6]), nevertheless, his uneasiness is not an assumption of fault on the part of the exercitant or a condemnation of him. At other times than the Spiritual Exercises, he is not in the least uneasy with those who do not experience many consolations, so long as they are praying as best they can, doing their work with a pure intention, seeking only God's will in everything, and growing in "solid virtues."[9] After a glowing passage in a letter to Francis Borgia in which he declares how we need the "gifts and graces" which are spiritual consolations in order to serve God, Ignatius concludes: "It is for this reason that we should desire these gifts, or some of them, and spiritual graces; that is, *insofar as they are a help to us*, to God's greater glory."[10] He goes on to illustrate how in some cases they may be a hindrance rather than a help.

On the basis of our general principle, we can now see better the significance of the "three principal causes" for desolation given by

---

8 *LettersIgn*, p. 18.
9 Ibid., pp. 254-255, 342; *Cons*, [260].
10 *LettersIgn*, p. 181 (emphasis mine).

Ignatius. We can see them as marks of God's merciful concern. If we miss that, we miss the whole point. However, if that is so, two questions arise. The first is this: From a practical point of view, is there any need for studying particular reasons? Is it not sufficient for dealing with desolation to believe that whatever God gives or allows, spiritual calm or desolation or consolation, is from his love and so should be accepted and made the most of? In fact, is not this simpler way also the better way? The answer is that to make the most of spiritual desolation, we must go against it vigorously and intelligently, using the means studied in Rules 6-8. Now, to do that we need to know as best we can why God is allowing this particular desolation, what he intends for us through it. Only in this way will we be able to respond as fully and wisely as we can. Consequently, besides meditation on the truth that God loves us and makes all, even spiritual desolation, work for our growth toward greater union with him, we need examination of our lives to see more particularly what God is saying to us through any particular desolation, or intending to do for us through it, so that we can respond accordingly.

Given that spiritual desolation, despite all appearance, is really the consequence of God's merciful concern, the second question that arises is this: Why then resist it? Are we resisting God's will for us, impeding the good he wants for us, by resisting desolation? Not at all. Recall that God does not actively prompt desolation. He withdraws consolation (which leaves us in spiritual calm) and *permits* the forces of evil, Satan or our sinfulness, to prompt it actively. He never wants us to accept desolation without struggling against it; to open ourselves to it without resistance would be to open up to those forces that tend to destroy our faith and hope in him and our love for him. His reason for permitting desolation is that *through resisting* we grow in courageous faith, hope, and charity in ways we could not in spiritual consolation or calm. It is when we fail to respond aggressively to spiritual desolation that it cannot fully serve his loving purpose in allowing it.

The first cause, Ignatius says, why we find ourselves desolate is our own fault, our tepidity, indolence, or negligence in our spiritual exercises. He is not saying that everyone who falls into tepidity or the like experiences spiritual desolation; and much less is he stating that everyone who experiences spiritual desolation has failed in this way. There is no necessary bond asserted between negligence in God's service and spiritual desolation. God's freedom is at work. Ignatius is saying that indolence and neglect in spiritual life comprise one possible reason among several principal ones why God leads us to spiritual desolation; and it should, therefore, be checked out. For spiritual desolation could be God's way of calling the desolate person to awareness of and conversion from the spiritually indolent way of life he or she has fallen into. God could, however, bring about a like effect in a different person through the gift of consolation of a sort to stimulate a more generous response. He might also achieve this purpose during spiritual calm by giving insights on the truths of faith and by leading the person to courageous and energetic resolution. God knows and gives whatever is best for each of us in each concrete situation of life. Desolation might be better for this person in this situation, not only because it will be more effective for repentance than consolation or light and resolution in calm, but also because there are other gains, for example, the teaching given in the third reason (which we shall take up in a moment), or the growth in sympathetic understanding of others in spiritual desolation.

If failure to be faithful and generous is the reason why God takes away consolation and allows desolation to overtake anyone, it is important for that person, through self-examination, to become aware of it. For then, the way to combat the desolation is obvious and will take on a different character than it would if something other than spiritual tepidity were the reason. So also, on the other hand, to think desolation is occasioned by one's failure to be generous when this is not the case could cause worse confusion and pain and prevent the desolate person from cooperating with God's providence working through the desolation.

The second reason God may have in mind for our spiritual desolation is said to be that desolation serves to put us to the test, thus giving us an opportunity to show how generous we will be in praising and serving him without the delights that reward past service and render present service sweet and easy. There are really two reasons here or, let us say, two sides to this second reason.

The first side is one we have already noted in Rule 7: Desolation serves as a challenge. Even one who is not tepid, indolent, and negligent in God's praise and service needs at times a challenge to draw out and develop potentialities which can grow best right now in desolation. This will happen under the inspiration and guidance of the Holy Spirit who is, as we saw, in reality though not in our perception, just as faithfully and lovingly and powerfully present to us in the darkness of desolation as he is in the light of consolation. When endured and struggled against with the courage, energy, patience, and discretion which the Spirit actuates from within our personalities, desolation helps to purify us of egoism, of childish need for rewards as a motive for praising and serving God. It demands actualization of a spirit of utter abandonment to God's will. It is the occasion for realizing a faith that is more purely faith in God alone, that seeks God in himself and for himself rather than seeking the consolations of God for our own selves. No one can grow as a Christian without any spiritual consolation, that is true; but it is also true that without spiritual desolation, we who are wounded by original sin would likely remain shallow—children, so to speak, spiritually spoiled.

We mentioned that there are two sides to the second reason for which God allows spiritual desolation. The other side of this second reason is closely related to the one we have just looked at: Through spiritual desolation we can be enlightened about our own love for God. If in desolation we are surprised by the selfishness in ourselves which we had not expected to see, such enlightenment will be an aid to humility. If we are surprised by the faithful love God's grace makes possible in us even in desolation, this enlightenment will encourage us. At one time we need one of these revelations and at another time the other. A word about each one.

In spiritual consolation we are carried along by our feelings. All is easy because all is sweet and satisfying to self. In some spiritual consolations, it is hard to determine (1) to what extent our praying and working with fervor and devotion, our dealing with others graciously and gently, result from loving God for his own sake and our neighbors with and in God for their own sakes, and (2) to what extent we are acting as we are because to do so brings us such warmth, sweetness, delight. During consolation most of us feel confident that it is the former because for the moment we *feel* so selflessly in love with God. When the feelings of consolation are withdrawn, then is the moment of truth.

We may find that we are like most who fall in love with another human person. Those who are in love feel utterly selfless, each in regard to the other. (Merely selfish desire for another as a sex object is not what I mean by being in love.) Those in love may be ready to risk or to sacrifice very much for the beloved. But the question stands: Is this, in ultimate analysis, principally for the beloved's own sake or for the lover's sake, the beloved being so desirable, so fulfilling to the lover? Are the lovers really loving each other because of the sweetness experienced in such love? Such love, it is true, can give rise to heroic exploits. But what is the ultimate object of love, the other or self? The truth comes out when feelings go dead for a prolonged period. How does one act toward the other and why? Does he or she continue to be gracious and generous, thoughtful, attentive, ready to serve, ready to sacrifice comfort or even life itself? Further, does the lover act this way out of genuine concern for the other or because he or she would be ashamed of self to do otherwise?

Romantic love is ordinarily, in ultimate analysis, self-centered, mainly if not totally so. Years of married life or of devoted friendship, years of working through periods of darkness, misunderstanding, mutual selfishness, years of mutual self-sacrifice and patience, with much reflection and prayer and struggle with self, all with the grace of God—these years are needed in order for what begins with falling in love to grow into any great measure of genuinely unselfish love of each for the other in and for his or her self.

There is a parallel here with our love for God. In consolation prior to the purifications of spiritual desolation, our love for God is usually, in ultimate analysis, mainly love for self: We find satisfaction and happiness in loving and serving him; and, whether we recognize it or not, that is why we do so—not only for that reason, but mainly so. In desolation, we *feel* unloved by God and *feel* unloving toward him. Light, sweetness, joy, peace, are lost. There is "nothing in it for me" now. At that time, how generous, devoted, faithful are we? That is the test. If we lose heart, slack off our prayer and work, grumble, become harsh toward others, thoughtless and neglectful, then we may well think that the overflowing feelings of love and the apparently unselfish generosity in time of consolation are perhaps only apparent or, at best, a transient thing completely dependent on having sweet feelings.

What can and does sometimes happen is that during desolation we continue to praise and serve the Lord just as faithfully and lovingly as during consolation. We may see this fact ourselves, without help; or, misled by our loss of the feelings of love in our affective sensibility, we may need a spiritual counselor to point out to us the facts that are obvious to anyone else. In either case, the Holy Spirit allows desolation in order that in this way he may show us the firmly rooted charity which he is creating in us, and thus lead us back to a consolation based on the experience of desolation. At times we need this latter kind of consolation to give us courage and joy in the realization that despite our weakness without God, he actually is with us, transforming us into his likeness, that our lives of prayer, sacrifice, striving, through his kindness and power are showing His glory.

The third of the principal reasons which God has, according to Ignatius, for depriving us of consolation and allowing desolation is also to enlighten us, to teach us a truthful, humble, attitude toward the experience of spiritual consolation. This reason presupposes that, although spiritual consolation is a gift of God, it can be misunderstood and misused. Of itself, as we have seen, it tends to support the growth of faith, hope, and charity; but it does not necessarily effect such growth. We can make it the occasion for vainglory, for thinking ourselves better than others, for attributing to ourselves the work of God, for failing to stand before God truthfully in utter dependence and gratitude for a gift that He alone can give.

In order to prevent or cure such twisting away from truth and turning to our harm what God gives to help us, he must acquaint us with the facts in a way that will be effective of a change of heart. To this end, he has to show us without any room for doubt that we ourselves can neither attain spiritual consolation when we wish and by our own efforts nor maintain it when it is given. We have to understand that God gives it and takes it away as he wills and that, in such consolation just as out of it, we are nothing apart from God's loving power. In order to have the lesson emphasized, we must know further that we cannot even keep from falling into its contrary, spiritual desolation, that we cannot even gain or maintain a state of spiritual calm merely by our own will and effort. In order for the knowledge to effect a change of attitude in us, it cannot be something taken from books of theology or accounts of others' experiences. It cannot be merely our own conclusions from reasoning on the truths of revelation. It has to be a knowledge from inner experience of desperate helplessness in the darkness of desolation. In that experience we know the truth by an "inward experiential perception." The despair to which the evil spirit wants to lead us through spiritual desolation is despair of God's love and help. The despair to which the Holy Spirit wants to lead us through spiritual desolation is despair of ourselves apart from him. The latter despair is truthful; it leads to humility and hope in God, to wonder and praise and gratitude when consolation is given.

To the three reasons which Ignatius gives in Rule 9 why God withdraws spiritual consolation and allows spiritual desolation, others may be added. One which fits with the whole spirit of the *Spiritual Exercises,* which corresponds with the ideal of love that Ignatius holds up to us, is the desire to be one with Jesus in his redemptive poverty, suffering, and humiliation. This reason could be seen as included in or drawn out of the second reason which Ignatius gives. But the redemptive aspect is not there, at least not clearly there, even by implication. In any case, it is well to make it explicit because the conviction that it is one of God's reasons for allowing our desolation can give a meaning to it that is a source of courage. Such a conviction gives us strength to endure suffering in union with Jesus desolate in Gethsemane and on Calvary—with him living in us and loving in us and filling up in us what is wanting to his suffering for his body the Church.

Another reason comes readily to mind when we read St. Paul's words to the Corinthians.

> Blessed be the God and Father of Our Lord Jesus Christ, the Father of mercies and God of all comfort, who comforts us in all our affliction, so that we may be able to comfort those who are in any affliction, with the comfort with which we ourselves are comforted by God. For as we share abundantly in Christ's sufferings, through Christ we share abundantly in comfort too. If we are afflicted it is for your comfort and salvation; and if we are comforted, it is for your comfort, which you experience when you patiently endure the same sufferings that we suffer. Our hope for you is unshaken; for we know that as you share in our sufferings, you will also share in our comfort (2 Cor. 1:3-7).

Desolation, just as consolation, is not only for ourselves. We are not our own; we are not merely for ourselves. We belong to each other in Christ, and each one's consolation or desolation is for the others. By enduring desolation in a Christian way we learn to understand and sympathize with others in desolation, we learn our dependence on others for comfort, we learn how to comfort others in their desolation. If Ignatius had never endured the terrible desolations he did endure, he would never have been able to teach us to understand our experience and to give us the encouragement and guidance that he does give.

191

In Consolation Prepare for Desolation: Rules I:10 and 11

After showing us why God's wise love allows, even leads us to, the experience of spiritual desolation, Ignatius turns to spiritual consolation and tells us in Rules I:10 and 11 what to do during that experience.

Among some there is a tendency to read these two rules as if they were merely parallel to Rules 5-9, rather than as continuous with them. In Rules 5-9, so this opinion goes, Ignatius has instructed us about our attitude toward spiritual desolation and what we should do while experiencing it; now in Rules 10 and 11 he will instruct us about our attitude toward spiritual consolation and what we should do while experiencing it.

If that were Ignatius' intention, however, the content of these Rules 10 and 11 would be disappointing; so much is omitted which we would expect if he intended to parallel his treatment of desolation. There is no instruction on the role of spiritual consolation in Christian life. There is nothing about the time of consolation as a time for finding God's will and coming to new decisions, no instruction on noting the impulses of the Holy Spirit at this time. There is no warning about being detached, not clinging to consolation or selfish satisfaction.

Hence to read Rules 10 and 11 merely as paralleling the advice on time of desolation would leave us disappointed. More than that, it would leave us puzzled. For all we find are two brief statements which speak about consolation entirely in relation to desolation, and which have no other direct purpose than to continue instructing us on how to combat desolation. In Rules 5 to 9 we are told how to oppose desolation while we are experiencing it. In Rules 10 and 11 we are told how to prepare during consolation for combating desolation when it comes, as come it surely will. We are to do this by laying plans on how to act in desolation, by building defenses against the temptations that come during it, by eliminating any attitude in us whereby we fail to see desolation as one of God's ways of teaching us. There is no treatment here of spiritual consolation as a topic of interest in its own right. But let us look at the rules themselves and see what is there.

Rule 10 consists of one compressed sentence addressed to a person in spiritual consolation.

Let him who is in consolation think how he will bear himself in the desolation which will follow, gathering energy anew for that time.

This sentence can be expanded into three distinct but related statements, each of which is worth careful attention: (1) Desolation will follow on consolation; (2) one in consolation should think about how to act when desolation comes; and (3) should renew his or her strength and energy to meet it.

If, during spiritual consolation, we are to take seriously and act on the advice to think about how we will face desolation when it comes and prepare to do so, we must first have a keen realization, or at least a firm conviction, that desolation will soon follow. This is not as easy as it sounds. Even if we easily give a notional assent to the proposition that desolation will soon follow, to realize the truth of it during consolation in a way that moves us to active preparation for coming desolation is almost as difficult as realizing during desolation that consolation will come again soon.

We saw in Rule I:8 how we tend, when desolate, to forget our past experiences of consolation (except when the remembrance adds to the desolation), and to feel it will never come again—though we could not make a reflective, critical judgment to that effect. In a parallel way, during consolation, we tend to forget desolation (unless the remembrance intensifies the present consolation) and to feel it will never come again—although we would never make such a critical judgment here either. At this time, God's presence and love, his providence at work in our lives, the grounds of our hope for the joy of perfect union in eternal life, God's beauty, the wonder of being in Christ—all these are lucid and certain to us. They make our way in life seem perfectly clear. They make all that is against God or irrelevant to seeking and finding him, to bringing about his knigdom among men, appear as obviously contemptible. The call to live in Christ for the Father and for our brothers and sisters in Christ is glorious. How then could anyone who believes as a Christian believes ever be down, depressed, gloomy, confused, drawn to mere earthly things, feel separated from God with us in Christ? So it is until the moment when desolation comes upon us. We are all somewhat like the Psalmist:

In my prosperity, I used to say,
"Nothing can ever shake me!"

Your favor, Yahweh, stood me on a peak impregnable;
But then you hid your face and I was terrified (Psalm 30:5-6).

Until God hides his face, we find it almost unreal to think that desolation can ever happen again. We have to make an effort to remember it has happened and to foresee that it will happen again.

Nevertheless, if I do not look ahead and prepare for that probably imminent moment, it will come upon me with the confusing shock of surprise added to all else in desolation and rendering me less able to bear the impetus of all else. Disappointed expectation may cause complete loss of composure, even bitterness with a tendency to accuse self falsely or to doubt God's faithfulness or to be angry with life, to flail about in any direction in order to take out my dismay and frustration on someone or something. At another time the unexpected shift from consolation to desolation may simply take all the wind out of my sails and leave me spiritually in a state of utter inertia. In every case, the desolation will find me unprepared to take immediate thought about how to meet the situation. Only after a serious struggle to recover from the unexpected collapse of consolation and to pull myself together will I be capable of any sustained and intelligent resistance. By then I may have wasted much time and emotional energy, failed others in need, perhaps forgotten entirely about Rule I:5 and made harmful decisions.

If, on the other hand, I do look ahead, expecting the loss of consolation and the coming of desolation as the normal course of events, I am in a position, with God's grace, to maintain control of the situation, and to render the impetus of desolation ineffectual against my prayer, work, and decisions. I am in a position to counterattack immediately with all the means at hand for doing so.

Before we consider how to prepare for desolation, we should note another attitude during consolation, one that is closely related to, even a contributing cause to, false expectations about the duration of consolation. That attitude is a selfish clinging to consolation for its own sake, because it is delightful, not because it helps to praise and serve God. Inasmuch as this selfish clinging to consolation is present we are unfree toward God's will, resistant to his molding and teaching us through spiritual desolation and spiritual calm as well as through spiritual consolation. In regard to the point of Rule 10, this attitude renders us unwilling to face the fact that

194

desolation will come. Consequently, it prevents us from thinking about how we will face it and from renewing our energy to do so. When desolation does come to one with such an attitude, or even when consolation declines into spiritual calm, the result can be irrational frustration, sadness, bitterness, a closing of the heart to the Holy Spirit's gift of courage, strength, and energy.

Presupposing that we are convinced that desolation is imminent and are ready to accept it from God's love along with the need for painful struggle against it, and presupposing too that we know that we should, while in consolation, prepare to meet it, how do we go about preparing? The first thing to do is to "think" (*piense*). Whether we are in desolation or in consolation, Ignatius continues to insist that we should think; that we should never let ourselves be carried along merely by feelings or desire or fears, but that we assert our intelligence by reflecting, evaluating our affections, and keeping a firm hold on the truths of faith, the realities of experience, and the demands of logical reason.

Ignatius gives no hint in Rule 10 about the content of our thinking except that it should bear on how to act in desolation. In context, he may justly assume that content to be evident; he has just given us five rules on what to do when in desolation. Preparation for desolation would surely include recalling and getting clear in our minds the practical directions given in Rules I:5-9 so that we will not be at a loss when desolation comes.

We can in fact also begin even during consolation to do some of those things which we are told to do in the preceding rules and, in this way, carry out the third point of Rule 10, "gathering new strength and energy for that time." We can, first of all, pray to be given courage, strength, and energy when we will need it. We can meditate on some of the truths of faith which will be a source of strength at that time, such as God's fidelity in love or his power. The present spiritual consolation can be a help to this if we do not merely seek to enjoy the sweetness of the gift but also attend to the love and presence of the Giver, deepening and making firmer our conviction of God's personal love with a reasonable hope that the conviction will survive without consolation to sustain it. We can, through meditation and prayer, build up other related intellectual convictions to support us in time of desolation. Thus, for example, we can think on the value of desolation for growth in faith, hope, and charity when the challenge is faced with fortitude and perseverance. We can reflect on our past experience to see the good that God has worked in us during desolations; we can give praise and thanks to him for this. We can put ourselves on guard against allowing desolation to impel us into changing decisions, recalling any stupid mistakes made this way in the past.

Two further preparations for spiritual desolation which can be made during consolation are explicitated by Ignatius himself in Rule 11:

> Let him who is [spiritually] consoled set about humbling and lowering himself as much as he can, reflecting on how pusillanimous he is in time of [spiritual] desolation without God's grace or consolation. On the other hand, let him who is in [spiritual] desolation keep in mind that, drawing energy from his Creator and Lord, he has great power, with the grace offered him, enough to resist all enemies.

The two preparations clearly hold each other in balance: The first, remembering our pusillanimity in earlier desolation and humbling ourselves, keeps us from being overconfident and careless as we look forward to desolation; the second, remembering God's power at work in us to overcome all hostile spiritual force, keeps the true sense of our own weakness from becoming tense and fearful as we anticipate desolation. Between the two we can maintain a quiet mind, alert and trustful, full of praise and thanks for what God has done in past time of desolation and full of hope for what he will do in the desolation to come.

Besides enlightening us on how to prepare for desolation which will come, Rule I:11, when read in coherence with rule I:9 on God's reasons for permitting spiritual desolation, is advising us about how to eliminate the third of those reasons. In so doing, it goes beyond preparing us for desolation to preventing the desolation that would come if it were needed for that reason. The third reason given in Rule 9 for spiritual desolation is to cure or prevent vainglory arising from spiritual consolation. It is true that spiritual consolation will never of itself lead to anything evil. However, the grace of spiritual consolation does not do away with human egoism or prevent the evil spirit from prompting our egoism to abuse even the grace of God, by giving ourselves credit for what is a gift of God, by trusting in our own strength to face temptations instead of trusting purely in God, by secretly or openly considering ourselves superior to others because we feel so much warmth or devotion.

The sort of response to the gift of spiritual consolation which Ignatius has in mind when he speaks of vainglory, and the reason why he is so concerned with it, can be shown in the gospel story of Peter:

> And Jesus said to them, "You will all fall away; for it is written, 'I will strike the shepherd, and the sheep will be scattered.' But after I am raised up, I will go before you to Galilee." Peter said to him, "Even though they all fall away, I will not." And Jesus said to him, "Truly, I say to you, this very night, before the cock crows twice, you will deny me three times." But he said vehemently, "If I must die with you, I will not deny you" (Mark 14:27-31).

We all know the sequel. If Peter in his time of consolation had humbled himself, acknowledged his weakness and need of God's grace to be faithful under trial, he might not have needed spiritual desolation with temptation and even actual failure to learn. God might have saved him from denying Jesus. If we have meditated on this passage and examined ourselves, we all see ourselves in Peter, here and elsewhere in the gospel story, as God schooled him in humility.

Very different from vainglory or pride and yet bearing a similarity to these, and sometimes a consequence of them, is another danger during consolation. It is one which Ignatius would likely have included here if his intent were to provide a treatment on how to act in consolation, and not merely of how to prepare in consolation for desolation. It might be well to call attention to this danger while we are still considering the dangers already mentioned in Rules I:10-11. This danger is mentioned among the instructions for the director of the Spiritual Exercises. If the director sees that the exercitant is having much consolation, he or she should prevent the exercitant from being carried away into making any precipitous and unconsidered promise or vow (*SpEx*, [14]). Here, as elsewhere, he insists that we take intelligent account of the realities involved: the person's circumstances in life, temperament, individual gifts or lack of them, the helps or hindrances likely to be encountered in carrying out the promise or vow, and the like. Someone in high consolation but inexperienced in the spiritual life can easily be carried away into impetuous and unreasonable commitments. Not every inclination experienced during spiritual consolation is by that very fact God's will. Ignatius' own cautiousness in following such an inclination, even when it comes frequently

197

and during very intense spiritual consolations, is strikingly evident in his *Spiritual Diary.*[11]

Demonic Style and Strategy. Rules I:12-14

The first set of rules is brought to a close with a group of three rules in which Ignatius calls attention to three characteristics of the evil spirit's manner of attacking us. He does so for the sake of putting us on guard, preparing us to meet Satan's attacks effectively by going contrary. This last group of rules is, then, continuous and overlapping with Rules I:5-11. All the rules in the first set after 1-4 form a unity: All of them are centered on how to counteract the action of anti-spiritual power manifest in spiritual desolation and head-on or deceptive temptations. Rule 12 is concerned with head-on and even violent temptation. Let us read it with this in mind:

> Rule 12. The enemy resembles a shrewish woman, being weak and willful; for it is connatural to such a woman in a quarrel with some man to back off when he boldly confronts her; and on the contrary when, losing courage, he begins to retreat, the anger, vengeance, and ferocity of the woman swell beyond measure. In like manner, it is connatural to the enemy to fall back and lose courage, with his temptations fading out, when the person perform- ing spiritual exercises presents a bold front against the temptations of the enemy, by doing what is diametrically the opposite. If, on the contrary, the person engaged in spiritual exercises begins to panic and to lose courage while suffering temptations, there is no beast on the face of the earth so fierce as is the enemy of human kind in prose- cuting his wicked intention with such swelling malice.

In the earlier rules Ignatius spoke of patience, of faith in God's help even when it is unfelt, of effort against desolation. In Rule 12, all this is involved but the tone and the stress are different. The tone is more buoyant and the stress is on the happy or terrible consequences of our response to the onset of the evil spirit: the happy consequences of facing the evil spirit promptly and boldly, by opposing him diametrically and aggressively; the miserable consequences of any timidity, hesitation, or compromising. The tone of this passage is not so much that of the teacher or even the strategist or tactician as it is that of the leader who has already struggled with this enemy may times; who knows by experience the enemy's terrifying strength and ridiculous weakness, his strange character and devious style; who has conquered fear in himself without growing careless and rash; who knows the divine power

---

11 *Spiritual Diary*, [1-153]; in W. J. Young's translation, pp. 1-34.

available to him and is confident of overcoming the enemy by that power; who can assure others of overcoming him if only their hearts will not fail.

But if the heart should fail, this enemy feeds and grows strong on our timidity, cowardice, discouragement. He quickly grows more ferocious than any beast on earth, incomparably more powerful than any earthly power, fiercely tenacious in his malignant purpose springing from his "damned malice" (*SpEx,* [331]).

On the other hand, when without hesitation one faces this enemy boldly, doing the very opposite of what he is aiming at, then his fierceness and power fade away. "Resist the devil and he will run away from you" (James 4:7). He is like a dog that barks and growls and makes as if to attack and actually does attack if one shows fear; but, when one turns on him, he runs away to yap at a safe distance, irritating but harmless. The conclusion is: Take heart, be bold, go contrary to the direction of Satan's temptations. Do so not merely with blind determination but with conscious trust in God, aware of his might, wisdom, and love.

> God is our refuge and strength, a very present help in trouble. Therefore we will not fear though the earth should change, though the mountains shake in the heart of the sea; though its waters rage and foam, though the mountains tremble with its tumult (Psalm 46:1-3).

Before a person with such a spirit, Satan will back off.

But he will be back again with a different approach. Rule 13 puts us on guard lest we think all is well when we have faced up boldly to the onset of desolation or temptation and conquered Satan's effort to make us turn back out of cowardice. When open, fierce, head-on attack does not frighten us, nor persistent crushing weight of desolation grind down our power of endurance, then the enemy takes to subtle seduction, to cunning, to deceit. The contrary response here has to be something more than prompt and bold.

> Rule 13. Likewise he behaves as a seducer does, in seeking to carry on a clandestine affair and not be exposed. When such a frivolous fellow makes dishonorable advances to the daughter of a good father or the wife of a good husband, he wants his words and seductions to be secret. On the contrary, he is greatly displeased when the daughter discovers to her father or the wife to her husband his fraudulent talk and lewd design; for he readily gathers that he will not be able to carry out the undertaking he has initiated. In like

199

manner, when the enemy of human kind insinuates into the faithful person his wiles and seductions, he intensely desires that they be received in secret and kept secret. It dispirits him greatly when one discloses them to a good confessor or to another spiritual person who is acquainted with his trickery and malice; for, when his evident trickery is brought to light, he gets the idea that he will not be able to realize the evil plan he has set in motion.

There are endless ways in which the evil spirit plays the impostor, offers counterfeit good in order to swindle us, offers a lesser real good for a better, distracts us, or allures us into a trap through our inadvertence or rationalization. In any artful human swindles or seductions, a principal point of method is to play the "confidence game." Through a false sense of intimate trust, through fear or avarice or some other motive, the victim is persuaded to keep quiet about what is going on—unless it be to consult another whose own ignorance of the ways of the world makes such a person incapable of giving sound advice, and perhaps even allows for his becoming an unwitting accessory to the crime. Once a knowledge-able and honest person is consulted, the deception is uncovered. So also in the evil spirit's fraudulent enterprises, it is essential to his purpose that the victim should speak to no one about the matter—unless it be to another who is inexperienced and unlearned in spiritual matters, and who may be counted on to give bad counsel—perhaps even to get burned himself.

That is why the way to expose and escape Satan has two elements: (1) our being open with someone about our spiritual life and (2) our being sure that the person with whom we are open is not only a good person who truly wants our good, but also a person with adequate learning and experience in the ways of good and evil spirits.

First of all, about our being open. It is true that the longer and deeper one's experience of spiritual life, the more one has reflected on it, the more one has grown in spiritual self-knowledge, in spiri-tual learning, and had experience also of spiritual counseling, both as counselee and counselor, the better can such a one deal with his or her own problems. However, persons who have had the opportu-nities and capacity for such experience, reflection, counseling, learning, are relatively few; and even they have some need of another to take counsel with. The rest of us have greater need, more or less, the more so the less our learning and experience and the more crucial the matter about which we are concerned. The first and most important step in being open to another is our coming to know reflectively with clarity what is going on in our lives. Very few people can come to this knowledge except by trying to tell someone else about it. Thus the two steps of gaining knowledge of what is going on in ourselves and of revealing it to another become fused into one. Often, simply coming to clarity about what is going on resolves the whole problem; it makes the solution obvious and brings peace. At other times, we need counsel.

Not everyone, however, knows how to listen well, how to make the other feel free to talk and talk honestly, by allowing the other to go at his or her own pace and get out in his or her own way what is really being experienced, by helping the other to get at significant matters when help is needed but without putting his or her own thoughts into the other, or without giving advice before listening long enough to really understand, or giving it at a time when the other is unlikely to accept it. Among those who know how to listen, not all have adequate spiritual learning or spiritual experience to understand what they hear or give sound spiritual counseling. They may, as a result, only compound the troubles of the one who seeks help. A good psychological counselor must not be mistaken for a good spiritual counselor, anymore than the other way around. One may, of course, be both. Ignatius is not recommending that we open our temptations to just any well meaning person, but only to "a good confessor or to another spiritual person who is acquainted with his [the evil spirit's] trickery and malice."

While openness with such a person is very helpful, and while our refusing or neglecting to avail ourselves of that help when it is available is refusing or neglecting the help which God offers through others, nevertheless it should be said that one who sincerely desires such help, prays for it, and looks for it—such a person need not be disturbed if the help cannot be found. The Holy Spirit can do immediately in him or her whatever he deigns to do through others, and he will himself counsel anyone of good will who cannot find human understanding and guidance.

What we have just been saying indicates that openness helps to self-knowledge, and self-knowledge in turn helps to openness, and both together help to overcome the deceits of Satan already set in motion. Self-knowledge has another related role to which

201

Ignatius points in Rule 14: It helps us to anticipate and prepare for Satan's attacks.

Whether Satan is trying to beat us down with desolation and violent temptations or trying to catch us with subtle deceptions while we are in desolation or consolation or calm, he does so with knowledge of our strength and weakness. He moves against our weak points and avoids our strength—except when our weakness makes it possible for him to use our own strength against us. To do this he has to know us. Rule 14 calls us to think on this and to draw a practical conclusion:

> So also, in order to conquer and plunder what he desires, the enemy of human kind acts like a caudillo. For, just as a military commander-in-chief pitching camp and exploring what the forces of a stronghold are and how they are disposed, attacks the weaker side, in like manner the enemy of human kind roves around and makes a tour of inspection of all our virtues, theological and cardinal and moral. Where he finds us weaker and more in need of reinforcement for the sake of our eternal salvation, there he attacks us and strives to take us by storm.

All that Rule 14 does is to describe how the evil spirit operates in preparation for attacking us, without drawing any practical conclusion. But surely Ignatius intends us to do that for ourselves. He is telling us about Satan in order to help us to oppose him intelligently as well as boldly. The obvious practical conclusion is that we need to know ourselves, our strengths and weaknesses, and be prepared for the evil one, unless we want to find our defenses penetrated before we know what has happened. We are back at the Ignatian emphasis on examination, reflection on our conscious lives, in order to take possession of ourselves for the service of God.

What this examination reveals will differ with each one. One may find that, like Peter in the Gospel, he believes in Jesus but is still too impetuous and thoughtless; or like John and James, zealous for the kingdom of God in a way that makes for impatience or unkindness: "Shall we call down fire from heaven?" One may find that he loves intensely but without much hope, easily gets depressed or discouraged. Another may be of a buoyant disposition and full of hope, but not really honest with himself or with others. One may be readily and constantly honest and kind in his personal relationships, but tend to be grossly dishonest and ruthless in business enterprises or politics, or be insensitive to social justice. One may strive strenuously and unselfishly for social justice and be harsh with individuals or have a weakness for drink or sex. One may be gentle and generous and have noble ideals but be vulnerable to fear of pain or of humiliation. One who is sympathetic and fearless may lack sound judgment. Wherever the weak point is, there is the likely point where Satan will make trial of us.

We need, then, to know our own strength and weakness in order to know what to pray for and strive to grow in, what situations to avoid, in what situations to seek support or guidance, for what situations to be prepared, and immediately to take a resolute stand, or even immediately to counterattack. It is also well to know where we are strong and where there is little or no imminent danger, so that, while we never get careless, we can free our attention and effort for what most needs it, and not get tense in our watchfulness and aggressiveness against evil in many directions, lest the strain become counterproductive.

Besides knowing the strengths and weaknesses of our temperaments and characters, it is, again, necessary to be aware of what has been going on in us and is going on. Where and how the power of evil will attack depends largely on what moves have just been made. (One could think of many analogies, not only with warfare, but with all sorts of competitive activities.) Thus, if we have just staved off temptation to unkind judgment of others by remembering our own failures and past misjudgments, the enemy may try to use the momentum of our counteraction and carry us on to a sense of false humility, to irrational self-disparagement, to discouragement. If we resist that temptation by meditating on God's great and forgiving love, he may try to lead us on to presumption. If we resist that by recalling God's justice and punishments for sin, he will try to push us into exaggerated fear of God. If we do good works for God, he will try to make us fall into vainglory. When we turn from that with abhorrence, he will suggest that it is better for us to omit good works and thus avoid the danger of vainglory, leaving the good works to others who are more humble people. So it goes, with him always trying to take advantage of every situation, to wear us down, to discourage us and turn us back from the way toward greater charity or closer following of Christ. We on our side have to be always aware of what is going on in each step and to oppose him by going contrary to what he is leading us to (*SpEx,* [349-351]).[12]

---

12 See also *LettersIgn*, pp. 19-22.

To sum up the practical conclusion to be drawn from this description of the demonic style of action against us as given in Rules I:12-14, we can say that effective resistance from our side calls for three things: (1) self-knowledge, of our strengths and weaknesses and of what is currently going on, understood in light of past experience; (2) prompt, bold, confident counteraction, with the confidence rooted in faith in God's power, wisdom, and love; (3) openness with someone who is able to understand spiritual experience, to listen well, and to offer sound counsel when it is needed and when it is time to do so. By God's grace working in us always, whether perceived or unperceived, we can, if we respond to our enemy's attacks in these ways, gradually grow into a balanced, integrated, usually tranquil spiritual life, filled with the glory of God. We can do this, not only despite desolation and temptation, but in a way by reason of them, that is, by meeting the challenge they pose with the discreet, courageous, energetic, faithful love which the Holy Spirit of Light ever present in the darkness of our spiritual desolation pours into the hearts of those who turn to him with trust.

Chapter 9

A SYNTHESIS THROUGH A GOSPEL STORY
Rules I:1-14

We have seen earlier how the appearances of Christ to his loved ones after the resurrection illustrate and confirm Ignatius' description of Christian spiritual consolation.[1] Every main point in his descriptions of spiritual experience, both of consolation and of desolation, and in his counsels on what to do about desolation, receives striking verification in the account of the two disciples on the way to Emmaus (Luke 24:13-52). This event is among everyone's favorites because it is so gracefully told by Luke, and also because we all find ourselves in it. To go through that story again will serve to pull together and illuminate what we have found in Ignatius' rules—and further, perhaps what we have found in the Ignatian rules will enable us to read the gospel narrative with greater insight.

These two disciples are precisely the kind of persons we described under the name of maturing Christians (Rules I:1-2). The central thrust of their lives is toward God. They are by no means yet persons of great faith, such as those whom we ordinarily designate as "saints." They are, in Christ's own words, "foolish men and slow of heart to believe" (Luke 24:25). Nevertheless, in the overall picture of their lives, they are men ascending from good to better, even though at present in one dimension of their lives they are regressing. It seems clear that despite their slowness to understand and believe what was in the sacred prophecies about the humiliation, suffering, and death of the Messiah, they still believe in Yahweh, still believe in the prophecy of a Messiah yet to come; and thus they still hope for the redemption of Israel, only not by Jesus. They are men capable of experiencing a spiritual desolation. If

1 See above, pp. 113-115.

they did not believe, if they did not love the people of God and hope for the redemption of Israel, if they did not love Jesus as a prophet of God "mighty in deed and word before God and all the people" (even though not the Messiah), their desolation would not be a spiritual one, any more than the desolation experienced by the followers of some political zealot or ambitious military man who had suffered defeat.

Let us look closely at their desolation, noting their feelings and the grounds of these feelings. All that comes out explicitly about their feelings is that they were looking sad (Luke 24:25). However, there is no difficulty in understanding what was going on in their hearts when we sympathetically enter into their situation. Their high hopes that Jesus would save Israel were shattered, certainly and to all appearances irrevocably. The focal point of their energies, the good news of the reign of God, was suddenly gone. The person whom they loved with great devotion and reverenced as a mighty prophet was tortured and killed by their own people. He was gone, the one who made God seem so real and so close, who made them experience God's love, who showed them in his person the beauty and power and gentleness of God, who gave them words of eternal life that burned in their hearts and illumined the darkness. He was gone, destroyed by wicked, worldly power. How could they not feel utterly gloomy, confused, deflated, aimless, discouraged, have a sense of faith and hope crumbling, and through all and worst of all, a feeling of separation from God as he had touched them in Jesus, his anointed, his beloved one, a feeling of separation from God because they were identified with the people who had again rejected and killed God's prophet?

There are, we saw in our analysis of consolation and desolation, consequences of the feelings which constitute these affective states. These feelings incline us, even impel us, toward thinking and acting in certain ways. In desolation we can, if we let ourselves, think that what our feelings imply is true and then yield to the inclination to change our previous decisions accordingly. We can begin to think that God really is far off and does not care, that we have cut ourselves off from him and he has rejected us; we can begin to lose faith and hope and love and can decide to turn back from the way on which we had set out to serve God. These actual consequences are not necessary ones; only the tendency in that direction seems necessary. We can resist and conquer the tendency. In the two disciples, we seem to have an example of those who lost heart and yielded to the tendency. While Jesus was with them visibly, speaking his powerful words, doing his mighty works, letting them experience the splendor and power of his personality, there was no problem about believing in him as the Messiah and hoping for the kingdom now. However, assuming they were like the Twelve and that their slowness to understand after Christ's death was there before, they could not even before the crucifixion grasp what Jesus was talking about when he prophesied his suffering and death. They would not let it come through. Here was "the weaker side" which Satan found while making his "tour of inspection." "Where he finds us weaker and more in need of reinforcement for the sake of eternal salvation, there he attacks us and strives to take us by storm" (Rule I:14). They were unprepared for temptation and desolation: They did not know their own weak point; they did not, would not, anticipate what Jesus told them time and again was coming (Rule I:10).

When the challenge to faith and hope came, they could not meet it with intellectual convictions, with courage and energy. Their faith and hope in Jesus collapsed. "We *had* hoped that he was the one to redeem Israel" (Luke 24:21). If they had listened to Jesus' warning and prepared, they might still, by his grace, have been hoping against hope during the darkness, anchored by faith in Jesus' own prophecy, perhaps even in the Old Testament prophecies through which Jesus will soon restore faith, hope, and consolation.

Before seeing how he does this, we should note also how these disciples appeared to be violating Ignatius' Rule I:5—the rule urging that spiritual desolation is no time to change decisions that seemed good in time of consolation or calm prior to the desolation, urging that spiritual desolation is a time to hold on in the directions chosen at those previous times. It fits with all that they say and do if we suppose that the two disciples are leaving Jerusalem because they have given up on the whole enterprise under Jesus' leadership. They are going back to pick up the threads of their lives, as best they can, where they left off to follow Jesus – exactly the decision which the evil spirit wants to bring about in anyone who dedicates himself or herself to close companionship with Jesus and total service of him and the gospel. This decision, which seems so reasonable during desolation, appears, when spiritual consolation or even spiritual calm returns, very stupid and possibly tragic. Jesus will come to save them from stupidity and tragedy. Only He can.

In these two men we have a typical image of ourselves in spiritual desolation, when we need "to change ourselves in ways contrary to spiritual desolation" (Rule I:6). They are utterly "pusillanimous" at such a time (Rule I:11). There they are, talking to each other but neither helping the other, probably digging themselves deeper into the pit of spiritual desolation with all its evil consequences in their lives; for neither one had enough faith or learning or understanding or spiritual experience to help the other. They needed to open themselves to someone who understood God's revelation better than they, who had come to understand the way spiritually good and evil powers work in our minds and hearts, who could understand what was going on in their minds and hearts and lead them to self-knowledge, who could give them guidance on how to resist and conquer the evil spirit, his desolations and temptations, through prayer, meditation, examination, and good works for others (Rule I:13).

Such a counselor was at hand even though they did not know it. They seemed to be left on their own without God's grace, without Jesus. But, as Ignatius says, "the divine aid...always remains" with one in desolation "even though he does not clearly perceive it" (Rule I:7). The Holy Spirit was in their hearts waiting to move them in response to Jesus who was now approaching them on the road unrecognized. "While they were talking and discussing together, Jesus himself drew near and went with them. But their eyes were kept from recognizing him" (Luke 24:15-16). Spiritual consolation seemed over with for the rest of their lives. What could ever give back to them the peace and joy in God which they once had, now that the source of it had been destroyed? How could they ever be glad again? Even the remembered peace and joy of former days was now a cause of bitter anguish. Whatever might be for other men and women of future times, when Yahweh might send his Messiah to save Israel, for them the darkness would be forever. The light of their world was gone, the flame in their hearts was dead forever. So it seemed. In reality Light was approaching unseen along the very road they walked, the Holy Spirit was ready to make their hearts burn within them, consolation was just around the next turn of the road! As Rule I:8 states, "...let him keep in mind that he will soon be consoled."

Now, let us watch how Jesus himself goes about the role of spiritual counselor for those in the depths of spiritual desolation. He begins by questioning them in a way calculated to draw out of them what was troubling them (Luke 24:17-19). Their account of their sorrows (19-24) is certainly a condensed version in Luke, even as is the account of Jesus' opening to them the Scriptures (Luke 24:27) once they had opened their hearts to him. Both must have taken considerable time. It is not until they have finished revealing themselves that Jesus says anything more. In the light of what they have themselves told him, he leads them to deeper self-knowledge, using the Scriptures to judge them and their response to the recent events. They are led through meditation on Scripture and examination of their hearts in the light of Scripture (Rule I:6) to see their own foolishness and slowness to believe what the prophets had spoken and what he had himself at least three times clearly told them before it happened (Luke 24:25). Beginning with Moses he took them through the prophets whom they had read or heard read over and over, showing them what their sluggish hearts, blinded by foolish assumptions and by fear, had not understood before, that it was "necessary that the Christ should suffer these things and enter into his glory" (Luke 24:26-27).

The result of this meditation and examination through which Jesus led them is to break the impetus of desolation, to restore the beginnings of faith and hope—or at least to remove disbelief and despair and to bring a flicker of faith and hope, with spiritual consolation grounded in understanding of Holy Scripture and tending to greater faith, hope, and charity. "Did not our hearts burn within us while he talked to us on the road, while he opened to us the Scriptures?" (Luke 24:32). They were now very likely responding much as the Twelve will when Jesus appears to them and for very joy they cannot quite believe (Luke 24:41). It seems too good to be true, though they cannot doubt either the overwhelming Scriptural evidence which Jesus presents or the evidence of their own senses.

When they draw near to their destination and Jesus makes as if to go further, they plead with him, "constrain" him to stay with them. Another effect of the meditation and examination through which Jesus has led them now appears. Their constraining Jesus (not yet known as Jesus) to stay with them reveals a desire rooted in hope, rooted in the flickering revival of faith. They want Jesus to stay—no doubt because they had grown to love this man who had pulled them out of the depths, but also because they desired to be more fully restored to life. They half believed it could be; and the desire burning in their hearts was a prayer for the greater faith and hope, the greater peace and joy of God from faith. (See Rule I:6 on prayer as the first response by a person in desolation.)

It is in answer to this prayer that Jesus brings them to what seems to be a full assent of faith to the truth of his resurrection and so to a consolation that impels them on the way back to Jerusalem, back to the little flock, back to the way of life they had chosen before tragedy and spiritual desolation had taken them unprepared and turned them away from it.

> So he went in to stay with them. When he was at table with them, he took the bread and blessed, and broke it, and gave it to them. And their eyes were opened and they recognized him; and he vanished out of their sight. They said to each other, "Did not our hearts burn within us while he talked to us on the road, while he opened to us the Scripture?" And they rose that same hour and returned to Jerusalem (Luke 24:29-33).

There in Jerusalem their newly revived faith is confirmed by the testimony of the Eleven and others (Luke 24:33-34) and by the appearance of Jesus to them all, giving further proof of his bodily reality (24:36-43), again opening the Scriptures (24:44-46), giving his mission (24:47-48), promising the Holy Spirit and power (24:49), and ascending to heaven (24:50-51). The whole mystery of Jesus is experienced and greater understanding of it is hoped for through the Holy Spirit. All are filled "with great joy" and are "continually...blessing God" (24:52).

Now the two of them would surely feel that they could never again experience desolation. How could they ever be desolate, now that they were sure Jesus had risen and promised to be with them always? But the seemingly impossible can happen and will happen. What Ignatius would tell them or anyone in a like time of consolation would be to expect desolation to come and to prepare for it. Do not let yourselves be taken again completely off guard and unprepared as you did before. Remember now how pusillanimous you were when in desolation, how utterly dependent on God's help to overcome it, how he was in fact lovingly and powerfully present when he seemed to have left you alone, how powerful you were against desolation and temptation when he came to your help through meditation and prayer.

Reflect on the whole experience, know your weakness, pray for help. If you are ready and open to the Holy Spirit of Jesus, he will enable you to endure with courage and energy, to enter even by desolation more deeply into the mystery of Christ; and he will bring you out again into the joy and peace of the risen Lord.

PART IV

THE EVIL SPIRIT

IN TIME OF CONSOLATION

Rules II:1-8

Chapter 10

DECEPTION BEGINNING IN SPIRITUAL CONSOLATION
Rules II:1-7

The purpose for the first set of rules, we said, is threefold: (1) to help us reflectively and discriminatingly to recognize, within the flowing mass of interior motions, those which are spiritual and those which are anti-spiritual; (2) to help us to understand respectively their characteristic features, their origin, and their consequences; and (3) finally and principally, to help us to remain actively receptive of the Holy Spirit's light—which during the darkness of desolation is experienced as dry but firm intellectual conviction of the central truths of faith, and as resolute trust, courage, and energy to withstand and counterattack the power of darkness, despite any and all *feelings* of doubt, of spiritual hopelessness and indolence and sadness, of coldness toward God and heavenly things.

Purpose and Theme of the Second Set of Rules. Rule II:1

The same threefold general purpose of the first set of rules, as given immediately above, remains present also throughout the second set. There is the same principal concern with recognizing and conquering the movements from the evil spirit and our sinful selves. But in the second set Ignatius now narrows his focus to one specific theme: the "specious arguments, subtle and persistently fallacious," which come from the spirit of darkness during a time of spiritual consolation. Clarity about this principal concern, and also emphasis on it, are necessary if we are to avoid reading Rules II:1-8 in a way that gives exaggerated significance to one or another element which is relatively minor when it is seen in perspective within the whole Ignatian teaching on discernment of spirits and discernment of God's will. Through such misreading we could all too easily undervalue more important elements, or even exclude

213

them from consideration; and thereby we could wrench Ignatius' whole teaching out of shape.[1]

In the title of the second set of rules and in Rule II:1, Ignatius himself states the overall purpose of these rules, specifies their theme, and shows their relationship with the first set:

> [328]. Rules for the same purpose [as the first set of rules], with more accurate ways of discerning spirits. These rules are more suited for use in the second week [of the Spiritual Exercises].
>
> 1. It is connatural for God and his angels, when they prompt inward motions, to give genuine gladness and spiritual joy, eliminating all sadness and confusion which the enemy brings on.[2] It is connatural for the latter to fight against such gladness and spiritual consolation by proposing specious arguments, subtle and persistently fallacious.

Deceptions were, we saw, involved in the desolations and the temptations dealt with in the earlier rules; but in the second series, they take on a special form. Their starting point, as we shall see more in detail, is not spiritual desolation and attraction to evil or to despicable things; instead, they begin from holy thoughts and spiritual consolations of two distinct kinds which are used as occasions for two distinct kinds of deceptions. Even in the first series (I:1-14), Ignatius shows that, while spiritual consolation of itself always tends to good, it can be misused as an occasion for a dangerously false sense of security (Rule I:10) or as an occasion for vainglory (I:9, 11). The use of spiritual consolation by the evil spirit can be more crafty than that. Anyone with any basic understanding and experience of the spiritual life can, if alert, easily recognize

---

1 A correct understanding of what Ignatius is intending to do in the second set of rules prevents false expectations and unfounded emphasis on the importance of consolation without previous cause in Ignatian discernment of spirits and discernment of God' will.

These rules are not a set of positive directives on how to find God's will through experiences of consolation and desolation and discernment of spirits. They are *directly* concerned only with two subtle diabolical deceptions that can hinder such discernment, deceptions which begin with one or other of the two kinds of consolation distinguished and described in the rules solely for the sake of understanding these deceptions. The fact that the distinction between consolation with and without previous cause is nowhere else so much as mentioned in Ignatius' writings suggests its unimportance to Ignatius outside this limited context. For further discussion, see Appendix IV below on pages 291-313.

2 It is only the sadness and confusion into which the enemy leads us which in the nature of the case is done away with by spiritual consolation. Other forms of sadness and confusion, spiritual and non-spiritual, may be left untouched by spiritual consolation, which, however, gives us greater ease in bearing these and finding meaning in them.

the ways of misusing consolation dealt with in the first series of rules. The ways treated in the second series can be so insidious as sometimes to test to the limit the resources even of those who are most experienced, perceptive, and learned in the spiritual life.

This shift of focus from spiritual desolation and discouragement, which flow from untrue thoughts, to spiritual consolation used by the evil spirit as an occasion for deception — it is this shift which calls for the second series of rules. The rules already given in the first series are inadequate for understanding and counteracting these more subtle moves of the evil spirit. In fact, without qualification and nuancing, in many instances the earlier rules would simply be wrong; and to follow them would be to play into the hands of the evil spirit. In Rules I:2, 4, and 5, spiritual consolation was, without qualification, said to be the effect and the sign of the Holy Spirit in a maturing Christian; and the thoughts which flow from it were also said to be from him. Now we will see that the evil spirit, for his evil purposes, can also prompt us to spiritual consolation and to good thoughts that lead ultimately to desolation or wrong thoughts (II:3-4). Or he can lead us to confuse our own thoughts, even those produced under his influence, with thoughts flowing from a spiritual consolation which he did not and could not prompt in us (II:8). The reason for the second set of rules is to alert us to these further dangers and to instruct us on what to do about them: how to discern the enemy trying to mislead us from the Holy Spirit trying to lead us on the way of truth and peace.

There is, then, no shift in the second set of rules from the main concern of the first set, namely, to note and to overcome by the light and power of the Holy Spirit our inner movements which come from the evil spirit and our sinfulness. The second set is continuous with the first, a coherent development of the latter. The reason for separating the rules into two sets, each one said to be more appropriate to one or another week of the Spiritual Exercises, is purely practical and extrinsic to the rules themselves, namely, the need of the persons being counseled (*SpEx*, [8-10]).[3]

3 Nothing whatever is said as to whether the second set of rules should be reserved till the Second Week of the Exercises, or whether the first set of rules should be explained before the Second Week begins. Explain them or not, according to the need of the exercitant (*SpEx*, [8])—that is the Ignatian rule from Annotation 8 by which one should guide oneself. Two conditions are set down which, taken together, indicate when the director should not bring up the second set of rules with a person engaged in the exercises of the First Week: (1) the exercitant is not versed in spiritual things

They will more likely, but not necessarily, need Rules I during the first week of the Spiritual Exercises and Rules II during the second week.[4]

Consolation With and Without Preceding Cause. Rules II:2 and 3

The two kinds of experience which put one in need of the second series of rules are the two experiences, mentioned above, of deceptions which take spiritual consolation as their occasion and starting point. Ignatius treats them in three main steps. First, in II:2 and 3 he distinguishes two kinds of consolation. Second, in II:4-7 he describes the way in which the person experiencing one of these kinds of consolations can be deceived, and how he can uncover and escape the deception. Third, in II:8 he briefly describes the other mode of deception connected with the other kind of consolation, and he shows how to avoid it. These three main steps comprise all the teaching which he directly intended in the second series of rules.

Let us turn now to the first step, constituted by Rules II:2 and 3:

> Rule 2. To give a person consolation without preceding cause is for God our Lord alone to do; for it is distinctive of the Creator in relation to the created person to come in and to leave, to move the person inwardly, drawing him or her totally into love of his divine majesty. I say without [preceding] cause, that is, without any previous perception or understanding of any object such that through it consolation of this sort would come by the mediation of the person's own acts of understanding and will.

> Rule 3. With a [preceding] cause, an angel, good or evil, can console a person. In doing so, the good and evil angels have contrary purposes: for the good angel, the person's progress, spiritual growth, ascending from good to better; for the evil angel, the contrary purpose—and, thereafter, to draw the person on to his damned intent and cunning trap.

Rule II:2 is notoriously difficult to interpret. One recent commentator prefaces his explanation with the following remarks.

and (2) he or she is tempted grossly and openly (*SpEx*, [9]). When neither of these two conditions is present and the exercitant could profit by understanding the second set of rules, it is in accord with Ignatius' instruction to explain them.

4 The reason which Ignatius gives is that subtle temptations, under the appearance of good, are more likely in the Second Week. For then the persons to be guided are exercising themselves in the illuminative way and, after the purgation of the First Week, are better able to stand firm against open temptations to sin or discouragement (*SpEx*, [10]).

Deception beginning in Spiritual Consolation. Rules II:1-7

Because both traditional and contemporary Ignatian commentators fail to present an intelligible, cohesive and unified presentation of the Ignatian CSCP [*consolación sin causa precedente*], one can easily understand and appreciate Suarez's candid admission relative to CSCP: 'I do not find it easy to understand these words.' J.H.T. van den Berg has noted that the explicit Ignatian formulation, 'without previous cause,' appears only in *Ex* 330 and 336, but not in Ignatius' *Autobiography*, *Spiritual Journal*, personal letters, nor even in his famous letter on discernment to Sr. Teresa Rejadell. We are forced to agree with K. Rahner that Ignatius 'has here accomplished a masterpiece of brevity but not of clarity.'[5]

Because of the lack of clarity in Rule II:2, many commentators handle the rule gingerly, merely paraphrasing Ignatius' words. Others make conjecture or declarations about what the rule means. Unfortunately, these bolder commentators do not agree among themselves.[6]

Without adopting any of the opinions already given or adding another, and yet doing more than merely paraphrasing or skimming lightly over the text, let us see if we can elicit from it some points that are clear in any reasonable reading. This may be enough at least to show some intelligible difference between consolation with and without previous cause. It may, consequently, enable us to understand the questions about consolation without previous cause that remain to be answered; further still, it may enable us to understand the difference between the two kinds of deception with which the second set of rules is concerned.

However debatable our interpretations on some aspects of the distinction between consolation with and without previous cause may be, there is no question about the fact that Ignatius himself states two main differences between the two forms of consolation. The first difference is that one of them has a "preceding cause" in the person's own acts, while the other does not. The second difference underlies the first: the consolation which has no preceding cause can come *only* from God and *immediately* from him. These two differences are extrinsic to the consolation itself: They refer explicitly to its origination, not to its intrinsic nature. In one opinion, there is a third difference implied by the unmediated influence of God in consolation without previous cause. There must be some difference in the consolation itself if it cannot be

---

5 H. Egan, *Mystical Horizon*, p. 32.
6 For a discussion of some contemporary conflicting interpretations of consolation without previous cause, see Appendix IV below on pp. 291-313.

mediated by any created agent or any acts of the person consoled. Another opinion contradicts this one: There is no such implication; all Ignatius is concerned about is the relationship to the previous cause, to the way in which the consolation arises. Let me for the moment put aside the question of intrinsic differences and look at the first two differences.

The first difference is perhaps the most obvious to the reader because it is the difference by which the consolations are named: consolation *with previous cause* and consolation *without previous cause,* sometimes contracted into consolation with cause and consolation without cause.[7] The preceding cause referred to is certainly not the prompting or instigating cause[8] who acts on the person to bring consolation, that is, God or his good angel or an evil spirit; that cause appears in the second difference. What is referred to here is the object of the person's antecedent acts (perception, understanding, willing), which through the mediation of these acts brings such consolation as the person experiences. It is the acts with this object or this object *precisely inasmuch as perceived or understood or volitionally responded to* that is the preceding cause referred to.

The general idea of "preceding cause" in this context seems clear. It may be made clearer still, if there is any need, by Ignatius' instructions in the *Spiritual Exercises.* He tells those making the Exercises that before beginning to meditate or contemplate they should ask for the grace desired, such as sorrow for sin and tears (*SpEx,* [55]), intimate knowledge of and love for Jesus ([104]), compassion for Jesus in his suffering ([203]), joy in his joy and glory ([221]). These experiences, which he calls spiritual consolation ([316]), are expected to come through meditation on truths taught in Holy Scripture, contemplation of Christ in the Gospels, consideration of God's gifts to each exercitant personally ([2]). It seems no exaggeration to say that every exercise in the Spiritual Exercises is calculated to bring consolation with preceding cause if God chooses to give it. Consolation without previous cause may be hoped for also, and the whole process of purification from sin and growing in love for Jesus disposes one to receive it if God wishes to give it. No spiritual exercise, however, can be devised which is calculated to mediate it. That would be a contradiction in terms.

---

7 See note 9 of ch. 2 above.

8 For the several meanings of the word "cause" in Ignatius' usage, see Daniel Gil, *La Consolación Sin Causa Precedente* (Rome, 1971), p. 30 (hereafter abbreviated as Gil, *La Consolación*).

The second difference between consolation with and without preceding cause refers to the prompting cause. If a consolation is ever recognized as certainly a consolation without previous cause, then one need be in no ambiguity about the originator: It cannot be anyone but God acting immediately on the person consoled. No evil spirit could possibly effect it in us, nor could any good angel, not even as an instrument of God. If, on the other hand, a consolation is recognized as having a previous cause, there is always some ambiguity about its originator which needs to be cleared up. It might be God alone, or God acting through a good spirit, or it might be an evil spirit. (There is no apparent reason, it might be added, why it could not be another human person.) It is true that Rule 3 mentions explicitly only good and evil angels; but it does not exclude God acting alone. It does not say consolation with previous cause is in every case from a good or evil angel; it says these agents *can* cause such consolation, whereas God alone is in every instance the cause of the other. In any case, it makes no practical difference. Even when God alone gives consolation with previous cause, it is such that it could be given by him through a good angel; and when it is given through an angel, it is still from God principally and given for his purposes. The purpose of the good angel could not be other than what God intends. The ambiguity about God alone or God acting through an angel to cause such consolation can never be resolved—nor is there any practical need for doing so.

Whatever else Ignatius may have meant by the distinction between consolation with and without preceding cause, this much is clear. Any consolation which is led up to and depends on prior meditation or contemplation, or on any prior affective experiences as its ground is consolation with previous cause. (All consolations looked for in the models of and instructions on meditation and contemplation in *The Spiritual Exercises* are such.) Consolation without previous cause may, however, in God's ordinary Providence, have some *extrinsic* and not necessary dependence on negative or positive *conditions*, the removal of obstacles or the actuation of good dispositions. Thus a person presently engaged in sinful sensual indulgence, or committing one cruelty after another, or totally distracted by profane concerns is not apt to experience such spiritual consolation; but innocence of life and concentration in prayer in which faith and love are intensely actuated prepare one to receive the gift. Consolation with previous cause may often or usually be such a disposition for consolation without previous cause. However, none of the dispositions will in any way serve to actuate or increase consolation without previous cause or mediate the act of God which effects such consolation. If a consolation should come through such mediation, it would be consolation with previous cause.

The reason given for saying that God alone can console without preceding cause suggests a third difference, an intrinsic one. It is, of course, possible that the *way* in which the consolation comes to be may, by itself, require that God alone effect it, without any mediation. In that case, no intrinsic difference from consolation with preceding cause would be called for in order to distinguish one consolation from the other. Nevertheless, it would not be surprising to find something intrinsic to consolation without preceding cause which is peculiar to it, something by which we could see why it cannot depend on our prior acts of mind or will as previous cause, and also why it cannot be effected by an evil or a good created spirit, but only by God without any created intermediary. Will there not likely be something intrinsic and peculiar to the experience which points to God's sovereign power over our most inward conscious life, the power by which he and he alone, without going through the process naturally required for the genesis of consolation, can effect it as he wills? Let us see.

Some think that there is an immediate, non-conceptual awareness of God implied by Ignatius' saying that God alone can effect the consolation and that it is without cause, that is, they say, without conceptual object. This gets us into difficult theological questions which had better be omitted now. What is clearly and explicitly in Rule II:2, however, are the words about God "drawing him or her totally into love of his Divine Majesty." The word "totally" seems to be a key word, pointing to what is most distinctive in our experience when such consolation is given. It belongs solely to God to enter the creature and to convert his or her love into a total love of God himself. The same emphasis recurs in a letter to Sister Teresa Rejadell where, it seems to many, Ignatius is discussing without naming what in Rules II:2 and 8 he names consolation without previous cause. In that letter he speaks of God lifting the person up "wholly to his divine love."[9]

In his *Spiritual Diary*, Ignatius speaks in the same terms of some

9 *LettersIgn*, p. 22.

of his own experiences, which might be consolations without preceding cause.

> Entering the chapel and overwhelmed with a great devotion to the Most Holy Trinity, with very increased love and intense tears, without seeing the Persons distinctly, as in the last two days, but perceiving in one luminous clarity a single Essence, I was drawn entirely to its love, and later, while preparing the altar and vesting, great devotion and tears, grace always assisting with much satisfaction of soul (*Spiritual Diary* [99, 100], March 3, 1544, page 22 in Young's translation).

> Later, the thought occurring to me that tomorrow I should say the Mass of the Most Holy Trinity, to determine what was to be done, or to end it altogether, many movements came upon me and tears, and from moment to moment over some space of time, great movements, sobs and floods of tears, drawing me entirely to the love of the Most Holy Trinity, with many colloquies (Ibid., [130], March 7, 1544, page 29 in Young's translation).

Perhaps it will help toward understanding this "drawing me totally into love of his divine majesty" if we recall the first description of spiritual consolation in Rule I:3 and the explanation given above in chapter 5 (pages 95-99). In that description, Ignatius says that the person in consolation is so "aflame" with love of God that, as a consequence, he or she "cannot love any created thing on the face of the earth in itself but only in the Creator of them all." Such love is, without doubt, a total love for God, leaving no room for any love even for self which is not in God, and rendering the lover free of any desire except the desire to do what God wills. We saw when discussing Rule I:3 that such purity of love is possible without consolation. But when consolation is given and includes such love, there is some reason for thinking it is what Ignatius calls consolation without preceding cause.

While what has been said gives no full and sure understanding of the distinction Ignatius makes between consolation with and without preceding cause, nevertheless, it gives some intelligible meaning to those terms—enough, I think, to enable us to understand (1) what the two deceptions are which Satan tries to effect by means of those two consolations, and (2) how to avoid them.

I do not know how to establish this assertion for the reader except by going ahead with the rules and letting its truth appear as we go along. I am not saying it would be of no great value to understand more clearly and certainly what Ignatius meant, with greater depth and fullness than we have. I am only saying that we need not wait for such knowledge in order to avoid the dangers he is pointing out.

Deception through Consolation With Previous Cause. Rule II:4

Both the deceptions which Ignatius deals with in his second set of rules usually happen in those whom he calls "devout" or "faithful" persons, and whom we have named maturing Christians. The deceptions occur to these persons when they have already learned how to understand spiritual desolation and temptation and how to guard against or counteract them by faith in God, when they are strong to resist and to overcome recognized attacks of the forces of evil from within or from without themselves. The first step in the evil spirit's attack on such persons is to catch them off guard by approaching as an angel of light who is bringing spiritual consolation and holy thoughts.

> Rule 4. It is characteristic of the evil spirit to take on the appearance of an angel of light, so that he begins by going the way of the devout person and ends with that person going his way. By that I mean that he first prompts thoughts which are good and holy, harmonious with such a faithful person, and then manages, little by little, to step out of his act [as an angel of light] and lead the person to his hidden falsehoods and perverse designs.

The importance to Ignatius of this mode of deception is indicated by the fact that descriptions and illustrations of it abound in his writings. One description of it that is clearer and more precise than the rule itself occurs in a letter to two of the early Jesuits who were sent on a difficult mission. There we find a surprising and interesting turn of thought. Instead of speaking about the spirit of darkness modeling himself on an angel of light, he advises his men to model their tactics for the good of others on the tactics of the evil spirit when he is trying to harm them. Such advice may sound sinister; but the whole letter could be summed up as advising his men to be like St. Paul, whose words he quotes: "I have become all things to all men" (1 Cor. 9:22). Ignatius' point is that Satan does the same, only for contrary purposes.

> Whenever we wish to win someone over and engage him in the greater service of God our Lord, we should use the same strategy for good which the enemy employs to draw a good soul to evil. He enters through the other's door and comes out his own. He enters with the other by not opposing his ways but by praising them. He

acts familiarly with the soul, suggesting good and holy thoughts which bring peace to the good soul. Later he tries, little by little, to come out his own door, always suggesting some error or illusion under the appearance of good, but which will always be evil. So we with a good purpose can praise or agree with another concerning some particular thing, dissembling whatever else may be wrong. After thus gaining his confidence, we shall have better success. In this sense we go in with him his way, but come out our own.[10]

To penetrate and reveal more fully the demonic deception of inserting darkness into light, we need to consider in more detail its starting point and then the process. The starting point consists of the good and holy thoughts which bring peace and consolation, or which flow from consolation. There is, in Rule 4 itself, no mention of consolation (and only an oblique mention of it in Rule 5); but the context leaves no doubt that it is to be assumed.[11] Nevertheless, what Ignatius wants to emphasize is the thoughts. It is the thoughts bringing consolation or coming from it and later leading to bad counsels or spiritual desolation which hold the center of attention. The good thoughts which begin the process have to be of a sort that the enemy foresees he can use, thoughts that offer an occasion for him to manipulate the unsuspecting person's thinking and affection through some known or hoped-for weakness of which he can take advantage. "It is his [the evil spirit's] way to suggest or propose a truth, or even several, in order to come off with a lie and entangle us in it."[12]

Some illustrations of starting points and the direction in which

---

10 *LettersIgn*, pp. 51-52.
11 The point of Rule II:3 is that the evil spirit can prompt consolation in order to deceive us. Rule II:5 gives as one of the criteria for judging thoughts to be from the evil spirit the fact that they end by destroying the peace and quiet of mind which the person had to start with. Rule II:6 is asking us to reflect on the whole experience to see how the evil spirit contrived to lead us gradually away from the "earlier sweetness and spiritual joy." Note in the letter just quoted in the text how the evil spirit is said to begin by suggesting good and holy thoughts "which bring peace to the soul." With this said for the sake of understanding this rule, it remains true that termination of a course of thoughts in thoughts that are evil, distracting, or less good marks the whole course as also being from the evil spirit when it begins without spiritual consolation. In fact, by a process of association or sophistical reasoning beginning from thoughts prompted by the good spirit, Satan can lead us into his trap. From a practical point of view, then, it is necessary to be always alert for such a deception. In some cases, however, especially when it is a matter of discerning God's will through consolation and desolation, it is important to know whether the original consolation was from a good or evil spirit.
12 *LettersIgn*, p. 195.

they can be turned in persons of a certain temperament or character or stage of growth will help us to recognize what Ignatius means when he speaks in general terms. Most of the experiences illustrated below and others like them are common enough, but most of us are not at all alert to what is happening when they take place. Accommodating himself to a good Christian who has a natural bent toward activism, the evil spirit may forcefully and persistently suggest thoughts about and plans for directly apostolic or other charitable works. Little by little, he will try to lead the intended victim to some harm to himself or others: to neglect of meditation and contemplation; to exhaustion and, if the works do not go as the person planned, to resentment, discouragement, withdrawal from dedication to a life of service to God's people. Finding one who is zealous but impetuous, the evil spirit may begin by suggesting thoughts harmonious with prudent zeal and then gradually lead the person to impetuous desires for immediate great undertakings, altogether beyond the reach of the person being tempted, for which he or she has neither the gifts nor the training. What disaster could follow is not hard to imagine. The temptation takes a reverse direction with someone who is shy and indecisive about action or of a contemplative bent: It begins with thoughts about the importance of contemplation in Christian life, stirs up consoling hopes for experience of God in prayer, and thus draws the person to neglect the works in accord with his or her vocation or the demands of charity here and now.

Someone with great business ability may be inspired with the thought of making a fortune in order to help others for love of God and then be led, little by little, to such an all-consuming drive for wealth as to become ruthless and unjust. Again, the evil spirit might inspire a preacher or theologian with the holy and consoling thought of making the gospel relevant to people of our time and then by imperceptible steps lead to emptying his or her teaching of what is essential to the Christian message.

Always, in such experiences, we must remember that the thoughts which the deception takes as a starting point are themselves good. They may not be good for this person, not what God is calling him to, at least not at this time; and in that case the whole idea should be dropped. But again, the original inspiration may be good, even very good, for this person; and withdrawing from it simply because the evil spirit has tried to misuse it would be granting a victory to the force of evil.

What has already been said makes plain what it means for the evil spirit to masquerade as an angel of light and the purpose of doing so. What of the process between the starting point and the achieved purpose? *How* does the evil one "lead a person [from good and holy thoughts] into his falsehoods"? The answer was already generally intimated in the first rule: by "specious arguments, subtle and persistently fallacious." He suggests apparently real but actually unreal advantages or real disadvantages for the praise and service of God. ([*SpEx*, 181-182]). He brings about the gradual isolation of a proposed truth from balancing truths, and thus he leads his victim even to a sort of destructive obsession. Through an intricate process of conceptual, imaginative, emotional associations which begins from the spiritually consoling thoughts, he leads a person to wrong conclusions. Or he instigates a more rational, and apparently logical, line of reasoning that is vitiated along the line by some ambiguous use of a word or concept, or by a false assumption of fact or principle. And so on.

One essential aspect of the experience has to be stressed; failure to keep it in mind will lead to serious confusion and error in judging our experiences. Ignatius is talking about a *process*, a series of thoughts and affections in which there is some continuity from the starting point to the termination. He says that from the first thoughts the evil spirit "leads" one into falsehood. He does so "little by little," each step leading on to the next, so that it will all "end up" in that which he aimed at from the start. The continuity does not have to be temporal, with no time lag at all between the steps. There may be minutes, hours, even days between the steps in the process. Nevertheless, there is continuity and process if each new step takes up from the earlier steps, builds on them, and develops from them toward the goal that gives them unity and purpose. Thus, a person may put aside a course of thoughts from weariness or because of other calls on his or her attention, only to take it up again later. Or a passing thought may come now, another at another time, and so on, but with all of them converging and building up an attitude of mind and heart. Or a thought comes and goes, and hours or days later comes back and by association leads to a different one, and so on until the person reaches the one the tempter intends. He or she may not even be aware that there is a continuity, a process, until after reflection on the whole experience.

Any thoughts which interrupt the process, whether they are opposed to it or simply unrelated by logic or association, are not parts of this particular deceptive process. The conclusions to which they lead, the affective acts and feelings to which they give rise or from which they spring, are not to be judged as coming from the prompting source of this particular process which they interrupt. They have to be assessed independently of it. They may be elements in another deception, or they may be from the Holy Spirit, or merely parts of a non-spiritual experience.

At the other extreme, there are deceptions in which the passage from the starting point to the bad termination is so immediate that these hardly seem to qualify as the sort with which Rule 4 is concerned; there is nothing of the "little by little" about them. However, even though the pattern is contracted, it is essentially the same. Consider this experience which Ignatius relates of himself. To understand it, we must keep in mind that by the crooked lines with which God is said to write straight, the Holy Spirit had, after many wanderings, led Ignatius to see that if he was to answer God's call to him, he had to get an education. He had just begun his studies.

> Returning to Barcelona he began his studies with great diligence. But there was one thing that stood very much in his way, and that is that when he began to learn by heart, as has to be done in the beginning of grammar, he received new light on spiritual things and new delights. So strong were these delights that he could memorize nothing nor could he get rid of them however much he tried.
>
> Thinking this over at various times, he said to himself: "Even when I go to prayer or attend Mass these lights do not come to me so vividly." Thus, step by step, he came to recognize that it was a temptation. After making his meditation, he went to the church of Santa María del Mar, near the house of his teacher, having asked him to have the kindness to hear him for a moment in the church. Seated there, the pilgrim gave his teacher a faithful account of what had taken place in his soul, and how little progress he had made until then for the reason already mentioned. And he made a promise to his master, with these words: "I promise you never to fail to attend your class these two years, as long as I can find bread and water for my support here in Barcelona." He made this promise with such effect that he never again suffered from those temptations.[13]

In this case, there were new and true spiritual insights which

<hr>

13 *Autobiog*, nos. 54-55; in *St. Ignatius' Own Story*, pp. 39-40. When Ignatius says that he was not troubled by these temptations again, he must mean on this particular occasion or during this time of his life in Barcelona; for later in life, as he tells us, he experienced the same sort of temptation and treated it in the same way (ibid., no. 82, p. 59).

brought spiritual consolation and also an immediate suspicious effect. What was gradual, "step by step," was not the course of thought but Ignatius' recognition of the deception. In a way, however, we might be able to say that the whole deception did take time; for although the thoughts did not have to develop over a period of time in order to arrive at a bad effect, the bad effect had to be produced over and over to become truly serious. One passing incident of this sort would cause no great impediment to Ignatius' studies. A similar temptation had come at an earlier time, one devised to cause harm to Ignatius' health and thus to his life of prayer and his apostolic work.

> Besides his seven hours of prayer, he busied himself with certain souls who came looking for him to discuss their spiritual interests. All the rest of the day he spent thinking of divine things, those especially which he had either read or meditated that day. But when he went to bed he received great illuminations and spiritual consolations which made him lose much of the time he had set aside for sleep, and that was not much. He looked into this matter a number of times and gave it some thought. Having set aside so much time for dealing with God, and besides that even all the rest of the day, he began to doubt whether these illuminations came from the good spirit. He concluded that he had better not have anything to do with them, and give the time determined on to sleep. And this he did.[14]

In all these experiences it is notable that Ignatius practices what he teaches. He is reflectively alert to what is happening in himself and questioning its source and direction. When he recognizes the signs of the evil spirit at work, he promptly goes directly and resolutely in the opposite direction.

Rule II:5 will instruct us on how to go about catching the evil spirit at work under his angel-of-light disguise. But before we take that next step, one question should be raised. It may seem at first purely academic, but the answer does turn out to have significant practical consequences and removes some otherwise likely confusions. The question is this: When consolation is prompted by the evil spirit, is it genuine spiritual consolation or only specious?[15]

---

14 Ibid., no. 26; p. 21 in *St. Ignatius' Own Story*. See also *LettersIgn*, p. 25, and relate these temptations described here with what he says in the rules for penance (*SpEx*, [84]).

15 Harvey Egan (*Ignatian Mystical Horizon*, pp. 61, 83) expresses what is probably a very common interpretation of St. Ignatius when he says that consolation from the evil one is only apparent, that only God and his angels can bring true consolation (see also notes 20 and 21, below). He appeals to Rules I:1 and II:1 (*SpEx*, [314,

Is it altogether inauthentic or only partially? There can, of course, be spiritual consolation which is certainly specious because it only appears to be rooted in living faith but really is not. Ignatius is not writing about that in Rules II:3-5. He is dealing with consolation rooted in good and holy thoughts, thoughts which presumably spring from living faith and are harmonious with the mind and heart of a sincere believer. This appears to be genuinely spiritual consolation, just as much as any spiritual consolation arising from listening with faith to a movingly eloquent preacher who may happen also to be a man leading a life of sin and motivated in preaching only by selfish ambition. When there is a genuine faith response issuing in peace and joy in the Holy Spirit, such consolation is from the Holy Spirit, the author of faith—even though it is the preacher or the evil spirit who provides the occasion. So, this consolation prompted by the evil spirit cannot be totally inauthentic.

Can we perhaps say that the consolation is genuine, authentic, but in some way impure, tainted, infected? We can say that the extrinsic source is tainted, but intrinsically the consolation is genuine and untainted. However evil the intention of the instigator, he is for the moment prompting thoughts and feelings and desires which arise only in one with living faith and which, of themselves, tend to the active expression and increase of faith. The evil prompter intends to lead them astray, but that does not affect what they are now.

329]). At first reading these rules seem to offer support for his assertion. On closer examination, however, this does not seem to be the case.

First of all, Ignatius in Rule I:1 ([314]) is writing about the effect of the evil spirit on the *regressing* Christian, who is going from sin to sin; there is no question here of the evil spirit trying to deceive such a person beginning from good and holy thoughts, harmonious with a faithful Christian, and from spiritual consolation, as Ignatius says he does in Rules II:4-5. In fact, the first series of rules is not concerned at all with deception by spiritual consolation, whether apparent or real. Secondly, in I:1, what Ignatius says the evil spirit causes are illusory gratifications or pleasures, which in the context are *evidently sinful*, without the least suggestion of being apparently from the Holy Spirit.

As for II:1, here Ignatius does *not* say that only God and his angels can bring true consolation. He says that it is connatural to them, characteristic of them, to do so. That does not exclude the possibility of the evil spirit also doing so. In II:3, it is said that an evil spirit can cause the same sort of consolation that a good angel can cause, with no indication of its being false consolation. And then in II:4 it is said that the evil spirit does in fact act as an angel of light, doing what is connatural to a good angel, i.e., prompting true spiritual consolation—in order finally to achieve his own purpose as an angel of darkness.

Perhaps it will be helpful if we push farther the parallel noted above with the human preacher. An eloquent speaker can play on people's religious beliefs, rousing genuinely good religious responses with the intention of swindling them of their money by a fraudulent appeal to their charity or, more like Satan, of twisting them little by little to violently uncharitable anger and mob action. Or think of the seducer Ignatius speaks of in Rule I:13. He might begin by playing on a woman's religious feelings, which are pure and of themselves lead only to what is pure, but subtly and gradually after getting her trust, lead her to his desires. In every such case, the instigator begins by prompting genuinely good and holy thoughts and affections in another but by doing it with a wicked motive, intending so gently and skillfully to induce a change in the character of the other's response that it will pass from what was genuinely good to being evil before the person is aware of what has happened. If the process ceases before it is directed awry, the evil spirit or the human swindler or seducer will, without wanting to, have benefited the intended victim. Then the situation will be very like that of a card shark who tries to take in his proposed victim by letting him get a taste of winning with the intention of leading him on to the big jackpot where he will be cleaned out. For the moment, the victim really is ahead of the game. If he suspects what is coming and withdraws from the game at that point, he will be richer than he was.

Strange as it may appear, we seem compelled to say that the evil spirit can and does prompt genuinely holy thoughts and genuinely spiritual consolations, which need not be repudiated in all cases after being discovered. We may withdraw from the game while ahead. The crucially important thing is to notice as soon as possible when and how the good thoughts and genuinely spiritual consolations shift to unholy thoughts and specious consolation or spiritual desolation. We will now see what Ignatius says about how to do that, in Rule II:5.[16]

16 Let it be clear, however, that whether consolation prompted by the evil spirit is a genuine or a specious consolation, we are left with the same problem. It may be expressed differently in each case, but it is fundamentally the same. On the supposition that origin from an evil spirit does not necessarily affect the intrinsic character of a consolation, that is, does not necessarily prevent it from being spiritual, the criteria arrived at in ch. 2 are adequate for discerning whether a consolation is genuinely spiritual; but they are not adequate for discerning whether it is prompted by a good or evil spirit. We still have to ask: What is the criterion for discerning whether the prompting agent of the genuine spiritual consolation is good or evil? On the suppo-

How to Expose the First Deception. Rules II:5 and 6

In Rule II:5, one of the most important among all the rules which Ignatius gives, we are led to see what is an *adequate* norm for judging the origin of those inner motions with which we are concerned, namely, consolations with previous cause; and thus we are enabled to guard against one of the most dangerous and common deceptions into which even well intentioned persons can fall in their spiritual life. Even genuinely spiritual consolation with previous cause is not an adequate norm. What begins as a truly spiritual consolation can, as we have just seen, be from the evil spirit, prompted for evil purposes. So, we need a norm for judging the origin of the spiritual consolation itself. If it leads to spiritual desolation, then it is marked as from the evil spirit. But even if it does not lead to spiritual desolation, there are other signs by which it is to be judged. Discernment of spirits is not done merely on the basis of spiritual consolation and desolation. For, although these are helpful norms for judging the origin of thoughts and impulses, the latter are equally norms for judging the origin of spiritual consolation. What Ignatius is telling us to look for as a sign of the Holy Spirit moving us is an *integral experience in which all the elements are mutually validating,* an experience of thoughts, feelings, and impulses to choice and activity, all related to each other as influencing or influenced, *all ultimately rooted in living faith and tending all through the temporal progression of the experience to expression of living faith and growth in it.* To accept an experience as one prompted by the Holy Spirit simply because it begins with what appear to be and even truly are holy thoughts or spiritual consolation or both together is to lay ourselves open to dangerous deception. A detailed and careful study of rule II:5 will help us to avoid such deception.

As in Rule II:4, the focus of attention in Rule 5 is not on the

---

sition that the consolation prompted by an evil spirit can be only speciously spiritual, the criteria arrived at in ch. 2 for the purpose of discerning a spiritual consolation are not yet adequate even for that purpose. An experience of consolation may seem to the person to fulfill all the cirteria set down there and still be only speciously spiritual. Therefore, we have to ask: What is the criterion for discerning whether the consolation is genuinely or speciously spiritual? Consequently, for the purpose of this rule, it makes no fundamental difference whether we think of the spiritual consolation in Rules II:4-6 as genuine or specious. Therefore I shall simply speak of a spiritual consolation without qualifying it as genuine or specious. No matter which way the reader qualifies it, we have to look for a further norm in order to decide whether the consolation and the thoughts which ground it or immediately flow from it are from a good or evil spirit. This is what Ignatius gives in Rule II:5.

consolation but on the thoughts; not, however, on the initial thoughts but on the progression of thoughts from the starting point and, above all, on the termination.

> Rule 5. We ought to pay close attention to the progression of thoughts. If the beginning, middle, and end of it are altogether good and tend entirely to what is right, that is a sign of the good angel's influence. It is, however, a clear sign that the line of thought originates from the influence of the evil spirit, the enemy of our spiritual progress and eternal salvation, if the thoughts which he prompts end up in something evil or distracting or less good than what the person had previously proposed to do, or if they weaken, disquiet, or confuse him, doing away with the peace, tranquillity, and quiet experienced beforehand.

The rule implies that we should allow the course of thought springing from spiritual consolation to progress freely until some clear sign of the evil spirit appears—as without any doubt it will if they are from his prompting (see below, pp. 237-242). To do otherwise would be useless for discernment of spirits, and also harmful to our spiritual life and psychological health. There is at the beginning of these thoughts and spiritual consolation no possibility of finding through any methodical discernment what spirit is at their source. (Perhaps one with a spiritual charism will perceive, at least in some instances, without methodical discernment; but then rules are not to the point.) Further, anxiety about these motions and immediate examination of them would only serve to close off all such movements from the Holy Spirit and put us under unbearable psychological tension, make us spiritual hypochondriacs. On the basis of what in general is a sign of the Holy Spirit as known from Rules I:2,3,5 and II:1, the person can presume that the present motions, holy thoughts and spiritual consolation, are from him, and *tentatively* but watchfully receive them as being from him until subsequent evidence proves the opposite or conclusively establishes the correctness of the assumption.

There is no reason to be fidgety about the possibility of deception, and much reason not to be. The initial thoughts and feelings are, in any case, good and holy, or at least harmless and possibly helpful. There is only reason to be alertly but calmly attentive to any sign of what may be from the evil spirit, as far as we can see at our present stage of spiritual growth, without undue strain. The Holy Spirit dwelling in us will make up for our limitations, directly or through those with whom he expects us to be open

(I:13). The real danger and just cause for uneasiness is failure to live an examined life as well as our capacity and circumstances allow. Here we have to note that this failure may not be general, but limited to one particular area of life where an individual is especially weak, where an otherwise generous and honestly reflective person draws the line and blinds himself or herself to what he or she does not want to see. Again, the way to prevent this failure is not to be worrisome about oneself, always uneasy for fear something of this sort is happening. It is rather to pray for the light of the Holy Spirit to reveal the truth about ourselves and, through regular examination and honesty with a director when needed, to open ourselves serenely to that light.

With an understanding of the right attitude toward the possibility of deception through spiritual consolation with good and holy thoughts, what we now need to examine more closely are the several signs of the evil spirit for which we should be alert. Ignatius' description of the criteria for judging spiritual consolations with previous cause are given principally in terms of what points to the evil spirit; if no sign of the evil spirit appears, then we are justified in taking the thoughts and the consolation and all that has continuity with them as being from the good spirit. For, as noted above, in the light of what was said earlier in the rules (I:1-3, 5; II:1), when there is a spiritual consolation or thoughts flowing from faith, hope, and charity, no further positive sign of the good spirit is needed in order to make a probable and tentative judgment that the experience is prompted by the Holy Spirit. What is needed to confirm the preliminary and tentative judgment is the absence of any contrary sign continuous with that starting point; for, if the experience originates from the good spirit, it will be all good in its beginning, middle, and end.

The course of thoughts about which the rule is concerned may lead to untrue thoughts; to evil desires, aversions, or fears; to thoughts or affections which distract us from prayer or good works, or which incline us to do something less good than what we had reasonably intended to do. These are all signs of the evil spirit. The Vulgate text of *The Spiritual Exercises* states them with brevity and exactitude: "What is of itself evil or diverts from good or impels to a lesser good than the person had previously resolved to do." Any one of these signs is enough. But, even without any of these, the evil spirit may betray himself in his influence on sensibility, with feelings of desolation replacing the earlier consolation.

If the beginning, middle, and end are all right and good, that, Ignatius says, constitutes a sign of the good angel leading us from the very start. Otherwise, the evil spirit has been at work. Clearly, then, what was said above regarding the continuity by which a number of partial experiences constitute a whole, a progression— that is of very great importance in judging whether the beginning, middle, and end are all good or whether something bad has happened. What occurs during the interruptions and is not included within the progression is not a factor for judging the experience as a continuous whole. Suppose I am moved to good and holy thoughts which bring me spiritual peace and joy. Then I become involved in some activity which gets my thoughts and affections centered in a way which has nothing to do with the previous thoughts and consolation. Suppose, during this time, I find myself thinking evil thoughts, laying selfish plans, or experiencing spiritual desolation. Afterwards, I recall the earlier good and holy thoughts and, by logic or association, I am led to further thoughts which are also good. The bad thoughts and spiritual desolation which came in between have no bearing on the experience which began with good thoughts and consolation. So far, all is well. So far there is no reason to think the consolation and thoughts come from an evil spirit.

Depending on the foregoing clarifications and keeping in mind such illustrations as those given in the comments on the preceding rule, we can now draw up a more elaborate statement of this rule than the one Ignatius gives, trying to be clearer and more precise regarding the general principle involved and its particular implications.

The main point put in general terms can be expressed in this way: An experience of good and holy thoughts springing from or leading to spiritual consolation can justifiably be judged as originating from the Holy Spirit immediately or through the mediation of an angel only if *all* the following thoughts and affections which have continuity with that starting point are free from any sign of the evil spirit. If any particular element in the continuous experience shows the influence of the evil spirit, the whole course of thoughts and affections from the very beginning is to be regarded as coming from him. In other words, no one element taken in isolation from the total experience can be a sign of the good spirit; only the total experience can be that. When the good spirit is at work the whole process bears his mark. When the evil spirit

233

is at work, not all will be evil, but some evil will appear as the termination to which the process leads.

Let us see what this means in regard to some particulars, even if doing so is in some measure repetitious. We are dealing with an experience of such importance, a deception that is so common in the lives of those striving to be better Christians, and one that can be so dangerous, that we need to understand as clearly and precisely as we can what transpires, and also to be able to close off as carefully as we can every avenue of error. First, then, consider what the general principle stated above means in regard to holy thoughts and desires. Obviously such thoughts and desires at the beginning are not yet sure evidence that we are moved by a good spirit. But a further point needs to be emphasized: Such thoughts and desires occurring in the middle *or at the end* of the process are not yet sure evidence either. Their value as a sign of the good spirit is nullified when they distract us while we are carrying out a good work to which God has called us. (Recall Ignatius' experience of intense spiritual consolation when he was trying to memorize his lessons or when it was time to sleep.) Further, even if the thoughts at the end evoke desires which are good but less good than this person had formerly and reasonably resolved upon, or if they cause desire for something that would be for the praise and service of God but as an alternative to what is for his greater praise and service, that also is a sign of the evil spirit.

What is more, even if these thoughts and desires are good, not distracting, and judged to be for the greater service and praise of God, they may still be marked as prompted by the evil spirit if they bring on *spiritual* desolation (truly spiritual desolation and not merely a non-spiritual disturbance, fear or sadness at the thought of what it may cost to do the service for God). On the other hand, if spiritual consolation endures from beginning to end of the experience, this is not by itself any reasonably sure evidence of the good spirit inspiring the thoughts and desires. At first blush it is (see I: 2 and 5); but its first-blush significance can be nullified, not only by thoughts and desires within the experience judged by reason as morally evil, but even by those judged to be distracting or less good, as was explained above. In short, to be a sign of the Holy Spirit, the process has to be integrally good, with every part validating and validated by the other parts of the whole experience.

The foregoing reflection on Rule 5 leads us to a significant conclusion: Ignatius did not think we have need of consolation without previous cause in order to make a reasonable judgment that we are being moved by the Holy Spirit, immediately or through a good angel—unless one makes the curious assumption that a good angel acts independently of what the Holy Spirit is working and may not be carrying out what God intends in us. For Ignatius says that if the beginning, middle, and end are altogether good and tend to what is altogether right, that is a sign of a good angel.

A warning, however, is in place. Just as a spiritual consolation with good and holy thoughts does not by itself assure me that the Holy Spirit is moving me, so also, even if the middle and end of a process so begun are also good and the whole experience is a sign of the Holy Spirit, this does not give valid assurance that an impulse or a plan of action that comes with the spiritual experience is thereby sealed and signed as God's will for me and counsel to me. This particular experience usually provides only some bit of evidence regarding God's will, not at all conclusive. Usually a number of such experiences, sometimes very many, are needed before I can reasonably think I have the *"much* light and understanding from consolation and desolation and discernment of spirits" (*SpEx*, [176])[17] which Ignatius calls for in this way of finding God's will. And further, all this evidence has to be integrated into a larger framework of thought regarding discernment of God's will. We mentioned above on page 12 that discernment of God's will overlaps with discernment of spirits in the Ignatian sense of that term, but also involves much more—so much, in fact, that the Ignatian teaching on the finding of God's will calls for another volume.

Learning by Reflection on Experience. Rule II:6

In Rule II:5 we have a way of detecting a deception based on an experience of spiritual consolation. Now, In Rule II:6, Ignatius

---

17 *The Spiritual Diary*, ([1-40], February 2—March 12, 1544; pp. 1-34 in Young's translation) shows clearly what a great accumulation of evidence from spiritual consolation Ignatius considered to be required for making the important decision he was facing. This document is instructive regarding Ignatian discernment of God's will not only by consolation and desolation but by other ways also. Notice, for example, the hours he spent considering the "reasons," the likely advantages or disadvantages of deciding one way or another as in his "third time" method of election. See *SpEx*, [181-182].

tells us what to do as soon as we have discerned the evil spirit at work if we want to grow in our power of spiritual discernment. He himself learned through prayerful reflection on his spiritual experiences; and in this rule he now calls us to do the same.

> Rule 6. When the enemy of human nature has been perceived and recognized by his telltale[18] train of thoughts terminating in the evil to which he leads, it is useful for the person who was tempted by him to look immediately at the course of good thoughts which were prompted in him, noting how they began and how, little by little, the evil spirit contrived to make him fall away from the earlier sweetness and spiritual joy until he led him to what his [the spirit's] own corrupt mind intended. The point is that observing such experience and taking mental note of it will be a safeguard for the future against these customary hoaxes of the evil spirit.

The self-examination called for here is another of the many forms of self-examination urged by Ignatius. Their main concern is, not so much with deciding where I failed and with what responsibility, but rather with getting a sure hold on the facts of what really happened, with understanding the facts; and then, through this understanding, with my coming to a knowledge of myself (my strength and weakness of character, my modes of reacting, and the like), and also to a knowledge of the Holy Spirit's loving and powerful care for me and of his ways of dealing with me; finally, to a knowledge of the evil spirit's base aims and ways of achieving them. How did the experience begin? What good thoughts does the evil spirit see as in some way or other related to my weakness and useful for manipulating me? How did he move me away from the good thoughts and spiritual consolation? By associations and sensible imagination or by concepts? By logic from a false principle not made explicit? By sophistical ambiguity of concepts or words? By gradually arousing emotion? How did the Holy Spirit bring to my attention what was going on? And so on. By questions such as these we may succeed in bringing to memory what happened and turn it into a profitable learning experience.

The purpose for doing this as soon as reasonably possible is that in most of us the memory of what happened quickly fades; it becomes hazy or jumbled or full of blank spots. Even when we reflect promptly, the task will sometimes be not at all easy. The

---

18 Although it would be a pun, telltale varied to "telltail" would catch Ignatius' metaphor, *conoscido de su cola serpentina* (*SpEx*MHSJ, p. 390).

process may have been spread over a long period of time with lengthy interruptions. The deception may have depended on associations so deeply hidden as to be hardly observable and only to be guessed at. There may be unexplicitated and unrecognized assumptions at work. Unearthing these subliminal and powerful sources of our thoughts and affections can be of incalculable value for taking possession of ourselves for God. Obviously in this enterprise we need the help of the Holy Spirit and should always undertake it in his presence and with prayer for his light.

If we do this we may hope not to be taken in again in this particular way. If we do this over and over, we may hope to grow in self-knowledge, to become more and more sensitive to the working of the Holy Spirit and of the evil spirit, and to be able to resist and go contrary to temptation before it becomes deeply rooted and dangerous, or before we have mistakenly done something harmful to others or to ourselves.

Assurance and Explanation. Rule II:7

One question may still bother the reader: Can we be sure that when the evil spirit prompts holy thoughts and spiritual consolation, he will in every instance betray his influence by one of the signs which Ignatius notes in Rule 5? This is the question which Rule 7 implies as a presupposition and to which it responds.[19] In answering this implied question, Ignatius first recalls and neatly formulates what he has declared earlier, especially in Rules I:1 and 2 and II:1, about the contrary ways in which the good and evil spirits affect persons according to the thrust of their lives as maturing or regressing Christians. To these declarations, he now

19 It must be admitted that Rule II:7 is puzzling. It does not *explicitly* raise or answer the question about the evil spirit always giving some sign that betrays his influence. Explicitly, it only repeats things said in Rules I:1 and 2 and II:1, and then adds an explanation. As noted earlier, this rule could, with perfect coherence, be inserted immediately after Rules I:1 and 2, as an explanation of them. Certainly, if Ignatius put Rule II:7 after II:6, he must intend something more than merely recalling what he had said in those early rules and now, near the end of all the rules, offering an overdue word of explanation, an afterthought that should have come up earlier. If we read Rule II:7 in context, letting the momentum of thought in Rules II:4-6 carry over into it, then we can see what Ignatius is getting at and why the rule is placed where it is. After reading those rules we may still be wondering whether the influence of the evil spirit will *always* or only sometimes show up in what follows on the consolation and holy thoughts with which the deception begins. Ignatius is now giving assurance that, and explaining why, even when the evil spirit comes as an angel of light, he is bound to reveal himself ultimately in *every* instance.

adds an explanation. It is this explanation which answers the question whether the evil spirit, no matter how cunning his deceptions, will alwaya finally betray himself.

> Rule 7. Persons who are going from good to better the good angel touches sweetly, lightly, gently, as when a drop of water soaks into a sponge, while the evil spirit touches sharply, with noise and disturbance, as when the drop of water falls on a rock. Those who are going from bad to worse the aforesaid spirits touch in a way contrary to the way they touch those going from good to better. The cause of this contrariety is that the disposition of the one touched is either contrary to or concordant with each of the said angels. For, when it is contrary, the angels enter perceptibly, with clamor and observable signs; when it is concordant, they come in quietly, as one comes into his own house through an open door.

The declaration of facts, how each spirit affects spiritually maturing or regressing persons, has already been dealt with in detail above in chapter 2. Therefore the first step in this Rule 7 may be omitted here and our attention centered immediately on the second, the explanation. The reason why a good spirit touches upon and enters into the consciousness of a maturing Christian sweetly, lightly, gently, quietly, as a drop of water enters a sponge, or as you come into your own house when the door is open—the reason is that the disposition of each is concordant with the other.[20] What does that mean? The disposition of maturing Christians is to "devote themselves intensely to purging away their sins and ascending from good to better in the service of God our Lord" (I:2). The disposition of the good spirit, what is "connatural" to him, is to go along with the thrust of life in which a maturing Christian's fundamental and dominant disposition finds expression. The good spirit and the maturing Christian move in the same direction. Insofar as you are a maturing Christian, you will experience the action of the Holy Spirit like a wind at your

---

20 Note that Ignatius is concerned with the consonance or dissonance of good or evil spirits with the already existing fundamental *disposition* by which a person is positively or negatively disposed toward spiritual growth. It is this consonance or dissonance which explains why consolation or desolation is generated when a good or an evil spirit affects the person. He is not, in this rule, concerned with the consonance or dissonance of an already generated *consolation* with a proposed plan or resolution. Rule II:7 cannot, therefore, be used in support of any understanding of Ignatian discernment of God's will by looking for the effect of different proposals on an already actual spiritual consolation. Whether that understanding of Ignatian discernment of God's will is right or wrong, any use of Rule II:7 to support it rests on a reading of the rule which goes far beyond anything which Ignatius explicitly says or implies in this rule.

back—ordinarily a gentle wind, lovingly adapted to you as you are now and helping you to move along easily, delightfully, peacefully, even increasing your velocity toward your goal. But the Spirit acts so gently, with such a light touch, as to be unnoticed unless your attention is centered on him acting in your life and your spiritual sensitivity has grown delicate and acute by pure and yearning love for God, so that you desire to hear and feel every slightest word and touch of his Holy Spirit.

Several qualifications, however, need to be kept in mind. First, an inspiration to such a person from the good spirit may be initially disturbing; but it then brings peace. On occasion, even the wind at your back can be disturbing, upsetting, when it comes suddenly and with too great a velocity to mesh with your present motion; but it is so only momentarily, until it has swept you into its own velocity, where you now move along again peacefully, easily. Second, the peace may be mingled with pain, fear, and the like, when the inspiration calls one to endurance of pain and to daring. Third, even a good person has dimensions of his or her personality not yet set toward God. When the good spirit touches on these there can be disturbance.

In the measure that a maturing Christian has grown sensitive to the Holy Spirit, he or she will also necessarily be sensitive to any contrary movement that conflicts with life in the Spirit. The disposition of the evil spirit is directly contrary to that of the maturing Christian and the Holy Spirit. It is connatural for him "to thrust obstacles in the way, disquieting with false reasons for the sake of impeding progress" (I:2). When he touches on and influences the consciousness of the maturing Christian, there is bound to be disturbance, clamor, observable signs, as noticeable as running into a headwind.

The whole case is reversed when we are talking about regressing Christians; for their disposition and the dominant movement of their lives concur with what the evil spirit connaturally tends to effect in them and runs head on against what is connatural for the Holy Spirit to effect.

All that we are saying squares readily with the first series of rules, but seems at first glance to be in disagreement with Rules 3-6 in the second series. If the dispositions of the evil spirit and the spiritually maturing person clash as they are said to do, producing perceptible disturbance and noise, then how can the evil spirit bring to such a person good and holy thoughts that yield spiritual consolation? How can he disguise himself as an angel of light?

Perhaps Ignatius is nuancing what he has been saying in the rules immediately preceding, in order to make it more accurate. Perhaps he is implying now that even when the evil spirit brings spiritual consolation, there is bound to be, right in the initial experience of thought and consolation from which the deceptive course of thought begins, some disturbance to indicate who is at work. Perhaps he means that if we become attentive and sensitive enough, and through reflection on spiritual experience wise enough, we will be able to perceive the evil spirit at work before he even gets started. The point of the rule would then be a warning and an assurance such as this: Beware of any spiritual consolation and good thoughts when mingled with some disturbance; and be certain that there will be immediately some such disturbance that is perceptible if the thought and consolation are from the evil spirit. Only be alert enough and you will find it. Thus this opinion runs; and at first glance such an interpretation of Rule 7 is logical and rather attractive as an elegantly simple solution of an apparent contradiction.[21]

However, close attention to what Ignatius says in Rules II:3-6 makes it difficult or impossible to accept this attractively simple solution of the problem. In these rules Ignatius seems to be saying that the evil spirit begins by successfully hiding all telltale signs, acting exactly like an angel of light. In Rule 3, he simply says that a good or an evil spirit can effect consolation with a previous cause. In Rule 4, he says that the evil spirit begins by prompting thoughts which are "good and holy, harmonious" with a devout or faithful person. This last phrase is especially pertinent. There is no suggestion of even slight discord, clashing, or disturbance of any sort; and to say that the thoughts are harmonious with the person would surely mean harmonious with his or her disposition as a maturing Christian. In Rule 5 (and 6), when directly attending to the signs of the evil spirit, Ignatius does not have us look for them in the beginning but in what terminates the progression of thought, what it ends up with. In Rule 6, where he instructs us to reflect on the

---

21 This seems to be Michael Buckley's interpretation (*The Way, Supplement* 20, pp. 32, 35). He assumes that there is some sign of the evil spirit right from the start, but too subtle for most persons to catch it.

whole experience, he wants us to note how it began with "sweetness and spiritual joy," and how *afterwards* the evil spirit contrived to lead us gradually away from sweetness and spiritual joy toward his intended goal.

Confronted with all this converging evidence, we seem forced to conclude that Ignatius does not think signs of the evil spirit are present and perceptible at the beginning of the kind of deception which he is describing. Accordingly, there is nothing at that point for even the most sensitive and spiritually experienced person to discern. The more likely or even the necessary interpretation of Rule 7 seems to be that while the evil spirit can begin his deception without any noise or disturbance, harmonizing fully with the disposition and fundamental life-movement of a spiritually maturing person, what he will not and cannot do is to sustain the angel-of-light act. Sooner or later, some sign will appear, some perceptible clash between him and the person whom he is touching. Some thoughts, some affective acts, or some affective feelings will betray his influence. He will not continue to effect what is in accord with the spiritual disposition of the person to be deceived without trying to lead that person by some stratagem to what is in conflict with a Christian disposition. To do so would be to promote Christian growth, a thing totally contrary to the evil spirit's connatural tendency.

A strong and interesting confirmation of this interpretation is that the resulting meaning of the rule becomes equivalently the same way of judging ordinary spiritual experiences which St. Theresa also used in judging her mystical visions. It appears time and again in her writings. One illustration will suffice. While she had easily recognized three or four visions of Christ as having a diabolical origin, there were others the origin of which she was not sure until she reflected on how they affected her life:

> ...for the difference was very great in every respect, and no fancy, but such as all could clearly see. As I had previously been so wicked, I concluded, I could not believe that, if the devil were doing this to delude me and drag me down to hell, he would make use of means which so completely defeated their own ends by taking away vices and making me virtuous and strong; for it was quite clear to me that these experiences had immediately made me a different person.[22]

22 *The Life of the Holy Mother Theresa of Jesus*, in *The Complete Works of St. Theresa*, translated by E. A. Peers (London, 1972), I, ch. 28, pp. 184-185.

The foregoing interpretation of Rules II:3-7 does not imply that there are no experiences of spiritual consolation with good thoughts which are accompanied by some sign of the evil spirit that is subtle enough to escape most persons' attention. All I am saying is that in these rules Ignatius is not talking about such experiences. However, these rules will serve for dealing with such experiences also. Michael Buckley has some excellent comments on the moments or stages through which a person may hope to grow towards sensitivity to any sign of the evil spirit at the very beginning of his intended deception. First, one learns to notice the evil or less good consequences, when they clearly appear, and to trace them back in memory, as Ignatius urges in Rule II:6. Second, by such repeated tracing in memory, one learns to note quickly when things begin to go wrong. Third, one finally learns to recognize the false tone even in the original experience of consolation.[23]

23 Michael Buckley, op. cit., p. 35.

Chapter 11

DECEPTION DURING THE AFTERGLOW
OF SPIRITUAL CONSOLATION
Rule II:8

Rule II:7 completes the treatment of deception by the evil spirit which begins in actual spiritual consolation with preceding cause. There are, we have seen, two steps in the deception. First, he does what is connatural to a good spirit and contrary to his own connatural mode of acting by giving spiritual consolation with good and holy thoughts. Secondly, beginning from those thoughts in spiritual consolation which seem prompted by God, he inspires a course of thought leading in one way or another to his evil purpose. Since consolation *without* previous cause can come only from God (II:2), it is immune from such deception. The evil spirit cannot prompt it nor influence the thoughts and desires that arise in it. Nevertheless, he has a way of using even that consolation to deceive us, and it is about this mode of deception that Ignatius in Rule 8 wants to warn us.

> Rule 8.   Granted that when consolation is without [preceding] cause, it has no deception in it, since, as has been said, such consolation is from God our Lord alone, nevertheless, a spiritual person to whom God gives such consolation should, with great alertness and attention, examine his experience to discern the precise time of the actual consolation [without preceding cause] as distinct from the following time, in which the person is still glowing and still graced by the residue of [actual] consolation that is now over with. The reason for making this distinction is that frequently in this second period, either through one's own reasoning about the relations of concepts and judgments and the conclusions to be drawn from them, or through the influence of a good spirit or of an evil spirit, various purposes and opinions take shape which are not given immediately by God our Lord. Inasmuch as that is the case, these purposes and opinions are in need of prolonged and careful examination be fore full assent is given to them or they are put into execution.

There is so much compressed into this rule, and each part is so dependent for its meaning on other parts, that a thorough and exact understanding demands an examination of each step seen in context, even if this entails some overlapping.

First Step: No Deception in Consolation Without Preceding Cause

The first step is a statement of what we may take for granted and the reason why we can: "Granted that when consolation is without [preceding] cause, it has no deception in it, since, as has been said, such consolation is from God our Lord alone." Two things in this statement need to be noted and commented on: first, the subordinate position and concessive character of what is said; and second, the interpretation of the phrase "no deception in it."

Calling attention to the subordinate position of the statement that consolation without previous cause is without deception will help us keep perspective and avoid reading into Ignatius what is not there. Ignatius is not directly concerned to show or emphasize the positive value of consolation without previous cause for discernment of spirits or discernment of God's will. The reason for bringing up the immediately divine source of consolation without previous cause and its consequent freedom from deception is simply to warn us about what can happen afterwards. Some recent writings on Ignatius' discernment propose that such consolation is the first principle for all discernment of spirits or discernment of God's will.[1] Certainly, if Ignatius thought so, he did not make it explicit in Rule II:8: and it is at least debatable whether such a view is implicit in that rule. As noted above on page 234, Rule II:5 seems clearly to imply that consolation with previous cause is a reliable sign of the Holy Spirit if no sign of the evil spirit follows in continuity with it. To say nothing of the fact that there are other and more fundamental signs of the good and evil spirits than spiritual consolation and desolation.

What Ignatius has in mind by "deception" when he states that consolation without previous cause has no deception in it is surely the deception that can be in consolation with previous cause, the

---

1 Foremost among those who hold that consolation without preceding cause is the first principle of all discernment are K. Rahner, S.J. and Harvey D. Egan, S.J. An account of their view and an evaluation of it can be found in Appendix IV below, pp. 291-313.

deception that he has been giving advice about in the preceding
four rules (II:4-7), which have just been explained in chapter
10. That is to say, the evil spirit cannot play the part of an angel
of light and prompt good and holy thoughts which are in accord
with faith, and then through these induce consolation without
previous cause. Such consolation is not mediated by our thoughts.
It is immediately from God alone. Hence, the thoughts or plans
which flow from such consolation cannot be deceptions.

Second Step: Distinguish Consolation from the Afterglow

"Nevertheless," Ignatius states, "a spiritual person to whom
God gives such consolation should, with great alertness and attention, examine his experience to discern the precise time of the
actual consolation as distinct from the following time, in which the
person is still glowing and still graced by the residue of actual
consolation that is now over with." Our very awareness of immu-
nity from deception in consolation without previous cause can
itself be an occasion for us to fall into deception in the time *immediately* following the actual consolation. That is why, in the second
step of the rule, Ignatius warns us to distinguish carefully between
the actual consolation and the time of afterglow. Leaving aside
for a moment the purpose of this warning, let us try to understand
what he is saying about the time immediately following consolation
without previous cause. We need to be clear on this if we are to
distinguish it from the actual consolation immediately from God.

What, then, is meant by saying the person is still glowing and
still graced by the residue of actual consolation? Our understanding
will be limited in some way by our uncertainty about the positive
characteristics peculair to consolation without previous cause with
which the afterglow is contrasted. However, by gathering all the
hints in the text and relating them with the structure of any
experience of consolation, we can reach a satisfactory understanding of what Ignatius means.

Recall the essential structure of any consolation whatsoever.
Recall that there are in the affective sensibility of the consoled
person feelings of delight, contentment, elation, peace, and the
like. These are grounded in the object of some cognitive and
affective acts. Now it is an ordinary experience that when the
source of a consolation ceases to actually influence the person's
awareness, the memory of it and the feelings, or even the feelings

alone, continue for a time, slowly dying, like the heat of metal removed from the fire, or like the freshness of flowers cut off from their roots. Think of someone who is consoled by great music or a sign of love from the beloved. When that which effects the consolation, the music or the sign of love in the illustrations just given, is no longer present except in memory, the delightful feelings of consolation may continue. In fact, when the person's attention is now entirely absorbed with something else, when there is not even a present actual memory of that which brought on the feelings of joy or exultation, the feelings may go on glowing.

What we see in all such experiences parallels what Ignatius is saying about the kind of actual spiritual consolation in which God influences the person without any mediation and about the afterglow of such spiritual experience. In Rule II:8, he is stating that when God's immediate influence ceases, the actual consolation of that sort is over with, ended, but the feelings can go on vibrating, glowing. In this situation, he warns us, unless we are alert, we can easily confuse this afterglow with the actual consolation from the immediate influence of God. Such confusion opens the way to a deception which he describes in the third step of the rule. Before examining that, let us take up a question which arises at this point and is of considerable significance for discernment of spirits and discernment of God's will through discernment of spirits.

A Question: Is the Afterglow a Spiritual Consolation?

Should this affective residue be called spiritual consolation? So long as we know that we are talking about an afterglow and not the actual consolation coming from the immediate influence of God, does it matter what we call it? There is good reason to think it does make a difference, and that difference explains why Ignatius does not call the experience spiritual consolation, not even spiritual consolation of a lesser degree or of a different kind, but only the residue, the glow that is left after spiritual consolation is ended (*pasada*).[2]

It is necessary to go carefully here. Immediately after the consolation without previous cause, the vivid memory of it and reflection upon it as a manifestation of God's love for me and

---

2 Karl Rahner calls it consolation without cause "of second degree" (in "The Logic of Concrete Individual Knowledge in Ignatius Loyola," *Dynamic Element*, p. 158). For discussion of this point, see Appendix IV below.

of his presence in my life may bring me consolation. This consolation is neither a spiritual consolation without cause nor merely its residue. It is plainly a spiritual consolation with cause. It arises from the present influence of the Holy Spirit intensifying my faith, hope, and charity *through the mediation of my memory, intellect, and will.* Consolation without previous cause is not so mediated; it is immediately from the Holy Spirit (Rule II:2). On the other hand, the mere affective residue or afterglow of such consolation is not mediated by my acts rooted in living faith, nor is it from any *present* immediate influence of the Holy Spirit. That is why it reveals nothing about what spirit is presently moving me and is of no use whatever for discernment of spirits, and is not, in Ignatian categories, a spiritual consolation properly speaking.

If we were to think of this afterglow as a spiritual consolation, it would have to be one which is neither without previous cause nor with previous cause in the Ignatian meaning of these terms. (To avoid confusion here, remember that "previous cause" in these phrases refers to the person's own acts of intellect and will toward a consoling object (II: 2), not to the prior influence of God or of any created spirit in prompting the acts of intellect and will.) Since the afterglow in Rule II:8 is the experience one has when spiritual consolation without preceding cause has ceased, it cannot be such consolation in a lesser degree; for such consolation is defined as immediately from God. While actual, such consolation has varying degrees of intensity, completeness, and the like; but what takes place in the following time, when God's immediate causation has ceased, is simply a different *kind* of experience, not a lesser degree of the original experience. Neither is it a spiritual consolation with previous cause. That is unthinkable on two counts: it is merely a *residue* of spiritual consolation, and what is more, it is a residue of spiritual consolation *without previous cause.* It is, then, not consolation from an actual object mediated by the person's acts of intellect and will. As shown above, spiritual consolation with previous cause might be experienced immediately after spiritual consolation without previous cause mediated by my memory of the latter and my thoughts about God's love for me. But that would be a different kind of experience from the residual glow of the unmediated actual consolation.

Should we then add a third category of spiritual consolation? Ignatius does not. There is strong reason for not doing so. If we did so, all that Ignatius says about spiritual consolation in general ought to hold for it, but could not. Any spiritual consolation, according to Ignatius, is at least, at first appearance, a sign of the Holy Spirit *here and now* influencing the thoughts and affective impulses toward decision and action which may come during and from its influence. Spiritual consolation with previous cause, it is true, can be prompted by the evil spirit disguising himself as an angel of light. But unless some sign of the evil spirit appears among the thoughts and affections which follow in continuity with that consolation, the consolation is to be judged as originating from the Holy Spirit (Rule II:5, 7). If, then, we call the residual glow of consolation without previous cause a spiritual consolation, we should be able to use it just as we use spiritual consolation with previous cause to evaluate thoughts and impulses as coming from the Holy Spirit. But nothing that Ignatius says in Rule II:8 shows that the afterglow of consolation without previous cause can serve such a purpose. Quite the contrary.

To serve as even probable evidence favoring a judgment that the thoughts (the "purposes and opinions") which come during it are from God, the afterglow of consolation without preceding cause would have to be seen as the result and sign of God acting on human consciousness at the very time of the experience; that is what justifies taking the thoughts or impulses which arise in consolation as being from God. But the very point of Rule 8 is that such divine action has ceased and the afterglow is not a sign of present actual divine influence on the human consciousness of the person involved. What he or she now experiences is precisely what Ignatius calls it, a "residue," a fading glory in the affective sensibility of a consolation which *was* from the actual immediate influence of God, an influence that has ended. That is why the afterglow is of no account whatsoever as evidence for discernment of spirits and gives no indication of any sort whatsoever about the source of the purposes and opinions which come to mind during it.[3] This is what Ignatius is telling us in the third step of his argument in Rule II:8. Let us look at it.

3 In complete consistency with his view that consoolation without preceding cause is the first principle of all discernment of spirits, Karl Rahner says that the time immediately following such consolation is the *only* time at which discernment of God's will can take place in Ignatius' second mode of election, by consolation and desolation and discernment of spirits (*SpEx*, [176]). It "is not just a possibility [for such discernment] but *the* possibility, as long as we are concerned with the Second Mode of Election at all" (*Dynamic Element*, p. 161).

Third Step: The Possible Deception

To get the full import of this third step, recall the first two steps:
(1) In actual consolation without previous cause there can be no
deception; and (2) we should, however, carefully discern in our
experience between the actual consolation and the residue. "The
reason for making this distinction," Ignatius now adds in the
third step, "is that frequently in this second period, either through
one's own reasoning about the relations of concepts and judgments
and the conclusions to be drawn from them, or through the influence of a good spirit or an evil spirit, various purposes and opinions
take shape which are not given immediately by God our Lord."
The clear implication is that we tend to overlook the passage from
actual consolation to mere afterglow and so assume that the purposes and opinions which come in the latter period are immediately
from the Holy Spirit.

How in fact do these purposes and opinions come? They are,
Ignatius says, from our own reasoning based on our own ways of
perceiving, understanding, relating ideas, and the like, or influenced by good or evil spirits. That is to say, it "frequently" happens
in this way. The implication of "frequently" is that it does not
always happen this way. So we may conclude that sometimes the
Holy Spirit himself does immediately inspire us without giving
any sign of actual spiritual consolation without previous cause by
which we could judge that he is inspiring the thoughts. So, the fact
that the purposes and opinions come during this glowing period
after actual spiritual consolation has ceased gives no hint at all
about whether they are prompted by the Holy Spirit or the evil
spirit or arise from our own dispositions and ways of thinking.

Further, by implication, the rule requires us to presuppose that
purposes and opinions are sometimes given in actual consolation
without previous cause, not merely after or before, and that when
they are so given, we may reasonably accept the consolation as
evidence that these are from God, without having to test them in
the way we have to test what comes in the following time. Otherwise, what is Ignatius' point in emphasizing that in the afterglow
as opposed to the actual consolation, there may be purposes and
opinions "which are not given immediately by God our Lord"
and as a consequence "are in need of prolonged and careful examination"? Is there not a clear assumption of purposes and opinions
which are immediately from God our Lord given in the experience

249

of actual consolation without previous cause? Otherwise, what is the deception that is special to the time following?[4]

This is, in fact, precisely the crucial point of the whole rule: Purposes and opinions arise both in actual consolation without previous cause and in the afterglow; actual consolation without previous cause is a sign that those purposes and judgments which will arise in it are immediately given by God; whereas the afterglow is not such a sign at all. It leaves open other possibilities, even the possibility of generating our purposes and opinions under the influence of the evil spirit playing on our ignorance, inattention, emotional weakness, and egoism.

Fourth Step: How to Avoid the Deception

So we see why Ignatius, in the fourth and final step of Rule II:8, counsels us: "Inasmuch as that is the case, these purposes and opinions are in need of prolonged and careful examination before full assent is given to them or they are put into execution." The point to clarify in this statement is the "prolonged and careful examination" by which we determine whether to give full assent and put into execution the questionable purposes and judgments. How do we go about such an examination? The afterglow during which they come is, as we have seen, of no help whatever; it even offers occasion for a deception. How, then, do we find out whether God wants us to assent to and execute the purposes and opinions in question? What are the norms for judging whether God is counseling us or not? What has already been said about the afterglow of consolation makes plain that we are then in the same general situation we are in whenever, in any concrete situation for choice, we wonder what God wants us to do and as yet have no convincing evidence for judging. So, our question can be turned into the more general one: What is the Ignatian teaching on how individuals can in a concrete situation discern God's will for their choice and action? The answer to this question goes beyond the limits of this book.[5]

---

4 Karl Rahner does not allow for any communication from God regarding our purposes or plans or any created reality during the actual consolation without previous cause (*Dynamic Element*, pp. 136-137). Harvey Egan, on the contrary, thinks the rule itself and the letter to Teresa Rejadell leave no doubt that there is such communication (*Mystical Horizon*, pp. 48-49). Egan's view seems well founded.
5 See above, pp. 12-13.

Summary and Conclusions

We have completed a detailed and somewhat complicated analysis of Rule II:8. It will now be possible to summarize our findings in a way that will more clearly and more precisely convey the meaning of the rule to anyone who has gone through the analysis.

1. Since spiritual consolation without previous cause can in fact (there is no question for now about what the recipient thinks) come only and immediately from God, it cannot be ambiguous or deceptive in the way spiritual consolation with previous cause can be. The latter bears at first sight signs of being from God or his good angel that were given in Rules I:2 and II:1; but it lacks sure evidence of its source, as is clear from Rules II: 3-4, until it has been tested as stated in Rule II:5. Before passing that test, there is the possibility that it is prompted by the evil spirit and is a misleading indicator for the source of the thoughts which cause it or spring from it. Consolation without previous cause, on the other hand, while it is actual (as contrasted with its afterglow), by right eliminates all doubt about its source in God (II:2) and, consequently, by right it eliminates any thought that it might be from the evil spirit. The thoughts and impulses that flow from it, therefore, also escape the possibility of being from the evil spirit and of terminating during the consolation in something which is to his wicked purpose.

2. Does such consolation also, in fact as well as by right, eliminate any uncertainty in the mind of the recipient? Is the recipient of the consolation made certain in the very experience itself that the consolation and the thoughts are from God immediately and are free from all deception, or is there need for instruction and assurance? Ignatius neither asserts nor denies that such certitude is given in the experience. Without any sure knowledge of what goes on in consolation without previous cause, beyond being drawn totally into love for God, we cannot make any reliable conjecture.

3. However, the main point of Rule 8 is not a certitude that consolation without previous cause is free of the aforementioned deceptions, much less the reason why it is so. All this is brought up as something taken for granted and leading to the main point, the warning that, *although* consolation without previous cause is

251

free of deception, nevertheless we must be cautiously on guard about the time immediately after it terminates. For then is the time at which a deception may set in. True, God may still be inspiring the thoughts which come at that time. God is not limited in his inspirations to time of consolation, much less to time of consolation without previous cause; it is we who are limited in our ways of telling when God is leading and guiding us. However, the thoughts that come then may be only the results of our own reasoning and even influenced by an evil spirit. If we give them immediate assent and put them into execution, we may open ourselves to error and harm to ourselves or others.

4. The means to avoid such deception, error, and harm is prayerful reflective examination of the experience. Ignatius says nothing of prayer in this rule, but all that we have seen before should make it perfectly clear that he would think us foolish to take on the spirit of darkness without prayer for light from the Holy Spirit. The examination itself involves two steps: (1) careful reflection on the whole experience in order to discern when the consolation ended and the period of affective afterglow began; and (2) if the thoughts under reflective consideration come after the consolation itself ended, subjection of these thoughts to prolonged scrutiny and to careful judgment by suitable norms, which are given elsewhere.[6]

5. It also seems that, although Ignatius does not state this anywhere that I know of, our understanding of this deception in relation to consolation without previous cause can call attention to the possibility of a parallel kind of deception in relation to consolation with previous cause. This one would differ from the deception noted in rules II:3 and 4, which begins during the latter sort of consolation, and can even be completed during it. For all we have noted about the structure of consolation in general and about the affective afterglow leaves no doubt about the experience of spiritual consolation with previous cause also having two moments: the moment of actual consolation, rooted in living faith here and now in act under the power of the Holy Spirit; and the moment of afterglow, the residue of the first moment. Here too we must be on our guard against confusing the residue with actual consolation. Only the latter can have the value for discernment of spirits and of God's will that Ignatius attributes to consolation

6 *SpEx*, [169-188, 333]; Autograph Directory III, [17-21] in *Dir SpEx*MHSJ, pp. 74-77.

with previous cause. We can be deceived at this time also if we fail
to distinguish between the two moments in our experience.

For example, I meditate on Sacred Scripture and I am moved
to spiritual consolation grounded in an actual response of enlivened
faith in God's amazing love for me revealed in Jesus Christ. Afterwards I go about my work. Without any present actual memory
of God's word or response to it, I am still feeling buoyantly glad.
During this time there comes to me some thought about and
impulse toward one side of a decision on which I have been deli-
berating. Does the fact that this thought and impulse came at just
this time provide any evidence, even partial and tentative, that the
Holy Spirit moved me to them, and that he is counseling me to
follow a certain course of action? There is no reason at all for
thinking so. The mere afterglow of the consolation is no sign that
thoughts and impulses or plans which come during it, even if
integral with it, are from the influence of the Holy Spirit. When
my feelings of peace, joy, and the like were flowing from an actual
response of living faith (not just temporally coincidental with it),
then there would have been sound reason for thinking that the
thought and impulse to a decision came from the Holy Spirit also.
I would have had some probable, partial, tentative evidence.
For only the power of the Holy Spirit can account for living faith.
When my feelings of peace and joy flow from an actual experience
of living faith, and are integral with it, then they too are spiritual.
When some purpose, some impulse, arises *within* this whole experience, *under the influence* of such faith and feelings, then and only
then can I think that I have any evidence that it comes from the
Holy Spirit. During the mere afterglow of spiritual consolation,
when there is no actual response of living faith, I have no reason
for thinking the feelings that remain without the actual faith
response rooting them are any sign whatever of the Holy Spirit
influencing me now. The residue of consolation (with as well as
without previous cause) has no positive significance for discernment of spirits or God's will; it has only a negative significance
as an occasion for a deception.

A Problem and a Proposed Solution

Whatever the reader may judge about the suggested extension
to consolation with previous cause of the deception which Ignatius
in Rule II:8 speaks of in relation to consolation without previous
cause, the extension neither helps nor hinders nor affects in any

way our understanding of that rule. We do understand enough to grasp the point which Ignatius is making and to know what he would have us do if we should have and recognize that we have the spiritual experience he is talking about. However, our grasp of what Ignatius means by consolation without previous cause is so incomplete that we cannot with any reasonable assurance recognize when we have or do not have such an experience and put that rule into practice. There are too many conflicting opinions without convincing reasons for any of them. There are too many unresolved questions, the answers to which are needed in order to make a sound judgment whether or not some particular spiritual consolation is what Ignatius means by consolation without previous cause.[7]

We do not want to act or to advise others rashly. How can we meet such a situation in the practical order while the exegetes and speculative theologians continue their efforts to bring us clarity? Even without adequate understanding of consolation without previous cause, what we have already drawn out of the earlier rules shows us a way of avoiding the deception against which Rule II:8 is warning us. (If what was said just now about a similar danger of deception in the afterglow of consolation with previous cause is true, then a general principle applicable to *all* spiritual consolation is needed and suffices: It will give a simpler, more unified directive for discerning spirits which is, as far as it goes, fully Ignatian.)

The deception warned against in Rule II:8 can take place only if the person being deceived makes several presuppositions, two factual and one theological. The presuppositions of fact are: first, that the consolation just now experienced is without previous cause and, second, that the thoughts arose during it and as integral with it. The theological presupposition is that, objectively, any thoughts which come in a consolation without previous cause cannot possibly be deceptive, because the consolation and the thoughts are immediately from God alone.

Let us allow the theological presupposition to stand unquestioned. If we simply decide never to assume the factual presuppositions to be fulfilled, then, without even concerning ourselves about the nature of Ignatius' consolation without previous cause, we can be

7 For further discussion, see Appendix IV below.

secure from any deception of the sort he speaks of in Rule II:8. If in our reflection on spiritual experience we simply subject all consolations and all thoughts that seem to come in genuinely spiritual consolation (whether with or without previous cause) to the tests already described in Rule II:5, we will be just as safe from deceptions as we would ever be with a thorough knowledge of what Ignatius means by his distinction of consolation with and without previous cause. By so doing we will not be departing from his own guidelines or taking any risk. We will simply be admitting our inability to go a step further and to excuse ourselves from the necessity of subjecting our thoughts and purposes given during a recognized consolation without previous cause to the tests required when thoughts and purposes come outside such consolation.

What is more, given human limitations in the concrete, even if we knew adequately and with certitude what, in general, consolation without previous cause is, and even if in some particular experience judged that the consolation just experienced was such, would it not be unwise for most of us, if not for all of us, most of the time if not all the time, to assent to and put into execution judgments and purposes which seemed to come during consolation without previous cause before subjecting them to thorough examination? It is so easy to misjudge our own experience. Could we be certain that what we thought was spiritual consolation without previous cause really was such? If it was, could we in many instances be completely sure the thoughts came during the actual consolation and not at a moment immediately after it ceased? If we sometimes can, are we sure that what we take now for the thoughts which came during the actual consolation are precisely the thoughts which came then? Are we sure that we have not missed some qualification that was in God's communication? Are we sure that we have not afterwards, without being aware of doing so, added to or taken away or wrongly interpreted something, and in so doing changed the whole tenor of the message?[8]

If we cannot be sure about all these matters, then the only way to avoid deception is to subject the thoughts to thorough testing. Then it seems to make little difference whether they came in consolation with or without previous cause; and so, it is of slight concern for the sake of avoiding deception whether we do or do

8 *LettersIgn*, pp. 22-23. See also what Ignatius says about prophets, ibid., p. 197; the parallel is obvious.

not know for sure what these consolations are or which one we have. It is enough: (1) to know that the consolation is a *spiritual* one, and (2) to see that the purposes and opinions which arise are truly integral with the consolation, and (3) to be sure they do not lead by some sort of continuous progression to any sign of the evil spirit (Rule II: 5). If these conditions are fulfilled, then we have sound reason for thinking that the consolation is prompted by the Holy Spirit and that we have at least some partial evidence (not ordinarily conclusive by itself) for judging any purpose and opinions which came in the consolation to be also from the Holy Spirit. If they in reality are from the Holy Spirit and if we do what lies in us to learn this, we can be sure that he will give us the further necessary signs to justify our reaching a judgment, insofar as this judgment is needed for living our faith-life for his glory.

PART V

APPENDICES

AND

REFERENCE MATTER

INTRODUCTION TO THE
APPENDICES

In a book written for a very much wider readership than the relatively small group of the Ignatian scholars, it seemed unwise to burden an already sufficiently difficult analysis of Ignatius' teaching with further difficult or lengthy topics, such as his teaching and the mystical doctrine of St. John of the Cross. For the same reason, it did not seem advisable to risk confusing readers with a consideration of conflicting interpretations of Ignatian teaching or conflicting theological opinions on Satan. However, it seems not only advantageous but even requisite at least to take note of and to comment briefly on some differing views of those who are all collaborating in a common search for a true understanding of spiritual experience, and of Ignatian teaching in particular. It is, of course, impossible to do full justice to these views in a few pages. Nevertheless, what is said now will at least serve to alert those without extensive background in Ignatian studies to the fact that there are differing, even widely differing, interpretations of Ignatius; and it will also serve to highlight by contrast critically important steps in the exposition of my own interpretation.

Appendix I

THE EXISTENCE OF SATAN AND DEMONS

Theological Opinions on It as an
Object of Christian Belief

Many Christians in our time feel uncomfortable with belief in created personal spirits, both good and evil ones. Two reasons for this feeling are obvious. First, belief in these spirits appears naive, primitive, to many in our scientific age. Second, belief in Satan and demons has had a dreadful history of accompanying superstition and cruelty.[1] But these are hardly sound reasons for renouncing belief in such spirits. Could not much the same reasons be alleged for renouncing belief in God?

It may be that the question regarding the existence of good and evil created spirits is not a question in the first order of importance among theological questions—though not all theologians would agree to that view, as will appear below (pages 268-270). In either case, there is no necessity to settle the question in order to use the Ignatian rules for discernment of spirits profitably, as was shown above (pages 34-37). Nevertheless it will be of value for those who want to use these rules to have some idea of what theologians are currently saying about faith in the good and evil spirits. Until quite recently theologians generally had no problem about the existence of such beings. Now, however, statements rather frequently occur in articles, books, discussions, and even lectures or homilies to the effect that many modern theologians doubt the existence of angels and devils. These statements, usually made in passing and without sufficient nuances or proofs, are unsettling to many of those who study or make or direct St. Ignatius'

1 See, e.g., Henry Ansgar Kelly, *The Devil, Demonology and Witchcraft* (Garden City, N.Y., 1968). Hereafter referred to as *The Devil*.

Exercises, or use his rules for discernment of spirits outside the Exercises.

Before detailing any theological opinions, I shall first formulate the question at issue as accurately as I can. After that, I shall present a spectrum of opinions of Catholic theologians.

Any lack of exactitude about the point at issue will inevitably lead to frustrating confusion in discussing answers to it. The question is not concerned with the mythological, imaginative, historically conditioned modes of representing angels, benevolent or malevolent, which are found in Sacred Scripture. No doubt demythologizing is needed in order to find the revealed message. But such demythologizing leaves untouched the core question, whether the existence of good and evil angelic beings, freed from mythological forms of representation, is part of the divine revelation. This distinction is very necessary lest some accept the mythological representations in a literal meaning and others discard the angels with the mythological material for no better reason than their having confused the two. Much less, of course, is our question concerned with the fanciful superstitions about angels, especially the wicked ones, which have flourished since the Scriptural times among Christians and others. Even the interesting and profound speculations of great theologians on the nature and action of angels are beside the point here.

Assuming the necessary demythologizing, then, we find that the chief point at issue is the existence of those good and evil, non-human, personal beings, spoken of in Scripture and ecclesial documents by such names as angels, Satan, demons, spirits, beings who can and do affect human persons to help or hinder salvation. The influence on human life and salvation to which we refer is not that of visions or diabolical possession or obsession or miraculous events or anything of that sort. It is principally their influence on the interior movements of human minds and hearts in hidden ways, and through these on the events of human history on a bigger scale, where good and evil are written large, in splendid or hideous ways. Even the foregoing statement and explanation of the question is not precise enough. For the question is not simply whether angelic beings exist and influence human life, but whether Christians should believe in their existence and influence as a revealed truth. Do Sacred Scripture, conciliar declarations, or the Church's ordinary teaching justify thinking that belief in good or bad angels is a matter of Christian faith?

Although the question necessarily includes the good angels, as it presents itself in our time it is focused especially on the evil angels, Satan and demons. Preceding and continuing during the recent unhealthy interest in the diabolic, some serious writing on the topic has been appearing for several decades. Most of it assumes the reality of evil spirits and discusses their nature and impact on human life. The exact question we are concerned with is touched on lightly or not at all. As mentioned above, one hears or reads many facile obiter dicta (more often from those who confidently wipe out belief in spirits as childish, not up-to-date). But any sustained, in-depth theological writing which bears on the precise question at issue, unconfused with related issues, aware of and competently evaluating the available theological evidence—this kind of writing is not plentiful.

Among those who have written on this question in a way to deserve some respectful attention, we find a spectrum of positions taken. Existence of angels (good and bad) is said to be: certainly a matter of faith; not beyond questioning but most probable, so that anyone who denies it is misinformed and misguided; uncertain, questionable; uncertain and improbable. Which opinion is more widespread among theologians and exegetes is a question for which there seems to be no solid evidence one way or the other. Again, confident assertions on both sides can be read, but I am not aware of any sound evidence for a majority opinion.

What does seem significant is that no reputable author, whether scriptural exegete or theologian, after serious examination of the theological evidence, is willing to say that the existence of angels is certainly not a matter of faith, is certainly not revealed. At least I have found no such conclusion, and neither have those whom I consulted who are theologically and scripturally more widely read than I am.

The farthest theologians seem able to go on the basis of analyzing theological evidence is to say that the existence of angelic creatures is not certainly a revealed truth to be believed by the faithful—which is very different from saying that their existence is certainly not a revealed truth or, in other words, certainly not an object of Christian belief

Appendix I. The Existence of Satan and Demons

A summary description of some contrasting views will serve to illustrate the spectrum of opinions mentioned above.

Although others have dealt much more fully with other questions about good and evil spirits, no one, to my knowledge, has dealt more fully or carefully with the core issue of their existence than Karl Rahner has. Let us look at the perspective in which he thinks we should approach this question and then at his conclusion and reason for it.

In an age when we readily suppose that there are other intelligent beings than man in the universe, Karl Rahner thinks it unreasonable to reject angels, provided they are purified of all mythological accretions and are regarded as "principalities and powers" of the cosmos, belonging to our one world by the very ground of their being. Thought of in this way, they are *in principle* not inaccessible to human knowledge, though not within the range of science. So, when speaking of angels, revelation is interpreting a reality of the universe in relation to God and his saving action in man, and all the statements of revelation about them belong to theological anthropology and Christology.[2] This perspective permeates Rahner's treatment of angels and demons: Even though not visible, if they exist, they are entirely integral with our visible world; their suprahuman influences on human history are subtly intimated to the human mind. Within this perspective, he thinks, the findiugs of comparative religion on the history of angels in human thought, its growth, variations, mythological expressions, and universality can become intelligible.[3]

For Rahner, the decisive evidence of the Church's teaching, which enables us to see the scriptural evidence as the Church does, is found in chapter 1 of the solemn profession of faith drawn up by the Fourth Lateran Council in 1215. Others, as we shall see, read this declaration of Lateran IV in a different way than Rahner, and it becomes a pivot of the debate. It will be well, therefore, to have the words of the Council before us.

> We firmly believe and profess without qualification that there is only one true God, eternal,...omnipotent, and indescribable: three persons but one essence...; they are the one and only principle of all things—Creator of all things visible and invisible, spiritual and

2 Karl Rahner, "Angels," *Sacramentum Mundi* (New York, 1968) I, pp. 28-29.
3 Ibid.

corporeal, who, by his almighty power, from the very beginning of time has created both orders of creatures in the same way out of nothing, the spiritual or angelic world and the corporeal or visible universe. And afterwards he formed the creature man, who in a way belongs to both orders, as he is composed of spirit and body. For the devil and the other demons were created by God good according to their nature, but they made themselves evil by their own doing. As for man, his sin was at the prompting of the devil.[4]

From this document, Rahner concludes: "The existence of angels cannot be disputed." "Consequently," he adds, "it will be firmly maintained that the existence of angels and demons is *affirmed* in Scripture and not merely assumed as an hypothesis which we could drop today." The affirmation, he says, is only of existence, not including the "mythological, historically conditioned, representational material" which may appear in Scripture.[5] Regarding the Devil (Satan) in particular, Rahner holds that he "is not to be regarded as a mere mythological personification of evil in the world; the existence of the devil cannot be denied."[6]

Since the Council was dealing with the Albigensians who believed in the devil as creator of corporeal reality, others interpret what the Council says as *assuming rather than explicitly declaring* the existence of good angels and the devil. Thus, Adolf Darlap says that, while explicitly declaring against the Albigensians only that everything other than God is created by God, the Council nevertheless also assumes and implies the existence of the angelic order of creation "and that this is guaranteed by the ordinary magisterium and tradition."[7]

Reading the declaration of Lateran IV as assuming or presupposing but not intending to declare explicitly and to define the existence of created spirits, Peter Schoonenberg is led to question the validity of apodictically concluding that the existence of such spirits must be an object of faith. For, unlike Darlap, he is not sure that the ordinary teaching of the Church, as for example in the encyclical of Pius XII, *Humani Generis,* or any other evidence from Scripture or liturgy or tradition settles the question. Schoonenberg

4 Denzinger-Schönmetzer, 800; Denzinger-Banwart, 428; English from *The Church Teaches: Documents of the Church in English Translation,* by J. F. Clarkson, S.J. et al. (St. Louis: B. Herder, 1955), p. 146.
5 K. Rahner, *Sacramentum Mundi,* I, p. 32.
6 "Devil," *Sacramentum Mundi,* II, p. 73.
7 Adolf Darlap, ibid., p. 71.

is careful not to go beyond questioning. He does not deny that good and evil angels exist or that their existence is an article of Christian faith. He only raises questions that theologians should ask themselves: whether they can claim without qualification that the existence of angels and devils is an article of faith, whether their existence is necessarily presupposed by any certainly revealed truths or is merely part of an historically conditioned world view in which those truths were revealed. Taking seriously the *possibility* of their existence, he then insists, as Rahner does, that, if they exist, they must be thought of as belonging to the one creation and so having a "causal connection" with our visible and evolving world. They can, he suggests, realize their fullness only by communicating themselves in some way or other to the visible world.[8]

With strong feelings on the question and great concern because of the harm he finds resulting from belief in the devil and demons throughout the ages, Henry Ansgar Kelly[9] gives an emphatic answer to Schoonenberg's question to theologians. Theologians, he says, cannot justly give or call for an unqualified assent of faith to the existence of evil spirits. He is willing even to assert that their existence is improbable. This opinion is declared on the first page of his book, but not until the last ten pages does he draw up his reasons for his opinion. Almost all of the book is given over to a critical account of demonology in the Old and New Testaments and in the history of Western thought since then. Besides this historical account, Kelly demythologizes many beliefs about the nature, origin, and activity of the devil and demons. He also highlights the harmful results of these beliefs in human life. All of this does, of course, indirectly bear on his answer to Schoonenberg's question and directly grounds his practical conclusion.

When he comes to the question whether we today should believe in the existence of these malignant creatures, he takes Schoonenberg's very condensed statement of reasons for questioning belief in them as his basis. He develops those reasons, and through them he seeks to undermine a number of commonly used supports for belief in Satan and demons. Finally he reaches a firmly held opinion that we have no grounds for a theological certainty about their existence.[10] (In the course of his argument, he seems not

---

8 Peter Schoonenberg, *God's World in the Making* (Pittsburgh, 1964), pp. 8-10.
9 See note 1 of this Appendix I, above.
10 H. A. Kelly, *The Devil*, pp. 122-131.

always to keep clear the distinction between disproving the existence of evil spirits and demythologizing the ways of representing them and their activities.)

However, as with others, the crucial issue seems to be how to interpret the declaration of Lateran Council IV. In his interpretation Kelly follows Schoonenberg, expounding it more fully than the latter does and explicitly setting his interpretation in direct contrast with that of Karl Rahner and Herbert Vorgrimler.[11]

When drawing his conclusions at the end of this line of thought, Kelly runs together (1) conclusions based on earlier chapters which dealt with other questions, and (2) the conclusion that follows from his argument in this final chapter. All his conclusions stated here regarding the need for demythologizing the Scriptural stories and representations of angels, and also all his conclusions regarding superstitions and diabolic possession can be fully accepted by those who respond affirmatively to the question whether the existence of the devil (and of good angels) is of the Christian faith. The only conclusion which Kelly draws from his reasoning on that question is that "although it is possible that evil spirits exist, at the present time it does not seem probable."[12] Perhaps a more just conclusion from the arguments which he gave would be that there is no certain answer to the question. Even assuming the validity of his interpretation of Lateran Council IV and his other arguments, they would seem to show no more than that the arguments from the other side are not conclusive, not that there is a greater probability on the negative side.

In any case, Kelly puts his *practical* conclusion firmly: Since the existence of evil spirits does not at present seem probable to him; and since belief in evil spirits does not seem necessary in order to cope with the problems of human life, the advantages claimed for

---

11 Ibid., pp. 128-129. Kelly was using an earlier work of Karl Rahner and Herbert Vorgrimler, *Theological Dictionary* (New York, 1965), pp. 126-127. It must be admitted that this article is at times obscure. Rahner has given us a much clearer and fuller statement of his opinion in his articles on "Angels" and "Devil" in his later work of 1968, *Sacramentum Mundi* (New York, 1968-1970), I, 27-35 and II, 73-75; and I have used this. If this later article had been available when Kelly published his book in 1965, some of his uncertainty about Rahner's opinion and, I think, his misunderstanding of it (perhaps justifiable in the circumstances) could have been avoided— unless Rahner has altered his opinion in his later work. The contrast between Kelly's and Rahner's views could have been made sharper, too.

12 H. A. Kelly, *The Devil*, p. 131.

such belief being attainable in other ways; since, further, great evils have, in the past, followed from this belief—for all these reasons Kelly concludes that "it would seem best to act as though evil spirits did not exist, until such time as their existence is forced upon us."[13] His reasons imply that even at that time, it would be best in the practical order to omit consideration of evil spirits unless it could be shown that some otherwise unattainable advantage would be entailed by bringing them into the picture. This practical conclusion, I have already pointed out, could be accepted by one who affirms belief in angelic beings who affect our human world. Let us look at one such person who, for different reasons than Kelly, offers similar practical advice.

Ernest Lussier, a scholar of Scripture, in a relatively recent article[14] gives an answer to our question based on Scripture and the ordinary teaching of the Church, though he asserts that the latter supports his conclusion without documenting or developing his assertion. He says nothing about Lateran Council IV. The Scriptural evidence is developed at length.

The whole article is pointed toward answering the exact question now being discussed. After a relatively full account of the Scriptural data and comment on it as it affects the question of Satan's existence, Lussier offers some carefully balanced speculative and practical conclusions. Belief in Satan and demons appears as an item of secondary importance in revelation and salvation history. Further, what is said in Sacred Scripture on Satan and demons calls for considerable demythologizing if we are to grasp without ridiculous distortions and superstitions the very jejune content of the real message, "practically nothing beyond the bare fact of the existence of evil spirits." Because the matter is so mysterious, belief in their existence is not "beyond the possibility of a practical doubt." Nevertheless, the most probable theological opinion is that evil spirits do exist, and any person who should hold the nonexistence of a personal Satan as certain would be "misinformed and misguided in abandoning the ordinary teaching of the Church." In the practical order, Lussier seems to imply, the question has little importance. Evil, he says, is not conquered by speculating on the existence of Satan, but by deciding with our freedom, in the con-

13 Ibid. And see pp. 117-118.
14 Ernest Lussier, S.S.S., "Satan," *Catholic Mind* (September, 1974), pp. 13-25.

crete situation, for goodness and against every sort of evil in our world.[15]

There are others who think that belief in the existence of Satan as a person is necessary for understanding the gospels and Christian life in this world. In a book which many theologians consider the best theological study of miracles ever written,[16] Louis Monden takes up the question of demonic pseudo-miracles.[17] Preliminarily to dealing with that problem, he faces the question about the existence of Satan. To present the detailed justification of his answer to this question is unnecessary here. His answer itself and the basic reason for it suffice; and they are expressed in the following passage:

> Actually, contemporary thought is prone to understand all mention of the diabolical in a figurative sense, and to look upon the Demon as a personification of the powers of evil. This personification of whatever symbolizes evil, found in the Old and New Testament literature, seems to them to be a part of that mythological garb in which God's entire message comes to us. In this matter, as in others, the existentialist theology of our day seeks to extract the marrow of Christian preaching from every myth, to free that preaching from outmoded conceptual schemes, and to translate it into a more authentic religious expression.
>
> However, if one reads the Scriptures with an open mind, not bound by preconceived notions, it is easy to see that one cannot eliminate the demon as a personal entity without changing the Christian message in its very essence. As far as the authors of the New Testament were concerned—even beyond that, in the thought of Christ himself—evil is, first of all, not some *thing* but some *one*. The struggle against "the Evil One" is of a strikingly personal character; and it is exactly for this reason that the battle on behalf of the Kingdom of God, like the battle which marks our own work-a-day lives, takes on an earnestness, an inexorable dramatic tension, which is the very touchstone of a true Christian life. The custom adopted by Christians, since the last century, of "demythologizing" Satan often, therefore, takes on the nature of a flight from the serious exactions of the Christian situation.[18]

In this brief essay, I have made no pretense of presenting a thorough survey of current theological opinions regarding the

15 Ibid., p. 25.
16 Louis Monden, *Signs and Wonders* (New York, 1966). For some indication of the extraordinary praise heaped on this book by reviewers, see Avery Dulles' Foreword to it, p. vi.
17 Ibid., pp. 139-168.
18 Ibid., p. 140.

question of Christian belief in the existence of demonic creatures. Much less have I intended to attempt any solution of that question. I have only tried to clarify the question and to present the opinions of a representative spectrum of contemporary theologians. However, what I have found seems to me to justify several conclusions which can provide reasonable, even if tentative, counsel for those who use the Ignatian rules for discernment of spirits.

First, given what the New Testament, when taken at face value (after removal of mythological accouterment), says about Satan and demons; given the declaration of Lateran Council IV; given the tradition among theologians, saints, and Christians in general up to very recent times—given all this, the burden of proof lies clearly on the side of those who deny or question the traditional belief in the existence of Satan and other evil spirits. Which belief (both views are beliefs) is true is not my point at the moment. My point is that those who deny or question the traditional belief bear the burden of proof and that, as yet, no reason they have offered and is generally known seems able to support that burden.[19]

Second, the reasons given for stating that we should not concern ourselves with evil spirits, even if we rightly believe in their existence, do not seem to justify such an unqualified statement. The statement unquestionably has a point, an important one: Ignoring evil spirits, even if they exist, is certainly better than becoming exaggeratedly concerned about them, filled with groundless fears and vicious superstitions that lead toward individual or social emotional derangement and cruelty. So, for some persons it is wise simply to put evil spirits out of mind. But to urge that in practical Christian living we should all ignore their existence and influence can have dangers and drawbacks. Given belief in the reality of Satan and evil spirits, the best way to deal with this belief is to keep it in its proper place within an integrated vision of Christian faith

19 Paul M. Quay, S.J., "Angels and Demons: the Teaching of IV Lateran," in *Theological Studies*, XLII, no. 1 (March, 1981), is an article bearing on the exact point of this Appendix and of great importance to it. Unfortunately, this article appeared only after this book was already in page proofs and hence we can give it only this brief mention. The author carefully studies the council's declaration in the light of the historical setting. Based on this study, he subjects to critical analysis the arguments of those theologians who hold that Lateran Council IV did not intend to define the existence of angels and demons as a matter of Catholic faith.

He concludes that "doubts or denials that the existence of angels or devils is an article of Catholic faith have been shown to be without serious grounding" (p. 45).

and the individual's psychological and spiritual development, his or her present needs and capacity. Within the perspective of Christian faith all is seen in relation to God's infinite love for each one, his wisdom, power, and personal providence over every human life. Within that perspective we see the need for being on guard against the personal powers of darkness, but we also see the limitation of those powers, and can live peacefully, without unhealthy fears, with ready confidence of overcoming evil by the loving power of God's Spirit working in us. (See also above, pages 198-204.)

Within this Christian vision, a sensible theologically sound attitude toward the demonic can have a positive influence, moving us to enter more seriously, generously, and courageously into the struggle against evil and also showing us how to deal with temptation and spiritual desolation wisely and serenely. Nevertheless, when account is taken of the individual's limited or unhealthy development, it may be wise in many instances to downplay attention to evil spirits or even to ignore them altogether. Those who are neurotic or who do not yet believe sufficiently in God's love for them personally and in his all-powerful providence over their lives may not be ready to deal profitably with belief in Satan and demons. (See above, pp. 34-37.)

A third conclusion is that there seems to be no foundation whatever for the broad statement often heard nowadays that contemporary scriptural and dogmatic theologians generally or mostly doubt or deny the existence of good and evil created personal spirits. In fact, there is some reason to wonder whether any highly reputable Catholic theologian has denied or does deny, at least in writing, that the existence of such spirits is an object of Christian belief. To be sure, some theologians do question the belief. But such belief is in truth not only still theologically permissible, but is even highly respectable.

Finally, from the foregoing conclusions it follows that those who employ the Ignatian rules for discernment of spirits, during the Spiritual Exercises or at other times, have no reason to feel embarrassed if they proceed on the basis of belief in the reality of good and evil created spirits. They are acting on the basis of what seems to be a much more solid theological position than those who beny or question what they believe. Only they should, of course, be careful to take account of the individual's capacity to deal with this belief, as we noted above when we were explaining the second conclusion.

"SPIRITUAL DESOLATION" IN ST. IGNATIUS OF LOYOLA
AND
THE "DARK NIGHT" IN ST. JOHN OF THE CROSS:
COMPARISON AND CONTRAST

There is an experience of desolation in the maturing Christian to which Ignatius does not advert in his rules but which should be taken note of if we are not to misuse his rules. For this desolation is radically different from the one described by Ignatius—in source, content, and consequences. It is a spiritual experience in a fuller sense than the desolation which Ignatius describes; and it never depends on the agency of the evil spirit. It comes at a more advanced stage of spiritual growth, and it is not as common an experience as the spiritual desolation described in the Ignatian rules. To discern this sort of desolation and its sources from the more common one, and to give counsel on how to respond to it when it is discerned, comprise a principal task of spiritual direction. Not everyone, perhaps even relatively few, of those whom we have called spiritually maturing persons experience the desolation of the dark night of the soul in its most painful forms. But it would seem to be frequent enough, especially in its less intense forms, to justify saying that no spiritual counselor is adequately prepared for his work who is not able to recognize it so as to give suitable counsel, or to send the counselee to someone who can do so. St. John of the Cross has some stern words for those who by their confident ignorance hinder God's work and cause unnecessary pain by wrong counsel to those who are suffering such desolation.[1]

The classic description of this second kind of spiritual desolation is that given by John of the Cross under the rubric of "the dark night," or more accurately, the passive, purifying, dark night

---

1 *The Living Flame of Love*, stanza 3, nn. 29-62 (hereafter referred to as *Living Flame*).

during its painful purgative periods. For it is necessary to distinguish the active from the passive dark nights and, within each of these, the night of the senses from the night of the spirit; and further still, within each passive night, its painful, purgative times from its delightful, peaceful times.[2] The whole night involves mortification of all the human powers in order to subject the sense powers to the spirit (the nights of the senses), and then to center the spirit on God by faith (the nights of the spirit).

In the active nights of the senses and of the spirit, the human person actively cooperates with God in achieving this twofold goal. John gives three reasons for calling this time of active striving toward union with God a "night."[3] First, the self-denial, the privation of so much that is desirable, is the point of departure toward union. To be so deprived is in some sense to be in darkness and emptiness. Second, the way to union is faith; and to the human intellect faith is a kind of dark night.[4] Third, the term of the striving, God, is to us in this life also like a dark night, a light beyond our power to see and thus a night to us.[5] Active purification for union with God can be painful to anyone in the measure that egoism and sensuality resist such discipline, but it does not of itself bring on that sort of pain which constitutes spiritual desolation. The experience of struggle and pain in active purification may be full of spiritual consolation, exhilaration, joy in conquering self by God's grace for love of him, for his glory. The instructions which John gives for this active night bear a striking resemblance to the thrust of thought in the *Spiritual Exercises* of St. Ignatius; and the desolations and consolations which occur during the active night also parallel what Ignatius describes.[6]

---

2 The active night is treated principally in the *Ascent of Mt. Carmel* (hereafter referred to as *Ascent*): in Book I, the active night of the senses; in Books II-III, the active night of the spirit. The passive night is treated principally in *The Dark Night* (hereafter referred to as *Dark Night*): in Book I, the passive night of the senses; in Book II, the passive night of the spirit.

3 *Ascent*, I, 2, 1. The reasons are for the active night of the senses, but they also and even more so hold for the active night of the spirit—as also for the passive night. Further reasons will be given for the latter.

4 On faith in particular as a dark night for the soul, see *Ascent*, II, 2-3.

5 As the purification of the human person during the dark night and the consequent conscious experience of God increases, the divine light becomes in one sense clearer and clearer; but as it does so, the recipient sees more and more clearly and realizes more and more deeply the infinite incomprehensibility of God and so enters, now joyfully and delightfully, into the night of the spirit—a night that is filled with light.

6 Note the parallel between what John says in *Ascent* I, 13 and the whole thrust of Ignatius' *Spiritual Exercises*: (the Principle and Foundation, the contemplation of

Appendix II. Spiritual Desolation and the Dark Night

In the passive nights of the senses and of the spirit, the fuller purification and centering of all the person's powers on God are achieved by God's action alone. The origin of both passive nights is the same: infused divine light encountering man's creaturely weakness and his sinfulness. It is this divine infusion which does the purifying. The human efforts at cooperation which are necessary in the active night only interfere with God's work in the passive night.

The two passive nights are ultimately one purification, one night; for, although the night of the senses precedes the night of the spirit, "the real purgation of the senses begins with" and is completed only in the latter "since all the imperfections and disorders of the sensory part are rooted in the spirit and from it receive their strength."[7] It is in the passive dark night that we find a spiritual desolation different from the one Ignatius deals with in the rules for discernment of spirits (or any that John sees in the active night).

For our purpose, it will not be necessary to keep the two passive nights distinct or to go into great detail about them. It will suffice to give a brief comparison and contrast of the desolation which is proper to the passive dark night with the spiritual desolation in the Ignatian rules for discernment of spirits. This can be done by setting down five factors we have found to be productive of or constitutive of spiritual desolation as Ignatius speaks of it and then looking at the five parallel factors in the passive dark night, especially the dark night of the spirit.

As already shown,[8] the desolation described by Ignatius is a spiritual as well as an anti-spiritual experience, that is, it has spiritual and anti-spiritual elements in conflict. It is this conflict which

Jesus, the colloquy of the Two Standards, the Three Modes of Humility). Both saints aim at a purification of faith, hope, and charity which prepares for the reception of God's infused light in the passive night of contemplation, if and when and in the measure God freely chooses to give it. It is significant that John, just as Ignatius, expects abundant spiritual consolation during the active night if one is generous (*Ascent*, I, 13, 7); but both John and Ignatius allow for spiritual desolation arising from the sinful, rebellious, dimension of self and the prompting of the evil spirit.

7 *Dark Night*, II, 3, 1, in *The Collected Works*, trans. Kavanaugh, p. 333. Note how far John is from any Neoplatonic understanding of matter, the sensible, as the source of evil. He sees clearly that the root or core of moral evil lies in the human spirit, in pride, egoism, not in the sensory part of human nature.

8 See ch. 6 above, esp. pp. 140-141.

accounts for desolation properly speaking, the desolate feelings. Inasmuch as the experience is spiritual, the *first* factor is the action of the Holy Spirit actualizing a *second* factor, living faith with its consequent desire and active striving to be free of sin and to go from good to better in praising and serving God. Spiritual desolation can be experienced only in a person with such an actualized attitude. Without it there would be no anguish over the experience of anti-spiritual thoughts and affections ("motions"), over the seeming loss of faith, hope, and charity, over the sense of separation from God. On the other hand, then, the anti-spiritual thoughts and affections arising from the person's sinfulness, the anti-spiritual dimension of his or her personality, constitute a *third* factor. The *fourth* factor is the evil spirit, who plays on the anti-spiritual dimension of a person in order to instigate temptation, desolation, and finally discouragement. To the mind of Ignatius the evil spirit is ordinarily active in spiritual desolation; but Ignatius was as well aware as anyone else that the sinfulness of the human person and the sinful world he or she lives in are adequate to explain particular experiences of temptation and desolation. It would not go against his way of thinking, so long as we did allow for the activity of the evil spirit as common, to let "evil spirit" in many contexts stand for the evil dispositions within our own selves and the evil influence of our world. Finally, as a consequence of the tension and friction of (1) the first and second factors with (2) the third and fourth, there is what we have called desolation properly speaking, the desolate feelings in affective sensibility: dark feelings, confused feelings, painful feelings of strain, sorrow, anguish, bitterness, emptiness, heaviness, estrangement from God. This is the *fifth* factor.

If in noting the parallel factors in the passive night insofar as it is purgative, we attempt to stay in touch with the text of John, it will be necessary to allow for overlapping in our exposition of them: that is the way they are treated by him, and the way we would expect them to be since they imply each other.

The *first* factor in the passive night is an infusion of divine light which, prior to and independent of any free cooperation of the recipient, illumines and purifies the latter for greater union with God by faith, hope, and charity. It is an "inflow of God," an "infused contemplation," a "secret wisdom," which instructs the soul in the perfection of love without the soul doing anything or understanding how it happens.[9] If it seems strange to call this divine illumination a night, John answers that it is called dark and a night, first, because divine wisdom exceeds the capacity of the human soul and, second, because it is "affliction and torment" to the soul.[10] This affliction and torment has many at least apparent similarities to the spiritual desolation Ignatius speaks of in his rules and John speaks of as occurring in the active night. The two desolations are, however, radically different. When or insofar as purified by this infused light, the recipient becomes capable of experiencing the light as unspeakably delightful. One and the same light is painful and oppressive or delightful and joyful, depending on the condition of the one receiving it.[11] Why and how this divine illumination, which John says is really in itself so "gentle," desolates and torments the human person John explains at length, as we shall see while making this comparison and contrast.

Let us look at what parallels the *second* factor in the spiritual desolation of Ignatius, the effects of divine illumination in the recipient. More than ordinary faith, hope, and charity are presupposed in the passive night, the faith, hope, and charity of one who has been led through the active night of the senses and of the spirit, to a far more than ordinary understanding of the mystery of Christ, purity of love and desire, and docility to the Holy Spirit; and this Spirit reaches so deeply into the person that the latter's effort at active cooperation becomes insignificant or can even, in some ways, at certain times, be a hindrance to what God alone can work in one who is willing to let him. If we leave aside the manifold ways in which this illumination and purification is completed, it will be enough to note its essential effects. These parallel the second factor in the spiritual desolation described by Ignatius.

There is from the very beginning an increase of what John calls "esteeming love" for God or "love of esteem" as distinct from what, he calls "burning love" or "the passion of love." The love of esteem is a love which, without passionate feelings, still values God above all and issues in urgent longing, a love so great that the lover would be eager to suffer and die over and over if only in this way he or she could please God.[12] Later, added to the esteeming love, is the infused burning passion of love—a spiri-

9 *Dark Night*, II, 5, 1.
10 Ibid., II, 5, 2.
11 Ibid., II, 13, 10; see also 12, 5.
12 Ibid., II, 13, 5.

tual passion, which resembles in some way a sensory passion but is as different from it as spirit is from what is bodily or sensory.[13] At the times when the touch of this spiritual fire is experienced, all human appetites are incapacitated for loving anything, for finding satisfaction in anything, apart from God. God is loved with all the mind and heart and soul and strength. Strangely, there is a sense of the Beloved's presence and of being strengthened, but all in darkness and anxiety, without satisfaction, a presence that kindles a torment of longing.[14] This burning passion comes and goes; in the early stages of purification during the dark night of the spirit, before great strengthening and purification have been achieved by the inflow of mystical contemplation, it would be too much to bear for long. In fact, during the earliest stages, "the divine fire spends itself in drying out and preparing" the soul for reception of the flame just as fire dries out and prepares damp wood for burning.[15]

The last essential effect to be experienced is the illumination of the intellect. When this happens—and it happens only after "many trials and a great part of the purgation"—the union of intellect and will in experiencing the inflow of God is an experience immensely rich and delightful, a beginning of the union for which the soul hopes and toward which all the painful purification leads. During it, the divine fire burns in the will like a "living flame."[16]

The *third* factor in spiritual desolation as Ignatius describes it is the anti-spiritual motions, more intense and persistent than ordinary, which are the subjective cause for the desolate feelings in one who loves God. These motions include severe temptations against faith, hope, and charity, gross inclinations "to contemptible and earthly things," and difficulty in and distaste for prayer, with

---

13 Ibid., II, 11, 1; 13, 4.
14 Ibid., II, 11.
15 Ibid., II, 10, 1-9; 12,5.
16 Ibid., II, 12, 5-6. It may seem strange to the reader that the infused fire of love is experienced before infused knowledge in the intellect. Recall that John does say, when describing the mystical passion of love, that there is a dark awareness of presence, of "someone." But he says (*Dark Night*, II, 12, 7) clearly that God can infuse love without knowledge to ground it and knowledge without consequent proportionate love. Why infused love (esteeming and passionate) precedes and is more frequent than infused knowledge he explains in *Dark Night*, II, 13, 3. An interesting parallel can be found in George T. Montague, S.M., *Riding the Wind* (Ann Arbor, 1974), pp. 57-62.

a consequent sense of separation from God and disc
about growing spiritually.[17]

There are, plainly, some similarities in the feelings and thoughts
that are experienced in this desolation and those of the passive
night, for example: a sense of declining in faith, hope, and love;
sadness; confusion; painful thoughts of being separated from
God; feelings of discouragement. But there are very great dissi-
milarities, especially in regard to the source of the desolation. The
fundamental explanation of why each one is desolate is quite the
contrary of the other and calls for contrary advice on how to
respond to the situation. Let us look at some of the differences.

In the passive dark night, the reason why the person cannot use
reason and imagination in prayer is not because of anti-spiritual
disturbances, but because of infused divine light. This light draws
the person's psychic energy away from the reason and imagination
into the depths of the spirit, where in the darkness of faith, God is
being experienced beyond all imagination and thought. The
person is not yet able to perceive what is happening in himself or
herself, and so is aware only of inability to pray as he or she did
at an earlier time and to experience the sweetness of God as in that
former mode of prayer. To the recipient of the divine light, all
seems darkness and absence of God. It is, however, in truth excess
of light and of intimacy that leaves the person in seeming darkness
and separation.[18] Consequently, any such active efforts as Ignatius recommends in Rule I:6 would be useless or even harmful
to one in the desolation of the passive night; they would be an
interference with what God is working and a cause of added pain
and tension to the person. John's recommendation to one in this
desolation is exactly the contrary of Rule I:6 and, as he notes,
exactly the contrary of his own advice to those in the active night.
He recommends doing nothing, keeping quiet and waiting in the
darkness of pure faith, abandoning oneself to God while he
accomplishes what he wills.[19] 12/5/93

What makes it impossible for those in the passive night to follow
this advice with peace is that their faith, hope, and charity appear
to them to be dwindling away, almost lost. The reason why they
see themselves this way is not, as it is in the earlier form of desola-

17 Rule I:4. See chapter 6 above.
18 *Dark Night* II 5,3; see also I, 9, 4.
19 Ibid. I, 9, 6-7; 10.

tion, disturbance and confusion from anti-spiritual motions, including direct attacks on faith, hope, and charity. The reason is that the acts of these virtues are becoming more pure and deeply interior, more fully centered on God in himself, beyond all images, symbols, concepts, reasonings. In consequence, these acts escape customary attention. What accounts for these acts becoming more pure, inward, and spiritual is the infused divine light. No matter how it appears to the recipient of that light, living faith is not really under attack as it is in the desolation Ignatius describes. It is, rather, more secure than ever before.[20]

So far from the more intense and persistent inclinations to earthly things disturbing those in the passive dark night and bringing on desolation, such inclinations are eliminated by the power of the infused divine light. While these persons cannot find satisfaction in God, neither can they find satisfaction in or experience attraction to anything other than God. It is God or nothing with them. This is one of the main signs by which John discerns the passive dark night from any other desolation, spiritual or non-spiritual.[21] There is, however, in this passive night a desolation based on the person's habitual, even innate, tendency to sin. By reason of the infused divine illumination this sinfulness, previously hidden, is now perceived with burning clarity and penetration and with acute sensitivity to the ugliness, the horror, of anything that is in opposition to the God toward whom such persons are now touched into agonizing love and longing. Until purgation and strengthening by the divinely infused light is accomplished, the evil revealed by it will make those who receive it feel unclean, wretched, utterly unlovable, ugly, and abhorrent to God and man, they against God and God against them. They think and feel this way even though they do love God immeasurably—which is the very reason for feeling so miserable at being unlovable in his sight and unloved by him, as they mistakenly seem to themselves.[22]

Added to this realization of sinfulness is the frailty of the human psyche, which cannot bear the intensity of divine reality. This is a source of pain and desolation as great as the sinfulness. Even without the sinfulness, so long as human nature is not supernaturally strengthened to bear such contact with God, the human person finds the experience an unbearable torment and source of deso-

20 Ibid., II, 16.
21 Ibid., I, 9, 1-2.
22 Ibid., II, 5,5; 7,7.

lation. So, until those in the night are fortified, in a way divinized, in spirit by this light of contemplation, which is in itself gentle and agreeable,[23] its touch so weighs upon their human frailty that they feel oppressed, crushed by it as by a mountainous weight.[24] Their spiritual substance is so "disentangled and dissolved" by its power that they feel melted down, undone, chewed up and devoured into darkness, dying, being emptied, annihilated.[25] In fact, something of the sort is happening in the conscious powers as their natural manner of operating is done away with so that they may become totally subject to the prompting of the Holy Spirit even in their very first movements.[26]

All these sufferings endured without recognizing their source seem unexplainable to the sufferers unless it is that they have angered God and he has abandoned them. To feel rejected by the one on whom all their power of love and longing is riveted, this is the core and supreme suffering of the whole night.[27] If they could be really assured that God does love them, that all the agony endured will turn out for his glory and their union with him, they could bear the pain and be glad because God is pleased to do this. The pain would remain but not spiritual desolation; in fact, they could even experience great spiritual consolation in the midst of their suffering.[28] No doctrine or spiritual direction can ever give them any assured sense of being pleasing to and loved by God.[29] They can with their rational judgment assent to logical conclusions from the revelation which they believe, but they cannot feel assured or control the judgments that flow from the feelings of rejection.

The worst of these sufferings are not constant. No one could bear them without cessation and live very long. There are more quiet times and even intervals when the darkness is lifted and the inflow of God is experienced only as illuminating and joyful, not painful and desolating. But these pass and the darkness comes again.[30] The dryness in prayer, a lack of satisfaction in God and the impossibility of finding satisfaction elsewhere than in God, the sense of

23 Ibid., II, 9, 10.
24 Ibid., II, 5, 6-7; see also 12, 4; 16, 1.
25 Ibid., II, 6.
26 Ibid., II, 9.
27 *Dark Night*, II, 6, 2.
28 Ibid., II, 13,5.
29 Ibid., II, 7, 3.
30 Ibid., II, 7,4.

darkness and desolation, all these vary in intensity but in some degree are relatively constant and last, John says, for longer or shorter times, usually a matter of years if really efficacious.[31] No counsel such as Ignatius gives in rule I:8 about expecting consolation to return soon could be given to anyone in the passive dark night.

If we are to understand what is happening and why, we have to keep reminding ourselves of two things, First, the infused light is *of itself* illuminating, loving, life-giving, delightful, strengthening, peaceful. However, before it has adequately purified and strengthened the human spirit, it is received in a sinful and feeble spirit. As a consequence, it is experienced as dark, painful, dreadful, desolating. The fuller the gift infused and the more deeply it penetrates, on the one hand, and the more the sinfulness or frailty of the person receiving it on the other, the greater or longer the darkness, the torment, and the feelings of desolation. Secondly, it is necessary to keep in mind the goal to which all the transforming process leads.[32]

One aspect of that goal is so astounding that one can easily read what John says about it without attending to its real significance. John is really saying, and saying over and over, that the natural way of operation in the memory, intellect, and will is actually done away with during those times when the purified person is most fully in union with God, and that these times can be quite prolonged. These powers of operation and their operations are divinized. The person is moved to act not by material sense stimuli or natural memory but by God alone. Consequently, even the very first movements are totally harmonious with God's will; and the person does with utter freedom whatever he experiences any inclination to do.[33] The most detailed expression of what happens can be found in *The Living Flame of Love*, where John says what happens in each of the natural powers and concludes with this amazing statement: "Accordingly, the intellect of this soul is God's intellect; its will is God's will; its memory is the memory of God; and its delight is God's delight; and although the substance of this soul is not the substance of God, since it cannot undergo a substantial conversion into him, it has become God through participation in God, being united to and absorbed in him, as it is

31 Ibid., II, 7, 3-4.
32 Ibid., II, 5; 13, 10.
33 Ibid., II, 4,2; *Canticle*, st. 27, 7; *Living Flame*, st. 1, 36.

in this state."[34] This is an approach toward eternal glory, as much as may be, short of the beatific vision.[35]

The *fourth* factor in the Ignatian description of spiritual desolation is the evil spirit. He may be an important factor in desolation during the active dark night, which does not of itself, of its very nature, involve any spiritual desolation, but during which the person may from time to time, because of sinfulness and the instigation of the evil spirit, experience such desolation. In the *passive* night, especially that of the spirit, the devil's action is not significant for the desolation which is proper to this night. If the evil spirit does cause desolation during the painful and purifying times of the passive dark night, that desolation is simply a contingent accretion to or aggravation of the desolation resulting from the impact of infused divine light on the ordinary sinfulness and natural frailty of human nature. Failure to distinguish the two contrary sources of two contrary kinds of desolation will lead to struggling against the infused light of God as if it were the power of evil, instead of yielding and waiting while the light painfully but lovingly purifies and gives life.

When, after much painful purification, the person begins to experience communion with God through "simple, loving knowledge" directly communicated by God, received passively without specific acts of intellect or imagination,[36] when, therefore, the person's actively meditating would be a distraction and a hindrance to what God is working, then the evil spirit will try to intrude, not with desolation but with "good knowledge and satisfaction [consolation]"—good, but so much less good as to be an incalculable harm to the person in whom he prompts such knowledge and satisfaction.[37] (Ignatius' Rule II:5 would apply to this experience.) During the later stages of the passive night, when the human spirit experiences deep peaceful solitude in God, the evil spirit will also try, more in accord with his proper style, to disturb by violence the inward peace and communion with God in whatever way he can. Sometimes he causes horrifying suffering,[38] but this is not spiritual desolation properly speaking. Least of all is it the spiritual desolation essential to the passive dark night.

34 *Flame*, st. 2, 34, in *The Collected Works*, trans. Kavanaugh, p. 608.
35 *Canticle*, st. 38, 3-4.
36 *Living Flame*, st. 3, 34.
37 Ibid., st. 3, 63-64.
38 *Dark Night*, II, 23, 1-9.

The *fifth* factor of Ignatian spiritual desolation is the affective feelings which arise at the spiritual pole or dimension of Christian consciousness because of what is experienced at the anti-spiritual pole or dimension. The corresponding factor in the passive dark night has already been described in conjunction with the third factor.

Even such a brief account as that which has just been given of desolation in the passive dark night and its differences from desolation in the Ignatian rules for discernment of spirits should make us aware that the Ignatian rules are not adequate to help us recognize it or to instruct those who experience it on how to conduct themselves during it. These rules could even prove harmful. Other criteria for discerning what is going on and other advice on how to respond are needed.[39]

39 To my knowledge, the book which is still the most sound, clear, and practically helpful source of the needed criteria and advice is A. Poulain, S.J., *The Graces of Interior Prayer*, 6th edition (London, 1950), chapters III-XIV. Poulain draws heavily on John of the Cross and enriches and clarifies John's doctrine from many other sources.

IGNATIAN "CONSOLATION" AND "DESOLATION":
SOME DIVERSE INTERPRETATIONS

The meaning one gives to the terms spiritual consolation and spiritual desolation in Ignatius' writing on discernment of spirits influences, and can even be decisive in, one's understanding of all that he says on this topic. The meaning given to spiritual consolation is more fundamental than the meaning given to spiritual desolation, since the latter is largely described as contrary to the former (*SpEx*, [317]). It is, then, of critical significance to be sure of what Ignatius means by spiritual consolation in its basic and general meaning, prior to making any distinction between consolation with and without preceding cause.

There are current understandings of consolation in Ignatius which differ from the one which I have worked out in this book.[1] Two of the most common understandings omit one or the other of the two aspects which my interpretation of Ignatius finds to be essential to his notion. The first does not take account of the spiritual character of the experience; the other does not take account of its consoling character.

The first misunderstanding, that overlooking the spiritual character of the consolation, is met rather often among persons not well trained in discernment of spirits. As far as I know, no writer of reputation and no respected student of Ignatius holds it. But I encounter it frequently in conversations; and other experienced directors tell me that they do too. That widespread acceptance which this opinion receives in practice by many only superficially acquainted with discernment of spirits is its only claim on our brief attention here. In this view, any innocent feeling of peace or

1 See especially chs. 4 and 6 above.

joy or satisfaction, exultation, delight, or the like, especially if it comes during the time of prayer, is taken for a sign of the Holy Spirit acting on the one who experiences it. The distinction between a spiritual and a non-spiritual consolation is ignored. This way of thinking misses the whole point of the Ignatian rules for discernment of spirits. It opens the way to confusing with a movement of the Holy Spirit any pleasant affective feeling that is entirely natural in origin, even a selfish one. If sinful responses should be excluded from those taken as signs of the Holy Spirit, we would still, in this view, have to think that, in Ignatius' teaching, the Holy Spirit directly inspires every euphoric affective response which is not sinful, or else that he gives no direct inspirations at all. Either conclusion would be plainly opposed to what Ignatius actually says.

The second interpretation of consolation and desolation in Ignatius is found among those with spiritual learning and understanding and deserves careful attention. Those who hold it so stress the spiritual character of these experiences that they let go the ordinary meaning of consolation and desolation; and they regard as a spiritual consolation or desolation in the Ignatian meaning what no one else would consider to be a consolation or desolation at all. They dismiss the delightful or painful, agreeable or disagreeable character of spiritual experiences as being outside the denotation of consolation or desolation in the Ignatian usage. Any movement of human affectivity is thought to be a consolation in the Ignatian meaning if it is directed to God; desolation is thought to be a movement in the contrary direction. In one variety of this view, the notion of consolation is more limited because of a focus on the phrase in Rule I:3 "every *increase* of hope, faith, and charity" (emphasis mine). With or without this limitation, these who hold this view see as nonessential to "consolation" in the Ignatian usage what all ordinary usage counts as essential to the experience referred to by that word.

The clearest and most forceful presentation of this way of thinking which I have read is that by Michael J. Buckley, S.J. His statement appears within an essay devoted to structural analysis of the whole body of Ignatian rules. He schematizes the factors involved in spiritual experience in order to show their relationships and their interactions.[2] What he says about the nature of consolation and desolation is not, therefore, his main point; but it is one that he develops with considerable emphasis. I doubt that we can find a better statement repre·entative of the interpretation which he accepts.

Buckley sees the concepts of consolation and desolation as two critically important concepts in terms of which Ignatius can "unify the multiform realities of affectivity"[3] for his purpose in the rules for the discernment of spirits. The use of the terms consolation and desolation by Ignatius must, Buckley asserts, be distinguished from their use in other spiritual authors[4] (and, one might add, from what anyone else would mean when using the terms in their ordinary meaning). In other words, Buckley is stating that for Ignatius consolation and desolation are words which he uses in technical meanings of his own—that is, jargon, even jargon peculiar to him. For, contrary to all ordinary usage and contrary also to the normal usage of spiritual writers, Ignatius, Buckley writes, dissociates from the essential concept of consolation any pleasant character, any note of being cheered or relieved of pain, any sense of sweetness, of delight; and he dissociates from the essential concept of desolation any contrary note of unpleasantness, bitterness, or pain. Buckley does not state this merely in passing; he insists on it over and over again. "Consolation and desolation do not identify necessarily with pleasure and pain." "In no sense does consolation merge with pleasure and desolation with pain."[5] The pleasure and pain excluded from the essential concept of consolation and desolation are not merely sensible but also spiritual: "they are obvious states of affectivity but they are not denoted by their sensible or even spiritual enjoyment."[6] What then is the essential difference between consolation and desolation in Ignatius? Buckley sees consolation or desolation as experiences of being drawn or driven in opposite directions, to or away f.om God. They are "states of affectivity...defined by the direction of the movement."[7] "Consolation is any interior movement of sensibility—irrespective of the

---

20 (Autumn, 1973), pp. 19-37. Those with a background in the history of religious experience and religious thought will find the introductory part, pp. 19-26, an especially brilliant demonstration of how Ignatius' teaching on discernment of spirits fits into that history.

3 Ibid., p. 28.
4 Ibid., p. 29.
5 Ibid.
6 Ibid.
7 Ibid., p. 28.

cause—whose direction is God...whether its presence is experientially pleasant or not."[8] "Consolation is any interior movement of emotionality, feeling, or sensibility whose term is God—a man is drawn or driven to God."[9] What this reading of Ignatius leads to in our understanding of desolation is graphically stated: "Men with their arms locked, singing bawdy songs on their way to the local whorehouse, are in desolation for Ignatius."[10]

The foregoing interpretation of Ignatius is in direct opposition with the interpretation given in this book. Any broad exegesis of the Ignatian text to establish this interpretation was impossible within the limits of Buckley's article, and was not to be expected. Nevertheless, it seems fair to say not only that such work is called for, but also that a special burden of proof lies on the side of an interpretation which attributes a meaning to consolation and desolation which bears no resemblance to ordinary usage, or to specialized usage among spiritual writers in any language with which Ignatius was familiar and which he used for communication. To my knowledge, no one has taken up that burden of proof and provided the requisite exegesis which would be set against that given above in chapters four through six. To compare, contrast, and evaluate reasons for the two positions is, therefore, not possible. What I can do, besides referring the reader to chapters four through six above, is to offer some reasons for thinking that any effort to establish the interpretation stated by Buckley would run into insuperable difficulties.

First, if what Ignatius had in mind when he wrote "spiritual consolation" or "spiritual desolation" was merely affective movements toward or away from God, spiritually good or evil movements, why would he not call them such rather than confuse his reader by using words which in common usage denote something else?

Even if the foregoing difficulty should not seem as cogent to others as it does to me, there are other more cogent grounds to suggest the futility of trying to establish a meaning for Ignatius of consolation and desolation (whether spiritual or not) other than that of common usage. There is, let it be said, one reason that could attract us to that interpretation: It makes the key notion of consolation much simpler to understand and, hopefully, much

8 Ibid., p. 29.
9 Ibid., pp. 28-29.
10 Ibid., p. 29

easier to work with in practice. But reflection on the text of Ignatius and on spiritual experience indicates that such simplicity is gained only at the cost of disregarding both the complexities of real experience (shown in de criptive analysis) and the tensions and complexities in the text of Ignatius. In presenting my own understanding of Ignatius, I was also aware of and have noted those passages in his writings which, if taken in isolation, could reasonably be read as supporting Buckley's opinion. I have already given reasons why, taken in full context, they should be read otherwise. What I will point out now are some striking inconsistencies and incoherences that would have to be attributed to Ignatius if we did not read consolation and desolation in their common meaning.

For instance, every description Ignatius gives of spiritual consolation and desolation is colored by such words as peace, joy, delight, sweetness, warmth, exultation, and the like—all denoting pleasant, enjoyable feelings to be sure. A contrary set of terms colors every description of desolation. These terms denoting pleasant or unpleasant experiences are to be found on every page of Ignatius' *Spiritual Diary*,[11] where Ignatius is describing his own consolations. These same terms are found in the *Spiritual Exercises*, [316, 317, 329, 335], and in the Autograph Directory for the *Spiritual Exercises*.[12]

In his letters these same modes of expression appear. When consolation is present, he writes in a letter to Teresa Rejadell, "all trials are pleasant and all weariness rest. He who goes forward with this fervor, warmth, and interior consolation finds every burden light and sweetness in every penance or trial."[13] In the same letter, consolation is contrasted with "darkness and sadness," as its contrary. Further, the assumption throughout is that we can go on believing and hoping and loving whether in consolation or desolation; consolation is spoken of as a help to these essential acts of Christian life, not as identified with them. Writing to Borgia, Ignatius describes "graces of consolation in which all darkness and restless worry are removed" and replaced by "contentment."[14] In another letter he sees consolation as the contrary of afflictions and misery.[15] For the encouragement of young Jesuits in their

11 See *The Spiritual Journal of St. Ignatius Loyola*, William J. Young, S.J., transl. (Woodstock, Md., 1958).
12 *DirSpEx*MHSJ, [11-12] on p. 72, [18] on p. 76.
13 *LettersIgn* pp. 21-22.
14 Ibid., p. 84. See also p. 18.
15 Ibid., pp. 318-319.

studies who find that studies seem to dampen spiritual consolation, Ignatius distinguishes consolation from acts of charity, humility, obedience, and the like. He assures them that, if these acts are taken care of, they need have little concern about how much consolation God gives. The latter is relatively unimportant.[16] He encourages another correspondent to trust God, to surrender himself, to let go willingly the consolations which he desires but God does not give. God, he assures him, will later give consolations as a reward for such persevering faith and love without consolation.[17] None of this seems to fit coherently with a reading of consolation as any affective responses having God as its term. Clearly Ignatius sees many affective responses to God without consolation in his ordinary meaning. Clearly consolation is conceived of as something involving spiritual pleasure, delight. He sees deeper affective experiences on which spiritual consolation depends but which can be without consolation.

Further, acceptance of consolation and desolation as concepts independent of pleasant or unpleasant feelings cannot work in Ignatius' teaching on discerning God's will. If we think of consolation as in essence independent of delight, pleasure, how can we make sense of *SpEx*, [177], where Ignatius describes a time of calm for finding God's will as distinct from a time of consolation or desolation? For in the tranquil time spoken of in that paragraph, Ignatius expects the one seeking God's will to have great faith, to be loving God with a purified love, and desiring only to know and to do his will (*SpEx*, [177, 179-180, 184]). Yet these affections terminating in God are not consolation; for by Ignatius' own definition (*SpEx*, [177]), this time of tranquility or calm is a time when one is not experiencing movements of the spirits, which is the same as to say not experiencing spiritual consolation or desolation.

Another difficulty arises concerning what Ignatius calls the "second time" for finding God's will, the time of consolation and desolation and discernment of spirits (*SpEx*, [176]). This mode of discerning God's will is not at all simple, and I am not intending what I say here to be at all an adequate statement of what is involved in it. All I will say is enough for those who have some familiarity with Ignatius' teaching on it to see the difficulty I am

16 Ibid., p. 342.
17 Ibid., p. 417.

raising about fitting into it a notion of consolation or desolation as any affective response toward or away from God—regardless of sweetness or bitterness, delight or pain, and the like.

In every situation for discernment of God's will as Ignatius is thinking of it, we have two (or more) alternatives, both of which appear desirable as ways of serving and glorifying God. One must see each alternative as in some way conducive to the glory of God (even in some respect more so than the other) and under that aspect desirable, or there would be no grounds for discernment at all. Before beginning to discern which one God wills, Ignatius wants the person to be moved by desire toward either alternative *only,* or at least predominantly, insofar as it seems to him or her more for the praise and service of God (*SpEx,* [23, 166, 169, 178, 184]).[18] The problem is to discern which of the desirable options is really signed by the Holy Spirit as more for the glory of God. Now the signs in this mode of discernment are consolation and desolation. Ignatius instructs us to go to prayer and, when God gives consolation, to note which alternative we feel more drawn to as to what God wills. The consolation is a sign of the Holy Spirit drawing us, moving us to prefer that one; desolation is a sign of the evil spirit, contraindicative.[19] The point of all this for our purpose is that Ignatius clearly assumes throughout that consolation is not just any affective response with God as its term; the affection by which one is drawn to a course of action precisely as God's will is not itself a consolation, but needs consolation as a sign of its origin.

A similar distinction appears in Rules II:3-5, where Ignatius is instructing us on how to tell whether a consolation, truly spiritual, is prompted by a good or an evil spirit. If it is from the good spirit, the desires which arise afterwards in continuity with it will be neither for what is evil nor even for what is less for God's service and praise than the desire which came during the original consolation. If they are, then they are from the evil spirit; and so is the original desire which came in consolation. Similarly, the original desire, which came in consolation, is thought to be from the evil spirit if it endures but by a continuous development the consola-

18 In the Autograph Directory for the Spiritual Exercises, Ignatius tells the director not to allow the exercitant to begin the "Election" unless the latter has clearly reached the "second mode of humility," and preferably the third (*DirSpEx*MHSJ, [17] on pp. 74-77). In the second mode of humility, the person is not inclined to any alternative for choice in itself but only inasmuch as it is for the service of God.

19 *DirSpEx*MHSJ, [18] on pp. 76-77. And see Rule I:5.

tion changes into desolation. Here also is a clear distinction between consolation and an affective response of desire for something
in order to glorify God. If consolation were merely any movement
of affectivity with God as its term, then in discernment of God's
will, every spontaneous desire for every opposing alternative motivated by love for God would be validated as an inspiration of the
Holy Spirit. Where would that leave the one discerning spirits?
And what would be the sense of Ignatius telling us to discern God's
will by consolation, desolation, and discernment of spirits?

In the light of the foregoing evidence, and with 'remembrance
of how Ignatius sees desolation as the contrary of consolation, it
should be clear also that in his usage there is no experience of
desolation which is not unpleasant, disagreeable, painful. Then,
although Ignatius would have compassion for the men whom
Buckley describes as going gaily to the local whorehouse, he would
in no way describe their sinful attitude as desolation, least of all
as spiritual desolation. In Ignatius' terms, these men, at least for
the time being, are very likely *incapable* of a true spiritual desolation. Not only is living faith presently inhibited from actuating
spiritual joy in their affective sensibility; such faith now seems to
be dead, or so little alive, that they can have no feeling of desolation
at separating themselves from God by withdrawing their own love
for him, and thus not accepting God's love.

None of the foregoing difficulties in reading Ignatius occur when
we understand consolation and desolation in their ordinary meaning,
grasp their essential structure by descriptive analysis, and specify
them as spiritual by relationship with living faith. Rather, we
find that, when describing consolation and desolation or when
using these notions in his letters of spiritual direction and in his
instructions on how to discern God's will, all Ignatius says fits
together with ready coherence.

IGNATIAN "CONSOLATION WITHOUT PRECEDING
CAUSE":
DIVERSE INTERPRETATIONS OF ITS NATURE
AND OF
ITS ROLE IN DISCERNMENT OF SPIRITS

There is a state of great uncertainty at present about the nature
of what Ignatius names "consolation without previous cause,"
how it functions in discernment of spirits, and how it functions in
discernment of God's will. This uncertainty becomes manifest
if we only think of some of the connected questions which are not
answered with anything approaching general agreement. Does it
differ from consolation with preceding cause intrinsically or only
extrinsically? That is, does it differ by reason of some features in
the content of the experience or only by its mode of originating?
If the difference is intrinsic, is the cognitive element in the consolation conceptual or non-conceptual? If non-conceptual, is it mystical
in the strict sense of the word? Does it bear within itself an objective
guarantee of its immediate origination from God alone, without
any created mediation? Is there a subjective certitude in the
recipient that it does so originate and is an experience of God?
Can there be any divine communication about a created object
during such consolation, for example, about something which
God wills the person to do? Do the answers about the cognitive
side of the experience and about the description which Ignatius
gives of the affective side allow for its being a frequent, even relatively ordinary, experience of good Christian life, or is it a rare
experience of a few persons? What is its relation to consolation with
preceding cause? What role does it play in discernment of spirits?
and then, in discernment of God's will?

Until recent years, the interpretations which were put on the
experience of consolation without previous cause, whatever they

were, had little impact on practical thinking about Ignatian discernment of spirits and discernment of God's will. But this situation has extensively changed since Karl Rahner in 1956 published his essay, "The Ignatian Logic of Existential Knowledge: Some Theological Problems in the Rules for Making an Election in St. Ignatius' Spiritual Exercises."[1] For Rahner, the question of consolation without preceding cause, its nature and role in Ignatian discernment, is not merely one question among others, not even just one very important question. It is the basic question. What is said on this question is decisive for all that he has to say on the process of discernment. What he says, moreover, is largely at variance with what has been traditional.

Through this essay Rahner has been a catalyst and the central figure in current study and discussion of Ignatian discernment. Some follow him wholeheartedly. Some accept his views with minor reservations and revisions. Others reject the main lines of his thought as being without foundation in the writings of Ignatius.[2] The questions which were asked at an earlier time, but which then never disturbed Ignatian scholars, spiritual directors, or directors of the Spiritual Exercises, have now become questions of great significance for discernment in theory and practice.

A Twofold Purpose

Within the present limits it is not possible to present a complete or even a broad survey in depth of the contemporary opinions. Neither is it necessary for the twofold purpose of this present discussion. One purpose is merely to give some impression of the disagreement and uncertainty regarding consolation without previous cause, which was what led me to offer the practical suggestions which I gave at the end of chapter 11 above. Another purpose is to expose in some detail the main lines of Karl Rahner's thought on Ignatian discernment of spirits and to evaluate it critically.

1 This is the literal and accurate translation of Rahner's own title as it appears in *Ignatius von Loyola: seine geistliche Gestalt und sein Vermächtnis (1556-1956)*, Friedrich Wulf, S.J., editor (Würzburg: Echter-Verlag, 1956), pp. 343-405. This essay has appeared in English, with an abbreviated title which is less communicative, "The Logic of Concrete Individual Knowledge in Ignatius Loyola," pp. 84-170 in *The Dynamic Element in the Church* (New York: Herder and Herder, 1964). A ten-page digest of the original German article, made by one of Rahner's pupils and approved by Rahner, is found in *Ignatius of Loyola: His Personality and Spiritual Heritage, 1556-1956* (St. Louis, 1977), pp. 280-289. Then (pp. 290-293) Rahner further develops his theory by replying to some questions raised by Avery Dulles.

2 See, e.g., Adrien Demoustier, S.J., in *Christus*, no. 99 (June, 1978), 378-379.

For this second purpose, a recent study by Harvey Egan,[3] made under Rahner's direction and published with a foreword by him, can by especially helpful. While Egan follows faithfully the fundamental lines of Rahner's theology, he also draws on a number of the most significant twentieth-century students of Ignatian thought and integrates their insights into his work. In an overall assessment, he seems to achieve a clearer and perhaps improved version of Rahner's transcendental theology of Ignatian discernment.

It should be noted also that Egan's study is more than merely a revised presentation of Rahner on discernment. Through this book he is reaching for an understanding of what he calls the Ignatian mystical horizon, "the fundamental mystical matrix... or the roots of all Ignatius' experiences of knowledge and love."[4] This mystical horizon he finds most fully and clearly written into the *Spiritual Exercises,* but illuminated by other writings of Ignatius, particularly his *Spiritual Diary* and the *Autobiography* in which he recounts the early years after his conversion. On the one hand, therefore, the scope of Egan's work reaches far beyond a study of consolation without preceding cause. On the other hand, he claims that this consolation is "an excellent miniature of the Exercises and the Ignatian mystical horizon," that it contains the main elements of that horizon "in a highly concentrated and experiential form."[5]

What is even more significant for our purpose, Egan also claims that consolation without preceding cause presents in a concentrated way what is most characteristic of *every* man's fundamental but usually anonymous stance in the grace of Christ. It "is essentially the becoming-thematic, the most explicit experience, of the mysticism of everyday life."[6]

All that Egan writes on consolation without previous cause is explicating what Rahner says or revising it under Rahner's supervision (but not necessarily with his agreement to the revisions). Therefore, we can at one stroke gain clarity and avoid repetitions if we simply join Egan's clarifications, developments, and revisions to the exposition of Rahner's opinions.

---

3 Harvey D. Egan, S.J., *The Spiritual Exercises and the Ignatiuan Mystical Horizon,* with a *Foreword by Karl Rahner, S.J.* (St. Louis, 1976).
4 Ibid., p. xviii.
5 Ibid., pp. xviii-xix, 31.
6 Ibid., p. 31.

In line with the first purpose stated above, that of giving some impression of the present uncertainty regarding consolation without previous cause, we will first look at Rahner's thought on the subject, including Egan's clarifications and revisions. After that we can make comparisons and contrasts with two other important views. A more traditional position that has points of agreement with Rahner but in final analysis is in deep disagreement can be found in Hervé Coathalem's *Ignatian Insights*,[7] a book that seems to be at present the most useful and most widely used commentary on the *Spiritual Exercises*. A recent study by Daniel Gil, S.J., entitled *Consolación sin Causa Precedente*,[8] offers an interpretation which sharply contrasts with both Rahner's view and Coathalem's. Since references will be to only one work of each author, it will be convenient to make citations in the text itself, using an initial and page number put in parentheses.

A. *Exposition*

Karl Rahner and Harvey D. Egan

While Rahner does intend to theologize on the basis of Ignatius' *Spiritual Exercises*, his essay is more theological speculation than exegetical study of Ignatius' text. Rahner uses his already developed transcendental theology to propose a way of understanding Ignatian discernment in which he sees everything depending on consolation without preceding cause. In his essay, the focus of attention is on Ignatian discernment of God's will; discernment of spirits and the role of consolation without preceding cause in it are treated in relation to discernment of God's will. The focus of my exposition and evaluation of Rahner is on his proposed understanding of consolation without preceding cause, its nature and function in discernment of spirits. What he says about Ignatius' ways of discerning God's will concerns us here only insofar as it is necessary for interpreting his views on consolation without preceding cause and discernment of spirits. A reasonably accurate presentation of Rahner's thought on discernment of God's will calls for more space than can be given here; and a critical evaluation of it will require an exegesis of the relevant Ignatian texts as detailed and extensive as has been made of the Rules for Discernment of Spirits in this present book.

---

7 Hervé Coathalem, S.J., *Ignatian Insights: A Guide to the Complete Spiritual Exercises*, 2nd edition (Taichung, Taiwan, 1971).

8 Daniel Gil, S.J., *La consolación sin causa precedente* (Rome, 1971).

The key to understanding Rahner's and Egan's transcendental theology of consolation without preceding cause is what they speak of as supernatural transcendence, the natural transcendence of human consciousness supernaturally elevated in the existential order. Itself remaining non-conceptual and implicit, natural transcendence is always involved as the horizon and condition for the possibility of any act toward a conceptual object (R, 145). Rahner's understanding of consolation without preceding cause cannot be grasped apart from supernatural transcendence; for in his view, such consolation depends on this transcendence becoming explicit as the center of consciousness (R, 151). This supernatural transcendence, in turn, cannot be understood except in terms of two aspects of its supernatural elevation by grace (E, 39).

Let us then see: (1) what these two aspects are; (2) how Rahner thinks we experience the transcendence becoming thematic (explicit and centered in consciousness); (3) what the "signal" is for this event; (4) what the criterion is by which to judge its genuinity; (5) what certainty we can have that God is immediately effecting it; (6) what forms it can take; (7) what its role is in discernment of spirits; and finally (8) how frequent or ordinary it is.

1. The natural dynamism of intellect and will, Rahner holds, is directed toward God as the term of human transcendence. In this way, God is always present implicitly and non-conceptually as the horizon of any explicit consciousness. In every act of knowing and loving, the human spirit returns to itself and has a "vague awareness of God" as the "pure and unlimited term of its dynamism." By reason of divine grace, this transcendence is elevated to a supernatural level. Further, because of the divine Word's incarnation, life, death, and resurrection, our human consciousness and our world are different. What Christ is by nature, the human person is by grace. We ourselves and our world are experienced differently than they would have been without the incarnation of Christ. This "metaphysical modification" also shows up in our conscious horizon. All this, let it be said, holds for *every* person in the world, antecedent to justification by grace. We live in a supernaturally oriented, Christ-affected world, and we have a supernatural orientation and horizon of consciousness (R, 124-125; E, 38-39, 42).

2. How does the supernatural transcendence, the implicit horizon of consciousness, become explicit, thematic, in conscious-

295

ness—not as an abstract object of theological reflection, but as the very focus of awareness? We are not yet concerned with describing the content of consciousness when this happens, its essential features, but only how it takes place, the way it happens.

Rahner thinks it is evident that supernatural transcendence with God as the pure and unlimited term of its endless dynamism can become more and more unmixed with the conceptual response of which it is the horizon. The conceptual object can become transparent, almost disappear, and become unheeded (R, 145). Then "the concrete, unique, intrinsic orientation toward God which constitutes the innermost essence of man" (R, 160-161) emerges into explicit awareness, ceases to be merely the implied condition for conceptual knowledge, the horizon of consciousness.

Harvey Egan gives a fuller statement of the way this comes about and, in doing so, proposes a way of relating in spiritual experience consolation with and without preceding cause, and then of bringing out the Christo-centric character of the latter. The grace-elevated horizon of human consciousness is, he says, ordinarily present to the knower only as a non-conceptual, vague, even if necessary, concomitant of consciousness. What if, he asks, the conceptual object in consciousness became transparent and the non-conceptual horizon moved into the center and became the focal point of consciousness, seen through the transparent conceptual object? If this occurred, one would have "an inexpressible, non-conceptual experience of his Christ-affected and supernaturally elevated transcendence." This experience, according to Egan, would be what Ignatius calls consolation without preceding cause (E, 40). Now, the conceptual experience Egan is thinking of is the graced experience of consolation *with* preceding cause, which comes when one is meditating on Jesus while making the Spiritual Exercises. In this way, by making the consolation with preceding cause which arises from meditat on on Jesus in the Gospels a sine qua non for consolation without preceding cause, Egan thinks to find a way of explaining how the Christo-centric orientation of human transcendence is rendered thematic and the consolation without preceding cause is a truly Christian consolation (E, 40-43).

3. Since consolation without preceding cause "begins in" consolation with preceding cause (E, 41), is "the fulfillment of" it (E, 57), the "normal crowning" of it (E, 56), and is experienced only when meditation and consolation with preceding cause be-

come transparent of the supernatural transcendence, and since the awareness itself is non-conceptual—for all these reasons, Egan thinks that it is oftentimes very difficult to distinguish in experience consolation without from consolation with preceding cause and to recognize that one is having the former. To do so "requires great skill, experience and understanding" (E, 153; see 44). Using an idea for which he commends Daniel Gil, he points out a "signal" which calls the person's attention to the beginning or ending of consolation without preceding cause. It is the disproportion between the experience of being drawn entirely into God's love and the consolation desired and expected from the particular meditation being made (E, 35-36, 56-57). The signal may be noticed when the consolation begins, but often only when it ends and the person feels "a temperature change," a dropping off of fervor (E, 57). This signal is not to be confused with the criterion for consolation without preceding cause, which is its quality, its intrinsic features. Let us now turn to these.

4.   Rahner distinguishes a negative side and a positive side of the consolation. "Without preceding cause," he says, really means "without cause"; and "without cause" means "without object." That is to say, the consolation is a non-conceptual experience (R, 132-133). This absence of object is utter receptivity to God, an inexpressible, non-conceptual experience of the love of God, the drawing of the whole person, with the very ground of his being, into the love of God as God, the divine majesty (R, 135-136). So total is this experience considered both negatively and positively that it allows for no concepts or judgments of any sort during it. It is experience of "the pure non-conceptual light of the consolation of the whole human person who is being drawn above and beyond all that can be named" (R, 136-137). Rahner wants emphatically, however, to exclude from his meaning any intuitive sight of God in the sense of the beatific vision or even of the Ontologists. God is in awareness as the term of human transcendence; it is supernaturally elevated transcendence which comes into awareness and "God as the term of this anticipatory reaching out in aspiration" (R, 148). The very nature of this experience explains why it carries within it an intrinsic certitude of its purely divine origin, why it possesses an irreducibly self-evident, self-sufficient character (R, 143). Also, pure openness and receptivity excludes nothing, makes no finite judgment that might falsely circumscribe God or attribute any opinion or purpose to him as its source; and so it cannot deceive (R, 149).

Three elements in Egan's development of these features are worth noting. Insisting, as Rahner does, on the drawing into God's love as the central and primary feature of consolation without preceding cause, he calls attention to this as a dying to self in a gratuitous and purely disinterested love, which profoundly tastes the mystery of the cross as its deepest calling, which is a flight from self-love, self-will, and self-interest, which is at the same time self-fulfillment (E, 36-37). "Whenever a person comes fully to himself, fully possesses himself, but fully surrenders himself to the loving Mystery of his life calling him beyond himself, he experiences CSCP [*consolación sin causa precedente*]" (E, 56).

5. The second notable element in Egan's reworking of Rahner is Egan's difference of opinion from Rahner's earlier statements on the certainty of consolation without preceding cause as accounted for by God alone. What Rahner says about the consolation as carrying its own intrinsic certitude of its purely divine origin, as being irreducibly self-evident, self-sufficient (R, 143), at least allows for understanding him to mean that the person who experiences such consolation is sure of its origin. If he does mean that, then Egan is taking issue with him. If he does not mean that, then Egan is at least providing a needed nuancing and clarification. If consolation without previous cause is actually given, Egan says, it is *objectively* speaking certainly from God (E, 44). The recipient, however, may have only greater or lesser "*subjective* evidence" that the actual experience is from God, depending on the quality of the consolation and the recipient's mature power of discernment (E, 45). In such cases, it is clear that Ignatius thought that the recipient of the consolation could reach certainty by reflecting on the experience and noting the change when the actual experience ceased (E, 44; *SpEx*, [336]). There are, however, some experiences of consolation without preceding cause which are in themselves and without reflection afterward subjectively as well as objectively certain. Egan points to Ignatius' letter to Teresa Rejadell as clear evidence of Ignatius' view (E, 47).

6. The third notable element in Egan's treatment of the features of consolation without previous cause is his answer to the question whether the non-conceptual awareness of God with a total drawing into his love totally absorbs consciousness, eliminating awareness of created conceptual objects and making any communication from God about them impossible while the pure consolation lasts. Rahner, as we saw, thinks so. Egan does not. The wording of

Rule II:8, he thinks, implies such communication; this rule and the letter from Ignatius to Teresa Rejadell, he says, leave no doubt that Ignatius is describing consolation without previous cause and is asserting that communications are sometimes given during it. Egan further speculates that, since there may be conceptual or non-conceptual communications or no communication, we ought to allow for three sorts of consolation without previous cause (E, 48-51).

7. Given the above description of consolation without preceding cause, how does Rahner see its role or function in Ignatian discernment of spirits? He sees the experience of consolation without preceding cause as the sine qua non of all Ignatian discernment of spirits, and of God's will also. All the other rules, he claims, are merely the application of the fundamental certitude in this consolation. It is, then, presupposed by them and makes them possible. It has, he declares, for spiritual discernment the same function as the first principles of logic and ontology have for the rest of knowledge (R, 130). "Everything depends on our recognizing the purely divine consolation as being of divine origin. It is the real and ultimately sole principle of the remainder of Discernment of Spirits and consequently the process of making the Election" (R, 164). More precisely, consolation without previous cause has the character of "primary, irreducible self-evidence," which enables it to function in the logic of concrete particulars as the most general principles do in the abstract realm (R, 142).

8, Attributing this role to consolation without previous cause has a number of important implications, which Rahner does not hesitate to draw. One of these is that consolation without previous cause is not at all unusual, that it is, in fact both "the foundation and high point of normal Christian life" (Foreword to E, xv). Egan is in full agreement with Rahner on consolation without previous cause as the first principle of discernment and as an ordinary experience of Christian life (E 43, 144).

Before offering an evaluation of the foregoing understanding of consolation without preceding cause, let us look at the two contrasting opinions of Hervé Coathalem and Daniel Gil.

Hervé Coathalem

In agreement with Rahner, Coathalem finds a striking intrinsic difference, a difference in content, between consolation with and without preceding cause. Like Rahner he also thinks that the latter experience bears "its own guarantee of authenticity," that is, of solely divine origin (C, 271). He goes beyond Rahner in declaring it to be a mystical experience. Rahner wants to leave aside the question of mysticism in its proper meaning, and seems to think that consolation without preceding cause at its lower degrees need not be mystical in that meaning (R, 151-153). Coathalem, on the other hand, thinks that every spiritual consolation *with* cause has "mystical overtones" and resembles, has a "practical equivalence" to, what St. Teresa of Avila calls *gustos*. In this way of thinking he joins himself with many eminent commentators on Ignatius' *Spiritual Exercises* (C, 256-257). When, however, he (with other commentators) wants to compare consolation *without* preceding cause to experiences described by Teresa and others, he does not refer to Teresa's *gustos*, but to a much higher and rarer form of mystical experience, to one which she names "prayer of union" or to what John of the Cross calls "substantial touch" (C, 271).

In judging that every consolation without preceding cause is such a high and rare mystical experience, Coathalem not only goes beyond Rahner but comes into conflict with two closely related key elements in the latter's interpretation of Ignatian discernment. In Coathalem's view, consolation without previous cause cannot be a common experience among good Christian people and so cannot be the first, the ultimately sole and necessary, principle of all Ignatian discernment. Rather, for Coathalem, such consolation is so unusual that rule II:8, which deals with how to guard against diabolical deception right after the consolation, "does not seem to have much practical utility" (C, 276).

What seems at first glance, therefore, to be an agreement between Rahner's interpretation of consolation without preceding cause and Coathalem's turns out to be a profound disagreement, implying head-on conflict about discernment of spirits, and consequently about discernment of God's will. What is understood by Rahner to be "the foundation and high point of 'normal' Christian life" and necessary for any spiritual discernment is for Coathalem very unusual, of peripheral interest, and not at all necessary for discernment of spirits or of God's will.

Daniel Gil

Daniel Gil thinks that there is, after all the years, no convincing exegesis of the Ignatian text. (This fact, he thinks, accounts for

Rahner's interpretation of consolation without preceding cause
(G, 90, note 11)—an interpretation which Gil considers erroneous.
Gil's own interpretation conflicts at a fundamental level with both
Rahner's and Coathalem's.

According to Gil, the distinction between consolation with and
without previous cause is not based by Ignatius on any difference
in the awareness of God (conceptual or non-conceptual, mystical
or non-mystical), or on any other feature intrinsic to the consolation itself. It is based solely on something extrinsic to the consolation and temporally antecedent to it. Either the consolation does
or does not follow from, with some dependence on, some object
of the consoled person's cognitive and volitional action. The consolation can be thought to follow from this object of these acts only
if there is a proportionate and adequate correspondence between
the consolation and the acts with their object. If there is, the consolation is with preceding cause; if not, it is without preceding cause.
Gil denies any evidence for Rahner's assertion that consolation
without preceding cause is experienced as indubitably from God,
purely and immediately. On the one hand, Gil says, any judgment
about an actual concrete experience of such consolation involves
a number of factors about which no absolute certainty can be
had and, so, the judgment is in every case only prudential. On the
other hand, all the necessary data are conscious and verifiable in
ordinary reflection on the experience, so long as the reflection is
carried out with careful and persevering attention. No highly
specialized methods are called for in order to reach a prudential
judgment (G, 31-36).

B. Critical Evaluation of Karl Rahner's Essay on Ignatian Discernment

1. Perspective for Evaluating This Essay: His Purpose and the Limits of This Evaluation

In order to evaluate Rahner's essay on Ignatian spiritual discernment, his expressed intention in writing must be noted and kept
in mind. After showing how theologians should approach the
Spiritual Exercises as a subject of theology without the assumption
that there is nothing in it they have not long since known, he says:

> So if a few, far from all, the *questions* are here propounded that the
> Exercises raise for a theologian who takes them seriously, the reader
> should not take it to be idle ingenuity, *nor should he complain if a ready-
> made answer is not supplied at the same time* (R, 89, italics supplied).

That propounding a few *questions* is really Rahner's aim is emphasized by a footnote to this statement in the text. He makes emphatically clear what he is not intending to do and the greater importance of what he is not doing.

> With limited purpose (everyone is permitted to choose his own theme) and in view of the space available, it goes without saying that it cannot be our purpose here to engage in an elaborate study of the sources for the life and writings of St. Ignatius and to expound and discuss the teaching of the commentators on the Exercises. Such things are necessary too. They are, in fact, more important than what we are doing here, and they alone can really accomplish the task to which a quite unpretentious stimulus is intended here, where *a question and only a question is propounded, even where, in order not to become too monotonous, it assumes the form of a firm statement* (R, 89, italics supplied).

Lest, in the course of reading his essay in which he does make many assertions, we should have forgotten his real intention, Rahner, at the end, recalls us to awareness of that intention and to how we should read his assertions if we are to truly understand him.

> In these last sections we have to all appearance made more assertions than we have propounded questions. But even so *the intention has really only been to permit the Exercises to put questions to theology*. Especially the question whether it is adequately equipped to expound and explain the religious activities that are described and above all prescribed in the Exercises (R, 169, italics supplied).

A careful reading of Rahner's own declaration of purpose in his essay does not permit us to think that he himself intended to reach, or considered his work to have reached, soundly established results based on exacting and trustworthy exegesis of Ignatius' writings. Two reasons come to mind which could account for a reader's mistaking Rahner's intention and his own evaluation of his work. The first is, on Rahner's own admission, his making so many firm assertions when all he really intended was to put questions. A second reason is that the proposed understanding of discernment which takes shape in the course of his theological questioning (in the form of assertions) is internally so fully coherent and is developed with such theological skill as to make the reader forget or not take seriously Rahner's repeated caution regarding his intention.

If I am mistaken in taking Rahner's declarations of the limits of his intention too seriously, then what I shall now say must be read as taking issue with him on some fundamental questions. If, however, I am correctly understanding Rahner's intention, then what I shall now say is to be read as offering answers to those fundamental questions—in the hope that what I say may be of some help to him and to other theologians, such as Harvey Egan, who are developing an Ignatian theology of spiritual discernment.

2. Two Fundamental Questions

Among the questions raised by Rahner in this essay, the only ones I wish to take up are questions of interpreting what Ignatius has written, while leaving aside any purely theoretical ones. Among these questions of interpretation, the focus of my attention is now limited to those which deal with Ignatian discernment of spirits, leaving aside those which deal with discernment of God's will except insofar as attending to these is necessary for discussing discernment of spirits. Further, among Rahner's questions regarding discernment of spirits, it will be enough for my purposes to attend to only two of them. The first of these seems to me to be *the* crucial question, the one on which the validity of Rahner's proposed interpretation as a whole depends, the one regarding the first principle of spiritual discernment. The second question will be taken up only because of its significance for answering the first.

Question 1. Is Consolation without Previous Cause the Principle of Spiritual Discernment?

What is it that leads Rahner to propose that consolation without previous cause is for Ignatius the first principle of all discernments of spirits and of God's will (R, 130; E, 43-64), the sine qua non, the "ultimately sole principle of the remainder of the Discernment of Spirits and consequently of the process of making the Election" (R, 164)? Is there some particular text or texts of Ignatius which he sees as clearly and cogently pointing to consolation without preceding cause as the first principle? If so, after many readings of Rahner's essay I have been unable to find any. Neither have I been able to find such texts in any of those writers who follow Rahner in this matter. Rather, Rahner seems to begin from his own premise that all discernment has to be founded on some *indubitably* divine motion within our experience. Given this premise, he then argues that there is no such indubitable divine motion mentioned in Ignatius' writings except consolation without previous cause, and that therefore this consolation must be for Ignatius the necessary foundation of all spiritual discernment (R, 123-131). Rahner asks:

> Is there for Ignatius a fundamental evidence and certainty which is presupposed by the various rules and techniques for Discernment of Spirits and which performs the same function as the first principles of logic and ontology for the rest of knowledge and which, distinct from the rules, makes them possible, so that they are the application and regulated putting into practice of this fundamental certitude? The rules would thus represent as it were a supernatural logic and themselves refer back to their own "first principle" (R, 130).

Rahner answers his own question (is his answer another question put as an assertion?): "clearly Ignatius has something of the sort in mind in the Rules for Discernment of Spirits in the Second Week" (R, 130). What he thinks Ignatius had in mind, of course, is consolation without preceding cause.

Is there any evidence that Ignatius would have accepted either of Rahner's premises or have drawn from them the conclusion that Rahner does? If so, Rahner does not present it. Rather, he moves immediately to a description of consolation without preceding cause. This description, even if it should be fully acceptable, can do no more than show that the consolation described is a possible candidate for consideration as first principle of spiritual discernment. It could not close off the possibility that this consolation is merely one privileged way of being moved by the Holy Spirit, giving a privileged kind of certainty, but not a requisite for all spiritual discernment nor even for most of it. So, it seems that we should consider what Rahner is doing here to be merely raising a fundamental problem for any theology of spiritual discernment and then asking whether, for Ignatius, consolation without previous cause is the solution to that problem.

When the questions involved in what Rahner says about consolation without previous cause as the first principle of spiritual discernment are sorted out and ordered, they can be stated in a sequence of three distinct questions, the first of which is theoretical and the other two historical and hermeneutical. First, does every discernment of spirits depend for its possibility on an experience of some self-evidently and indubitably divine movement which is the first principle of all spiritual discernment? Second, do the writings of Ignatius give evidence that he saw any need for such an experience as the first principle of every spiritual discernment? Third, if we should assume an affirmative answer to the second question, is there also evidence that Ignatius thought that consolation without preceding cause is the experience which constitutes the first principle?

Of these three questions, it is only the third that I propose to answer: Did Ignatius explicitly or even implicitly teach that consolation without preceding cause is the first principle in every genuine discernment of spirits? In my reading of Ignatius' writings, I have found no evidence that would allow me to give an affirmative answer to this question. Neither does the evidence allow me to remain in doubt about the answer. What Ignatius said and what he did not say compel me to give a negative answer; an affirmative answer appears to me clearly incompatible with his teaching.

Consider first what Ignatius did *not* say. It is true that the argument from silence is often not a very convincing one. There are, however, some cases in which is is very convincing. This appears to be one of them. Make the supposition that Ignatius saw consolation without preceding cause as the first principle of spiritual discernment, necessary for the very possibility of it. Would he not tell us so explicitly? Would we not expect him to remind us of it over and over, warning us never to attempt discernment of spirits or God's will by any indication whatever, whether of reason or affectivity, apart from consolation without previous cause? The fact is that such consolation is never mentioned anywhere in Ignatius' writing—neither in the *Spiritual Exercises* nor elsewhere—except in Rules II:2 and 8; and in these two rules we do not find any clear implciation that we are dealing with a first principle of all discernment, much less any explicit statement to that effect. Nowhere in all the directories for the Spiritual Exercises written by the early disciples of Ignatius does anyone seem to have found a clear indication to that effect. Can we really believe that Ignatius and those whom he trained entirely overlooked declaring explicitly what he considered the one thing absolutely necessary in order to discern spirits, or to employ his modes of discerning God's will? Is such incomprehensible negligence really credible?

But even if we allow for this very improbable possibility, what Ignatius does in fact say seems clearly to eliminate any idea of consolation without preceding cause as the first principle of discernment. For in the second set of rules he spends most of his time (Rules II:4-7) showing how we can discern what spirit is moving us in consolation *with* previous cause (II:4, 5), and why we can be confident of doing so (II:7), and what we are to do when we have discerned the evil spirit at work (II:6). This series of rules clearly implies that we have no need of consolation without previous cause in order to discern spirits.[9]

The consolation about which Ignatius is speaking in Rules II:4-7 is obviously *with* cause, the consolation already described in Rule II:3. For the question these rules are to help us answer is whether a good or evil spirit is the prompter of a consolation which could come from either source, whereas neither an evil spirit nor a created good spirit can prompt consolation without previous cause. Ignatius indicates in II:4 that the evil spirit can for his unholy purpose cause good and holy thoughts; and in II:5 Ignatius assumes feelings of "peace, tranquility, and quiet" along with these thoughts. Rule II:5 shows us how to find "clear" signs of a good or evil spirit prompting these thoughts and feelings and thus to reach a trustworthy conclusion. Rules II:6 and 7 confirm this way of understanding Rule 5. Rule II:6 assumes that we have detected what spirit is at work and, when it is the evil spirit, urges us to examine the whole process in order to grow in understanding of how he works. Rule II:7, read in context with Rules 4-6, assures us that when the evil spirit is influencing a person who is progressing in God's service, there will inevitably, even if not immediately, be "clamor and observable signs" which betray him. When no such signs arise, but all is "delicate, gentle, delightful" from the beginning to the end of the process, then it is surely the good spirit who is acting. Nowhere in this whole series of rules for discerning the prompting source of consolation *with* previous cause is there any hint that we need consolation *without* previous cause in order to do the discerning; rather, there is a clear and strong declaration that we can do so in other ways.

Question 2. The Frequency of Consolation without Previous Cause

Closely related to the preceding question regarding the role of consolation without preceding cause in Ignatian discernment of spirits is the question of frequency. Is this sort of consolation a rare experience in Christian life or is it a more or less ordinary one? Ignatius himself makes no clear and explicit statement on which we could base an answer to this question one way or the other.

9 For a detailed analysis of these rules, see above, pp. 222-242; and notice especially p. 235.

There is one passage in a letter to Teresa Rejadell (letter of June 18, 1536) to which appeal is made (E, 55); but I shall try to show that it is at best very dubious evidence regarding Ignatius' thought on the frequency of consolation without preceding cause.

As a consequence, we have to look for an answer by drawing implications from Ignatius' description of consolation without preceding cause and from the clear and generally granted assumption throughout his writings that spiritual discernment is something we need to be doing day in and day out if we are to mature as Christians.

If consolation without preceding cause is a rare experience and yet necessary for any spiritual discernment, then spiritual discernment will necessarily be rare. Ignatius and those in the Ignatian tradition see discernment of spirits and also of God's will as an ongoing and very important part of the spiritual life. Therefore those who think that consolation without preceding cause is rare do not think of it as necessary for spiritual discernment; whereas those who do see it as the first principle of all discernment think of it as an ordinary experience. Thus we find Egan asserting that such consolation belongs to the "normal perspective of spiritual life"; that it is hardly more extraordinary than the other consolations during the Spiritual Exercises; that it is, in fact, to be expected as the normal crowning of consolation with previous cause (E, 55-56). We may assume that Egan is speaking for Rahner as well when he makes these statements. Rahner also implies that for Ignatius consolation without preceding cause is an ordinary experience among maturing Christians. For he interprets Ignatius to be teaching that, apart from the "first-time election" (which Rahner sees as a divine revelation [R, 107]), no discernment of God's will is possible unless it at least terminates in discernment by consolation and desolation, as in the "second time." This mode of discernment, according to Rahner, can take place only during the time immediately following the actual experience of consolation without preceding cause (R, 95-96, 160-161). If this is an accurate interpretation of Ignatius' thought, then he must also think that consolation without preceding cause must be as ordinary as he thinks discernment of God's will should be in the life of a maturing Christian.

While this idea that consolation without preceding cause is a common occurrence fits nicely with the idea that it is the first principle of discernment, if the latter idea is seen to be unfounded, the former loses its importance; and it can readily be let go if a strong reason moves us to do so. There is, at least at first appearance, a strong reason based on the intrinsic features of consolation without preceding cause which are explicit in Rules II:2 and 8 and on those features which are developed by Rahner and Egan as implicitly in these rules. For all these features point to an experience that is not at all ordinary, not even among very good Christians.

Among these features we noted that it is without preceding cause and is certainly from God immediately and solely. Rahner develops this to means an explicit, non-conceptual, unmediated awareness of God as the term of supernatural transcendence, subjectively as well as objectively certain as an immediate experience of God (but not always subjectively certain according to Egan). There can, it is true, be degrees of intensity, clarity, and certainty in such an experience. But even the low degrees seem to be unusual with respect to the large body of good Christians. Do we have any other experiential evidence to go by than that offered by those who have gone through the stages of spiritual life from the lower to the highest, or those who have been the spiritual directors of these persons? Does not the converging evidence from them .indicate that even the lowest degree of non-conceptual, immediate experience of God comes ordinarily only to those who have lived a prolonged and intense life of prayer and striving for purity of heart? Is there any evidence of such experiences being ordinary except among those who have been led by God from discursive prayer gradually simplified to the beginnings of passive or infused contemplation commonly called by Teresa's term "prayer of quiet"? And does such religious experience at these lower degrees or stages have the feature of consciously being drawn into total love for God? Is the experience during the earliest stages of the prayer of quiet clear and certain enough to be of any service as a first principle of discernment? Until these questions have been dealt with, any assertion of a *commonly experienced* non-conceptual and self-evident immediate awareness of God must remain highly improbable.

We have so far only hinted at a yet more cogent reason against the frequency of consolation without preceding cause. Leaving aside the feature of immediacy to God and certainty of it, let us focus attention on the central experiential element in Ignatius' description of consolation without preceding cause. Here is something that can in no way be thought of as ordinary, namely, the "drawing him or her totally into love of his divine Majesty" (Rule II:2) or the "lifting up totally to his divine love" (letter of June 18, 1536 to Teresa Rejadell). What was said in chapter 10, on pages 220-221 above, regarding these phrases is of decisive importance. Further, Rahner and Egan count these phrases of Ignatius as essential and crucial for understanding what he means by consolation without preceding cause (R, 135; E, 36). The descriptions of the consolation which they draw from these phrases make even more difficult the acceptance of it as an ordinary Christian experience.

Rahner speaks of the *whole* person drawn into love of God as God (R, 135), the *whole* human prson drawn above and beyond all that can be named into the love of God (R, 137). This experience, he says, lays hold of the soul *completely* (R, 153). So totally absorbing of consciousness is it that no judgments or concepts are possible during it (R, 136, 158). In it, there is as it were a "perception" or a "sense" of God, by which it is *irreducibly and irresistibly self-evident as immediately from God* (R, 143, 153-154). How could such an experience be thought of as usual or normal in Christian life? Most of us, I think, would be more likely to say we have never had such an experience.

What Egan says, if read in full seriousness, could never suggest anything but a rare, a very rare, experience. Remember that, like Ignatius, he and Rahner are describing events in consciousness, events which take place at an experiential level. Egan says that in consolation without preceding cause God takes *full* possession of the consoled person by bringing the deepest spiritual center into express, thematic, awareness (E, 37). So the person comes *fully* to self, *fully* possesses self, *fully* surrenders self (E, 56). The "*total* body-person" (italics mine) is rendered connatural with grace by God's love penetrating all the layers and dimensions of the person and unifying him or her to the very roots (E, 61-62). *Total* unification of all layers and dimensions of the personality, *full* possession and *full* surrendering of self—that an experience with these features should be called normal (even among very unusual persons) is hard to accept.

Let me be clear. I have no difficulty with these elaborations of Ignatius' phrase. I think they very likely draw out accurately the implications of what Ignatius is saying: that the person is drawn totally, wholly, to love of the divine majesty and, in order to be so drawn, has to be for the moment fully integrated and surrendered. What I cannot understand is how an experience so described can be thought of as anything other than a most extraordinary experience, which very few Christians, if they really understand the force of "completely," "totally," "fully," and the like in these descriptions, could say that they have ever had. The only experiences these descriptions seem to fit are not only mystical in the strict sense of passive or infused contemplation but also very high and rare ones even among such mystical experiences.

It is, I take it, the anticipation of this very difficulty which leads Rahner to speak of different levels or degrees in the experience of consolation without preceding cause. He presumes that it will not be wrong to think that the experience "can occur on very different levels without prejudice to its identity of nature" (R, 144). The awareness of God as the term of transcendence and love for him can become increasingly intense, pure, and unmixed (R, 145-146). It is only the lowest levels or degrees of the experience which Rahner thinks are not rare. At what level or what degree of intensity and purity the consolation becomes mystical, infused contemplation, this is a question which Rahner puts aside as unimportant in working out the fundamental outlines of a theology of discernment (R, 151-152).

At first glance this appeal to levels of experience gives promise of a simple and satisfying solution to our problem. On more careful consideration, however, doubts arise. How can one be totally drawn into love of God in a slight degree?—be fully self-possessed and fully self-surrendered in a slight degree? Most difficult of all, how can one be fully unified, fully integrated, in a slight degree? It would seem that one simply is or is not totally drawn into love, is or is not fully unified and surrendered. Perhaps, however, we can let the words "totally" and "fully" refer only to the undividedness and present indivisibility of love, "low degree" refer to the intensity of love. It is conceptually possible that a love of low intensity be an undivided love for God, free from any accompanying love for self or any creature which is not wholly assumed into love for God, free for the moment even of the possibility of any such accompanying love. The concept of a love for God which is undivided and even for the moment indivisible is not incompatible with the concept of a love of slight intensity. But is a love with these two features a likelihood in the real order? If it is possible, it is surely a rarity.

In any case, is it not true that those who have come to a deep knowledge of what goes on in their own hearts and in the hearts of other persons tend to agree with Bernard of Clairvaux when he gives it as his opinion that in this life only the great saints, and they only for passing moments, reach a love so totally integrated and pure as to exclude even any self-love which is not fully taken up into love for God (p. 96 above)?

Perhaps the ordinariness of consolation without preceding cause can be saved if we assume that Ignatius, Rahner, and Egan are all employing hyperbole when they use the word "totally" or "fully" in their descriptions of this kind of consolation. For, given that assumption, we can understand them to mean that in such consolation the person is drawn into a notably (but not totally) pure love of God with a high or a low intensity of love. It may be possible for this experience to be sufficiently frequent to allow for adequately frequent spiritual discernment.

Is the assumption of hyperbole in the use of the word "totally" a reasonable one? It is at least questionable as an interpretation of what Ignatius says when Rule II:2 is read in context and seems not at all compatible with the statements of Rahner and Egan when they describe consolation without preceding cause. What is more, it would require the renunciation of any intrinsic difference in the affective dimension of consolation with and without preceding cause, a renunciation which I doubt Rahner and Egan would be willing to make.

One last appeal could be made, an appeal to Ignatius' letter to Teresa Rejadell which was mentioned above when the question of frequency of consolation without preceding cause was first raised (on page 307 above). In that letter Ignatius declares:

> For it frequently happens that our Lord moves and urges the soul to this or that activity. He begins by enlightening the soul; that is to say, by speaking interiorly to it without the din of words, lifting it up wholly to His divine love and ourselves to His meaning without any possibility of resistance on our part, even should we wish to resist.[10]

10 *LettersIgn*, p. 22.

With good reason this passage is commonly interpreted as a description of consolation without preceding cause during which God gives an impulse toward some course of action, marked by the consolation as a divine impulse to that action. This interpretation is strengthened by what follows in the text; for there Ignatius warns Teresa about the deception which can occur during the time immediately subsequent to the described experience, just as he does in Rule II:8 (see above, pages 243-252). At first glance, the passage could easily be read as evidence that Ignatius saw consolation without preceding cause as a frequent, even ordinary, experience of Christian life.

Careful reflection, however, shows that the passage is so ambiguous as to be useless for our present problem. Assuming that we are correct in thinking that Ignatius is talking about consolation without preceding cause, the passage is patient of a number of different meanings which would nullify it as evidence for the opinion that such consolation is to considered as usual, ordinary, in the life of a maturing Christian. Frequency and infrequency, it is necessary to remember, are relative terms. When they are used, we can understand what is meant only if we know in relation to what something is frequent or infrequent. For instance, Ignatius could mean that for persons like Teresa who are intensely dedicated to a life of contemplation and to doing God's will in all details of life, the occurrence of the experience he writes about is frequent even though it is rare in relation to the large body of those who are good Christians but not so fully and intensely dedicated as these others. Or he might be saying that among all maturing Christians the occur ence is frequent in the same way that we say serious accidents are frequent on the highways, despite the fact that by far most drivers never have one; or in the way that we say tornados happen frequently in a certain area, meaning that they occur on an average of once or twice a year, which is frequent relative to other areas where they happen once every five or ten years.

It could even be that Ignatius is not directly concerned at all with the frequency of the consolation, He may, rather, be saying that many of the times when God does in fact give this consolation (which may be infrequently in relation to the whole body of maturing Christians), he also gives with it some movement or urge to this or that course of action. That is, even if the consolation described is a very unusual experience among Christians generally, relative to the number of times it is given, the times when an impulse to this or that act accompanies it are frequent—much as we say that among those Christians who undertake a vowed life in a religious congregation (a rare undertaking in relation to the whole body of Christians), it frequently happens that they grew up in families where Christian faith and the expression of it were lively.

These possible meanings of the passage under discussion do not eliminate the possibility that it could also mean that consolation without preceding cause is a frequent occurrence in the lives of all maturing Christians. It simply leaves the meaning so uncertain that the interpretation has to be controlled by the implications of what is said elsewhere.

Conclusion

What Ignatius does say elsewhere, we have seen, leads to the conclusion that he did not see consolation without preceding cause as an ordinary event in the lives of maturing Christians in general, certainly not at all adequately frequent to make possible the ongoing discernment of spirits and of God's will which he thought should characterize their lives. If this conclusion is true, then it offers a strong confirmation of the answer given to the first question, whether consolation without preceding cause is in the teaching of Ignatius the first principle of all discernment of spirits and of God's will, necessary for the possibility of such discernment.

However, even if my conclusion regarding the second question, that about the frequency of consolation without preceding cause, should be mistaken; and even if this consolation could be shown to be ordinary according to the mind of Ignatius, this would not require any change in my answer to the first question. One added reason would be lost; that is all. The basic evidence on which my answer to the first question rests has no necessary dependence whatever on the answer to the second.

A SELECTED BIBLIOGRAPHY

Chiefly of Works in English,
on Discernment of Spirits

Even after taking note that this is a selected bibliography, readers may be surprised by a number of omissions, unless they keep in mind that the limits of the bibliography correspond with the limits of the present book.

This is not, then, a bibliography on discernment of God's will, but only on discernment of spirits. Further, it is not a bibliography on discernment of spirits in general, but only on the kind with which Ignatius deals in his Rules for Discernment of Spirits.

Still further, even within those limits it is intended almost exclusively for the reader of English. To those who desire a bibliography which includes works in other languages we recommend the bibliographies in the volumes, listed below, by Harvey D. Egan, S.J., and Daniel Gil, S.J.

The publishers are listed for works still in print.

Asselin, David, S.J. "Christian Maturity and Spiritual Discernment." *Review for Religious*, XXVII (1968), 581-595.

Augustine, St. *The Confessions of St. Augustine*. Trans. by John K. Ryan. Garden City, N.Y.: Image Books, 1960.

Bernard of Clairvaux, St. *De Diligendo Deo*. Patrologia Latina, Vol. 182. Paris, 1854. English Trans. by Terrence Connolly, S.J. *St. Bernard on the Love of God*. New York, 1937.

Buckley, Michael, S.J. "The Structure of the Rules for Discernment of Spirits." *The Way. Supplement 20* (Autumn, 1973), 19-37.

Clarkson, J.F., S.J. et al., trans. and eds. *The Church Teaches: Documents of the Church in English Translation*. St. Louis, 1955. (Available from Tan Books and Publishers, Rockford, Illinois.)

Coathalem, Hervé, S.J. *Ignatian Insights: A Guide to the Complete Spiritual Exercises*. Trans. by Charles J. McCarthy, S.J. Second edit. Taichung, Taiwan: Kuangchi Press, 1971.

Costa, Maurizio, S.J. "Spiritual Discernment," *Progressio*, 48th Year (January, 1979), 3-12, 21-29.

Darlap, Adolph. "Devil," *Sacramentum Mundi: An Encyclopedia of Theology*, I, 70-73. New York, 1978.

315

Saint Ignatius' Rules for the Discernment of Spirits

Delmage, Lewis, S.J. *Spiritual Exercises of St. Ignatius Loyola.* New York, 1968.

Directory to the Spiritual Exercises. London, 1925.

Dubay, Thomas, S.M. *Authenticity: A Biblical Theology of Discernment.* Denville, New Jersey: Dimension Books, 1977.

Egan, Harvey D., S.J. *The Spiritual Exercises and the Ignatian Mystical Horizon.* St. Louis: The Institute of Jesuit Sources, 1976.

English, John J., S.J. *Choosing Life: Significance of Personal History in Decision-making.* New York: Paulist Press, 1978. Chapters 3, 9, 10.

———— *Spiritual Freedom: From an Experience of the Ignatian Exercises to the Art of Spiritual Direction.* Guelph, Ontario: Loyola House, 1973. Chapters 8, 12.

Futrell, John Carroll, S.J. *Making an Apostolic Community of Love: The Role of the Superior according to St. Ignatius of Loyola.* St. Louis: The Institute of Jesuit Sources, 1970.

———— "Ignatian Discernment." *Studies in the Spirituality of Jesuits,* II, no. 2 (April, 1970). St. Louis: The American Assistancy Seminar on Jesuit Spirituality, 1970.

Gagliardi, A., S.J. *Commentarii seu Explanationes in Exercitia Spiritualia.* Bruges, 1882. Pp. 107-197.

Gil, Daniel, S.J. *La Consolación Sin Causa Precedente.* Rome: Centrum Ignatianum Spiritualitatis, 1971.

Guibert, Joseph de, S.J. *The Jesuits: Their Spiritual Doctrine and Practice.* Trans. by William J. Young. Chicago and St. Louis: The Institute of Jesuit Sources, 1964 and 1972.

———— *The Theology of the Spiritual Life.* Translated by Paul Barrett, O.F.M.Cap. New York, 1953. See esp. pp. 129-144 on The Discernment of Spirits.

Guillet, Jacques, S.J., et al. "Discernement des esprits," *Dictionnaire de Spiritualité Ascétique et Mystique,* Vol. III. Paris, 1957. English trans. by Sr. Innocentia Richards: *Discernment of Spirits.* Collegeville, Minn.: The Liturgical Press, 1970.

Ignatius of Loyola, St. *Exercitia Spiritualia: Textus.* Monumenta Historica Societatis Jesu. Eds. J. Calveras and C. de Dalmases. Rome, 1969.

————et al. Directoria Exercitiorum Spiritualium (1540-1599). Ed. I. Iparraguirre. Rome, 1955.

————*The Constitutions of the Society of Jesus: Translated, with an Introduction and Commentary,* by George E. Ganss, S.J. St. Louis: The Institute of Jesuit Sources, 1970.

————*Letters of St. Ignatius of Loyola.* Selected and Translated by W. J. Young, S.J. Chicago: Loyola University Press, 1959.

————*The Spiritual Journal of St. Ignatius of Loyola.* Translated by W. J. Young, S.J. Woodstock, Md., 1958.

————*St. Ignatius' Own Story as Told to Luis Gonzalez de Camara.* Translated by William J. Young, S.J. Chicago, 1956. Reprint, Chicago: Loyola University Press, 1968.

John of the Cross, St. *The Collected Works of St. John of the Cross*. Translated by Kieran Kavanaugh, O.C.D. and Otilio Rodriguez, O.C.D. with Introductions by Kieran Kavanaugh, O.C.D. Washington, D.C. Institute of Carmelite Studies, 1973.

Kelly, Henry Ansgar. *The Devil, Demonology and Witchcraft*. Garden City, N.Y.: Doubleday, 1968.

Kyne, Michael, S.J. "Discernment of Spirits and Christian Growth," *The Way, Supplement 6* (1968), 20-26.

Lussier, Ernest, S.S.S. "Satan," *Catholic Mind*. LXXII, no. 1285 (Sept., 1974), 13-35.

MacNutt, Francis, O.P. *Healing*. Notre Dame: Ave Maria Press, 1974.

O'Leary, Brian, S.J. "The Discernment of Spirits in the Memoriale of Blessed Peter Favre." *The Way, Supplement 35* (Spring, 1979).

Montague, George T., S.M. *Riding the Wind*. Ann Arbor, Mich., 1974.

Penning de Vries, Piet, *Discernment of Spirits: According to the Life and Teachings of Ignatius of Loyola*. Trans. by W. Dudok Van Heel. New York: Exposition Press, 1973.

———— "Quaker Experience and Ignatian Principles," *Spiritual Life*, XVIII, no. 2 (summer, 1972), 128-135.

Peters, William A.N., S.J., *The Spiritual Exercises of St. Ignatius: Exposition and Interpretation*. Jersey City, 1967. Reprint, Rome: Centrum Ignatianum Spiritualitatis, 1978.

Poulain, A., S.J., *The Graces of Interior Prayer*. 6th edit. London, 1950.

Pousset, Edouard, S.J. *Life in Faith and Freedom: An Essay Presenting Gaston Fessard's Analysis of the Dialectic of the Spiritual Exercises of St. Ignatius*. Translated by Eugene L. Donahue, S. J. St. Louis: The Institute of Jesuit Sources, 1980.

Puhl, Louis J. S.J. *The Spiritual Exercises of St. Ignatius: Based on Studies in the Language of the Autograph*. Westminster, Md., 1951. Reprint: Chicago: Loyola University Press, 1968.

Quay, Paul M., S. J. "Angels and Demons: the teaching of IV Lateran." *Theological Studies*, XLII, no. 1 (March, 1981), 20-45.

Rahner, Hugo, S.J. *Ignatius the Theologian*. Trans. by Michael Barry. New York, 1968.

Rahner, Karl, S.J. *The Dynamic Element in the Church*. Trans. by W.J. O'Hara. New York, 1964.

————"Angels," "Devil," *Sacramentum Mundi: A Theological Encyclopedia*, I, 27-35; II, 73-75. New York, 1968.

————and Vorgrimler, Herbert. "Devils," *Theological Dictionary*. Ed. by Cornelius Ernst, O.P. Trans. by Richard Strachan. New York, 1965. Pp. 126-127.

Richards, Sister Innocentia (translator from *Dictionnaire de spiritualité*). *Discernment of Spirits*. Collegeville, Minn:. the Liturgical Press, 1970.

Roustang, François, S.J. *Growth in the Spirit*. New York: Sheed and Ward, 1966. Ch. 4, pp. 95-120.

Saint Ignatius' Rules for the Discernment of Spirits

Sheets, John R. "Profile of the Spirit: A Theology of Discernment of Spirits," *Review for Religious*, XXX, (1971), 363-376.

Smith, Herbert F., S.J. *The Pilgrim Contemplative*. (Collegeville, Minn.: the Liturgical Press. Book Two, chapters 14-16.

Schoonenberg, Peter. *God's World in the Making*, Pittsburgh, 1964.

Theresa, St. *The Complete Works of St. Theresa*. Trans. by E. Allison Peers. London, 1972.

Toner, Jules, S.J., *The Experience of Love*. Washington, 1968.

Wulf, Friedrich, S. J. (ed.), H. Bacht, A. Haas, Hugo Rahner, Karl Rahner, J. Stierli, and other Jesuits. *Ignatius of Loyola: His Personality and Spiritual Heritage, 1556-1956. Studies on the 400th Anniversary of His Death*. St. Louis: Institute of Jesuit Sources, 1977.

EDITORIAL NOTE

---

on the Term "Spiritual Exercises"

Throughout this book, as was pointed out in footnote 5 of chapter 1 on page 9 above, *Spiritual Exercises* (in italics) refers chiefly to Ignatius' book, and Spiritual Exercises (in roman type) to the activities of an exercitant within a retreat. The term "Spiritual Exercises" gives rise to many editorial problems, which are handled according to the procedures shown by exemplification in the following paragraphs.

Long before Ignatius various spiritual exercises, such as attendance at Mass or recitation of the Office, were common. He gradually composed directives for a sequence of such exercises. Before 1535 his companions Xavier and Favre made his Spiritual Exercises for a period of thirty days. Ignatius assembled his notes in his *Spiritual Exercises*, which was (or were) published at Rome in 1548. To make references easier, in modern editions since that at Turin in 1928 a number in square brackets has been added to each paragraph of the text; for example, the purpose of the Exercises is stated in *Spiritual Exercises*, [21] or, in our abbreviation, *SpEx*, [21]. The Introductory Observations (*Anotaciones*) are in [1-20]. Important meditations or other exercises in his book are the First Principle and Foundation ([23]), the Call of the King ([91-100]), which is an introduction to the Second Week or division of the *Exercises*, the Three Modes of Humility ([238-260]). Since 1548 the *Spiritual Exercises* have been read or made by many persons. These Exercises are often a stirring spiritual experience.

The Rules for the Discernment of Spirits form one section of the *Exercises*. Ignatius composed these rules in two sets, the fourteen rules ([313-327]) often "more" (but not at all exclusively) appropriate for use during the First Week, and the eight rules ([328-336]) often "more" (but not at all exclusively) useful during the Second Week. We shall designate these as Rules I:1-14 or Rules II:1-8, or—for example—Rule I:3, or Rule II:5, or more simply when the context is sufficiently clear as I:3 or II:5.

INDEX

The numbers refer to pages

Self knowledge, why difficult to attain, 41-42
—— necessity of, for discernment of spirits, 39-41
for defense against evil spirit, 201-203
Sentir, Ignatius' meaning of, 22-23
Sorrow, when and when not a spiritual consolation, 100-103. *See also* Spiritual consolation
Spirit. *See* Holy Spirit; Good spirit; Evil spirit; Angels; Satan
Spiritual consolation:
No satisfactory substitute for this term, 79
interpretation of it crucial for interpretation of Ignatian rules, 283
some disregard the spiritual character of, 283-284
some disregard the consoling character of, 284-290
—— description and analysis of:
Ignatius' description of in Rule I:3, 24
Ignatius' assumption and intention in describing, 81-82
his paradigm of, 99
his widening definitions of, 108-109
essential and contingent, 62, 90-92
Ignatian rules concerned with contingent, 92-93
dynamic structure of, 109-112. *See also* Consolation; Motions
in causative sense, 84-85, 109-113
in proper, restricted, sense, 84-85, 86, 177-178, 287-290. *See also* Affective feeling; Consolation
in broad sense, 87

is a God-centered experience, 111
is rooted in faith, hope, and charity, 109-113
is not, in its proper meaning, identified with faith, hope, and charity, 98, 102, 110, 177-178
in what way it is "an increase of faith, hope, and charity." 60, 103-107, 177-178
integrated summary of factors in, 112
illustrations in Gospels, 113-115
some difficulties in distinguishing it from non-spiritual consolation, 115-121
—— its relation with sorrow:
presupposes sorrow, 112-114
sorrow rooted in living faith can be a form of, 101-102
does not exclude concomitant non-spiritual sadness, confusion, etc., 214
can be integrated with sorrow and pain, spiritual or non-spiritual, 119-120
two characteristics of Christian, 102-103
—— its relation with spiritual desolation:
will soon be followed by spiritual desolation, 193, 210
the difficulty of remembering this, 193
importance of remembering it, 194-195
how to prepare for spiritual desolation during, 195-196, 210
can be concurrent with spiritual desolation, 91-92
can be integrated with spi-

——*See also* Desolation; Motions
Spiritual discernment
  need for a teacher of, 5
  St. Ignatius a preeminent
    teacher of, 7
  See also Discernment of spi-
    rits; God's will
Spiritual Exercises
  texts of, 21
  immediate context of Rules
    for Discernment of
    Spirits, 9, 14, 20
  editorial policies on problems
    with the term, 319
  passim
Spiritually maturing persons,
  meaning of, 51-54,
  205-206
  effects of evil spirit on, 56-59
  effects of good spirit on, 56,
  60-70
  See also Holy Spirit; Good
    spirit; Evil spirit;
    Motions
Spiritually regressing persons,
  meaning of, 50-52,
  53, 54
  effects of evil spirit on, 54-55
  effects of good spirit on, 55
  See also Holy Spirit; Good
    spirit; Evil spirit;
    Motions
Spiritual motions. *See* Motions

Stars, Ignatius' contemplation of, 116

T

Tears, 99, 100, 106
Temptations of evil spirit and
  how to deal with. *See*
  Evil spirit; Deception
  by evil spirit
Tranquility, different meanings
  in different contexts of
  Ignatius' writing, 89
Trust and act, principle of
  explained, 157-160
  a variant formulation of, 158
  operative throughout Igna-
    tian teaching on spiri-
    tual life, 157-159
  primacy of trust and prayer,
    159-160
  relation with principle of
    counterattack, 160.
    See also Counterattack
  application to overcoming
    spiritual desolation,
    162-174

W

Warfare, Ignatius' metaphorical
  use of, 31
"Week," meaning of in *Spiritual
  Exercises*, 23